INTELLIGENCE AND U.S. FOREIGN POLICY

INTELLIGENCE AND U.S. FOREIGN POLICY

Iraq, 9/11, and Misguided Reform

Paul R. Pillar

COLUMBIA UNIVERSITY PRESS NEW YORK

Columbia University Press
Publishers Since 1893
New York   Chichester, West Sussex

Library of Congress Cataloging-in-Publication Data
Pillar, Paul R., 1947–
    Intelligence and U.S. Foreign Policy : Iraq, 9/11, and Misguided Reform / Paul R. Pillar.
      p.   cm.
    Includes bibliographical references and index.
    ISBN 978-0-231-15792-6 (cloth : alk. paper)—ISBN 978-0-231-15793-3 (pbk. : alk. paper)—
    ISBN 978-0-231-52780-4 (e-book)
    1. Intelligence service—United States.   2. Iraq War, 2003–   3. September 11 Terrorist
Attacks, 2001.   I. Title.
JK468.I6P55   2010
327.1273—dc22   2010048141

Columbia University Press books are printed on permanent and durable acid-free paper.
This book was printed on paper with recycled content.
Printed in the United States of America

Cover design by Michael Gibson

To Veronica,
who puts her intelligence to good use

CONTENTS

9/11	September 11, 2001
9/11 Commission	National Commission on Terrorist Attacks Upon the United States
ASAT	antisatellite
BJP	Bharatiya Janata Party
CBRN	chemical, biological, radiological, or nuclear
CIA	U.S. Central Intelligence Agency
CTC	Counterterrorist Center
DCI	director of central intelligence
DNI	director of national intelligence
DRV	Democratic Republic of Vietnam
ExComm	Executive Committee
FAA	Federal Aviation Administration
FBI	Federal Bureau of Investigation
IAEA	International Atomic Energy Agency
ICA	intelligence community assessment
INR	Bureau of Intelligence and Research
MACV	U.S. Military Assistance Command Vietnam
NASA	National Aeronautics and Space Administration

NCTC	National Counterterrorism Center
NIC	National Intelligence Council
NIE	national intelligence estimate
NSA	National Security Agency
NSC	National Security Council
ODNI	Office of the Director of National Intelligence
PCTEG	Policy Counter Terrorism Evaluation Group
PNAC	Project for the New American Century
SALT	strategic arms limitation talks
SLBM	submarine-launched ballistic missile
UNMOVIC	United Nations Monitoring, Verification, and Inspection Commission
VFW	Veterans of Foreign Wars
WMD	weapons of mass destruction

March 29, 1973, found me aboard a C-141 transport plane, along with fifty other U.S. servicemen, returning to the United States after duty in Vietnam. The flight was the last in the withdrawal of U.S. military forces under the terms of the peace agreement that the United States and North Vietnam had reached in Paris two months earlier (not to be confused with the much more hazardous and chaotic exodus of the few remaining Americans when the agreement broke down and Communist forces overran South Vietnam in April 1975). I was on that final flight because my assignment since arriving in Vietnam the previous April was at a replacement depot called Camp Alpha at Tan Son Nhut Air Base on the outskirts of Saigon, which during the last year of the war was the processing point for almost all U.S. military personnel entering or leaving Vietnam. Once the peace agreement was reached, those of us who did the processing at Camp Alpha had to send the other remaining troops on their way before we ourselves could leave.

What had once been an American force of more than half a million was down to about twenty-four thousand when the Paris Accord was signed. The withdrawal of that residual force (except for a few embassy guards and members of a joint military commission to monitor implementation of the agreement) was supposed to be synchronized with the repatriation of American prisoners of war from North Vietnam. The withdrawal proceeded in fits and starts because of disagreements over implementation of the agreement. Sometimes we would load a plane with soldiers who happily thought they were within minutes of leaving Vietnam, only to be ordered to unload it because an aircraft with prisoners of war had not taken off on schedule from Hanoi. The biggest hiccup occurred with two weeks to go in the withdrawal, when our flight operations were suspended altogether. Once the underlying problem was resolved, we had three days to ship out the last five thousand troops. And we had to do this while signing over remaining property to the embassy, making final payments to our Vietnamese employees, packing our own bags, and trying to keep the compound we were about to vacate from being looted. I got almost no sleep during those three days and as a result slept most of the way across the Pacific.

We at Camp Alpha had it easy, however, compared to those we processed—and many more before them—who had experienced directly the stresses and horrors of combat. Other than two Viet Cong rocket barrages against the airbase, I saw not enemy fire but instead some of the other ways the Vietnam War inflicted damage on the army as well as on American society. U.S. troops' burgeoning use of narcotics had become a particular problem by that late stage of the conflict. The most important piece of processing we did with soldiers exiting Vietnam was a urinalysis to identify the disturbingly large number of heroin users.

After landing in California, we on that last flight exited the plane onto a red carpet and along a receiving line that included several generals. The arrival festivities were partly a celebration of the end of an eight-year-long national nightmare. Later that night I joined my battalion commander and one of our noncommissioned officers to participate in another ceremony at the since-closed army base in Oakland to deactivate our unit, the Ninetieth Replacement Battalion. The unit had first been created to serve the American Expeditionary Force in World War I and had later seen service in World War II. A reporter at the ceremony asked for my thoughts. I expressed hope that the battalion was furling its colors for the last time and would never need to be activated again.

These events were to have connections with subsequent professional endeavors, including ones I never could have anticipated at the time. Having participated at the low end of an effort to extract the United States from a war, I became interested in how things work at the high end. This interest led to a doctoral dissertation, which I later turned into a book, on the principles and dynamics of peace negotiations and the role that military force plays as an accompaniment to them.

Later in my career I worked on counterterrorism, and that subject would have a more personal connection with my experience in Vietnam. One of my most effective and valued colleagues at Camp Alpha was an experienced master sergeant named Max Beilke. Max was a paragon of calm and good judgment, with a low-key and effective way of bringing order out of confusion. When the last hectic days of the troop withdrawal ended, and it was time for the remaining few of us to get on our aircraft, a North Vietnamese colonel was waiting on the tarmac to mark the occasion with a gift—a rattan-backed painting of a pagoda—to whoever was the final soldier to leave. It was decided that Max, as one of the most senior enlisted men to board our flight, should receive the honor. And so he became formally and officially the last American combat soldier to depart Vietnam.

Max retired from the army shortly afterward and as a civilian worked in a variety of capacities on issues of concern to military veterans. I did not stay in regular contact with him—we got together for lunch a few years later—but I knew he eventually went to work with the personnel staff at the Department of the Army. Thus, I thought of him when hearing news that offices used by this staff were in the part of the Pentagon hit on September 11, 2001. Max was in fact there that morning, making him one of two people with whom I had ever worked who perished in the 9/11 attack. The other was John O'Neill, the former FBI counterterrorist chief who, having started a second career as director of security at the World Trade Center, was in one of the towers when it collapsed.

A different sort of connection to the end of the Vietnam War came in my last few years of government service. I was the national intelligence officer for the Near East and South Asia during a period (2000–2005) in which the war in Iraq was sold, launched, and became a quagmire. Thus, two tragically ill-conceived military expeditions were bookends to my thirty years of public service (two in the army and, after an interval as a student, twenty-eight in the intelligence community). The perches from which I observed the end of one misguided war and the beginning of another were quite different—a junior army officer in the field in one, a senior intelligence officer in Washington in the other—although I hardly had any more influence on events in one job than in the other. The significance of these two wars in my life has prodded my thinking about why the

United States gets into such costly misadventures. This book addresses what is commonly, even if mistakenly, perceived to contain much of the answer to that question.

My career in the U.S. intelligence community provided a vantage point for observing directly many of the patterns discussed in this book. That vantage point also made clear that an extraordinarily large proportion of public commentary about intelligence is ill informed. This pattern in part reflects the special qualities of intelligence, which combines an unavoidably large amount of secrecy and opacity with a fascination and intrigue that have made it a favorite subject of writers of fiction and nonfiction alike as well as of writing that unfortunately blurs the two.

My experiences in intelligence brought pride and satisfaction. I entered the profession for reasons similar to the corny but commendable ones I hear from my students who are interested in entering it—wanting to serve the public interest and hoping to have a favorable impact on public policy and address problems that present as much intellectual challenge as any inside government. As parts of this book make apparent, any young officer who enters the profession with expectations about saving the world through brilliant intelligence will quickly have such expectations deflated. But I had my share of high points on a wonderfully diverse set of issues. For example, I accompanied Director of Central Intelligence William Webster as his executive assistant when he became the first director to visit eastern European countries shortly after Communist rule crumbled. Several years later I had the satisfaction of being the lead (and originally the sole) intelligence officer in the initial rounds of secret talks with Libya that led Colonel Muammar Qadhafi's regime to give up its unconventional weapons programs and become an ally rather than an enemy in efforts against international terrorism.

I am not primarily an intelligence officer by sentiment or temperament, however. I was trained as a political scientist, the profession I currently practice as a university professor. During my career in government service, I often felt like an academic trapped inside a bureaucrat's body. This book is written less from the perspective of a former intelligence officer than from the perspective of a concerned citizen and scholar of foreign policy who happens to have additional insights gained from previous experience in intelligence.

I have known and worked with many of the officials and former officials who populate this book, in addition to the few about whom I explicitly mention such a personal connection. Some of my former colleagues may dislike some observations that appear to question their usefulness and even their integrity. That is not my intent. Others may interpret some of my observations as an attempt to exculpate the U.S. intelligence community, to obscure its shortcomings, and to shift to others the blame it has incurred for past failures. That also is not my intent. This book will have achieved its main purpose if it helps to get Americans away from blame games altogether and leads them to ponder how the making of their country's foreign policy is really—not just theoretically or ideally—informed and guided and what this understanding implies for making that policy better guided.

I owe thanks primarily to the many colleagues inside and outside the intelligence community with whom I worked while a public servant. As a citizen, I salute them for contributions to the national interest that are almost entirely unknown and too often unappreciated. More personally, I thank them—especially those who at one time or another were my subordinates—for helping me do my own jobs and for being so congenial in the process. Any attempt to name specific individuals would surely entail many inadvertent omissions and might also be a complication for some still in government.

Since I retired from public service, Georgetown University and its Center for Peace and Security Studies have furnished me with a stimulating professional home. I have benefited in intellectual enrichment and other ways from interaction with the students, staff, and my fellow faculty members at the center and its associated Security Studies Program. I am grateful to Daniel Byman, a remarkably energetic scholar and academic leader who, as program director, was most responsible for bringing me to Georgetown. I also thank Robert Gallucci, then dean of the Walsh School of Foreign Service, for acceding to Dan's idea of taking me on board. I have continued to benefit from the leadership of the current program director, Bruce Hoffman, and the current dean, Carol Lancaster.

I have honed the ideas in this book in informal discussions about intelligence with sundry friends and associates from either my first or my second career. Several are regulars in the intelligence salon led by Jennifer Sims of Georgetown. The salon critiqued a draft of one chapter of the book. Richard Betts, who has long been one of the most insightful scholars of intelligence, read the entire manuscript and offered helpful suggestions. I have profited from exchanges of ideas over several years with Robert Jervis, another perceptive academic observer of intelligence and contributor to the literature on it. Eva Brown, Alissa Gordon, Stephen Ryan, and Samantha Vinograd provided research assistance.

I have presented some ideas in this book in different form in articles in *The National Interest, Foreign Affairs, Intelligence and National Security*, and the *SAIS Review*. I thank the editors of those journals for their invitations to develop my thinking on the subject and to present some of the results in their publications. I also thank Anne Routon and Leslie Kriesel, the editors at Columbia University Press who have shepherded this book, and Annie Barva, who copyedited the manuscript.

As a condition of my former government employment, the CIA has reviewed this book to ensure that it contains no classified information. That review has not affected the substance of the book. I am solely responsible for its contents. Nothing in this book reflects any position of or authentication or endorsement by the CIA or any other part of the U.S. government.

My family has exhibited exemplary forbearance in the face of my preoccupation with this project. My wife, Cynthia, has provided support in ways too numerous to list while stoically observing that retirement from the government did not seem to reduce my working hours. My daughter, Veronica, and son, Lucas, have exhibited patience in other ways, for which I also am grateful.

Washington, D.C.
January 2011

INTELLIGENCE AND U.S. FOREIGN POLICY

CHAPTER ONE

INTRODUCTION
A Comforting Explanation for Calamity

Why does the foreign and security policy of the United States so often seem to be not just unsuccessful but misguided, being based on incomplete or otherwise mistaken images of the outside world? Some of the most memorable episodes in America's relationship with the world have included debilitating wars—Vietnam and Iraq being the leading examples—in which the decisions to wage war appear to have been based on incorrect perceptions of those countries. They have included placing bets on ill-fated regimes, such as that of the shah of Iran. They have included falling victim to surprise attack, most notably at Pearl Harbor in 1941 and in New York and Washington, D.C., sixty years later. How can the United States—powerful and resourceful as it is, with its leaders surely able to call on the best possible sources of insight and information—be so badly and sometimes tragically mistaken about events beyond its borders?

The impression of chronic error is partly a matter of selective retrospection. One can easily find offsetting successes. Along with the debilitating and inconclusive wars have been victorious ones, including the two world wars of the twentieth century, the Cold War, and the war to expel Iraq from Kuwait. Losing bets on specific countries or regimes are offset by winning ones such as the Marshall Plan, whose payoff came in the form of stable and strong European allies. And although the converse of a surprise attack is a nonevent and thus inherently less visible, favorable nonevents such as attacks that did not happen have also been a part of the history of U.S. relations with the rest of the world. A fair appraisal of the more than two centuries of that history suggests that, on balance, well-conceived and well-guided policies have added to the good fortune of geography and resources to help put the United States in the enviable position it reached by the opening decade of the twenty-first century. One of the most perspicacious students of American foreign relations, Walter Russell Mead, observes that overall "the United States has had a remarkably successful history in international relations."[1] Many of the successes have depended not only on sound judgment and skillful execution but also on accurate underlying images of the foreign reality with which the policymakers have dealt.

Regardless of whether the bottom line of the U.S. foreign-policy balance sheet is colored black or red, how can it be improved in the future? Bad foreign policy has numerous possible ingredients, but among the more important presumably are the images that policymakers hold of the foreign situations to which their policies are a response. Those images include the policymakers' perception of current reality, their understanding of the forces and dynamics at play, and usually their sense of where the events in question are heading. The whole package is a construct that, whatever its origins, is tied more closely to the decision maker's mind than to the outside world that the decision maker believes it represents. It is accordingly more appropriate to call this construct an image rather than knowledge.[2]

In one sense, there has been plenty of attention to this ingredient in discussions of U.S. policy. Anguish in recent years over the twin traumas of the terrorist attack of September 11, 2001—commonly known as 9/11—and the Iraq War has been expressed chiefly in terms of mistaken images: of threats that supposedly were underrated in one instance and overrated in the other. But most of the anguish has an extremely narrow focus that overlooks the most important inputs to the images policymakers hold and how images actually shape policy, if they shape it at all. That narrow focus has been on what are termed "intelligence failures" and on the need to fix or reform intelligence. Narrowing the focus even more, intelligence gets equated with the output of certain elements of the U.S. government that have the word *intelligence* in their names or that have the gathering of intelligence as their primary mission.

This very constricted form of attention to the causes of misguided pol-icy stems in part from how the making of foreign and security policy is *supposed* to work. The textbook model of the policy process involves de-cision makers dispassionately reflecting on the information and analysis available to them—the principal source being an equally dispassionate intelligence service—and then selecting a course of action based on that reflection.

The narrow focus of attention stems at least as much from emotion and public psychology as it does from textbooks. We like to attribute woebegone wars and shocking surprise attacks to the shortcomings of intelligence ser-vices because this explanation is easily understandable and because it of-fers the comforting prospect that by fixing such shortcomings, we can pre-vent comparable calamities from occurring. It would be far less comforting to conclude that mistaken images underlying failed policies had sources less susceptible to repair, that relevant misperceptions resided more in our own heads or the heads of political leaders we elected than in unelected bureaucracies, or that some of the most important things we did not know were unknowable to anyone on our side, even if we had the most exemplary intelligence service.

These tendencies are especially marked for Americans. It is natural to assume that the superior capabilities that have enabled the United States to do so well in so many other endeavors apply also to the forming of ac-curate images of the outside world. If the United States could win world wars, put a man on the moon, and do all the other marvelous and diffi-cult things it has accomplished, then according to reason it should be able to perform just as well the task of determining what is going on in other countries.

The tendency toward exceptionalism—the idea that the United States is not only good at many things, but also better than anyone else—contributes to this pattern. This tendency obscures inconsistency between how other countries are believed to form their images of the outside world and how America is believed to form its. Many Americans see nothing contradictory in believing that foreigners are prisoners of parochial biases, but that they themselves are not.

These perspectives color Americans' attitudes toward their own institu-tions, including governmental institutions. The opening words of the U.S. Constitution set the tone in referring to the formation of "a more perfect union." Perfection being an absolute, "more perfect" does not make semantic sense. But the constitutional preamble captures well an American outlook that combines unbounded faith in what institutions ought to be able to do along with an engineer's problem-solving perspective that when difficulties arise, the machinery of government needs to be and can be fixed. The American belief in the "indefinite perfectibility of man" that Alexis de Tocqueville observed in the nineteenth century extends as well to a belief in the indefinite perfectibility of American institutions.[3]

A consequence of this outlook is a strong belief that if the relevant institutions are working well, the United States ought to hold accurate images of the outside world. A more specific consequence is the persistent American tendency to attribute failures of U.S. foreign and security policy to the policymakers' having been misguided, to attribute the misguidance to failures of intelligence institutions, and to believe that the proper response is to fix intelligence.

A major refrain in discourse about making U.S. foreign and security policy better is thus intelligence failure and intelligence "reform." (I often put the term *reform* in quotation marks because as generally used it refers to any change to intelligence institutions not initiated by the institutions themselves rather than to improvement per the dictionary definition of the term.) The refrain has been heard for decades in a huge flow of official pronouncements and unofficial commentary. The flow is unending. It implicitly promises a reformist nirvana in which, with the right fixes, Americans finally can stop fretting about the ineffectiveness of their intelligence services. But the nirvana is never reached.

The fixation on intelligence failure and reform sustains several misconceptions that this book aims to dispel. Among the realities that are contrary to broadly held belief and that later chapters demonstrate are:

• Despite intense attention to an infamous intelligence estimate in 2002 on Iraqi unconventional weapons, most prewar intelligence analysis on Iraq was good, especially regarding the prospective consequences of the war. The policy implication of the intelligence community's work on Iraq was to avoid the war, not to launch it.

• Despite near-universal acceptance of the 2004 report by the National Commission on Terrorist Attacks Upon the United States (9/11 Commission) as thorough and careful, the commission misrepresented much of the intelligence community's pre-9/11 strategic work on terrorism and never mentioned large portions of it. This misrepresentation and elision distorted a record in which the intelligence community successfully identified and described the threat from al-Qa'ida and imparted that threat to policymakers.

• Notwithstanding some instances (such as with terrorism) of intelligence enlightening policy, the overall influence—for good or for ill—of intelligence on major decisions and departures in U.S. foreign policy has been negligible. Most notorious intelligence failures have similarly had almost no effect on U.S. policy or U.S. interests.

• Policy has shaped intelligence more than vice versa. This relationship has entailed significant corruption of intelligence through politicization, but official inquiries have refused to recognize this influence.

• The intelligence community—contrary to its common image as a stodgy bureaucracy that must be pushed into reform—has exhibited nearly continuous internally driven change and adaptation. Almost every subject raised by would-be reformers outside the community has already been a focus of concentrated attention by the community itself.

• The most important sources of images guiding policy and thus the leading opportunities for making those images more accurate have nothing to do with intelligence and instead lie within the political strata of government.

Whatever solace the common beliefs about intelligence have provided to Americans looking for reassuring explanations for past setbacks, they have done almost nothing to make American policy better informed and more intelligently formulated. Hence, the main message of this book is:

Efforts to make U.S. foreign and security policy better guided, based on the notion of intelligence reform, are themselves misguided. They miss the sources of mistaken images underlying failed policies, misconceive the intelligence–policy relationship as the reverse of how it often works, produce "reform" that does not improve intelligence and in some respects makes it worse, misperceive the limits to understanding the outside world, and encourage foreign policies that are unsound because of the failure to recognize those limits.

The dominant approach, focusing on intelligence failure and reform, to making U.S. policy better informed is misguided in part because actual formulation of policy is far different from the textbook model. Even though intelligence makes important contributions to national security every week on matters ranging from ferreting out terrorist cells to monitoring enhancements to foreign military forces, it has not had anything close to the guiding role in policy that it does in the model. One reason why it hasn't is that images of the world abroad, from whatever source, are only one input to foreign-policy decisions and not necessarily the most influential. Other factors, from presidential neuroses to domestic political interests, are often more powerful. Another reason is that to the extent that images of the world abroad do shape policy, intelligence is only one possible source. It is much less influential than sources that are closer to the policymakers' minds and hearts. The latter sources include individual leaders' personal experiences of other leaders (such as Harry Truman's likening of Stalin to Truman's former patron, Kansas City political boss Tom Pendergast)[4] and entire generations' historical experiences (for example, Hitler's serving as a repeatedly invoked analogy for other foreign dictators).

Those more personal and formative sources of images have a much greater chance than any report from an intelligence service to break through and to mold worldviews—which in the political realm are usually called "ideologies"—that shape our perceptions of the world around us.[5] This shaping is how our brains avoid being paralyzed by the torrent of information our senses continually gather and the inconsistencies within it. We discard or distort new information to fit into a preexisting worldview far more than any new information changes the worldview.[6] This is at least as true of political leaders, who lack time for contemplation and reeducation, as of the rest of us. Doris Kearns Goodwin has noted this pattern, which she saw firsthand in Lyndon Johnson but can be applied to political leaders generally: "Worldviews, once formed, are difficult to change, especially for politicians. Always reacting and responding, their life largely one of movement among and contact with others, politicians are nearly always bound to the concepts and images formed in their minds before taking office, or those evolved from well-established and therefore safely followed sources of knowledge and guidance. If their ideas about the world sometimes sound like assumptions from a forgotten age, it is, in part, the price they pay for a life of continual motion."[7]

In addition to the more personal sources of images of the outside world and to the personal and political considerations that influence policy regardless of the images, policymakers share with their countrymen whatever peculiar ways of looking at the world flow from their nation's history, physical circumstances, and culture. The very distinctive history and circumstances of the United States has made for some distinctively American ways of looking at problems in the rest of the world. It therefore should be no surprise that inputs from an intelligence service have had so little influence in guiding American foreign policy. There simply is no contest be-tween someone's memorandum or briefing, on the one hand, and the deci-sion maker's political and psychological well-being, the belief system that got that decision maker to a position of power, and the accumulated effects of more than two centuries of American history, on the other.

The fixation on intelligence reform also is misguided in that it fails to recognize the very large amount of uncertainty that is an unavoidable in-gredient in policymaking, no matter how effectively an intelligence service may be performing. The uncertainty is inevitable for two fundamental reasons. One is that adversaries (and sometimes friends) withhold informa-tion, and there is no reason to expect them to be any less adept than we are at keeping secrets and uncovering those of others. The other reason is that much of what would be nice to know while formulating policy is essentially unknowable (even without anyone keeping secrets) because it is the result of processes too complex to fathom. This is especially true of the anticipa-tion of future events, which result not only from unfathomable complexity but also from decisions that others have not yet taken.

The fixation on intelligence failure and reform feeds on itself. It has become part of a worldview that most Americans share. As with other worldviews, information is selected, discarded, or distorted to fit existing beliefs. And thus many specific misperceptions add to the more basic mis-conceptions about what intelligence influences, what it should be capable of knowing, and how it currently functions.

The theme of intelligence failure fits comfortably into characteristically American ways of thinking about politics, policymaking, the U.S. encoun-ter with the world, and the nature of the United States itself. The theme is firmly entrenched in American political discourse—so firmly and so con-tinuously that it is a safe bet it will remain entrenched indefinitely. Refer-ences to failures of intelligence and the need to fix intelligence are a kind of throat clearing—an obligatory preliminary to ensure that one's contri-bution will be accepted as in touch with mainstream thinking on national security.

Although the theme has been entrenched in American discourse for decades, failures—or perceived failures—of intelligence inevitably occur from time to time, thereby sustaining the theme, adding to the related lore, and giving participants in the discourse material that helps them to sound fresh and current. More important, it enables them to sound responsive to genuine and sometimes deeply felt anger among the American people over national tragedy or trauma. Playing this role far more than any other sub-jects in recent years have been the terrorist attacks of September 11, 2001, and the presumed Iraqi unconventional weapons program that the George W. Bush administration used to sell the Iraq War. The searing effects of both 9/11 and the Iraq War on the American consciousness account for the fact that these two topics overwhelm almost everything else the intelligence community has done during the past couple of decades in shaping popular American perceptions of that community's performance.

The fact that the terrorist attack and the souring of the Iraq War oc-curred in rapid succession amplified the impact of both. One event is only one event; two events are taken as a pattern. The 9/11 attack and Iraqi weap-ons of mass destruction (WMD) have become a two-verse mantra whose utterance is now another required part of mainstream discourse on security issues. The details of what intelligence did or did not do or say or of how it did or did not affect policy related to these events do not seem to matter. The two tragedies are repeatedly invoked as a widely understood shorthand reference to the equally widely accepted common lore about how U.S. in-telligence is broken and needs fixing.

That lore, along with all of the associated perceptions about intelligence guiding policy and about bad intelligence being responsible for failed poli-cies, functions as a national myth, which in turn is a component of main-stream American ideology about foreign affairs and national security. All nations have myths, which serve a variety of cultural, psychological, social, and political functions. They are mainly a source of reassurance about shared problems and the nation's ability to overcome them and a reinforcement of faith in the people themselves and in what is most important to them. The mythology about American intelligence provides a sense that the problems (in this case, destructive policies and shocking loss of life) and their causes (presumed faulty intelligence) are understood. It provides a sense that every-one agrees that the problems should be fixed. It offers assurance that as long as the fixes are made, the people will elect leaders who will follow sound policies and will protect them from harm, thus bolstering the people's faith in the worth and effectiveness of their political system. And like some other aspects of national culture, the myth strengthens national cohesion, giving people of different political persuasions something to agree upon even if they disagree on other things.

An unrealistically high expectation for what intelligence should be able to achieve is a major element of U.S. mythology about intelligence.[8] Americans expect that an intelligence service that is performing properly should be consistently accurate and accurate in detail about a wide range of questions. That range may have become even wider in recent years. Former director of central intelligence (DCI) George Tenet thought so when he reflected on criticism of the intelligence community for not predicting the timing of Indian nuclear tests in 1998. The "field of expectation had changed," he said; when the adversary was the USSR, the community had not been expected to predict or prevent weapons tests, but now it was.[9] Like so much else about criticisms of U.S. intelligence, however, inflated expectations are not altogether new. When Walter Bedell Smith was appointed DCI in 1950, he insightfully noted the impossible expectations he would face. "American people expect you to be on a communing level with God and Joe Stalin, and I'm not sure they are so much interested in God," Smith observed. "They expect you to be able to say that a war will start next Tuesday at 5:32 p.m."[10]

Myths are not necessarily false in their entirety. Most national myths are at least based on truth, and in the case of intelligence there is the truth of actual intelligence failures. But the myth typically departs from reality in ways that preserve the myth's ability to reassure. The myth may encourage policymakers to act differently from how they otherwise would have acted. Myths thus can have major downsides even though they serve important purposes. The Cold War myth that America's Communist foe was a single, global movement intent on imposing its ideology throughout the world helped to sustain national will to wage the Cold War for four decades, but it also helped to misguide the United States into the Vietnam War.[11]

The mythology of American intelligence damages U.S. interests in several ways. One is to pursue fruitless intelligence "reform" that is at best a diversion of national time and attention and at worst a disruption that impedes an intelligence service's work in the short term and might even make it less effective over the longer term. As a spasmodic reaction to a few salient national tragedies, such "reform" is based on truncated and distorted perceptions of U.S. intelligence that miss not only most of what intelligence is doing right, but also much of what it is doing wrong.

The mythology misses the fact that images of the outside world flow from preferences more than preferences flow from the images. That is how worldviews and ideologies work. Because the mythology further misses how policy influences intelligence more than intelligence influences policy (especially on high-profile foreign-policy issues regarding which sentiments are strong), it fosters blindness to the politicization that infects intelligence and to those possible reforms that would help to correct the problem.

Mistaken notions about the influence of intelligence on policy lead to inattention to what really influences policy and to changes that would have the best chance of making policy better guided in the future. The mythology of intelligence ignores the much larger role of other sources of images of the world abroad, in particular ones within the policymaking layers of government. This means overlooking yet another possible avenue of reform that, unlike the endless tinkering with the intelligence community, actually might make U.S. foreign policy better guided.

The most damaging consequence is to encourage the making of policy that is prone to fail because it exceeds the limits of our knowledge. The mythology does not recognize those limits. So we embark on policies that would work well only if certain things we believe—but do not know—were true, and then we curse our lack of knowledge when these things turn out to be false. Or rather, we curse the intelligence service we expected to provide the knowledge. We fail to appreciate that some of our images, no matter how carefully they are constructed and no matter how much the intelligence community has been reformed, will be wrong. The reformist nirvana will never be reached because it does not exist. The mythology diverts us from the truth that sound policy needs to take account of unavoidable uncertainty and to be designed to advance the national interest no matter what way that uncertainty is ultimately resolved.

Intelligence often fails, sometimes demonstrably. But illusions about the reasons and ideas for reform based on such illusions and on naive expectations about what can be done risk producing different failures at least as bad as those we have already seen. Intelligence mythology leads to policy pathology. Real improvement—rather than feel-good pseudo-solutions that have been peddled and in some cases unfortunately implemented—requires cold-eyed appreciation of many unwelcome realities that human psychology and emotion make difficult for policymakers and citizens alike to grasp. This book presents such an appreciation, based on long study of the problems and many years of personal experience with them.

Chapters 2 through 4 address a recent and extreme illustration of some of the main propositions in this book and one that has contributed heavily to the mythology: the George W. Bush administration's decision to invade Iraq in 2003. Intelligence, which figured prominently in the selling of that decision, played almost no role in making it. The war was launched in spite of, not because of, most of what the U.S. intelligence community said about Iraq. The U.S. Congress went along for the political ride, and its passivity provided incentive for its own later contribution to the mythology about intelligence and the war.

Iraq is an especially strong example of the irrelevance of intelligence to the making of a major U.S. foreign-policy decision, but it is hardly the only one. Chapter 5 reviews how several of the other biggest departures of U.S. policy since World War II, including successful as well as unsuccessful ones, exhibit the same pattern.

Chapter 6 discusses how politicization has been a fact of life for the U.S. intelligence community and a major blind spot in the mythology of intelligence and associated agitation for reform. The Iraq War provides an extreme example of politicization, but earlier episodes foreshadowed it.

The narrow focus on intelligence failure as an explanation for misguided policy has become so narrow that discourse on the subject loses sight of whether intelligence has any impact on policy at all. Intelligence has become a spectator sport, with selected bits of intelligence output being scored as successes or failures not because they matter for U.S. interests, but instead because they happen to be easy to score. As chapter 7 shows, some of the most notorious intelligence failures have had virtually no impact on U.S. policy or U.S. interests.

The theme of intelligence failure and reform has been sounded for so long that it raises the questions of why this theme has such persistence and why something that supposedly has been broken for so long still has not been fixed. Chapter 8 examines the possible answers to these questions. The most commonly voiced answers, consistent with the mythology, have some grains of truth but ultimately are unable to explain the theme's persistence. More cogent—though less comforting—explanations are that intelligence failures are inevitable, that the performance of intelligence is perceived as worse than it is, and that the theme of intelligence failure serves purposes that no amount of reform can ever serve. Providing a reassuring explanation for calamity is the theme's chief but not sole purpose. Others are the diversion of blame from political interests and the sustenance of what amounts to an intelligence reform industry.

Chapter 9 turns to the other (besides the Iraq War) great shaper of contemporary U.S. perceptions of intelligence: the 9/11 attack. It was one of the most traumatic episodes in U.S. history, so the need for comforting explanations was greater than ever. The impulse to make intelligence failure the chief explanation for tragedy and intelligence reform the chief hope for preventing a recurrence was thus stronger than ever. Accounts of events surrounding 9/11 were bent as necessary to furnish such a reassuring explanation. The chief bender was the 9/11 Commission, which became a vehicle for achieving postattack national catharsis. It accomplished that mission with a highly politicized inquiry and report that fostered the false impression that U.S. intelligence had neither recognized the threat underlying 9/11 nor conveyed appreciation of the threat to policymakers. The strength of the nation's appetite for the catharsis and reassurance that the commission provided was further manifested, as chapter 10 describes, in the unthinking, adulatory acceptance of the commission's account and recommendations.

The centerpiece of those recommendations was an intelligence reorganization scheme that Congress adopted after cursory consideration in 2004. As discussed in chapter 11, the reorganization was an exercise in which Americans deluded themselves that redrawing lines on the intelligence community's organization chart would somehow make them safer. It has not. That chapter also addresses how recurring themes in intelligence reform pay little attention to what the intelligence community already does along the same lines or to the reasons it does not do more.

Possible reforms that offer genuine hope for better guiding policy are few, and the probable impact of most is limited. Chapter 12 discusses one type of reorganization that actually might improve intelligence on the most significant and controversial policy issues, but that has been completely ignored by mythology-based "reform": making the intelligence community more independent of executive-branch policymakers and thereby reducing politicization. The same chapter also addresses the single reform that would be most likely to improve the accuracy and objectivity of images that come before policymakers and are most likely to influence their policies: a substantial paring down of the unusually large political layer of the executive branch.

No matter what reforms are enacted, substantial and unavoidable uncertainty will forever characterize the making of foreign and security policy. Much about the outside world we will never know, regardless of how intelligence performs. The makers of policy should accept that fact and shape policy in recognition of it. Chapter 13 sets out principles for doing so.

CHAPTER TWO

WEAPONS OF MASS DESTRUCTION
AND THE IRAQ WAR

The most extraordinary aspect of the George W. Bush administration's launching of a war in Iraq in March 2003 was the absence of any apparent procedure for determining whether the war was a good idea. There was not just a poor policy process or an incomplete one or a biased one; there was *no* policy process. In the years since the invasion, investigative reporters have uncovered many details about discussions on Iraq within the administration, but they have found no meeting, no options paper, no debate in the White House Situation Room, or anything else that addressed whether an invasion of Iraq was in U.S. interests or not as input to a presidential decision on whether to invade. Many discussions addressed how to sell the war to the public. Others—in retrospect, perhaps not enough—addressed how to implement the decision to invade. But none addressed whether the war should be launched at all. Deputy Secretary of State Richard Armitage, when asked after leaving office whether the process for making policy on Iraq was broken, replied, "There was never any policy process to break, by Condi [Rice] or anyone else. There never was one from the start. Bush didn't want one, for whatever reason."[1]

A major implication is that any analysis that the intelligence community or any other part of the bureaucracy might have offered could not possibly have guided the decision to go to war because there was no opportunity to offer such analysis. The intelligence community, the military, and other parts of the executive branch were never asked for input to the decision whether to invade Iraq. They also had no forum in which they could even volunteer insights while speaking directly to the issue of whether the United States should initiate such an expedition. The issue was never raised; it was never on any meeting's agenda.

The bureaucracy could volunteer relevant analysis only partially, indirectly, circumspectly, tardily, and thus ineffectively. Some such analysis—for example, concerning likely postinvasion division and disorder in Iraq—was offered in discussions about implementing the decision. But there was no chance of influencing the decision itself, which had already been made. Queries from skeptical members of Congress provided other opportunities to offer some relevant images about Iraq, but the implications for whether it made sense to go to war could not be spelled out without openly aligning with the administration's opponents and blatantly subverting a policy course already set.

The absence of a policy process has obscured, even to this day, the true reasons the Bush administration invaded Iraq. There simply is no record of deliberation on this question. The director of policy planning at the State Department at the time, Richard Haass, was later asked why the administration launched the war. "I will go to my grave not knowing that," he replied. "I can't answer it."[2]

Rhetorical smokescreens have exacerbated the challenge of identifying the genuine reasons for the invasion. The Bush administration released the thickest of these smokescreens as part of its huge effort to muster public support for the war. The effort had to be huge because of the extraordinary nature of the step the administration was taking. The invasion of Iraq was the first major offensive war the United States was to wage since the war against Spain more than a century earlier. All of America's foreign military expeditions during the twentieth century had been either minor operations such as those in Panama or Grenada or, in the case of major wars, interventions in ongoing conflicts that had begun with someone else's aggression. In Iraq, the United States would be the aggressor.

The administration realized that a tremendous, no-holds-barred sales job was needed to persuade the American public to support this departure from a tradition of nonaggression. A successful sales campaign required focusing on whatever themes would resonate best with the American public regardless of whether they reflected actual reasons for waging the war or not. The campaign also needed to portray a war of choice as a war of necessity instead, based supposedly on hard, cold, frightening facts. The direct result was a hyping of the twin specters of terrorism and WMD. The campaign was supported by a relentless effort to dig up whatever bits of reporting could be construed as showing that Iraq was an immediate threat on both counts.

An indirect result was obfuscation of the true reasons for going to war. The themes of the sales campaign were so relentlessly sounded and so dominated public discussion before the invasion and afterward that they have been widely taken as being not only sales themes, but the actual reasons for the invasion, or at least the main reasons for it. Bits of reporting used to support those themes have been mistakenly regarded as images that drove the decision to invade. An example of the latter outlook is the subtitle of one journalist's book about an infamously fraudulent source for allegations about an Iraqi biological weapons program: *Curveball: Spies, Lies, and the Con Man Who Caused a War.*[3]

The difficulties that U.S. forces eventually encountered in Iraq and the consequent reduction in public support for the war that the Bush administration encountered within the United States extended the obfuscation. Recriminations and rationalizations flying from several directions added to the confusion. The administration tried to slide from one rationale to another in maintaining that the war was still a good idea, while letting the intelligence community absorb most of the hits for errors regarding unconventional weapons programs. For others who were seeking to rationalize their own support for the war, emphasizing the weapons issue as a supposedly overriding reason had a similar attraction, enabling them to claim that if they had erred, it was only because they had been misinformed.

THE NEOCONSERVATIVE DREAM

Concern about WMD was not the principal driver of the Bush administration's decision to invade Iraq, and the famously flawed intelligence analysis on the subject had no or almost no influence on the decision. A major indication of this conclusion is that the decision was made well before the analysis was produced. The movement for war had gained momentum much earlier.

The roots of the decision to use military force to overthrow Saddam Hussein extend back a decade, to the previous war that the United States—led by George W. Bush's father—had waged against Saddam Hussein's Iraq. Operation Desert Storm in 1991 swiftly accomplished its mission of reversing the Iraqi conquest of Kuwait but left in some mouths the bitter aftertaste of unfinished business. One of those bothered by Saddam's remaining in place was Paul Wolfowitz, then undersecretary of defense for policy, whose later obsession with removing Saddam would make him (as deputy secretary of defense) probably the most passionate advocate of war among senior policymakers in the younger Bush's administration. As Desert Storm was concluding its mission, Wolfowitz opposed announcing a cease-fire and, along with Secretary of Defense Richard Cheney, warmed to an abortive proposal to place U.S. troops inside western Iraq.[4]

The theme of removing Saddam Hussein acquired more momentum in neoconservative circles during the mid- to late 1990s. A crescendo of commentary, much of it by neocons who would obtain senior positions in the younger Bush's administration, addressed the subject. By the latter part of the decade, the theme of ousting Saddam had been translated into open calls to accomplish the goal through war. An article by Wolfowitz and Zalmay Khalilzad in the *Weekly Standard* in late 1997 called for the "substantial use of military force" to accomplish the goal. The authors recommended "sustained attacks" against elite Iraqi military and security forces as well as other measures, such as arming and training Iraqi exile groups.[5]

In January 1998, the Project for the New American Century (PNAC), a neocon-dominated advocacy group chaired by *Weekly Standard* editor William Kristol, published an open letter to President Bill Clinton calling for a new strategy that "should aim, above all, at the removal of Saddam Hussein's regime from power." This meant, the letter made explicit, "a willingness to undertake military action as diplomacy is clearly failing."[6] Another open letter in February, including many of the same neocon signatories and additional heavyweights such as former secretary of defense Donald Rumsfeld, declared that "Saddam must be overpowered; he will not be brought down by a coup d'état." The statement called for a series of forceful measures, including sustained air bombardment, to exploit what the letter asserted was a situation "ripe for a broad-based insurrection." The letter did not prescribe an immediate ground war, but it recommended the positioning of equipment for U.S. ground forces so that as a "last resort" such a campaign could be waged.[7]

The history of the neoconservatives' march to war thus began well before the advent of the George W. Bush administration. The impetus for that march could not have been any intelligence or any other input laid before that administration. Two years into the war, in 2005, Robert Kagan commented on this subject as it related to the evolution of his own thinking and that of his fellow neocons: "I certainly never based my judgment on American intelligence, faulty or otherwise, much less on the intelligence produced by the Bush administration before the war. I don't think anyone else did either. I had formed my impressions during the 1990s."[8]

DEMOCRATIZING THE MIDDLE EAST

The chief purpose of forcibly removing Saddam flowed from the central objectives of neoconservatism. At the core of this ideology is the proposition that the United States should use its power and influence to spread its own freedom-oriented values, including open politics and free-enterprise economics. The PNAC's founding statement listed promotion of "the cause of political and economic freedom abroad" as one of its main goals.[9] The chief objective of the war to oust Saddam Hussein—bearing in mind that no single objective explains everything and that the relative importance of different objectives varied from one proponent of the war to another—was not only to bestow free politics and free economics on Iraq, but also, through regime change there, to catalyze the spread of those freedoms through the rest of the Middle East.

In a speech to a friendly audience—the American Enterprise Institute— in February 2003, three weeks before U.S. forces invaded Iraq, President Bush emphasized that the proposed war was about the spread of freedom and democracy. He presented a democratic domino theory, in which Iraq would be the first in a row of dominoes in the Middle East. "A liberated Iraq can show the power of freedom to transform that vital region," the president said, "by bringing hope and progress into the lives of millions." A spread of democratic values is in everyone's interest, the president continued, and he perceived a Middle East that would be receptive to those values. The mission for the United States in overthrowing Saddam was clear: "A new regime in Iraq would serve as a dramatic and inspiring example of freedom for other nations in the region."[10]

Nearly two years into the war, President Bush (and his speechwriters) eloquently spelled out this objective further in his second Inaugural Address, in which he declared that "it is the policy of the United States to seek and support the growth of democratic movements and institutions in every nation and culture, with the ultimate goal of ending tyranny in our world."[11] Some critics of the administration dismissed the rhetoric as an after-the-fact scramble for a rationale for the war following the nondiscovery of the unconventional weapons programs that earlier had been the chief selling point. But the theme of democratic transformation and reform was too fully developed in the administration's statements, too prominent a part of the administration's overall policy toward the Middle East, and too much at the core of neoconservative doctrine to be merely rhetorical rationalization. The Bush administration certainly scrambled to maintain support for the war when earlier rationales proved defective, but that does not make the later rationales any less sincere than earlier ones. The earlier rationales were chosen because of salesmanship, not sincerity.

Other signs pointed to the preeminence of democratic values as a motivation to launch the war, despite this motivation's being eclipsed in the prewar sales campaign by the fear-laden themes of terrorism and WMD. Vice President Cheney, in a conversation one month after the invasion about what was most important to the president in making war, said, "Democracy in the Middle East is just a big deal for him. It's what's driving him."[12] As for the supporting cast of intellectuals whose push for the war did so much to create the climate in which the president made his decision, a good indication of motivations comes from one of the more honest and thoughtful neocons, Joshua Muravchik, in an article in 2006. Remaking the politics of the Middle East was indeed the main purpose of the war, said Muravchik, who argued persuasively that even though America's troubles in Iraq may have been due not just to poor execution, but to the war's having been a bad idea from the start—an unusual admission from a neocon—political reform in the Middle East was still needed because the region's unreformed politics help to breed extremism and terrorism.[13]

Political and economic transformation in the Middle East was the chief but not sole objective in invading Iraq. Another purpose was the exertion of American power as a demonstration of the U.S. ability and willingness to use that power, thereby increasing deference to U.S. interests worldwide and deterring adversaries and would-be troublemakers from opposing those interests. This objective was a matter of the United States capitalizing on its position as the sole remaining superpower, as columnist Charles Kraut-hammer had urged in a much-noticed article on "the unipolar moment" when that moment was beginning in the immediate aftermath of the Cold War in the early 1990s. "Our best hope for safety," wrote Krauthammer, "is in American strength and will—the strength and will to lead a unipolar world, unashamedly laying down the rules of world order and being pre-pared to enforce them."[14]

This objective, like that of spreading political and economic freedoms, was at the core of neoconservative ideology. In this sense, Iraq became for neocons a sort of test case for their much larger ideas about U.S. power and leadership worldwide.[15] But the concept did not solely belong to the neo-cons. It probably was a major motivation for Vice President Cheney and Secretary of Defense Rumsfeld, who are best labeled not as neoconserva-tives, but instead, according to one study of policymaking in the Bush ad-ministration, as "assertive nationalists."[16]

The twin objectives of spreading freedom in a region and sending mes-sages farther afield about American strength and willpower constituted an offensively oriented counterpart to the defensive objectives that were the main reasons the United States under Lyndon Johnson went to war in Viet-nam in the 1960s. The version of the domino theory applied to Asia in-volved a feared succumbing of successive neighboring states to communism; the new version applied to the Middle East featured a hoped-for succumbing of successive neighboring states to the attractions of freedom and democracy. As for sending a message about American strength and will, the Vietnam-era policymakers were concerned chiefly with maintaining the credibility of de-fensive commitments. With Iraq, the objective was similar but with more emphasis on expanding U.S. influence and not just protecting a status quo. In both cases, the country over which war would be waged—Vietnam or Iraq—was less an end in itself than a means to achieve something larger.

The neoconservatives focused on the Middle East because in addition to energy resources, strategic location, and other reasons the area held their interest, it was (and still is) conspicuously deficient in the freedoms that they wished to spread. The region also is dominated by largely unreformed, state-centric economies characterized by subsidies and heavy dependence on extraction of natural resources. The Middle East has been an annoying affront to the idea—part wish and part perception—that the Western vic-tory in the Cold War had opened the way for Western values to win ac-ceptance around the globe.

Several attributes of the Iraqi regime, such as Saddam's brutality and record of aggression, helped to make a war in Iraq a more sellable proposition than a war elsewhere in the region. More basic to the neocon agenda, however, was Iraq's importance in the Middle East. Its place in regional affairs made it a promising lodestar for regionwide political and economic change. It was an Arab state, which made it more capable than non-Arab Iran of setting an example for other Middle Eastern countries. Iraq has been one of the traditional centers of Arab culture and power, dating back to the Baghdad-centered Abbasid Caliphate that arose in the eighth century. It is one of the most populous Arab states and more centrally located than other relatively large Arab countries.

In short, Iraq combined positive and negative attributes that made it an especially attractive target for anyone interested in changing regimes and spreading freedom in the Middle East. On one hand, Iraq was significant enough to the Arab world for it plausibly to function as the lead domino whose fall would help to knock over other reconstructed political systems in the region. On the other hand, it was ruled by an especially abhorrent dictator—the perfect foil whose overthrow would be the immediate objective of a war that could be portrayed as just and necessary. For an administration "determined to change the strategic equation in the Middle East," note Michael Gordon and Bernard Trainor in their chronicle of the war, "Iraq was not a danger to avoid but a strategic opportunity."[17]

OIL

Two other subjects are sometimes mentioned as motivations for the war, although public discussion of them has tended to obscure more than to illuminate. Raising them at all risks being misunderstood, which is why in shorter descriptions of the objectives that drove the decision to launch the war I have referred only to the primary objective of remaking the Middle East's politics and economics and have not attempted to address other motivators.[18] One of those other subjects is oil. Mentioning this subject risks giving credibility to some of the more primitive accusations against the Bush administration—namely, that the war was all about seizing control of Iraq's oil and, in the crudest versions, that this control was sought in the financial interests of the U.S. oil and oil services industries. Closely related is the fallacious accusation heard in the Middle East that the United States was out to plunder Muslims' resources.

Setting the primitive accusations aside, however, there are two respects in which oil figured into the decision to launch the war. One is that Iraq's oil resources are part of what gives Iraq disproportionate influence in the Middle East. Its more than one hundred billion barrels of oil reserves are larger than those of any other Middle Eastern producer, including Saudi Arabia and Iran, so its petroleum accentuates its clout and regional importance. Along with geography, demography, and history, oil is part of what made Iraq appear to be a promising catalyst for regionwide political and economic change.

The other respect was the belief among some proponents of the war that occupation of Iraq could be done on the cheap because the country's oil wealth would help the occupation pay for itself. I return to this belief in the next chapter.

ISRAEL

Another subject that, even more than oil, is hazardous to raise is the extent to which sympathy for Israel and its interests—or, more precisely, certain interpretations of its interests—helped to drive the decision to invade Iraq. Temperate, open discussion of this topic is almost impossible in the United States because of the vituperative responses elicited by any discourse that questions the wisdom of unflinching U.S. support for Israel, points out daylight between U.S. and Israeli interests, or explains why such responses occur.[19]

Despite the hazard of venturing close to this third rail of American politics, the subject simply cannot be ignored in any complete examination of why the United States went to war in Iraq. The effects of pro-Israeli sympathies on U.S. policies in the Middle East are too conspicuous and substantial to dismiss the possibility that they helped to guide the most significant U.S. policy initiative in the region in recent years.

U.S. and Israeli interests in Iraq and the Iraq War are in some respects parallel, but in other respects diverge. The divergence is all the greater when U.S. interests are compared not with an outsider's objective rendering of what is in Israel's best interests, but instead with the particular conception of those interests—associated with the Israeli political Right—that tends to influence U.S. policies more than other conceptions.

The most obvious point of divergence is that the war has expended American—not Israeli—blood and treasure. Whatever the benefits that proponents of the war in either country hoped for, the expected costs for each country were quite different. The direct costs for Israel were essentially zero. Thus, from an Israeli perspective even vague or tenuous benefits might tip the balance of pros and cons in favor of the war, even if from a U.S. perspective alone they would not.

For a U.S. operation in Iraq to become a new center of attention in the region could benefit Israel by diverting attention and opprobrium from its own military occupation of the West Bank and conflict with its Arab neighbors. To some extent, this diversion did happen. Before the war, the Israeli–Palestinian issue was the one topic that Arabs throughout the region (and some Muslims elsewhere) would repeatedly raise as a grievance. After 2003, it became one of two such persistent themes, the other one being the U.S. occupation of Iraq. For the United States to use large-scale military force in the name of the "war on terror" also helps Israel to justify its own use of military force against adversaries it describes as terrorists.[20]

Given that the Israel factor is a matter of sentiment at least as much as strategy, it tended to affect the thinking of U.S. policymakers on the Iraq War in very personal ways. It probably was significant for some policymakers, but much less so for others. One for whom it appears to have been a major consideration was Douglas Feith, who was undersecretary of defense for policy from the start of the Bush administration in 2001 until mid-2005. Feith's principal intellectual endeavor in the mid-1990s was to advocate a hard-line policy for Israel that would kill the peace process based on the Oslo Accord and have Israel indefinitely retain the occupied territories.[21]

In 1996, Feith participated in a study group convened by a right-wing Israeli think tank to offer advice to Likud Party leader and incoming prime minister Benjamin Netanyahu. The group included other American neoconservatives who would ardently promote the Iraq War: David Wurmser, who later worked for Feith in the Pentagon, and Richard Perle, who led the study group and would chair the Defense Policy Board in the Bush administration. The study group's report continued the theme of rejecting the trading of land for peace. "Our claim to the land," the group wrote, "to which we have clung for hope for 2000 years—is legitimate and noble." The group's report stressed the need to remove Saddam Hussein's regime not only as "an important Israeli strategic objective in its own right," but as a means to remake the regional balance of power in Israel's favor. The report talked about a restoration of the Hashemites (who include the Jordanian monarchy and the Iraqi monarchy that was overthrown in a coup in 1958) in Iraq as leading to an Israel–Turkey–Jordan–Iraq alignment that would isolate and squeeze Syria and reduce the influence of Hizballah and Iran.[22]

Netanyahu did not follow all of the group's advice (Feith, in a later article, chided him for not explicitly abrogating the Oslo Accord),[23] but the authors of the study group report did not give up. Wurmser developed the report's themes further in a 1999 book that portrayed Iraq and the Palestinian resistance to Israel as parts of the same problem, lauded Ahmed Chalabi's Iraqi National Congress, and suggested the Congress could ally with King Hussein, with post-Saddam Iraq becoming part of a federation with Jordan. If diplomacy could not accomplish this, Wurmser concluded, "we will eventually be forced to revert to war, to end Saddam's regime and occupy Baghdad."[24] A subtext to all of this was that by revising the regional balance of power and stripping the Palestinians of sources of support, Israel would not have to negotiate a withdrawal from the Occupied Territories.[25]

Feith's dedication to Israeli interests had an intensely personal foundation. His father had lost his parents and several siblings in Nazi death camps. Feith spoke of policy in explicitly religious terms that few others, especially Gentiles, would dare to do. "The surprising thing is not that there are so many Jews who are neocons," he said, "but that there are so many who are not."[26]

Another architect of the Iraq War with connections to Israel was Deputy Secretary of Defense Wolfowitz. Like Feith, Wolfowitz had lost relatives in the Holocaust.[27] His older sister married an Israeli and took up residence in Israel.[28] The *Jerusalem Post* reported that when Wolfowitz, whom it noted was "considered a strong supporter of Israel," was appointed deputy defense secretary, "the Jewish and pro-Israel communities [jumped] for joy."[29] In 2003, the *Post* made Wolfowitz its inaugural selection as "Man of the Year."[30]

Beyond a few individual officials such as Feith and Wolfowitz, any influence that sympathy for Israeli interests had on the Iraq War decision was more indirect, in the form of the clout of broader constituencies for whom Israel had special importance. Broader constituencies in this case did not necessarily mean Jewish Americans, who according to polls—even if this pattern may have surprised Feith—supported the Iraq War less than the American population as a whole.[31] Religion was relevant, however, in that some Christian evangelicals, as a matter of religious doctrine, have been among the most strongly pro-Israel elements in American politics. The evangelical doctrine in question holds that the establishment and protection of the Jewish state is a critical intermediate step toward the Second Coming.[32] The evangelicals were in turn among the most important parts of George W. Bush's base of support.

Sympathy for Israeli interests probably was not the principal motivator in the decision to launch the Iraq War, but it did play an important supporting role. Images of a foreign problem such as Iraq that are most important to U.S. interests are not necessarily those most important to the interests of Israel or any other foreign state. Thus, some policymakers probably gave less attention or weight than U.S. interests warranted to, say, the American human and material resources required for the postinvasion occupation of Iraq because they had Israeli interests (or their particular conception of those interests) and not just U.S. interests at heart.

THE EARLY FOCUS

The preoccupation with Iraq and with forcibly ousting Saddam Hussein, which became so prominent in commentary of the late 1990s, continued unabated when some of the commentators entered office under George W. Bush. Ten days after becoming president in 2001, Bush met for the first time with his national security principals, with "Mideast policy" as the advertised subject. The biggest, longest-running topic in U.S. policy on the Middle East, the Arab–Israeli conflict, was disposed of in short order, with the president remarking that the United States should disengage from that issue. When the president—in what several present took to be a previously arranged exchange—asked his national security adviser, Condoleezza Rice, what they should discuss instead, Rice replied, "How Iraq is destabilizing the region, Mr. President." By the end of the meeting, the president had levied several tasks concerning Iraq. Secretary of Defense Rumsfeld and the chairman of the Joint Chiefs of Staff, General Hugh Shelton, were to "examine our military options" and "how it might look" to use U.S. ground forces to challenge Saddam Hussein. DCI George Tenet was charged with reporting on how to get more intelligence on Iraq.[33]

When the principals reconvened at the beginning of February, Rumsfeld cut more directly and explicitly to the objective that was driving the agenda. Amid a discussion about sanctions against Iraq, he said, "Sanctions are fine, but what we really want to think about is going after Saddam." Rumsfeld extolled the further benefits of doing so: "Imagine what the region would look like without Saddam and with a regime aligned with U.S. interests. It would change everything in the region and beyond it. It would demonstrate what U.S. policy is all about." Secretary of the Treasury Paul O'Neill, who was at the meeting, later aptly characterized what he was witnessing: "From the beginning, we were building the case against Hussein and looking at how we could take him out and change Iraq into a new country. And, if we did that, it would solve everything. It was all about finding a way to do it. That was the tone of it. The President was saying, 'Fine. Go find me a way to do this.'"[34]

From the first days of the Bush administration, the impetus for forcibly removing Saddam Hussein was strong and coming from senior policymaking levels. The most energetic promoters of the cause were within the office of the vice president and the civilian policymaking structure of the Department of Defense. The president himself evidently favored the cause from the beginning, even if he was not the prime mover. Policymakers were not choosing an objective in response to dangers and demands being made known to them, regarding WMD or anything else. Instead, as O'Neill correctly described the process, they were "building the case" for the ouster of Saddam Hussein, which they already sought. A military invasion was the most certain way of achieving that goal and the goal of politically remaking Iraq—as well as the assertive nationalists' goal of demonstrating "what U.S. policy is all about." In the first eight months of the administration, however, the case was not yet built. More important, there would not have been sufficient support among the American public for the drastic step of launching an offensive war at this time.

Exploiting 9/11

The situation changed abruptly and dramatically on September 11, 2001. Not because the terrorist threat that materialized that day had not earlier been thoroughly understood by those responsible for countering terrorism; it was. Not because Iraq was working with those responsible for the terrorist attack; it wasn't. Instead, it was because 9/11 drastically changed the mood of the American public. Americans suddenly became more militant and far more willing to pay prices, bear burdens, and assume risks in the name of national security than they had been previously. They felt a strong urge to lash out, strike back, and "do something"—preferably several forceful things—in response to the horrifying attack. Americans became far more receptive than before to even something as extreme as an offensive war.

The proponents of a war to oust Saddam at last had their opportunity, and they realized it immediately. On the afternoon of the attacks, aides to Secretary of Defense Rumsfeld took notes on his staccato thoughts as he led a meeting in the National Military Command Center: "Best info fast. Judge whether good enough to hit S. H. [Saddam Hussein] at same time. Not only UBL [Usama bin Ladin]. Go massive. Sweep it all up. Things related and not."[35] In a National Security Council (NSC) meeting the following day, Rumsfeld argued that any effort against global terrorism inevitably would take the United States someday to Baghdad.[36]

Deputy Secretary Wolfowitz, who within minutes of fleeing his Pentagon office was also talking about going after Saddam, pressed the issue four days later in a meeting of President Bush and his national security team at Camp David. Wolfowitz said there was a 10 to 50 percent chance that Saddam had been part of the 9/11 plot, but that wasn't even the main reason he argued for attacking Iraq immediately. It would be, he argued, an easier war than one in Afghanistan. Intervention in Afghanistan would mean chasing elusive al-Qa'ida cells in mountainous terrain; invading Iraq would be a straightforward toppling of a corrupt and vulnerable regime.[37]

When the director of operations for the Joint Chiefs of Staff, Lieutenant General Gregory Newbold, returned from an overseas trip a few days after the attack, he threw himself into planning for the military response. With the smell of smoke still in the Pentagon corridors, he assured Undersecretary Feith that his staff was working hard on Afghanistan. Feith—although he later would deny making this remark—responded, "Why are you working on Afghanistan? You ought to be working on Iraq."[38]

Proponents of the war outside the administration cranked up their agitation in favor of knocking over Saddam. An open letter to President Bush signed by several prominent neoconservatives, among others, on September 20 stated, "It may be that the Iraqi government provided assistance in some form to the recent attack on the United States. But even if evidence does not link Iraq directly to the attack, any strategy aiming at the eradication of terrorism and its sponsors must include a determined effort to remove Saddam Hussein from power in Iraq."[39] In November, Wolfowitz asked the American Enterprise Institute to put together a study group on terrorism. The resulting report—which, bizarrely for the product of a private think tank, was labeled "secret" and hand delivered to selected cabinet members—conflated diverse lines of conflict in the Middle East and wound up focusing on Iraq because it was considered a more tractable target than Saudi Arabia, Iran, or Egypt. Saddam Hussein was deemed vulnerable, and the Ba'athist ideology of his regime was described as "an Arab form of fascism transplanted to Iraq."[40]

The opportunity for the warhawks had arrived, but time was needed to develop and exploit the opportunity. Wolfowitz's Camp David urging to topple Saddam Hussein right away was rejected because the other Bush administration seniors realized that, even amid the suddenly more militant climate in America, an invasion of Iraq then would have been too obviously contrived a response to a terrorist attack by a group based in Taliban-ruled Afghanistan. A yearlong effort to condition public opinion, based on the notion that invading Iraq would be part of a global "war on terror," was needed to make the Iraq War sellable.

Preparations, however—for the war itself as well as for the selling of it—could begin without delay. The day after the 9/11 attack, President Bush collared White House counterterrorist chief Richard Clarke and some of his staff and said, "I know you have a lot to do and all . . . but I want you, as soon as you can, to go back over everything, everything. See if Saddam did this. See if he's linked in any way." When Clarke replied that repeated previous examinations had uncovered no connection between al-Qa'ida and Iraq, the president responded—"testily," according to Clarke—"Look into Iraq, Saddam."[41] On November 21, 2001, nine days after the Taliban was driven from Kabul, Bush directed Rumsfeld to construct in secret a fresh plan for going to war against Iraq. When Rumsfeld suggested he should bring DCI Tenet in on the planning, the president denied him permission to do so, saying that could be done later.[42]

U.S. Central Command (CENTCOM) did the planning the president had ordered. On December 28, its commander, General Tommy Franks, presented to Bush at his ranch in Texas a full briefing on a plan to invade Iraq. In a press conference after Franks's visit to the ranch, the president discussed Afghanistan but did not mention Iraq. None of the journalists present asked about Iraq. Over the next several weeks, the war plan that

Franks briefed was revised in repeated exchanges between him and Rumsfeld.[43]

In his State of the Union Address on January 29, 2002, Bush applied the famous label *axis of evil* to Iraq, Iran, and North Korea. He also established what would be the main war-selling rhetorical theme for the next year and beyond: terrorism and WMD, mashed together into a single, indivisible, scary threat. Rogue regimes "could" give advanced weapons to terrorists, he said, and so the goal had to be "to deny terrorists and their state sponsors the materials, technology, and expertise to make and deliver weapons of mass destruction."[44] The inclusion of Iran and North Korea (the subject of one sentence each in the speech) provided cover for the focus on Iraq (the explicit subject of five sentences). An earlier draft of the speech had mentioned only Iraq, with the axis of evil referring to the dual threats of terrorism and WMD. Condoleezza Rice and her deputy, Stephen Hadley, added Iran and North Korea to reduce the chance that the planning for a war against Iraq would be discovered.[45]

The gradually increasing public rhetoric about Iraq as well as accumulating signs of the secret planning for the war and the selling of the war became more noticeable to officials within the executive branch over the next several months. Haass, the State Department's policy planning chief, initially did not read much into these signs, but by early July he took them seriously enough to raise Iraq in a regular meeting with Rice on foreign-policy issues. When Haass began to express the department's reservations about a war with Iraq, Rice interrupted him. "Save your breath, Richard." she said. "The president has already made up his mind on Iraq."[46]

By the following month, the administration's determination to go to war had also become evident to its allies in the British government. The head of the British Secret Intelligence Service, Sir Richard Dearlove, reporting on a recent visit to Washington, told Prime Minister Tony Blair and his senior national security aides in a meeting on July 23 (minutes of which later leaked as the "Downing Street memo"), "Military action was now seen as inevitable. Bush wanted to remove Saddam, through military action, justified by the conjunction of terrorism and WMD." Foreign Secretary Jack Straw agreed that "Bush had made up his mind to take military action, even if the timing was not yet decided." The intelligence chief further observed that "the intelligence and facts were being fixed around the policy," the Bush administration "had no patience with the UN route," and "there was little discussion in Washington of the aftermath after military action."[47]

The Bush administration had strong reasons to dissemble about its commitment to invade Iraq. To complete the necessary selling of the war, it needed to maintain control over the conditioning of public opinion. Most Americans, even in their post-9/11 militancy, might be hesitant about a measure as extreme as an offensive war unless their government first spent a year inculcating in them the belief that Saddam Hussein was a serious menace. To unveil the war option too clearly and too soon would give arguments against the war a chance to build momentum and support. The arguments would include ones from both outside and inside the government, with the latter always posing the threat of leaks. The Bush administration's most successful act of preemption was not against Saddam Hussein—who was not on the verge of attacking U.S. interests—but instead in domestic politics by keeping its intentions unclear long enough to prevent effective opposition to the war from mobilizing.

An additional incentive to dissemble was to preserve the fiction that the administration's principal objective was not the ouster of the Iraqi regime, but instead an end to its menacing behavior, particularly with respect to the development of unconventional weapons. This was especially important in keeping on board the British, who believed a war would be difficult to justify without first attempting to resolve the weapons issue through United Nations–mandated inspections. The fiction eventually would break down completely in the final days before the invasion as the administration shoved the inspection process aside, but by then it was far too late for any opposition to the war to have a chance.

President Bush maintained the deception by saying repeatedly in 2002, both publicly in press conferences and privately to members of his cabinet, that there were "no war plans on my desk."[48] That may have been literally true in terms of what documents lay on furniture in the Oval Office, but it misrepresented the state of decision making of a president who months earlier had clearly ordered the development of such plans and had been fully briefed on them by the theater commander.

In sum, most senior members of the administration who already had favored forcibly ousting Saddam probably concluded very quickly after 9/11 and the resulting sea change in the American political climate that the time had come to do so. That another year and a half would pass before U.S. forces attacked Iraq was not because of indecision or contemplation of intelligence on Iraq, but instead because of the need to prepare public opinion for the war. President Bush's thinking is somewhat harder to track but appears to have followed a similar timeline. Given his early instructions to prepare military plans and to search for any Iraqi links to the terrorist attacks, he probably also effectively decided in the first weeks after 9/11 to wage the war, which was possibly still contingent to some degree in his mind on how effective a public case could be made. It is highly likely that by midsummer 2002—about the time Rice was telling Haass to save his breath and Dearlove was telling his superiors in London that military action was inevitable—the decision was firm.

No Alarm Bells

The history of the march toward war in Iraq makes it clear that intelligence did not guide or propel that march, however much the Bush administration drew on intelligence in making its public case for war. Other indications confirm that, including statements that the war makers themselves made on the few occasions when guards were lowered and candor emerged. Paul Wolfowitz, near the end of a long interview for *Vanity Fair* in May 2003, indicated that the weapons issue was a convenient consensus selling point rather than the prime mover that the sales campaign made it appear. "The truth is," said Wolfowitz, "that for reasons that have a lot to do with the U.S. government bureaucracy we settled on the one issue that everyone could agree on which was weapons of mass destruction."[49] Douglas Feith remarked in 2006 about the weapons issue, "My basic view is, the rationale for the war didn't hinge on the details of this intelligence even though the details of the intelligence at times became elements of the public presentation." With the cavalier attitude he had so often displayed in selling the war, he continued, "The administration sold it the way it sold it. That's history."[50]

As the Bush administration entered office, neither the intelligence community nor any other part of the bureaucracy presented it with alarms about Iraq, any statement about imminent danger from Saddam's regime, or anything else that could be interpreted as a spur for use of military force against that regime. The DCI never walked into the Oval Office and said, "Mr. President, there's a problem regarding Iraq's weapons programs that needs your attention" or anything even remotely resembling that. To the contrary, in the early months of the Bush administration (before 9/11 and the decision to go to war) the dominant theme of what the intelligence community and State Department were saying to policymakers was one of downplaying the immediacy or severity of any threat from Saddam and specifically any threat based on unconventional weapons.

This pattern was evident in a briefing DCI Tenet gave to President-elect Bush shortly before the inauguration. Tenet's number one topic was the threat from Usama bin Ladin and al-Qa'ida. Other subjects included rising China and weapons proliferation in general. Tenet barely mentioned Iraq.[51]

In early February 2001, Tenet presented to Congress the intelligence community's comprehensive annual statement on worldwide threats. After the lead topic of al-Qa'ida and terrorism, the statement addressed weapons proliferation. The sole mention of Iraq in this section was a single sentence saying that Iraq probably was conducting work on ballistic missiles and that, if it received foreign assistance, it could develop an intercontinental ballistic missile capability "sometime in the next decade." The section of the statement on weapons went on at length about biological, chemical, and nuclear threats, addressing many other countries, but with no further mention of Iraq. In a later section addressing the Middle East, a passage on Iraq discussed how higher oil prices had helped Saddam to fend off domestic pressure and how he was using diplomacy to reduce his isolation. The statement emphasized, however, the constraints on Saddam's power. His economic infrastructure was in "long-term decline," his ability to project power outside Iraq was "severely limited," and international sanctions were keeping his diminished military from operating effectively even inside Iraq. The statement did refer to "the likelihood that he will seek a renewed WMD capability," but the only developments cited were refurbishment of civilian facilities that could be diverted to military use related to chemical or biological weapons or ballistic missiles. The possibility of Iraqi nuclear weapons was never even mentioned. Nor was there mention of any stockpiles of biological, chemical, or other unconventional weapons.[52]

Intelligence briefings presented privately to policymakers were consistent with the publicly delivered picture. In a meeting President Bush had with his senior national security team in May, Tenet stressed how much was unknown about Iraqi activities and that it was only speculation that Saddam Hussein had WMD or active programs to build them.[53] My corner of the intelligence community produced nothing during the first year of the Bush administration that could be construed as an impetus for more aggressive action against Iraq. When I joined the National Intelligence Council (NIC) in October 2000, the council was on the verge of completing a paper on Iraqi weapons programs; the main judgments in that paper were essentially the same—as of course they should have been—as those in the worldwide threat statement delivered in February.

In May, Secretary of State Colin Powell told a Senate committee that Iraq was pursuing programs to develop WMD, but that "the best intelligence estimate suggests that they have not been terribly successful." Powell's bottom line was that the Iraqi regime "has been contained."[54] Intelligence judgments about Iraq and Iraqi weapons programs were clearly not driving any decisions on more forceful action against Iraq. The later sordid story of intelligence, the issue of WMD, and the selling of the war is a tale about policymakers pulling, not of intelligence services pushing.

PULLING ON INTELLIGENCE

The interaction between Bush administration policymakers and the intelligence community about Iraqi weapons programs was entirely one of the administration's pressing the community for juicier tidbits that would make more of an impression on the public when talking about Iraqi weapons programs. It was this kind of pressing that led to George Tenet's famous "slam dunk" comment at a meeting at the White House in December 2002. Deputy DCI John McLaughlin had carefully reviewed for the president the available information on Iraqi unconventional weapons. The president's response was, "That's not good enough." He didn't mean that it wasn't good enough to launch the war, a decision that had already been made, but that it wasn't a good enough sales pitch to the public. "Nice try," said Bush, but "it's not something that Joe Public would understand or would gain a lot of confidence from." When the president then asked Tenet if this was the best material he had to offer, the intelligence chief responded with his immortal remark about a basketball shot. In this and other dialogue with intelligence officers, policymakers never asked whether thinness of the evidence might warrant a reappraisal of judgments based on it, let alone a reappraisal of the wisdom of going to war with this material as one of the principal rationales. It was all about selling the war to the public.[55] The most famous tidbit the administration extracted concerned an alleged purchase by Iraq of uranium ore from Niger—famous because it became the subject of a public refutation by a former diplomat who investigated the matter, a subsequent effort by the office of the vice president to discredit this diplomat and his

U.S. Central Intelligence Agency (CIA) officer wife, a cover-up of the discrediting, a criminal conviction of vice presidential aide I. Lewis Libby for committing perjury during the cover-up, and a presidential commutation of Libby's prison sentence. This item had special attraction to the war makers because it was something that might resonate with the masses. Unlike technical details such as the thickness of aluminum tubes, buying uranium was something even Joe Public could understand or thinks he understands. The policymakers did not care that even if Iraq had purchased ore in Niger, it would have made little or no difference to an Iraqi nuclear program given that Iraq already had a large stockpile of uranium oxide. What mattered to them was not any implication for analysis of whether Iraq had such a program but instead what would help them to sell a war to the American public.

The rhetorical attraction of the report about uranium ore led policymakers to push repeatedly to include it in public statements about Iraq, despite the intelligence community's repeated advice that they not use it because of its doubtful credibility and authenticity. One such occasion was a presidential statement in the Rose Garden about Iraq; Condoleezza Rice agreed to delete a reference to the report after the CIA raised the issue when reviewing a draft of the statement.[56] The most significant occasion came during preparation of Bush's biggest speech on Iraq, in Cincinnati in October 2002. The White House once again included the suspect item in its draft. This time DCI Tenet called Deputy National Security Adviser Hadley to urge him to delete it. Hadley resisted, saying this line was one of the more important in the speech. Tenet did not back down, and again the item was removed. The CIA followed up this conversation with a memorandum to the White House explaining more fully why it distrusted the report. Besides the fact that Iraq's stock of uranium ore made a further purchase unnecessary, the sourcing of the report was weak, and other information about the uranium mines in question suggested they could not have been involved in any such transaction. The CIA's memo also noted that its analysts had made these same points to their British counterparts and to Congress.[57]

After pulling on several doors in the intelligence community, the administration finally found one that would open. Despite the previous warnings, the White House once again put the item about uranium in the draft of a speech—the 2003 State of the Union Address. The NSC's senior nonproliferation official, Robert Joseph, called Alan Foley, the chief of the intelligence community's nonproliferation center, and proposed that the report be cited while attributing it to the British.[58] Foley's acquiescence was the reaction of an intelligence officer accustomed to dealing with many reports of uncertain credibility and being comfortable doing so as long as the sourcing was specified and unjustified conclusions were not explicitly built on them. It was not the reaction of someone wise in the ways of speech-writing gamesmanship and the public manipulation of images. So the White House finally got to use its uranium-purchase zinger, making it sound like credible information by using as its formulation in the final version of the speech not "a report the British collected," let alone "a report the British collected and about which U.S. analysts have major reservations," but instead "the British government has learned that."[59]

The later recriminations over this episode contributed significantly to the ill will between the Bush administration and the intelligence community and in particular between Rice and Tenet. It made for some good Washington theater, but most of the audience did not seem to reflect on what Rice was essentially saying when she tried to shift blame for the episode onto the CIA: "You failed to prevent us from misusing intelligence when, despite your repeated previous efforts and warnings, we insisted on doing so." Or, more succinctly, "It's your fault because you didn't keep us from misbehaving."

This posture should have provoked howls, but it did not because the administration's public misuse of intelligence on Iraq was so extensive for so long that it shifted the entire frame of reference for interpreting what was taking place and evaluating the participants' performances. What was happening was less akin to theater than to a football game, in which the Bush administration was the offense attempting to run as far and as hard as it could with its chosen pieces of reporting. It was left to the intelligence community to play defense. Even if on the previous couple of downs the defense had stopped the play for no gain, when the offense found a weak spot (think of Foley failing to tackle Joseph) and gained yardage, the defense would later be criticized for this one failure. With the clock for war winding down, the offense also was continually trying to go out of bounds. The defense was expected to keep the offense in bounds. Its failure to do so was again a source of later criticism.

The metaphor of a football game accurately describes not only how spectators in the public and the press came to view the relationship between the Bush administration and the intelligence community, but also the actual relationship. In this sense, the spectator-critics were viewing the game appropriately. But almost no one asked, "What's wrong with this picture?" Or "Why is this game being played at all?" Policymakers and intelligence officers are supposed to be on the same team. Intelligence services are supposed to help resist the offensive thrusts of foreign adversaries, not the offensive thrusts of their own political leaders. In the game being played, an intelligence service was being relied upon to perform a task it was not created, organized, or trained to do—a task that made no sense in any sound process for making foreign policy. The intelligence community thus came to be judged not only for whether it got things right, but also for how vigorously it resisted when policymakers insisted on getting things wrong.

The Infamous Estimate

Not only did the neoconservative campaign for a war predate the Bush administration, but the administration's own pro-war campaign predated the most infamous intelligence product on which it supposedly was based: the ill-starred national intelligence estimate (NIE) on Iraqi weapons programs, which was completed in October 2002. As the documented history of the policymaking indicates, the president reached his decision to invade Iraq well before that point—and even before work began on the estimate, which was produced in three weeks.

The campaign to *sell* the war moved into high gear before the estimate was ever written. In August 2002, White House chief of staff Andrew Card set up the White House Iraq Group to plan and coordinate the sales effort.[60] Most of the planning and script writing was done by the end of the month, even though most of the implementation would take place after Washington and the country returned from summer vacations. As Card observed, "From a marketing point of view, you don't introduce new products in August."[61] The de facto keynote for the campaign, a major speech by Vice President Cheney to the Veterans of Foreign Wars (VFW) on August 26, jumped the postvacation gun a bit. Besides taking advantage of a friendly audience at the VFW convention, the accelerated timing of the vice president's speech evidently stemmed from Cheney's concern that he needed to counter arguments against the war that such luminaries as Brent Scowcroft and James Baker recently had made.[62]

Because calendars do not run backward, it was impossible for the October 2002 NIE to have influenced the war decision already made. It also was impossible for it to have influenced arguments that the vice president and others already were making and that were centered on the specter of WMD. Such chronological details tend to get lost amid the passage of time and the swirl of recriminations. Looking back at those politically charged events is like watching a creatively edited movie filled with flashbacks, and the audience is taxed to its limits in trying to keep track of which scenes took place before which other scenes.

The Bush administration did not request the estimate about weapons programs, which is consistent with its record of not having requested any intelligence assessments about Iraq prior to its decision to invade the country. Democrats on the Senate intelligence committee requested the estimate—on a rush basis as they faced a vote on a resolution to endorse the war. The committee's chairman, Bob Graham (D–Fla.), said he was "stunned" to learn that the administration itself had never requested such a paper.[63]

President Bush never read the entire estimate, and neither did National Security Adviser Rice.[64] Presidents rarely read NIEs, but this one concerned what Bush's administration was using as one of the biggest selling points for the war that would be by far the biggest initiative of his presidency. And Bush was a president whose willingness to read would later take the form of a book-reading contest with his political adviser, Karl Rove. According to Bush, in the first year of the competition (2006), he read ninety-five books totaling 37,343 pages.[65] The unread estimate on Iraqi weapons was ninety-two pages.

Bush's and other senior policymakers' lack of use for this intelligence estimate, notwithstanding the enormous public attention it would receive, showed two things. It was one more indication that the weapons issue had little role in leading the Bush administration to war, despite its huge role in selling the war. It also demonstrated the imperviousness of the policymakers on the Iraq War to intelligence as an input to the images shaping their policies. Secretary of Defense Rumsfeld repeatedly made clear his doubts and suspicions about intelligence. He contended that intelligence generally understated problems or failed to detect them at all.[66] Vice President Cheney warned in his VFW speech, "Intelligence is an uncertain business, even in the best of circumstances," and a dictatorship adept at deceit was far from the best circumstances. Cheney referred to intelligence underestimates of the progress Iraq had made on a nuclear program prior to Operation Desert Storm in 1991. He went on to present judgments about current

Iraqi programs that were markedly different from those of the intelligence community (which I discuss further later).[67]

The flawed intelligence analysis on Iraqi weapons programs tended to serve the Bush administration's war-selling purposes, particularly in the dumbed-down, greatly oversimplified "Saddam has WMD" form in which it became absorbed in the public consciousness. But even the faulty October NIE contained important judgments that, if they had been noticed and heeded, would have provided the foundation for strong arguments *against* invading Iraq. One such judgment was that the Iraqi regime probably was still years away from possessing any nuclear weapons—the most important type of unconventional weapon and the basis for the scary images of mushroom clouds of which President Bush and Condoleezza Rice spoke.[68] There was no urgency and nothing impending to preempt. If Iraqi weapons developments were the concern, there was ample time to try other policy responses short of the drastic one of an offensive war. The message that Vice President Cheney conveyed in his speech in August was far different. "Many of us are convinced," he said, "that Saddam will acquire nuclear weapons fairly soon."[69]

Cheney expressed in the same speech a degree of certitude going well beyond what could be gleaned from the intelligence community's product, including even the infamous NIE: "*We now know* that Saddam has resumed his efforts to acquire nuclear weapons," said the vice president. "Simply stated, *there is no doubt* that Saddam Hussein now has weapons of mass destruction."[70] Even just the dissents that individual agencies registered in the NIE, regardless of the language expressing the majority views, were sufficient to show that there were many doubts on this subject, at least within the U.S. intelligence community.

Cheney continued his supremely confident, "no doubt" tone in speaking of the likely use that Saddam Hussein would make of any WMD he did have. "There is no doubt he is amassing them to use against our friends, against our enemies, and against us," Cheney declared. "And there is no doubt that his aggressive regional ambitions will lead him into future confrontations with his neighbors—confrontations that will involve both the weapons he has today, and the ones he will continue to develop with his oil wealth."[71] Donald Rumsfeld had exuded similar certainty three months earlier when he told a Senate subcommittee, "In just facing the facts, we have to recognize that terrorist networks have relationships with terrorist states that have weapons of mass destruction, and that they *inevitably* are going to get their hands on them, and they would not hesitate one minute in using them."[72]

On this issue there were not just doubts; Cheney and Rumsfeld's declarations were directly counter to the intelligence community's judgment regarding likely disposition and use of such weapons. In response to a question from Senator Carl Levin (D–Mich.), a member of the Senate Select Committee on Intelligence as well as chairman of the Senate Armed Services Committee, the intelligence community included in the October estimate its judgment on the issue. The judgment was that Saddam probably would not use either conventional or unconventional weapons against the United States, unless a U.S. attack against him was inevitable and thus there was nothing left for him to deter. The last-gasp scenario of a U.S. invasion toppling his regime also was the only situation in which the intelligence community envisioned Saddam considering the extreme step of helping Islamist terrorists to conduct a WMD attack against the United States in order to bring down as many victims as possible along with himself.

Levin, Graham, and other Democratic skeptics on the Intelligence Committee correctly seized on this judgment as important. In a closed hearing the committee held in early October with several of us who had been involved with the estimate, the senators understandably—and somewhat angrily—said there was no less reason to make this judgment public than to broadcast to the public all the alarums, supposedly based on intelligence, that the administration was raising about Iraqi weapons programs. The judgments about likely usage were chiefly my responsibility. It was left to me and my colleague Bob Walpole, the national intelligence officer who covered nuclear programs and directed the overall estimate, to negotiate with the senators as to what to do about the issue. (George Tenet had been present for an earlier part of the lengthy hearing but left for another commitment.) We agreed to draft an unclassified statement that incorporated the portion of the estimate the senators had highlighted as well as related excerpts from testimony at the hearing. Such a statement, after being revised in Tenet's office, was released five days later as a letter from the DCI to the committee chairman and was published in full in the New York Times.[73]

We will never know, of course, if the judgment in question was sound because Saddam Hussein did not have the feared weapons in the first place. But anyone who cared to take notice would realize that the judgment stood the Bush administration's entire campaign about Iraqi WMD on its head; the only event likely to make those weapons a threat to the United States would be the very war for which the administration was campaigning. Despite the efforts made by the skeptical senators on the Intelligence Committee, whatever notice this issue received was drowned out by the incessant drum beating about what Saddam "could" do with WMD. The administration did not miss a beat. On the day the letter went to the committee, President Bush delivered a major speech about the "grave threat" Iraq posed, hitting all the scripted themes about mushroom clouds and how Saddam Hussein might give WMD to terrorists.[74]

FALSE EQUATIONS

Another indication that the invasion was all about regime change and not about WMD was the administration's unwillingness to take yes for an answer regarding international inspections of Iraq's weapons-related activity or suspected activity. In an NSC meeting in September 2002, Cheney expressed opposition to international inspections out of fear that anything less than a damning inspection report would weaken the case for deposing Saddam.[75] Douglas Feith put it more bluntly in another comment he later denied making: "In crafting a strategy for Iraq," said Feith, "we cannot accept surrender."[76] Saddam's readmission of inspectors from the United Nations Monitoring, Verification, and Inspection Commission (UNMOVIC) and the International Atomic Energy Agency (IAEA) to Iraq in November 2002, after a gap of four years, thus posed a hazard to the administration's plans. Hans Blix of UNMOVIC and Mohamed El Baradei of IAEA reported to the United Nations Security Council in February that although the regime still had to account for many banned weapons, it was cooperating well, and no WMD had been found.[77] In subsequent reports in early March 2003, Blix and El Baradei cited further progress and said no proscribed activities had been discovered.[78] If the concern really were with prohibited weapons, there was every reason to let the inspection process proceed. But the Bush administration was instead set on ousting the regime. This time it was Washington, not Baghdad, that kicked weapons inspectors out of Iraq, advising them to leave three days before the invasion.

Yet another sign that WMD were not the chief motivation for the invasion was that nuclear weapons programs were more advanced and posed more immediate worries in countries other than Iraq that the Bush administration was not planning to invade. These countries included the other members of the axis of evil, especially North Korea, the one place where, given the erratic and bankrupt dictatorship of Kim Jong Il, the much-hyped scenario of a government giving (or more likely selling) fissile material to a terrorist group begins to be plausible. As of the first year of the Bush administration, the intelligence community assessed that North Korea had produced enough plutonium for one or two bombs.[79]

Iran—although not presenting the same kind of danger as the mercurial North Korean regime—was in other respects at least as timely a focus of nonproliferation concern. When the Bush administration was escalating its rhetorical campaign for invading Iraq, Iran had a more advanced nuclear program, and there was more detailed information about that program than anything that had come to light about any similar program in Iraq, but Iran—unlike North Korea—probably did not yet have a deterrent in the form of an extant nuclear weapon. Technical problems in the late 1990s had slowed Iran's nuclear program enough to invalidate earlier U.S. estimates that Tehran would have a bomb by the end of the decade. But revised estimates spoke of 2005 as a date when it might achieve that goal.[80] And in the summer of 2002, thanks to revelations from an Iranian dissident group, the world learned of the existence and location of Iran's principal facility for enriching uranium.

The most fundamental reason the weapons issue was not the chief motive for the war was that the presumed existence of Iraqi WMD and programs for producing them simply did not equate logically or empirically with a case to invade the country and overthrow the regime. The most obvious evidence of that nonequation is that many in the United States and abroad who shared the mistaken perception of active Iraqi programs nonetheless opposed the war. This group included not only many Americans who opposed it, including probably most members of Congress who voted against the war resolution in 2002, but also many foreign governments such as those of France and Germany. When President Bush accurately and repeatedly pointed out, as he was later questioned about the WMD that never materialized, that the mistaken prewar consensus about Iraqi weapons programs had been very broad, he failed to address how it could be that so many who were part of that consensus nevertheless believed that the war was unwise and unjustified.[81] Even some who were part of that consensus and joined the U.S.–led coalition did not believe that a war was the best way to deal with any problem regarding unconventional weapons. That was the case with the most loyal of allies, Tony Blair's government in Britain, which joined the coalition to preserve its all-important strategic relationship with the United States despite grave misgivings centered on likely postinvasion problems in Iraq and the insufficient attention the Bush administration was giving to those problems.[82] The Bush administration's public drumbeat equating WMD with the need to topple Saddam was so loud and went on for so long that we sometimes forget there was not an equation at all.

A LIE

Despite the huge part the WMD issue played in selling the invasion of Iraq, it was not the principal or even a major reason the Bush administration went to war.[83] Policymakers in the administration almost certainly shared the broadly held perceptions about Iraq's having active weapons-development programs, but the issue was at most a subsidiary motivator of the policy. To the extent it was even a secondary consideration, it did not depend on specific images of what Saddam Hussein had or was doing, but instead—just like the public rhetoric—on what he "could" do. Vice President Cheney said that if there were even a one percent chance of something awful such as terrorists getting their hands on a nuclear weapon, one had to act as if it were a certainty. "It's not about our analysis, or finding a preponderance of evidence," said Cheney. "It's about our response."[84] Such an outlook obviates any assessment from the intelligence community or from anybody else of what an adversary probably is doing. It discards probabilities altogether in favor of mere possibilities. Almost nobody, even among those most skeptical about the administration's case, would have denied there was so much as a one percent chance that Iraq had ongoing unconventional weapons programs that threatened U.S. interests.

Journalists and others have sometimes attempted to draw me out about whether the Bush administration "lied" in bringing the country into war. I usually have eschewed that word, mostly because it oversimplifies a deception that was more complicated than a straightforward matter of falsehood versus fact.[85] But on a few questions the term can confidently be used. When White House spokesman Gordon Johndroe said in April 2007, "The president made the decision to remove Saddam Hussein for a number of reasons, mainly the National Intelligence Estimate on Iraq and Saddam Hussein's own actions, and only after a thorough and lengthy assessment of all available information as well as Congressional authorization," that was a lie.[86] Not only was there never any "thorough and lengthy assessment" or anything close to it, but it was also impossible for the intelligence estimate in question—which did not even exist until after the president had already decided on the war and the campaign to sell it to the country had shifted into high gear—to have been a basis for the decision.

ALTERNATIVE VISIONS OF THE IRAQ WAR

The Bush administration's launching of the Iraq War was even more disconnected from intelligence on other Iraq-related issues than on WMD. These issues included the one other major theme in the pro-war sales campaign—supposed ties between the Iraq regime and al-Qa'ida—and other issues that would prove to be much more consequential as the United States sank into the costly quagmire that the war became. The war makers' posture toward intelligence went beyond mere disregard; it became one of rejection, hostility, and attempts to discredit.

THE IMAGINARY ALLIANCE

Unlike with WMD, there was no broad consensus about a relationship between the Iraqi regime and al-Qa'ida. There was no such issue until the war makers in the Bush administration manufactured it—not quite out of whole cloth, but out of scraps they assiduously collected in an effort to stitch such an issue together. The impression that the administration cultivated with the public, that Saddam Hussein's regime was an "ally" of al-Qa'ida,[1] did not come from any input reaching the administration from the bureaucracy

or anywhere else, and it contradicted the intelligence community's judgments. The administration manufactured the issue to exploit the national
anguish over 9/11—the public reaction to which was what had made the
Iraq War politically feasible—by associating Iraq with the perpetrators of
that terrorist horror.

The high priority that the U.S. intelligence community had placed during
the Clinton administration on monitoring and understanding al-Qa'ida
had led it to investigate all possible sources of support and cooperation for
the group, Iraq included. That is why Richard Clarke was able to report,
when Bush instructed him after 9/11 to look at this relationship, that such
a look had already been done and that nothing significant was found. A
few inconclusive contacts between bin Ladin's associates and officers of
the Iraqi regime had occurred in Sudan in the early 1990s, and there were
some other crossings of paths that the pro-war campaigners would point to
in arguing that "links" existed, but there was nothing approaching operational support or cooperation, much less an alliance. This lack of connection should not have been surprising. Although Saddam Hussein may have
been willing to make a pact with the devil if he saw tactical advantage in
doing so, his secular dictatorship was part of the very power structure in
the Middle East that bin Ladin was seeking to overthrow.

The edition of the annual *Patterns of Global Terrorism* report—the government's most authoritative public statement on international terrorism—
released in April 2001 said nothing about any links, even of the most modest or inconsequential sort, between the Iraqi regime and al-Qa'ida. Like
the previous several editions, the report referred to the activities that appropriately kept Iraq on the list of state sponsors of terrorism: its cooperation with the violent Iranian opposition group Mujahedin-e Khalq and
with some semimoribund Palestinian groups as well as its hunting down of
exiled Iraqi dissidents.[2] Even the edition of *Patterns* released the following
spring, after the Bush administration had begun its year-long talking-up of
the Iraqi threat, had nothing to say about any relationship between Iraq
and al-Qa'ida. The closest it could come was to note public commentary by
the Iraqi regime that failed to condemn the 9/11 attacks and that expressed
sympathy for bin Ladin after U.S. military strikes in Afghanistan.[3] Classified assessments by the intelligence community were consistent with the
summaries in *Patterns*. And both public and classified assessments were
consistent with what we now know about the subject.

The supposed alliance between Saddam's regime and al-Qa'ida clearly did not drive the Bush administration's decision to launch the war because the administration was receiving no indications that any such alliance existed. Given that this fact did not stop the administration from nonetheless promoting publicly the notion of such an alliance, it is highly likely that even if intelligence judgments on the WMD issue had been different, this would barely have slowed down the administration in using WMD as one of the themes in its fear-based campaign to sell the war.

The campaign succeeded in linking Iraq and al-Qa'ida in the minds of many Americans despite the absence of supporting intelligence judgments. Popular belief extended to the idea that the Iraqi regime had been involved in 9/11—a belief that had no basis in the findings of investigations into the attack. Opinion polling showed that although only 3 percent of Americans believed in the immediate aftermath of 9/11 that Iraq was the leading suspect, by August 2002—after several months of the administration's rhetoric about Iraq—a majority thought that Saddam Hussein had been "personally involved" in the attack. By August 2003, after another year that included the most intensive selling of the war, more than two-thirds of Americans thought Saddam had been involved in 9/11.[4] Some of this belief was due to innuendo such as the vice president's repeated references to a phantom meeting in Prague between an Iraqi and 9/11 hijacker Mohammed Atta. It was due mostly to the administration's rhetorical drumbeat that repeatedly mentioned Iraq, 9/11, and "war on terror" in the same breath. The impact on public opinion was in part a tribute to the strength of the bully pulpit and in part a demonstration of the power of rhetorical themes—especially themes laden with fear and emotion—to overwhelm substantive judgments, whether those judgments come from the intelligence community or from anywhere else.

The Case-Building Shop in the Pentagon

The center of the Bush administration's efforts to dredge up as many links as possible was a small unit that Feith established within the Department of Defense, the Policy Counter Terrorism Evaluation Group (PCTEG).[5] Some reporting indicates the PCTEG was Wolfowitz's idea.[6] At one point, Wolfowitz expressed impatience with the rate at which the group was generating material for the pro-war campaign. He complained in a memo to Feith, "We don't seem to be making much progress pulling together intelligence on links between Iraq and al Qaida."[7]

The PCTEG came to have two specific objectives. One was to compile as much material as possible that could be used in the public effort to associate Iraq with al-Qa'ida. The other was to discredit the intelligence community's contrary judgment that the only contacts between Saddam's regime and al-Qa'ida consisted of "two organizations trying to feel out and exploit each other" and that there was no conclusive reporting about any collaboration on terrorist operations.[8] This was the conclusion of the most comprehensive intelligence assessment on the subject, a CIA paper completed in September 2002 and titled *Iraq and al-Qa'ida: A Murky Relationship.*

Feith's attempts to defend the PCTEG's existence and activities reflected his difficulty in juggling different rationales. He told members of Congress in 2003 that the group was not doing intelligence. He said its purpose instead was "to help me develop proposals for Defense Department strategies for the war on terror, which is a policy exercise, not an intelligence activity."[9] When the inspector general of the Department of Defense issued a report four years later noting that the PCTEG had in fact been disseminating alternative intelligence assessments and that this activity was inappropriate for a policy office, Feith took a different tack. The PCTEG was fulfilling a need to question and challenge intelligence judgments, he said.[10] This assertion, like similar ones from other Bush administration policymakers, obliterated the major distinction between open-minded questioning of intelligence judgments, which is a proper role for policymakers and a useful tool for finding weaknesses in those judgments, and the quite different close-minded pressing of intelligence agencies to support the policymakers' favored line, which is what Feith and the other makers of the Iraq War were instead doing.

Feith's accusation that CIA analysts had "excluded reports" and were "suppressing" information was ridiculous to anyone who had looked at the work in question. Because the Bush administration policymakers placed such high importance on uncovering whatever possible connections between Iraq and al-Qa'ida could be uncovered, and because they pressed intelligence officers so long and so hard on the matter, there probably was no other topic during that administration that the intelligence community investigated more painstakingly. Everything of possible relevance was scrutinized, particularly in the CIA *Murky Relationship* assessment. With so much potential for pleasing policymakers with useful finds and for displeasing them by coming up empty-handed, the incentives were all in the direction of scouring for information rather than suppressing it. The correct translation of Feith's accusation was that the intelligence community, having done all that scouring, arrived at a conclusion the policymakers did not favor and in so doing found some reports bogus and others outweighed or contravened by other reporting. The community can be criticized for how it handled this subject: not for suppressing information, but instead for devoting so many analytic and management resources to serving the needs of the administration's pro-war campaign—resources that otherwise could have been working on analyzing actual terrorist threats.

That the PCTEG's work was about discrediting intelligence judgments rather than improving them is demonstrated by how it designed and handled its product (as well as by the fact that its work provided the content for leaks to the likes of the *Weekly Standard*). In August 2002, the group presented to Tenet and the Defense Intelligence Agency director, Vice Admiral "Jake" Jacoby, a briefing on relations between Iraq and al-Qa'ida. The briefing's argument was that there was a "mature, symbiotic, relationship" that included "cooperation in all categories"—a view that, as the Defense Department inspector general later noted, was quite at odds with the intelligence community's judgment. The briefing also treated questionable reporting as if it were established fact; the alleged meeting with Mohammed Atta in Prague, for example, was described as a "known contact."[11]

In September, the PCTEG presented its briefing at the White House, with Hadley and vice presidential aide I. Lewis Libby as the most important recipients—except that this time it added a slide titled "Fundamental Problems with How Intelligence Community Is Assessing Information."[12] The supposed problems were application of a "juridical" standard of evidence, "consistent underestimation" of the importance that Iraq and al-Qa'ida would place on hiding their relationship (this bullet on the slide included Rumsfeld's dictum that "absence of evidence is not evidence of absence"), and an "assumption that secularists and Islamists will not cooperate." These accusations would have bemused counterterrorist analysts in the intelligence community, who are acutely aware from their regular dealings with law enforcement colleagues that intelligence standards (including what they were using on Iraq) are different from juridical standards, who every day confront adversaries' deception and operational security as their biggest analytical challenge, and who themselves have written about cooperation between secularists and Islamists. But intelligence officers' reaction did not matter because the PCTEG never raised these issues with them. The accusations were instead being raised at the White House to provide rationales for rejecting an intelligence community judgment that was so inconveniently at odds with one of the main themes of the public campaign in favor of war.

The briefing and the PCTEG's accusations were raised at a closed hearing of the Senate Select Committee on Intelligence in February 2004. I participated, as did Ben Bonk, a colleague from the CIA who at the time held my former job as deputy chief of the DCI Counterterrorist Center (CTC). Senator Levin, whose energetic inquiries into the PCTEG revealed much of what later became publicly known about the group, had before him a copy of the briefing slides presented to the White House. Ben had a copy left from the presentation to Tenet and Jacoby. Levin asked about the "fundamental problems" the briefing said were plaguing the intelligence community's work on the subject. Ben riffled through his copy, trying to find the reference. Levin described the accusatory slide in more detail. More riffling. "We don't seem to have that slide," Ben said. When Levin's aide walked a copy to the witness table, it was the first time any of us had seen the accusations or had been made aware of a modified version of the briefing being given to the White House. The challenging and questioning that supposedly were designed to improve intelligence had never been communicated to the intelligence community. It took a Democratic senator—and one with Levin's bulldoglike tenacity—to serve as mailman.

The attitude of Feith's apparatus toward the intelligence community's work on the Iraq/al-Qa'ida issue was encapsulated in a covering memo it appended to the CIA's *Murky Relationship* assessment, which Feith forwarded to the secretary and deputy secretary of defense. The memo advised, "The CIA's report should be read for content only, and CIA's interpretation ought to be ignored."[13] Not questioned, not debated, not examined critically, not made the subject of substantive dialogue with the intelligence officers who prepared the assessment—just ignored. Meanwhile, went Feith's advice, these Defense Department officials should read the paper just in case the CIA analysts' digging into the subject uncovered any more publicly usable nuggets that the PCTEG and others may have missed.

Among the many reasons for bemusement over the rationalizations that Feith and other Bush administration policymakers have used for their abuse of intelligence—which took one of its most egregious forms in the PCTEG—is what turned out to be true and what turned out to be false. Given everything known now, the intelligence community's characterization of relations between Iraq and al-Qa'ida was largely correct. The PCTEG's image of a mature, multifaceted, cooperative relationship was badly incorrect.[14] If the community had allowed itself to be swept up any more than it did in this part of the pro-war campaign, it would only have added to the errors it committed regarding unconventional weapons.

The struggles between policymakers and intelligence officers over the issues that played such large roles in the public campaign to sell the Iraq War can be summarized quite simply. Where the intelligence community was largely wrong (regarding active Iraqi unconventional weapons programs), policymakers did not challenge the community's judgments at all. They instead pushed to make juicier tidbits public. To the extent they succeeded in doing so (as they eventually did regarding the alleged purchases of uranium ore), it just made the publicly conveyed image even more wrong. Where the intelligence community was largely right (regarding the non-alliance between Saddam's regime and al-Qa'ida), policymakers either ignored or discredited the community's judgments and conveyed to the public their own alternative—and wrong—image.

Pressing the Case

Although I was not working directly on counterterrorism at the time, I was exposed to some of the policymakers' labor on this subject on the weekend in early February 2003 when Secretary of State Powell's presentation on Iraq to the United Nations Security Council was being prepared. I was fortunate in not having to participate in that preparation. Those who did participate—including Secretary Powell, his aides from the State Department, and a contingent from the vice president's office—took up temporary residence in the same seventh-floor suite at CIA headquarters in Langley where I had my office. I was in my office that weekend, trying to get ahead on my own work, when a former colleague from the NIC, Barry Lowenkron, walked in with something he wanted me to read. Barry was then deputy director of the Policy Planning Staff at State and part of Powell's team working on the United Nations briefing. The paper he gave me had come from the vice president's office. It was about the Iraqi regime's supposed connections to Islamist terrorists—a script the vice president's people wanted to be a prominent part of the secretary of state's presentation. "Take a look at this," said Barry. "Let me know what you think."

The paper was dozens of pages of artful spinning of a terrorist conspiracy out of the thinnest gossamer. It paid almost no attention to the credibility or noncredibility of its material. It made no mention of available material that would point in different directions but dwelled at length on threads that possibly could imply some connection between regime and group. It took no account of much of what was known about the objectives and operations of the regime and group in question. It did not consider alternative explanations, let alone which explanation made the most sense, for the bits and pieces of reporting it highlighted. It bore no resemblance to any serious intelligence analysis. Although much work had obviously gone into the paper, it bore no resemblance to any kind of serious analysis aimed at understanding the issue at hand and uncovering the truth about it. It consisted of suggestions based on possibilities based on innuendo. It struck me as a brief from an industrious and creative trial lawyer who was doing his best with the material available to him to plant thoughts in the minds of jurors.

That evidently was the spirit in which the document was written. Libby, who reportedly wrote the paper, told Powell he had prepared it as something a lawyer might present in a courtroom.[15] When I shared my reaction to the paper with Lowenkron, he said he had reacted similarly. The secretary of state expressed the same view more forcefully. "I'm not reading this," Powell said while throwing Libby's script into the air. "This is bullshit."[16] The few minutes given to terrorist links near the end of the final version of the presentation (most of which was devoted to unconventional weapons) was the minimum that Powell felt obliged to include given the strong pressure from the vice president's office, supported by the civilian policymakers in the Department of Defense, to make such a case.

For years after the invasion of Iraq, the Bush administration's public statements continued the obfuscation about the supposed role of WMD and terrorist links in the decision to launch the war. The smokescreen was as thick as ever in a valedictory address on the Middle East that the president delivered a month before he departed office, in which he claimed to have left the region a better place than he found it and, although admitting with understatement that his "efforts have not always gone according to plan, and in some areas we've fallen short of our hopes," offered no hint of regret about his decisions. He referred to Saddam Hussein's having "refused to resolve the issue [of WMD] peacefully," as if it had been Iraq rather than the United States that had cut short the international inspection process in March 2003. And although he issued the requisite disclaimer that Saddam had not been connected to the 9/11 attacks, he proceeded to deliver more of the rhetoric that had led most Americans to believe there was such a connection. "The decision to remove Saddam from power cannot be viewed in isolation from 9/11," Bush declared. "In a world where terrorists armed with box cutters had just killed nearly 3,000 of our people, America had to decide whether we could tolerate a sworn enemy that acted belligerently, that supported terror, and that intelligence agencies around the world believed had weapons of mass destruction."[17]

A Disdain for Expertise

The nonuse of intelligence in making the decision to launch the Iraq War was part of a larger pattern of dismissing relevant sources of insight and expertise. Across the entire range of issues pertinent to the war, the war makers not only did not seek input from such sources, but also consciously excluded it. Insights from the civilian and military bureaucracy were ignored or rejected, as were the perspectives of experts outside government (except for a very few whose policy preferences already were safely in line with those of the war makers).

The absence of a policy process and the pointed exclusion of expert input conformed to President Bush's decision-making style of trusting his instincts as he confidently moved in the direction his gut told him to go. When Bush did listen to others, he heard not so much the substance of what the other person was saying but rather what his instincts were telling him about the person's reasons for saying it. He fancied himself a good judge of people and considered this ability at least as important as being conversant with the ideas and information that people conveyed. This approach shaped his interactions with foreign leaders, as when he looked Vladimir Putin in the eye and got "a sense of his soul."[18] He would use the same eyeball-scrutinizing method with the new Iraqi leadership. He told U.S. troops in Iraq during a visit in June 2006, "I have come not only to thank you but to look Prime Minister [Nouri] Maliki in the eyes—to determine whether or not he is as dedicated to a free Iraq as you are. I believe he is."[19] The same basic approach shaped Bush's interaction with experts inside the U.S. government. This approach meant deeply discounting input from the intelligence community on any potentially controversial subject because of the community's presumed overriding motive of protecting its own interests and presumed lack of support for Bush. The president's response to one CIA briefing a few months after taking office was, "All right, you've covered your ass now."[20]

The president reached his decision on Iraq without hearing the views of any of his senior advisers, save for the vice president and possibly the national security adviser, about whether it was wise or not.[21] He never asked DCI Tenet for a judgment about going to war.[22] Neither did he ask Secretary of State Powell or even Secretary of Defense Rumsfeld. When Bob Woodward later raised this subject with Bush, the president replied, "I didn't need to ask them their opinion about Saddam Hussein or how to deal with Saddam Hussein. . . . I think we've got an environment where people feel free to express themselves."[23] This statement was astounding in light of the punishment meted out to those who did dare to express themselves, especially publicly, in directions contrary to the administration's preferred line. A prime example is what happened to army chief of staff General Eric Shinseki, who in response to a question at a congressional hearing assessed that "something on the order of several hundred thousand soldiers" would be needed for success in Iraq.[24] Two days after Shinseki's answer, Wolfowitz testified to a Senate committee that the army chief of staff's estimate was "wildly off the mark."[25] Rumsfeld and Wolfowitz subsequently sidelined Shinseki as a lame duck through the unprecedented tactic of announcing his successor eighteen months in advance and further snubbed him by boycotting his retirement ceremony. The treatment of Shinseki silenced any other military officers who might have had ideas about questioning dogma concerning required military resources. An air force officer involved in planning for the war said, "After seeing Wolfowitz chew down a four-star, I don't think anyone was going to raise their head up and make a stink about it."[26]

The barrier between the president and any skeptical input about the war was so high that it constrained even Powell—who enjoyed the highest reputation of anyone in the administration—and even as it related to private advice to the president. In August 2002, after General Franks had briefed the latest revision of the war plan, Powell asked to confer with the president to address some important issues he thought had not yet been discussed. In the resulting meeting in the White House residence, Powell raised concerns such as the destabilizing effects of a war on the region, the damaging picture of a U.S. military occupation, the uncertainties over how long the occupation would last and how success would be defined, and the diversion of attention from everything else. When the president said, "What should I do? What else can I do?" Powell mentioned going to the United Nations. The concerns the secretary of state expressed amounted to an argument not to launch the war at all, but he did not directly voice that conclusion because that option was not on the table. Powell's thinking, as channeled by Woodward, was that "he had to play to the boss and talk about method. It was paramount to talk only within the confines of the preliminary goals set by the boss. Perhaps he had been too timid." When asked later about Powell's reservations, Bush's oddly unresponsive reply was, "And my reaction to that is, is that my job is to secure America. And that I also believe that freedom is something people long for."[27] Two months before the invasion, when the secretary of state gently raised again some of his worries about the war, Bush played the loyalty card. "Are you with me on this?" he asked Powell. "Time to put your uniform on."[28]

The intelligence community's judgments on the course and consequences of a U.S. occupation of Iraq were neither sought nor heeded (more about those judgments in a moment). Since 2000, I had been the member of the NIC responsible for political, economic, and other nonmilitary and nontechnical issues relating to the Near East and South Asia. As the national intelligence officer for the region, I would have been the recipient of any requests for intelligence community assessments or estimates on issues in my area and would have supervised the production and coordination of such papers. No Bush administration policymaker asked my office for any classified assessment on anything having to do with Iraq until a year into the war.

The intelligence community was not the only source of insight inside the government that the Iraq War policymakers rejected. Another was a major State Department project called the Future of Iraq. When the head of the project and another State Department officer involved in it began attending meetings at the Defense Department on postinvasion needs, Secretary Rumsfeld ordered them barred from the Pentagon.[29] The professional military did not fare any better. The rejection of their input was related to the determination of Rumsfeld, Wolfowitz, and their aides to exert tighter control over the uniformed services than the Clinton administration had.[30] Rumsfeld's purpose would be served each time a general bent to his will or to his opinion.

War makers in both the White House and the Pentagon responded similarly to analytic efforts outside government. One such effort was a proposal from the Council on Foreign Relations to convene a panel of experts to study postinvasion Iraq.[31] Additional efforts included the work of almost all experts in academia—that is, other than the select few who were firmly on board with the policy.[32]

The Bush administration's remarkably closed and contorted decision-making on Iraq[33] surfaced in some other foreign-policy departures during the Bush presidency. One such departure was the jettisoning, during the first year of the administration, of the Agreed Framework on North Korea that had been negotiated under President Clinton, which led to several more years of North Korean nuclear development and Pyongyang's detonation of a nuclear device before the United States returned to diplomacy. One analyst of that episode states that it demonstrated "that the president had very strong instincts about issues—and that those instincts would override the policy process, even making the whole notion of a process quite beside the point once the president was sure of what his 'gut' was telling him."[34]

The war makers' broader rejection of expert input reflected a disdain for expertise per se, rooted in a hubristic sense of possessing some higher form of wisdom. As a four-star general observed, "There was a conscious cutting off of advice and concerns. . . . The people around the president were so, frankly, intellectually arrogant."[35] An analyst who helped to write a study by the army's Strategic Studies Institute on postwar Iraq (another of the useful analyses on the subject that the policymakers ignored) said of Wolfowitz and the other proponents of the war, "They didn't have to listen to us. Somewhere along the line they had decided they were smarter than the rest of us."[36] Douglas Feith exemplified the war makers' outlook when he sniffed at what he termed the "intellectual class," which he believed had been on the "wrong side" of the Oslo peace process and much else. Expertise about an area, said Feith, "is not a guarantee that you will have the right strategy or policy as a matter of statecraft for dealing with that area. You see, the great experts in certain areas sometimes get it fundamentally wrong."[37]

A final reason the makers of the Iraq War eschewed a process for assessing the costs and risks of the war and rejected input that would normally have been part of such a process was the challenge of keeping the campaign for war on track and selling the expedition to the public. Candid appraisals inside the government of the consequences of the war would have raised doubts about the wisdom of the whole enterprise. Even worse from the war proponents' standpoint, such appraisals and doubts probably would have leaked at least in part, making the mustering of public support for the war even more challenging.[38] The Iraq adventure was initiated by a small number of neoconservative intellectuals and assertive nationalists, ultimately backed by George W. Bush's gut. The numbers were small enough for Powell's longtime assistant Lawrence Wilkerson to refer plausibly to a "cabal" as being responsible for the war.[39] If the invasion to overthrow Saddam Hussein ever were to take place, the selling of the war would have to take overriding priority over any assessment of its advisability. And it did.

The Other Intelligence Assessments

The notorious estimate about Iraqi weapons programs was only one of three classified, community-coordinated assessments about Iraq that the intelligence community produced in the months prior to the war. The other two addressed issues that not only were more related directly to the main motivations for the war, but also spoke to the reasons the expedition would become such a prolonged, bloody, and expensive mess. As such, these assessments proved to be more important than the weapons estimate, notwithstanding the notoriety the latter paper would achieve. One of the assessments, *Principal Challenges in Post-Saddam Iraq*, addressed the political, economic, and security difficulties that would be encountered within Iraq once the dictator was gone. The other, *Regional Consequences of Regime Change in Iraq*, concerned the ramifications of overthrowing Saddam for the rest of the Middle East, including effects on extremism and terrorism and on the prospects for political change in other countries.[40]

I initiated those other two assessments. Part of an intelligence service's function—more specifically, part of a national intelligence officer's job—is not just to sit back and wait for requests but instead to anticipate, with self-initiated products, the needs of those who make or execute policy. The need to understand the can of worms the United States would be holding once it had ousted Saddam would clearly be immense. Even if those launching the war were turning a deaf ear to anything the community of analysts might offer, someone—an American general, an American ambassador or proconsul, or perhaps an Iraqi leader acting on American advice—would eventually need to deal with and thus to understand the aftermath.

Despite the obvious need, the assessments required circumspection. If even Secretary Powell felt he could not address directly whether the war was advisable, the constraints on intelligence officers—who are not supposed to opine about U.S. policy at all, especially without being asked—were all the greater when dealing with any material implying that the war was inadvisable. I chose the "principal challenges" formulation for the assessment about internal Iraqi issues as a way to address the severe problems the United States was likely to encounter in Iraq while keeping it in the mode of a paper designed to support the mission. After all, don't all complex operations, even ultimately successful ones, encounter "challenges"? I also employed a device that intelligence officers (especially those of us on the NIC) often employed to seem more responsive to policymakers' needs and less as if we were subverting the policy: to get a policy office (in this case Richard Haass's Policy Planning Staff at the Department of State) to agree to be the "requestor" of record on the title page, thus making it appear that the assessments had not been self-initiated.

The circumspection also affected the timing of the assessments. I put the community of analysts to work on them as summer moved into fall in 2002, about the time the administration fully activated its opinion-molding campaign on Iraq. This also was close to the time that Powell, having heard the war plan briefed, first raised his concerns with the president. For those of us in the intelligence community who had no access to the plan even then, it would have been difficult to have initiated anything like these two assessments earlier in the year—when war was ostensibly not even an option under consideration—without appearing to attempt our own brand of preemption. War had become a certainty before it became an option. So the calendar, the administration's strategy of preemption and deception in planning the war, and the sensitivity involved in any intelligence component offering ugly prognoses about the consequences of possible policies combined to frustrate any earlier completion of these assessments.

One thing I was determined not to do was to emulate the three-week rush job that produced the weapons estimate. Unlike with that paper, we did not cut procedural corners. The preparation was comprehensive and careful. My deputies assembled the assessments using contributions from analysts throughout the intelligence community. We solicited input and critical comments on drafts of the assessments from multiple outside experts, including ones we expected would hold views diverging from our own. Coordination of the drafts was thorough and laborious enough to achieve full concurrence of all the participating agencies without punting difficult issues or resorting to least-common-denominator conclusions. The outcome was the best possible representation of expert judgment, from inside as well as outside government, of the results of forcibly overthrowing Saddam Hussein.

The first "key judgment" in *Principal Challenges in Post-Saddam Iraq* was that the greatest of those challenges would be the building of a stable and representative political system—a process that would be "long, difficult, and probably turbulent" amid an authoritarian political culture that does not foster liberalism or democracy. The next judgment was that any post-Saddam authority would face a "deeply divided society with significant chance that domestic groups would engage in violent conflict with each other unless an occupying force prevented them from doing so."[41] This prospect was based on the incompatible goals of Sunni Arabs facing loss of their long-standing privileged position, Shia seeking power commensurate with their majority status, and Kurds trying to secure control over oil resources in northern Iraq.

The third judgment was that notwithstanding Iraq's oil, the country's economic options would be "few and narrow," with economic reconstruction requiring measures akin to a Marshall Plan. The fourth judgment spoke of the major outside assistance that would be required to meet humanitarian needs, with a refugee problem and civil strife combining to strain Iraq's already inadequate public services. The final judgment, which addressed foreign and security policies, looked beyond the assessment's three- to five-year time frame to note that Iraq's threat perceptions and self-image as a regional power would, without the right security guarantees, revive its interest in WMD. The more immediate security challenge would be al-Qa'ida or other terrorist groups operating from Iraqi territory if Baghdad were unable to exert control over the countryside.

These judgments were not selected pieces of bad news. They were the main points, expressed in a summary section of less than two pages at the front of the thirty-eight-page assessment, that the intelligence community believed would be most descriptive of post-Saddam Iraq.

The assessment did not venture a prediction on how Iraqis would regard coalition forces when they first invaded, but it did assess what would shape Iraqi attitudes after the first few weeks or months. Those attitudes, according to the assessment, would depend above all on the coalition's performance in providing security, stability, and basic public services. Insofar as it failed to provide them—which proved to be the case for much of the first few years of occupation—Iraqis' traditional antipathy toward foreign occupation would manifest itself in hostility toward the latest occupiers.

Regional Consequences of Regime Change in Iraq judged that the war would give a regionwide boost to political Islam, including its extremist variants. Al-Qa'ida would exploit the conflict. Any violence in Iraq would serve as a magnet for extremists elsewhere in the region. The regional assessment also judged that even if the experiment in politically reconstructing Iraq were successful, there would not be (with the possible exception of Iran) the hoped-for "democratic domino" effect; political and economic reform in other Middle Eastern countries would continue to face significant obstacles and would be influenced chiefly by conditions within those countries.

The overall implication of these assessments for the advisability of launching the expedition was summed up by one of my colleagues on the NIC as the papers were undergoing final review. No one who accepted and reflected on the assessments' conclusions, he commented, could possibly think the war was a good idea. Quite so, and that would be true even if one also accepted the judgments in the weapons estimate.

The judgments in the two assessments reflected not special insight in the intelligence community, but instead broader expertise about Iraq and the Middle East that the administration, if it had wanted, could have tapped in many other ways. The community nonetheless was audacious to offer the assessments given the inherent difficulty of forecasting events as complex as those in postinvasion Iraq and given how much U.S. decisions yet to be taken would affect those events.

The assessments received wide dissemination throughout the executive branch and were provided to Congress. Consistent with our purpose of assisting those who would have to deal with the aftermath of the invasion, I briefed the conclusions to members of the Office of Reconstruction and Humanitarian Assistance, the Defense Department's body for postwar planning, when that office came into existence shortly after the assessments were published. None of us who worked on the assessments was under any delusion that the papers would derail the war train that already had been

gathering steam for a year. With still two months before the invasion, however, there was still plenty of time for second thoughts. I do not know if
anyone who favored the war and read the assessments had second thoughts
as a result. I do know that Deputy DCI John McLaughlin peddled copies to
policymakers in the White House Situation Room. The only feedback I
received from a senior policymaker—via his morning briefer and referring
to the regional consequences assessment—was, "You guys just don't see the
possibilities."

NAIVE OPTIMISM

The images about Iraq that policymakers held and that underlay the decision to launch the war were quite different from those in the intelligence
assessments. A particularly important image guiding the policy was of a new
Iraqi political order, more liberal and more democratic than the norm for
the Middle East, falling into place more smoothly than the "long, difficult,
and probably turbulent" process envisioned in the *Principal Challenges*
assessment. The war makers and especially the president expressed confidence in their sunnier image of an untroubled transition to democracy, not
only publicly (as in the president's speech to the American Enterprise Institute), but also privately. Two months before the invasion, for example,
Bush told Tony Blair it was "unlikely there would be internecine warfare
between the different religious and ethnic groups."[42]

Perhaps historical analogy—in this case, to the successful post–World
War II occupations that yielded stable democracies in Germany and Japan—
played a role in shaping the war makers' expectations, as such analogies
often do in molding policymakers' beliefs. If so, the analogy overlooked
major differences between those cases and Iraq, including a previously
well-established democratic culture in Germany and the demographic homogeneity of Japan.[43]

Ahmed Chalabi and other Iraqi exiles who won the war makers' favor
probably contributed to the image of a trouble-free political transition in
Iraq. The myopia of dealing face to face with Chalabi, an operator who was
as smooth as the transfer of power he promised he could achieve, led the
policymakers to believe the exiles had far more support inside Iraq than
they ever did. The *Principal Challenges* assessment made it clear that Chalabi's Iraqi National Congress lacked sufficient support to speak, as it

claimed to, for the Iraqi opposition. The assessment's principal judgment about the exiles in general was, "The external opposition does not have the popular, political, or military capabilities necessary to play a leading role after Saddam's departure without significant and prolonged external economic, political, and military support."[44] The years following the invasion amply demonstrated the exiles' lack of support among Iraqis.

The chief source of the policymakers' belief that Iraq would easily give birth to democracy was probably simple faith in democracy itself, in its appeal to people everywhere, and in the ability and willingness of people everywhere to make it work once they get it. The Bush administration declared in a national security strategy in September 2002, "The United States must defend liberty and justice because these principles are right and true for all people everywhere. No nation owns these aspirations, and no nation is exempt from them."[45] Bush returned repeatedly to this theme during the war, suggesting that anyone who doubted that stable democracy would take root in Iraq was guilty of ethnocentric condescension. In a speech in October 2005, he declared, "As Americans, we believe that people everywhere—everywhere—prefer freedom to slavery, and that liberty, once chosen, improves the lives of all. And so we're confident, as our coalition and the Iraqi people each do their part, Iraqi democracy will succeed."[46] Ideology created the image. The holders of the ideology did not let disturbing details about Iraq's history, demography, and culture get in the way.

One of the beliefs policymakers conveyed most openly—and with great assurance—was that Iraqis would regard U.S. forces as liberators rather than as occupiers. Wolfowitz testified a month before the invasion, "I am reasonably certain that they will greet us as liberators."[47] At about the same time, Rumsfeld said of U.S. forces, "There's no question but that they would be welcomed."[48] Cheney stated on the eve of the invasion, "The read we get on the people of Iraq is there is no question but what they want to get rid of Saddam Hussein and they will welcome us as liberators."[49]

As the occupation wore on amid increasing attacks on U.S. forces and numerous other indications of a more hostile attitude, the policymakers resisted in varying ways any acknowledgment of error on this subject. Rumsfeld denied ever having made such an optimistic prediction, snapping at a journalist who referred to his earlier statement, "Never said that. Never did. You may remember it well, but you're thinking of somebody

else."[50] When similarly challenged, Cheney invoked the Nixonian concept of a silent majority: "I think the majority of Iraqis are thankful for
the fact that the United States is there, that we came and we took down
the Saddam Hussein government."[51] Douglas Feith propounded a variation of that view, theorizing that some Iraqis were still too intimidated
by Ba'athist remnants to express their views openly, but that "they had
flowers on their minds."[52]

Exposure to the skewed sample of Iraqi exiles and Iraqi Americans who
had access to the policymakers probably again helped to shape the belief
that U.S. troops would be welcomed as liberators. Wolfowitz talked of how
listening to pro-war Iraqi Americans in the Detroit area had bolstered his
optimistic view on the subject.[53] Failure to anticipate hostility to U.S.
troops during the occupation also stemmed from failure to anticipate inadequate postinvasion security and breakdowns of public services—which, as
the *Principal Challenges* paper assessed, would in large part determine Iraqi
attitudes toward the occupiers.

The belief in a smooth transfer of power also led to optimistic images of
the troops and money required. The slapping down of Shinseki and his
inconvenient estimate of several hundred thousand troops reflected not
just the policymakers' need to maintain public support for the war, but also
their private sense of what really would be needed. In the month prior to
the war, Wolfowitz was telling senior army officers to plan on reducing U.S.
troop strength in Iraq to between thirty and thirty-four thousand within a
few months of the invasion.[54] Besides the policymakers' Pollyannaish views
of an easy change of regime, their unrealistically low perception of the
necessary forces may also have been an artifact of the Rumsfeld doctrine of
the U.S. military's doing more with less, especially less of a ground force.

With regard to money, the Eric Shinseki role was played by Bush's chief
economic policy adviser, Lawrence B. Lindsey, who in an interview in September 2002 estimated the cost of the coming war to be $100–200 billion—
at the time an embarrassingly high set of numbers.[55] The White House
budget director subsequently declared Lindsey's range to be much too high
and said $50–60 billion was the right estimate.[56] Lindsey had been a Bush
appointee and loyalist, but as punishment for his cost estimate he was fired
and further insulted as White House aides passed word to reporters that the
president had been unhappy about the portly Mr. Lindsey's personal appearance and lack of exercise.[57]

It was not the intelligence community's business to make cost estimates, but its sense of the cost of just one segment of the mission—economic reconstruction of Iraq—could be inferred from its reference to the need for a Marshall Plan. The original Marshall Plan cost $12.7 billion, which would be about $96 billion in 2003 dollars. By the end of fiscal 2009, the total direct cost of the Iraq War, most of which was for continuing military operations and other security needs and not for reconstruction, was more than $700 billion—with the meter still running and not counting the ultimately greater indirect costs.[58]

Visions of Iraqi oil revenues contributed to the policymakers' gross underestimation of the war's costs. Wolfowitz repeatedly referred to Iraq's oil as the salve that would soothe any discomfort to the American taxpayer. In testimony a month before the war, he said, "There is a lot of money there," which could be put to "a good use instead of building Saddam's palaces."[59] Private beliefs again mirrored the public assurances. When Jay Garner, the retired general who was initially given the thankless job of overseeing postinvasion reconstruction, sought guidance from Rumsfeld about how much money the United States was willing to devote to the task, the secretary of defense replied, "Well, if you think we're spending our money on that, you're wrong. We're not doing that. They're going to spend their money rebuilding their country."[60] The naive image of an occupation of Iraq paying for itself appears to have stemmed from nothing more than the simple combination of the ideas that oil means money and Iraq has lots of oil, coupled with a disbelief in the security problems that would both escalate the bill for the occupation and depress Iraqi oil exports.

Another image that guided the decision on the war was the democratic domino effect: the idea that the introduction of a more liberal political and economic order in Iraq would stimulate similar change in other Middle Eastern countries. Perhaps this image, like the earlier version of the domino theory that underlay the intervention in Vietnam, stemmed in part from the simple appeal of the imagery itself. Isn't it natural to assume that knocking down anything, be it a domino or a regime, also will disturb similar nearby objects? Perhaps the image also stemmed from earlier waves of democratization in other regions—in Latin America in the 1980s and, most conspicuously, in eastern Europe with the collapse of communism and Soviet domination there. Like the image of successful political transformation within Iraq, it probably came mostly from faith in the strength and universal popular appeal of liberal democratic values.

DAMNING THE CONSEQUENCES

Incredible though it may seem—given the magnitude and importance of the war about to be launched—policymakers gave little indication of bothering to think at all about many of the consequences of what they were undertaking, as if they didn't care. In fact, they did not care about most of those consequences, given the nature of what they were setting out to do. They were dragon slayers, not nation builders. They did not worry about the instability they would cause in Iraq and in the Middle East because destabilizing the existing order was part of their purpose. They had faith enough that whatever emerged from the debris would be better than what they were destroying that they did not see value in spending time contemplating the debris or gaming out the emergence of a new order. As for the assertive nationalist goal of intimidating and deterring others by throwing U.S. weight around, the throwing was much more important than any direct consequences of it.

After the war went sour, the war makers realized the need to make a show of having given more careful thought to consequences. Five years into the war, Feith called attention to a three-page memo that Rumsfeld had produced in October 2002 on what could go wrong in the expedition.[61] The memo was merely a list of things that might happen, not an analysis of what likely *would* happen, much less an application of any such analysis to the question of whether the war should be launched at all. The throwaway nature of the memo was underscored by Rumsfeld's observation at the end of it: "It is possible, of course, to prepare a similar illustrative list of all of the potential problems that need to be considered if there is no regime change in Iraq."[62] In Rumsfeldian terms, the message was, "Stuff may happen no matter what we do, and we've decided what we want to do." The memo was reminiscent of a document McGeorge Bundy prepared for a meeting that Lyndon Johnson held with the Joint Chiefs of Staff and civilian secretaries of the military services in July 1965. Bundy's memo recited a list of arguments why the decision Johnson had just taken to intervene in Vietnam could be considered a bad idea. The purpose of the memo was not to revisit the decision, but instead, as Johnson made explicit to the contingent from the Pentagon, to brace for criticism and to be prepared to defend the war policy.[63]

If the three-page length of Rumsfeld's memo were not enough to demonstrate that it was not a serious analysis of consequences, there was further indication that it was still about the selling of the decision to invade Iraq rather than about the advisability of the decision. Number one on Rumsfeld's list of things that could go wrong was, "U.S. could fail to find WMD on the ground."[64] Of course, the hazard to military operations and other U.S. interests would have been greater if there *were* WMD. The only hazard of not finding such weapons was to the administration's sales campaign.

Passion and Personality

Beyond the Pollyannaish prognostications and disregard for consequences, the invasion of Iraq was for some of the war makers a matter more of obsession than of calculation, of personality than of prediction. That was most conspicuously the case with Wolfowitz, who campaigned for the war so long and so fervently that the distinctions between reason and rationale, between purpose and propaganda, became very blurred. As one official who worked with him on the war remarked, "Paul Wolfowitz, for all his good qualities, has an unfortunate ability to delude himself because he believes so passionately in things."[65] Wolfowitz's strong commitment to overthrowing Saddam Hussein not only contributed to delusion but also turned the war into a personal crusade that he seemed determined to pursue regardless of the underlying beliefs.

The personal attributes and interests of the policymaker who mattered most, George W. Bush, in addition to the aforementioned decision-making method of trusting his gut, shaped in several important ways his decision to launch the war. Bush's personal history as a born-again Christian who had overcome an earlier problem with alcohol probably contributed to the image he held of a troubled Iraq being reborn as a liberal democracy. The experience of individual reformation inspired a faith in societal reformation.[66]

An additional interest for the president, having nothing to do with images of Iraq, was the domestic political effect of leading the nation into war. Like other initiators of war, he benefited from a rally-round-the-flag effect. The stratospheric approval ratings that Bush enjoyed in the immediate aftermath of 9/11 declined over the next sixteen months to the high fifties before getting a new bounce when the Iraq War began. By mid-April 2003, about the time Baghdad fell to U.S. troops, Bush's numbers were back up to the midseventies—before gradually declining, as the painful reality of Iraq set in, to historic depths by the time he left office.[67]

Bush's unique personal impact on the policy had at least as much to do with psychology as with politics. As commander in chief during a major war, he acquired a sense of direction and purpose that had eluded him in his early months in office. The 9/11 attacks would have helped in that regard anyway, but a metaphorical "war on terror"—which necessarily centered on less visible police and intelligence activity, even if supplemented by the military intervention in the Afghan civil war—would not have been nearly as effective in sustaining his "wartime president" mode as would a conventional military operation to overthrow a despised dictator.

Bush's religious faith confirmed his convictions, quieted any doubts, and strengthened his resistance to contrary ideas. Spreading freedom and democracy through regime change in Iraq was for him a divine mission. In a speech to a religious broadcasters' convention in the month before the invasion, Bush proclaimed, "Liberty is God's gift to every human being in the world. America . . . [is] called to extend the promise of this country into the lives of every citizen who lives here."[68] The president returned to this theme during the 2004 election campaign. In one of the candidates' debates, he spoke at length about the importance of his religious faith and said, "I believe that God wants everybody to be free. That's what I believe. And that's been part of my foreign policy."[69] No less an authority than Bush's father confirmed the sincerity of such statements from his son. "This thing about his faith—I mean, this is real for him," George H. W. Bush remarked in an interview in 2001. "It's something that is in his heart."[70]

The elder Bush unwittingly provided two additional drivers of the younger Bush's decision to invade Iraq. An openly stated one was that Saddam Hussein had attempted to assassinate the former president through (fortunately inept) agents in Kuwait in April 1993. In speaking at a fundraiser in September 2002 about the need to do something about Saddam, George W. Bush commented, "After all, this is a guy that tried to kill my dad at one time."[71] The unstated driver was that deposing Saddam was the most conspicuous way in which the younger Bush could outdo his father, the former president whose foreign-policy achievements included the successful conclusion of the Cold War. And the war was not the only method through which George W. Bush, whose knowledge and experience in foreign affairs appeared paltry in comparison with those of the elder

Bush, sought to escape his father's shadow. He also did so through his appointments—particularly of Rumsfeld, who had had an awful relationship with George H. W. Bush.[72] But to knock off the dictator whom the elder Bush had left standing in 1991 would be the clearest and most emphatic way for George W. to eclipse George H. W.

God and the father—divine will and Oedipal anxiety: what a potent combination. There is a good book yet to be written about the inner George W. Bush that will do at least as much to explain why the Iraq War happened as has any commentary about politics and strategy in the Middle East and much more than any commentary about WMD or intelligence.[73]

BLIND DETERMINATION

Two patterns regarding intelligence and the Iraq War are clear. One is that intelligence did not guide the decision to go to war. The other is that if one were to draw an implication for policy from the judgments that the intelligence community offered, it was that an invasion of Iraq was unwarranted and unwise. The community assessed that the Iraqi regime was probably years away from acquiring a nuclear weapon; that it did not have any alliance with al-Qa'ida; that the only circumstance that might lead Saddam Hussein to use any unconventional weapons he did have against the United States or to give them to terrorists was an invasion of his country; that any attempt to establish democracy in Saddam's wake would be difficult and turbulent; that sharp and violent confrontations among competing factions would characterize post-Saddam Iraq; that a costly reconstruction effort and large refugee problem also would characterize it; that violence in postinvasion Iraq would stimulate terrorism; that the war would boost political Islam throughout the region; that even if democracy were established in Iraq, it would be unlikely to spread through the rest of the Middle East; and that over the longer term even Iraqi production of WMD would not be prevented.

These patterns are ironic in view of the strong public association of the Iraq War with faulty intelligence judgments and the still prevalent belief that those judgments led the United States into the war. The irony is redoubled by noting not only that the war makers in the Bush administration were not guided by the intelligence community, but also that they considered themselves to be in an adversarial relationship with the community and believed that intelligence officers were trying to subvert their policy.

The Iraq War was the realization of a narrow idea held by a small number of people. It would never have occurred without a unique combination of circumstances that included the placement of several of those people in positions of power, the enjoyment by the United States of its unipolar moment, the peculiar needs of a popular but inexperienced president, and extraordinary national trauma inflicted by a major terrorist attack. Even with those circumstances, the war still would not have occurred if any decision to make war had to grow out of—in the words of the Bush administration's false claim—a thorough and lengthy assessment of all available information.

Not only was there no assessment of relevant and available information and images, but the war makers also consciously and forcefully rejected them. Those with contrary insights were not just ignored but punished. Any thoughts about whether the war was advisable were quickly exterminated so as not to complicate the selling of the war.

The fear-laden themes that dominated the sales campaign originated not with threat assessments from a government agency, but instead with the war makers' sense (correct, as it turned out) of what would sell most readily. An assiduous year-long effort to condition public opinion successfully capitalized on the post-9/11 militancy. The campaign shaped perceptions that in important respects were contrary not only both to fact and to the judgment of government agencies, but also to logic—especially in falsely equating presumed Iraqi weapons programs with a need to overthrow the Iraqi regime through force. The next chapter addresses how enough of Congress, the press, and the American public were swept up in the mood that the Bush administration successfully manipulated to enable the neoconservatives to undertake their great experiment in sowing democratic values through the barrel of a gun.

The decision to invade Iraq carried to extremes some patterns that have appeared to lesser degrees in other cases. What was most extreme was the complete absence of a process for arriving at the decision, with everything this implies regarding the uncompromising rejection of relevant input. The United States invaded Iraq with blind determination unequalled in modern American foreign policy. It may be hard for Americans to believe that the publicly stated rationale for the war was so different from the actual reasons for the invasion, but it was. And Americans may also have difficulty believing that their government made such an enormous and costly commitment with so little attention to so many of the considerations that should have given it pause, but it did.

CHAPTER FOUR

CONGRESS AND THE POLITICS OF
THE IRAQ WAR

What drove the war makers in the Bush administration to invade Iraq is most but not all of the story of why the United States got enmeshed in the war. The remainder of the story concerns the rest of the country's willingness to acquiesce to the administration's decision, including the role that the issue of WMD played in that acquiescence. Intelligence on that or other issues was no more decisive in guiding other players in the political process than it was in guiding the administration.

SUBMISSION ON CAPITOL HILL

The most important act of acquiescence was the joint resolution in Congress in October 2002 authorizing the president to use military force against Iraq. The resolution passed the House by a vote of 297 to 133 and the Senate 77 to 23. All but a handful of the nays were from Democrats, including a majority of Democratic members of the House.

The WMD issue, given its prominence in the administration's sales campaign, clearly had a large role in swaying Americans' opinion. But the influence of the administration's sales pitch was quite different from the influence of intelligence. The grossly oversimplified "Saddam has WMD" view of the subject provided many members of Congress with cover and a rationale for voting the way they had strong political reasons to want to vote. Intelligence products, with all of the complications and detailed implications for what did and did not pose threats to U.S. interests, had little influence on the voting and very little on passage of the resolution. The political environment surrounding Congress during that autumn killed whatever chance there might otherwise have been for the legislative branch to function as an independent source of deliberation and decision regarding Iraq.

The 535 politicians who constitute Congress are habitually attuned more to the politics of issues than to the substantive details, especially technical details. Whenever an issue gets attention and discussion—whether because of the administration's agitation, as in the case of Iraq, or any other reason—members of Congress need to be seen paying attention to it and responding to it, regardless of what substantive views, if any, they previously had on the subject. Only rarely does Congress set on its own a significant course in national security policy—the work of Senators Sam Nunn (D–Ga.) and Richard Lugar (R–Ind.) on controlling nuclear material in the Soviet Union is an example—and even then only a few long-serving members who have specialized in foreign and security matters are involved and understand the topic.

Members of Congress faced in October 2002 not a de novo examination of Iraq as a possible security threat, but instead the political problem of how to respond to the challenge that President Bush had presented in calling on them to get aboard the war train. For members of both parties, several realities defined that problem. One was the still bellicose post-9/11 public mood. Another was the president's popularity, which had soared after the terrorist attacks. Yet another was the administration's conditioning of public opinion about Iraq as a threat, which had been ongoing since the beginning of 2002 and, under the war marketers' strategy of post–Labor Day pushing of the product, had become ever more intense in the weeks immediately before the vote. Finally, there were looming midterm elections. The impact of the first three factors on the fourth would be reflected in the Republicans gaining seats in both houses and retaking control of the Senate.

As the partisan breakdown of the vote on the war resolution suggests, party loyalty was a very important factor for Republican members. Probably typical was the perspective of the House majority leader, Dick Armey (R–Tex.). Armey had earlier expressed reservations about the prospect of a war and had been left unimpressed by a briefing, complete with overhead photographs, that Vice President Cheney had given to him and other congressional leaders. "If I'd gotten the same briefing from President Clinton or Al Gore," Armey recalled, "I probably would have said, 'Ah, bullshit.' You don't do that to your own people."[1]

Democrats—always more vulnerable, however unfairly, than Republicans to charges of being wimps on national security—felt a different sort of pressure. A particular burden for Democrats was the history that most of them had voted against the resolution that authorized the war in 1991 to reverse the Iraqi conquest of Kuwait. They had followed Nunn's lead, as they did on many military issues. But after Operation Desert Storm's smashing military victory, they felt burned. They did not want to repeat the mistake.

The only Democrats who would be presidential or vice presidential nominees in the next three elections—Bill Clinton (Ark.), Al Gore (Tenn.), and Joseph Lieberman (Conn.)—had been in their party's minority in supporting the 1991 war.[2] The lesson was not lost on those who still aspired to be president. Four of the six Democratic members of Congress who would run for president in 2004 voted in favor of the war resolution in 2002: Lieberman, Senator John Edwards (N.C.), Representative Dick Gephardt (Mo.), and the eventual nominee, Senator John Kerry (Mass.). (Bob Graham and the Ohio Congressman from the party's left wing, Dennis Kucinich, voted no.) The additional members who, besides Edwards and Kucinich, would seek the Democratic presidential nomination in 2008— Senators Joe Biden (Del.), Hillary Clinton (N.Y.), and Chris Dodd (Conn.)— also voted for the resolution. Probably a major reason (besides senatorial constituencies being more heterogeneous than House members' constituencies) that a majority of Democratic senators (29 out of 50) supported the war resolution even though most House Democrats opposed it was that there were more presidential hopefuls in the upper chamber.

Democratic members got additional reinforcement for voting the way their political interests inclined them to vote from some former Clinton administration officials such as Kenneth Pollack, who argued in favor of war in his influential 2002 book *The Threatening Storm: The Case for Invading Iraq.*[3] The frustrations those officials had encountered in handling Iraq-related issues made them receptive to the idea that Saddam Hussein was a problem worth doing away with once and for all. One of the most persuasive briefers for Democratic members was former weapons inspector David Kay, who would gain headlines with his later trumpeting of how wrong the assessments about Iraqi weapons programs had been. Before the war, however, Kay argued that toppling Saddam was the only sure way to prevent the Iraqi dictator from acquiring nuclear weapons.[4]

Just as the Bush administration would show it was not serious about pursuing a solution to the weapons issues when it shoved international inspectors aside to clear the decks for the invasion of Iraq, the U.S. Senate had a chance to show its seriousness when Carl Levin and other members introduced a substitute resolution saying that Congress was ready to consider the use of force, but only if an additional United Nations resolution calling for Iraqi cooperation with international inspections was not adequately observed or enforced. Lincoln Chafee (R–R.I.), the sole Republican senator to vote against the war resolution, recalled in 2007 that the arguments in favor of Levin's substitute "fell on deaf ears in that emotionally charged, hawkish, post-9/11 moment, less than four weeks before a midterm election." The Senate voted down the substitute 75 to 24 shortly before it passed the war resolution. "It was clear that most senators were immune to persuasion because the two votes were almost mirror images of each other," Chafee observed. "Their minds were made up."[5]

Whereas Republican members maintained party loyalty and followed their popular president, most Democrats just wanted to finesse the issue with minimal damage and to return as quickly as possible to domestic topics that offered more fertile political ground for their party to till. This meant not only that many of them would cast the politically safe "yes" votes that would ensure passage of the war resolution, but also that consideration of the resolution was superficial and short. The Democratic caucus in the Senate voted in September to get the vote over with as soon as possible in order to allow the maximum amount of time pass between the vote and the election. "Members were intimidated," said Senator Robert Byrd (D–W.Va.). Attendance of House and Senate members at the cursory debates on the war resolution was never higher than 10 percent.[6] Byrd—whose nearly half-century tenure in the Senate had given him plenty of previous debates with which to compare—stated on the Senate floor a few weeks before the invasion, "This chamber is for the most part ominously, dreadfully silent. You can hear a pin drop. Listen. You can hear a pin drop.

There is no debate. There is no discussion. There is no attempt to lay out for the nation the pros and cons of this particular war. There is nothing." [7]

As for the notorious NIE on Iraqi weapons programs, which had been rushed to completion to meet the members' desire to get their vote out of the way as soon as possible, it did not attract any more readership in Congress than it did among policymakers in the executive branch. No more than six senators and a "handful" of House members looked at the estimate, according to staff members who kept custody of the copies.[8] Some staffers who read it tried unsuccessfully to get their members to do so as well, realizing that the details and uncertainties laid out in the document were markedly at variance with the ominous certitude about Iraqi weapons that the Bush administration was expressing in its pro-war campaign. "The dissents leaped out—they're in bold, almost like flashing light," recalled the scientific adviser to the Senate Foreign Relations Committee. "I remember thinking, boy, there's nothing there. If anybody takes the time to actually read this, they can't believe there actually are major WMD programs."[9] Bob Graham, the Senate Intelligence Committee chairman who was one of the few members of Congress to bother to read the estimate, reacted similarly. He was struck by the "vigorous dissents" on issues such as whether aluminum tubes Iraq had procured were intended for use in centrifuges to enrich uranium and by the judgment—to which there was no dissent—that Saddam was unlikely to use any unconventional weapons he had unless the United States attacked Iraq.[10] Graham's reading of the estimate was one of the considerations that led him, despite his presidential aspirations, to vote against the war resolution.

Most members did not take this approach. Congress's overall role in getting the nation involved in war in Iraq was not the analytic one of independently assessing the merits of the expedition, but instead the political one of stepping nimbly enough to avoid getting run over by the train that the war makers in the Bush administration had already sent accelerating down the track. Images pertinent to Iraq and the coming war accordingly did not determine most members' position or vote, regardless of whether those images came from the intelligence community or from some other source and whether they concerned WMD or some other topic. Images that were any more specific than the dumbed-down "Saddam has WMD" had almost no influence on most members; the very few who, like Graham, took the time to scrutinize the more specific images were, as a result of such scrutiny, at least as likely to oppose the war as to support it.

Congress's submissive behavior in the run-up to the war has been noted in only a few of the finger-pointing inventories of responsibility for landing the United States in the mess in Iraq. Journalist Thomas Ricks, who addresses the subject in his book on the war, writes that "the failures in Congress were at once perhaps the most important and the least noticed."[11] But affixing the label of "failure" in this instance as in any other is not the same as understanding why something happened. To blame Congress for responding as it did to the political realities its members faced in late 2002 is almost like blaming a dog for chasing squirrels. The response is part of the animal's nature. The responses of the political animals who inhabit Capitol Hill are understandable even if they are not commendable.

The inattention to the infamous NIE was all in a day's work for most members—even though this inattention was astounding for anyone who thought about the high stakes and the ostensible rationale of the war that the Bush administration was about to launch, and even though the inattention makes the later hair-splitting, exegetical recriminations about this estimate ring hollow. Members of Congress, after all, are busy people who routinely rely on the simplest cues (such as from a party leader, a staff assistant, or a lobbyist) to decide which way to vote on legislation about which they know next to nothing.

I had reason to reflect on this fact after an open hearing of the Senate Armed Services Committee in March 2004, at which I back-benched the DCI's annual testimony on worldwide threats. At the hearing, Senator Bill Nelson (D–Fla.), who had voted in favor of the war resolution, complained about a classified prewar briefing that in his view had not fully apprised him of disagreements about whether Iraq's unmanned aerial vehicles were intended for the delivery of biological weapons. DCI Tenet replied—accurately—that all the disagreements had been spelled out in the written estimate. Nelson acknowledged that he "subsequently" found out what was in the estimate and a moment later remarked, "I have noticed as I have been sharing my thoughts with you that there have been several quizzical expressions on the faces of your staff there." The quizzical expressions reflected our astonishment at hearing a senator admit in a televised hearing that he had not bothered to read the document on which his vote on a highly important matter supposedly had been based. As Nelson went on to say, if he had been alerted to the issue he was raising, "I would have gone and gotten that NIE and looked at it."[12] It occurred to me later that the senator saw nothing astonishing in the idea that he should not have to read a document unless a colleague, a staffer, or someone else pointed out to him the political hazard he incurred if he didn't.

CONGRESSIONAL RATIONALIZATION

As the Iraq War went sour and American casualties mounted, many members of Congress from both parties faced the problem of explaining away their earlier support for the expedition. Because the Bush administration had centered its selling of the war on WMD, and because the subsequent nondiscovery of WMD or active Iraqi programs to produce them represented what everyone agreed was an intelligence failure, then intelligence mistakes about Iraqi WMD would serve as the politically necessary explanation. "We were misled" became the battle cry of congressional rationalization, with the specific focus on intelligence and WMD. Those members who had supported the war could blame bad intelligence. Senator Hillary Clinton, in her subsequent campaign for the Democratic presidential nomination, came under the strongest pressure to rationalize in this way, but except for her presidential aspirations she was no different from many other members who had backed the invasion—including, as noted earlier, most Democratic senators. As for members who had opposed the war from the beginning, they had less political incentive to point out anything good about intelligence work on Iraq than to claim credit for seeing sooner than their colleagues what was bad about it.

That it was the Senate Intelligence Committee and not its House counterpart that launched an inquiry into intelligence work on Iraq should not be surprising, and not just because it was members of the Senate committee who had requested the intelligence estimate that would become the centerpiece of the investigation. It was in the Senate, not the House, that majorities on both sides of the aisle had backed the war. The most salient feature of the Senate committee's inquiry was that although it ostensibly was about all aspects of intelligence on Iraq, it focused narrowly on—and beat its drums loudly about—only one aspect: work on unconventional weapons and even more narrowly the infamous estimate the intelligence community delivered to the committee in October 2002. The committee's biggest splash was the release in July 2004, with a press conference and much fanfare, of a report of more than four hundred pages.[13] Three-fourths of the report was about unconventional weapons, with most of that a dissection of the October estimate. A smaller portion of the report addressed intelligence work on Iraqi involvement in terrorism, and an even smaller part was about other threats Saddam Hussein's regime may have posed.

The report's title, U.S. Intelligence Community's Prewar Intelligence Assessments on Iraq, sent the message that it covered all of the community's work on Iraq or at least all of it pertinent to the war. If citizens want to judge how intelligence performed on Iraq, the committee was saying, here is the whole performance. The message of the hoopla associated with the report was the same or an even narrower message that the work on WMD was the whole performance. But missing from the report and the hoopla was the entire other side of the equation of war-related issues: what the community assessed was likely if the United States went to war, not just what was likely if it did not. Of the three classified, community-coordinated assessments the intelligence community had produced on Iraq in the months before the war, the committee's report wallowed line by line in only one of them—on the weapons programs—and ignored the other two: on the challenges the United States would face in post-Saddam Iraq and on the regional repercussions of the war.

This highly selective treatment of the intelligence community's work reflected the political purpose of the Intelligence Committee's inquiry. To give any attention at all to intelligence assessments that pointed to the strife, violence, and counterproductive effects likely to ensue from the invasion obviously would not have helped members to rationalize their support for the war. To the contrary, such attention would have underscored the other considerations that members should have applied to their decisions on the war but failed to do so. Such attention would have been particularly unwelcome for Republicans because it would have highlighted the decision-making failures of not only members of Congress, but also the Bush administration.

The committee could not with a straight face ignore permanently the intelligence work on postinvasion consequences. It said this work would be addressed later in a "phase two" of its inquiry. The committee's Republican majority still had an interest in delaying attention to that work as long as possible. So the majority sat on phase two. Months went by. Years went by. The slow rolling was not even well disguised. As the official who had initiated and supervised the two major assessments the committee was holding in occultation, I was a prime interviewee. I had a lengthy interview with committee staff as phase two was supposedly getting under way. A couple of years later, after I had retired from government service and Democrats had agitated for movement on phase two, I was asked to return for another staff interview. The CIA congressional liaison officer who relayed the request did so apologetically, noting that as a retiree I was under no obligation to comply. I said that didn't matter; it was an important topic, and I would do the interview. The second interview was essentially a repeat of the first one, serving only to restore what the intervening passage of time had lost because of staff turnover, misplaced notes, or dulling of memories. The experience demonstrated how much the tardiness of a phase two report was a politically motivated hold rather than anything to do with investigative work in progress. There was very little to investigate in the first place, and there were far fewer security complications concerning public discussion of intelligence sources and methods than the weapons estimate had presented.

If Democrats had not won a majority of the Senate in the 2006 election, there is no telling how much longer the intelligence work on postwar consequences would have been kept under wraps. But the change in party control was sufficient to tip the balance in favor of finally putting something out—more than four years after the start of the war. The partisan division continued to be so intense that the "report" the committee issued contained no single evaluation of the intelligence community's work on the subject because committee members could not agree on one. Instead, the release consisted of redacted versions of the two community assessments I had supervised, a summary of judgments in the assessments, an overview of related work by individual intelligence agencies, and separate comments by Democrats and Republicans.[14] The two sides even argued over whether to include in the release the distribution list for the assessments. Democrats wanted to include it to show how widely the documents had been disseminated within the Bush administration. Republicans countered that if that list were to be released, then the names of all members of the congressional intelligence committees, which also received the assessments, should be included as well. Democrats had the deciding vote, and so the executive-branch recipients were listed, but members of Congress were not.

Democrats and Republicans still had enough shared interest in assigning blame to the faulty intelligence work on WMD, however, for neither side to want the prescient intelligence analysis about postinvasion consequences to upstage their earlier drum beating about the weapons issue. The rollouts of phases one and two of their inquiry could not have been more different. There were no press conferences and thus no page one headlines for phase two. The committee quietly put this report on its Web site on a Friday as Americans were beginning a holiday weekend. The different treatment was an excellent example of sustaining the mythology of intelligence by playing up failures and obscuring successes. In this case, with almost three years passing between the two releases by the committee, most Americans had already firmly equated intelligence work on Iraq with nonexistent WMD and did not believe there was anything else to learn. Very few ever noticed phase two.

The Senate committee's lopsided attention to the different Iraq-related issues did not reflect each issue's intrinsic importance to the war and to decision making on the war. Suppose that everything the intelligence community said about Iraq before the war—including about WMD—turned out to be true. Assume also that the Bush administration and the American people anticipated the costly mess that would follow a toppling of Saddam—completely consistent with the community's assessments about the postwar consequences, but with additional crystal-ball detail, unobtainable in the real world, about American costs and casualties. Under those assumptions, it is highly unlikely the administration would have proceeded with its plan for war and inconceivable that Congress and the American people would have gone along if it had. (And that is without even considering the prospect, which the intelligence community identified, that Saddam would use his assumed WMD in response to the invasion and thereby make the war even more costly.) The United States instead would have relied upon means other than war to deal with the problem of Saddam and his unconventional weapons. Even as committed a neocon as Richard Perle says that if he could have foreseen the course of the war—which he blamed on poor execution—"I probably would have said, 'No, let's consider other strategies for dealing with the thing that concerns us most.'"[15] What would happen once Saddam was toppled was always more important to the war than the scary possibilities of what he "could" do if he were not toppled, even though that is not how the Bush administration sold its decision or how the politics of the decision played out.

The Senate Intelligence Committee also promised another part of phase two, which would examine the use of intelligence in statements by the president and other administration leaders. Not surprisingly, this part also became a bone of partisan contention and subject to indefinite delay. The eventual product was mostly a mechanical comparing of individual lines from speeches with intelligence reporting; it did little to address the larger patterns in the administration's sales campaign and the nature of how it abused intelligence.[16] Released more than five years after the start of the war and nearly four years after the fanfare surrounding the phase one report, the committee's product—like its other phase two installment—barely detracted from the dominant and by then well-established theme about intelligence and the Iraq War: that it was a story of the intelligence community screwing up on WMD.

GUERRILLA PARSING

The phase one report had real faults to address in the community's work on Iraqi unconventional weapons, of course, particularly in the ill-starred 2002 estimate. The congressional report writers made the most of the opportunity with their extended excoriation of that one intelligence product. But the committee report also reflected some other common tendencies, repeatedly encountered as well in the unofficial commentary, that can make any intelligence failure seem more egregious than it really is.

The estimate on weapons programs, for all its faults, was a transparent document. It laid out—for anyone who took the trouble to read it—the disagreements and doubts within the intelligence community. It presented all sorts of possibly relevant information, including the dubious (such as the reported purchase of uranium ore) and the not so dubious, while indicating what could be confirmed and what could not. Readers of the estimate were given a good sense of the variety of reporting that the analysts were seeing and could use that to reach their own conclusions if they were so inclined. The rushed schedule on which the estimate was produced contributed to its inclusiveness, and in that peculiar sense the rush may have been beneficial. Like Blaise Pascal, who wrote a long letter because he did not have time to write a short one, the intelligence analysts delivered an estimate with an everything-but-the-kitchen-sink quality because they lacked the time to craft something more concise (or to resolve any more of their disagreements and doubts).

This quality makes oft-heard recriminations against the intelligence community that highlight the dissents and that raise issues of where the expertise on certain issues did or did not lie strange and illogical. The dissents and the different perspectives within the community were all part of the package it delivered to Congress, to be used and assessed as anyone who bothered to read the document saw fit. If one believed, for example, that the Department of Energy had the preeminent expertise on whether the captured aluminum tubes could be made into gas centrifuges, then one could pay attention to the department's judgment on this issue and ignore everyone else's judgments. The estimate was one more "for what it's worth" submission by the intelligence community, even though in this case the submission was made in a highly charged political environment with extra pressure to offer bottom-line judgments. The judgments were offered, but only as part of the larger package—with doubts and dissents, warts and all. Full use of the package did not require members of Congress to play intelligence analyst—only to assess, as did Senator Bob Graham, whether a subject with this much doubt and this little direct evidence constituted as compelling a reason to go to war as the Bush administration claimed it did.

Much of the Senate Intelligence Committee's many pages of exegesis of the weapons estimate consisted of matching up analytic judgments with the underlying intelligence reporting or lack of reporting. The committee's report repeatedly criticized judgments because there was no single report that said the same thing as the judgment. This technique can be applied to *any* intelligence judgment, no matter how sound and accurate, and for that reason the technique is empty and meaningless. The essence of intelligence analysis is to go beyond what the reporting says and certainly beyond any single report. If the intelligence community never were to offer any judgment beyond what can be found in a report from the collectors, then it could save resources by dismissing all the analysts and making do with reports officers and editors. Much of the committee's critique was thus a mindless, line-by-line assembling of sticks with which to beat the community rather than a serious and informed evaluation of the shortcomings of the analysis.

The committee used a similar approach in a chapter of its phase one report that addressed an unclassified paper that the intelligence community had also produced in 2002 on Iraqi unconventional weapons. Addressing this product in tandem with the classified estimate was misleading from the start. It nurtured the misperception that this paper was an "unclassified version" of the estimate, although it had an entirely different provenance. Democratic senators requested the classified estimate; the Bush administration had tasked the community much earlier in the year to prepare the unclassified paper. The scope of each paper also was different. The classified estimate included other judgments as requested by the senators, especially about likely Iraqi use; the unclassified paper was always only about weapons and programs to produce them.

In response to the administration's task, analysts in the CIA had written the unclassified paper. The NIC had then obtained coordination from other community agencies. (Because my office—for reasons of spreading the workload in the NIC—managed the coordination and subsequent production, my name became associated with the paper even though weapons were not my bailiwick.) And then the paper had lain fallow for several months. The administration had waited until the peak of its pro-war campaign in early autumn before telling the community to release it.

The paper was an unusual, though not unprecedented, product for the intelligence community. The clearest precedent was a "white paper" on the same subject the community had produced in 1998 for the Clinton administration, which used it as an aid to U.S diplomats in persuading foreign governments to maintain sanctions on Iraq. The 1998 paper had no markings to identify who produced it, which led CIA lawyers to object, warning that such a paper could be construed as an unauthorized covert-influence operation. To avoid that legal complication, the 2002 paper departed from its predecessor in one respect, which was to add to the cover the DCI seal. Otherwise, it retained the format of the earlier paper. This meant that, unlike classified intelligence community assessments, there was no listing of participating agencies, which in turn meant no use of the first-person plural ("we judge" or "we assess"), which is typical verbiage in classified assessments.

The administration's holding of the paper for several months had required an additional adjustment. By the time it was about to be released, the classified estimate on Iraqi weapons was in preparation. Despite the lack of any previous connections, two papers with largely overlapping subjects coming out at about the same time would inevitably invite comparisons. Avoiding both the appearance and the reality of inconsistent messages was important. It was too late to do anything about the main body of the unclassified paper, which had an entirely different format from the estimate. But we did scrap the unclassified up-front summary of the unclassified paper and replace it with a key judgments section that tracked as closely as it could the corresponding section of the estimate, within the limits of one paper's being top secret and the other unclassified. This effort to maintain as much consistency as possible between the classified and unclassified worlds only seemed to facilitate another form of mischief by the Senate Intelligence Committee staff.

The committee report lined up all the differences in wording between the two papers that could be found and strove to portray them as differences in substance. Not using the formulations "we judge" and "we assess," the report said, "changed many sentences in the unclassified paper to statements of fact from assessments."[17] The committee never explained how this editorial alteration constituted such a change. Most editors not steeped in the stylistic habits of the intelligence community probably would consider the alteration to be a desirable elimination of redundant words. The committee did not explain how omitting "we judge" from a sentence can make any difference when it is part of a section headed by the title "Key Judgments" (not "Key Facts") in large, boldface font. The unclassified paper used *probably, could, suggests,* and other weasel words in all the same places as the estimate. In that respect, its language also was similar to that of the 1998 white paper, which as the committee report itself noted—evidently with approval—"contained other words which expressed the uncertainty behind the IC [intelligence community] judgments without using the word 'we.'"[18] Although individual agencies were not named, the issues on which there was disagreement on the 2002 paper were clearly identified as ones on which "most analysts assess" one conclusion, whereas "other analysts assess" a different conclusion.

The committee report claimed that "caveats were removed" when the classified key judgments from the estimate were converted into unclassified ones.[19] In fact, no caveats to any judgments in the unclassified paper were removed. The only language removed was classified or applicable only to what was classified. For example, the committee complained about deletion of the phrase "although we have little specific information" from a judgment about Iraq's presumed stockpile of chemical weapons. The words were part of a sentence that gave a specific numerical range for the size of the stockpile: one hundred to five hundred metric tons, with the further statement that much of it was "added in the last year." The specifics about how many tons and recent additions had to go because they was classified, and so the clause that qualified that judgment and was part of the same sentence went with it. The unclassified paper was left, as its only judgment about chemical weapons stockpiles, with the weaker and vaguer sentence, "Saddam probably has stocked a few hundred metric tons of CW [chemical weapons] agents." Incredibly, the committee report stated that this change "portrayed the IC as far more certain" about Iraqi chemical weapons stocks and programs than it was.[20] As this example demonstrated, the changes necessitated by declassification instead resulted in language that, if different at all, was mushier and less specific than what was in the classified estimate. But the notion that the unclassified paper expressed more certainty than the estimate was a stick with which the committee had decided it would beat this part of the intelligence community's work. It kept beating, line by line, even where the notion clearly made no sense.

Although the committee's guerrilla parsing lapsed into silliness on such issues, it served the political purpose of boosting and perpetuating an image of intelligence community malfeasance that went beyond the actual errors in the community's work on Iraqi unconventional weapons. Themes in the committee's long and loudly trumpeted phase one report were replayed in the unofficial commentary. The canard about removing caveats, for example, still gets heard. Meanwhile, though, the committee ignored larger and more important questions, including whether any of the details over which the committee spilled so much ink mattered at all in the Bush administration's ability to sell the war.

Probably only a tiny proportion of even well-educated Americans ever read any of the unclassified paper; the public was many times more exposed to the statements made on Iraq by Bush and other administration leaders (and the White House issued its own "white paper" on Iraq, replete with "intelligence reporting" on WMD as well as on all the well-worn themes about terrorist connections[21]). Moreover, no one who did bother to read the intelligence community's paper would have had his views about an Iraqi threat shaped by stylistic details such as whether a sentence included the words *we judge* and the like. But this unclassified paper illustrates another more basic question that the committee ignored and on which it could have been helpful if it had wanted to be: What business did the intelligence community have in producing such a paper in the first place? Unclassified intelligence assessments for public consumption have legitimate functions, although they also raise difficult issues that I touch upon again in a later chapter. But the Bush administration's purpose in this paper was not just to educate the public; it was to muster support for a policy initiative—a controversial one at that. That is not a legitimate intelligence community function, and for that reason it is regrettable the paper was ever produced.

Being regrettable does not mean being avoidable—not in the real world in which intelligence officers have to work. The difference in legitimacy between the 1998 paper and the similar one in 2002 is that the former was intended to support diplomacy aimed at foreign governments (a function that the intelligence community regularly performs in many other ways), whereas the latter was intended to influence domestic U.S. public opinion in support of a particular policy. If the leaders of the intelligence community had refused to comply with the Bush administration's request, however, the response would have been easy to predict and difficult to counter: "So when the Clintonites ask you for a paper, you do it because their policy toward Iraq was to use multilateral sanctions. But when we ask you for the same kind of paper on the same subject, you refuse because you see our policy as one of using military force. And you claim that your own policy preferences aren't affecting your work?" This action by the intelligence community is properly labeled "politicization," but the label points to no realistic and effective alternative course for the intelligence officers to follow.

In an ideal world, in which congressional intelligence committees diligently perform their function of helping to establish policies and principles for the use of intelligence resources, the Senate committee would have squarely addressed this issue. It would have declared that it is improper to use intelligence resources to try to influence American public opinion on policy issues under debate and that if intelligence officers find themselves in a similar situation in the future, they should run, not walk, to the committee to raise the problem.

No such declaration was made. Republicans had no interest in highlighting the Bush administration's politicization of intelligence, and Republicans and Democrats alike shared an interest in keeping attention focused on the intelligence community's errors concerning WMD as an explanation for their own misguided support of the Iraq War. Principles for the proper use of intelligence resources did not enter into the committee's lengthy report because that was not the purpose of the exercise. The purpose concerned politics, not propriety.

Another way to understand that purpose is to ask how much of the committee's phase one report could have been issued *before* the war. The answer: most of it—including everything about the unclassified paper and how it compared to the estimate, a subject that required no investigation, but only the reading of two documents the committee had in its possession as of early October 2002. If the intelligence community were misleading the public or anyone else, the committee had five more months to warn or complain about it before U.S. troops rolled across the Iraqi border. The report was done after, not before, the invasion because it was only later that there arose a political need to explain away previous support for a war gone bad.

PASSIVITY IN THE PRESS

The inadequacy of congressional review of the administration's decision to go to war made it less likely the other major intermediary between government and the people—the press—would challenge that decision either. With no public hearings (not even cursory ones like those preceding passage of the Gulf of Tonkin resolution in 1964, which served as congressional authorization for the Vietnam War) and no critical witnesses, the press lacked easily acquired material. As one Capitol Hill veteran put it, "The media didn't stand up because they had no one to quote. So, in combination, the two institutions [Congress and the press] didn't work."[22]

After the war went sour, the fourth estate began issuing mea culpas. In 2004, the editors of the *New York Times* published an extraordinary statement in which they cataloged what they considered in retrospect to have been their own errors in giving too much attention to unsubstantiated assertions about threatening Iraqi weapons programs and insufficient prominence to qualifications, retractions, and refutations. "We wish we had been more aggressive," the editors lamented.[23] The *Washington Post*'s ombudsman described in 2005 the failure to challenge diligently the administration's rationale for war as "by far the single most important and most disappointing performance by the press, including the *Post*," during his five-year tenure.[24] One of the most recognized figures to straddle journalism and politics, Bill Moyers, released in 2007 the episode "Buying the War" on *Bill Moyers Journal*, the main theme of which was that war makers in the Bush administration relied on "a compliant press, to pass on their propaganda as news and cheer them on."[25]

The media's backward-looking self-criticism has been so extensive that the only fair thing to add is that, as with Congress, there were admirable exceptions to the general failure. Although the absence of hearings made material harder to get, such material was not impossible to get. The work of Warren Strobel and Jonathan Landay for what was then the Knight-Ridder newspaper chain is a good example of healthily skeptical coverage of the administration's pro-war case.[26]

Also as with Congress, merely allocating blame—whether on oneself, as the mainstream press has done, or on others, as with most of the finger pointing associated with the Iraq War—does not equate with understanding the dynamics of politics and opinion that helped to make the war possible. The press was subject to the same post-9/11 militant mood as nearly everyone else in the United States. To the extent that the press conveyed themes that were helpful to those selling the war, it was more a matter of mood and atmospherics than of specific reporting or detailed analysis.

This pattern has occurred previously, including before the Vietnam War. The images of what was at stake in Vietnam, involving the domino theory and the idea that backing away from the commitment there would encourage aggression or subversion elsewhere, were widely shared outside the government. They were part of a received wisdom accepted by the vast majority of Americans across the political spectrum, including journalists who later would win fame for writing about what was wrong with the war and with how it had been launched.[27] An example was David Halberstam, whose 1969 book *The Best and the Brightest* depicted how smart people could get involved in a stupid conflict.[28] In an earlier book that Halberstam had published just as the ground war was getting under way in 1965, he had shared—despite the book's discouraging title, *The Making of a Quagmire*— all of the Johnson administration's fatalistic sense that despite the likely costs and difficulties the United States needed to forge ahead. Withdrawal from Vietnam, according to Halberstam, would mean "that the United States's prestige will be lowered throughout the world, and it means that the pressure of Communism on the rest of Southeast Asia will intensify. Lastly, withdrawal means that throughout the world the enemies of the West will be encouraged to try insurgencies like the one in Vietnam." Halberstam went so far as to state that Vietnam was "perhaps one of only five or six nations in the world that is truly vital to U.S. interests."[29]

Another *New York Times* reporter, Neil Sheehan, who would become the recipient of the leaked *Pentagon Papers* and would win plaudits for his critical coverage of the war, including his later book *A Bright Shining Lie*,[30] expressed views similar to Halberstam's before the U.S. intervention. In a long piece in the *Times* in August 1964 in which Sheehan conveyed his own analysis and was not just citing official sources, he wrote that there were two basic reasons for fighting in Vietnam: the United States was "the only western power capable of meeting the Chinese Communist challenge for hegemony in Asia," and there was a need "to demonstrate to the rest of the world that this country has the desire and the ability to defeat the Communist strategy for expansion." Most of the article was an elaboration of the domino theory. A fall of Southeast Asia because of the repercussions of an American defeat in Vietnam, declared Sheehan, "would amount to a strategic disaster of the first magnitude."[31]

To the extent that press coverage of Iraq four decades later got into specifics, these details did not match the specifics of the intelligence community's output, including all the qualifications and dissents that were part of that output. This mismatch is part of what the *Times* editors were referring to when they acknowledged that assertions friendly to the administration's case received prominent coverage on page one, but that doubts and other views were relegated to the back pages if they got any coverage at all. A long article by Michael Gordon and Judith Miller in the *Times* in early September 2002 highlighted the aluminum tubes as a prime piece of evidence that Iraq had "stepped up its quest for nuclear weapons," while giving no hint of expert disagreement about the tubes' purpose.[32] Even before 9/11 and before Bush became president (but after neoconservatives had begun agitating to overthrow Saddam), some press treatment of the weapons issue went beyond any intelligence judgments. Tim Weiner published an article in the *Times* in 1999 that, citing various private analysts, talked up the weapons threat as a counterpoint to the patient long-term containment of Iraq that was the Clinton administration's policy toward Iraq. Saddam Hussein "may be as close to building a nuclear weapon—perhaps closer—than he was in 1991," wrote Weiner.[33] The U.S. intelligence community, as I noted earlier, was not saying any such thing.

The principal source for the most prominent press coverage of Iraq and the weapons issue was the Bush administration itself, which had its own favored sources, such as Ahmed Chalabi's Iraqi National Congress. The principal source was not the intelligence community, and it was not war skeptics. The relationship between the press and the administration became one of co-optation in some instances and intimidation in others—both being ingredients of politicization, the subject of chapter 6.

In short, the WMD issue certainly figured prominently in what the American public read in the press about Iraq in the run-up to the war, but for the most part it figured in the same crude, tub-thumping way in which it figured into the Bush administration's overall sales campaign. Most of the coverage did not reflect the fine points of intelligence judgments that later would provide such grist for recriminating postmortems, and most of it did not attempt to look carefully beyond the most general "Saddam's weapons are a threat" theme that the campaign featured. To the extent the press got into specifics, it was mostly specifics that the administration was happy to feed to the press.

WORLDS WITHOUT ERROR

To appreciate how much difference the intelligence community's judgments about Iraqi weapons programs made—or did not make—in gathering support for the war, imagine how the discourse about Iraq would have played out if the judgments had been sound. As the stiffest possible test, start with the extreme—and thus impossible and unreasonable—assumption that the community's judgments corresponded exactly with everything we know now about Iraqi policy and programs based on what was uncovered after the invasion. Although this accuracy would have been beyond what even the most magnificent intelligence service could have achieved, thinking about such a hypothetical extreme can have heuristic value.

The most thorough statement of what we know now about prewar Iraqi unconventional weapons activities is the report of the study group led initially by David Kay and subsequently by Charles Duelfer, based on exhaustive field investigations and interviews in Iraq during the first year and a half of the occupation. Among the key findings of the Duelfer report were that Saddam Hussein saw strong advantages in having WMD and intended to re-create Iraq's WMD capability once he got out from under the yoke of international sanctions. His aspirations included a nuclear capability, "irrespective of international pressure and the resulting economic risks." Moreover, Saddam was close to the point of being able to restart his programs. "By 2000–2001," the report concluded, "Saddam had managed to mitigate many of the effects of sanctions and undermine their international support. Iraq was within striking distance of a *de facto* end to the sanctions regime, both in terms of oil exports and the trade embargo, by the end of 1999."[34]

Perfect prewar judgments from the intelligence community about the state of Iraqi weapons programs would have necessitated some modifications in the Bush administration's sales campaign. Vice President Cheney presumably could not have declared with a straight face, for example, that there was "no doubt" that Iraq had WMD. But it is remarkable how much, even under this unrealistically extreme assumption, would *not* have to be changed in the campaign. The administration continued to invoke well into the war (even after the nondiscovery of WMD) many of the themes of that campaign, which had centered at least as much on intentions and possibilities as on extant capabilities. Cheney himself cited the Duelfer report as support in arguing three years into the war that the invasion was justified and that the dangers from what Saddam Hussein could do with WMD had been one of the reasons justifying it.[35]

The crumbling of the sanctions regime was an important factor because continued containment of Saddam, with international sanctions being a major part of the containment effort, was widely seen as the main alternative to a war to oust the Iraqi dictator. Awareness of how much the system of sanctions had already grown weaker was a major consideration for nonneocons among the policy elite who came to believe that a war would be worth the costs and risks. Conclusions identical to those in the Duelfer report might possibly have been used to argue for a renewed effort to bolster the sanctions regime. But it is at least as likely that the report's conclusions would have provided ammunition to those arguing that such efforts had been made already and had failed and that there was thus no recourse left but forceful removal of the Iraqi dictator. Even with perfect intelligence judgments, the Bush administration still would have beaten the drums about Saddam Hussein's intentions regarding WMD, about all the awful things he "could" do with WMD once he got them, and about the need to take action to eliminate such a threat before the threat materialized.

And even if somehow, in this impossible counterfactual world, omniscient intelligence analysts had rendered completely accurate judgments, there would remain the question of how the analysts arrived at those judgments and whether they might be wrong. Hypothetical prewar judgments identical to the Duelfer report are not the same as the Duelfer report itself, which was based on a trove of postinvasion, on-the-ground information far beyond anything available to analysts before the war. In making judgments before the war, the intelligence community could not *know* what it was saying. Cheney, Rumsfeld, and other advocates of the war would still highlight how badly the intelligence community had underestimated progress in Iraq's nuclear program prior to 1991 and how foolish it would be to hinge policy on the judgments of an intelligence service that had proven to be so wrong about such things in the past.

Despite the adjustments the Bush administration would have to make to its pro-war campaign, even under this extreme scenario of intelligence omniscience the campaign probably would have succeeded. With Congress paying more attention to politics than to substance and more to themes than to details, the administration likely would have lost a few votes but still would have had a good chance of getting its resolution endorsing the war.

The probable outcome is even clearer in a much more realistic alternative scenario of the intelligence community's performing the best possible analysis given the unavoidably incomplete information available to it. One version of such a scenario comes from the scholar Richard Betts, who points out that "no responsible analyst" could have concluded in 2002 that Iraq did *not* have the feared WMD.[36] Betts suggests the following as the proper key judgments of any estimate on the subject in the fall of 2002:

- Iraq is probably hiding stocks of chemical and biological weapons and active programs to develop and produce chemical, biological, and nuclear weapons;
- That conclusion is deduced primarily from its obstruction of UNSCOM [United Nations Special Commission], the failure to account for destruction of stocks known to exist in 1991, and some other circumstantial evidence;
- There is very little direct evidence, and no highly reliable direct evidence, to back up the deduction.[37]

The best-possible analysis might have discouraged the administration from highlighting some of the tidbits of reporting that in the actual scenario of flawed analysis were misinterpreted or fraudulent, involving such things as aluminum tubes or biological weapons trailers. But flawless intelligence analysis certainly would not have precluded such use, as indicated in the actual scenario by the administration's insistence on using the fraudulent report about Iraq purchasing uranium ore in Africa.

The best-possible analysis would have changed almost nothing else in the Bush administration's campaign for war, which would still be replete with scare-mongering themes of mushroom clouds and dictators giving WMD to terrorists. Hardly a word would have been different in Cheney's

August 2002 VFW speech. The same would be true for President Bush's major prewar statement on the subject, his speech in Cincinnati in October 2002, as well as for the torrent of other administration statements designed to condition public opinion. Indeed, the tone of agnosticism in Betts's suggested judgments would have provided the perfect foil for everything the administration actually said about how dangers can lurk in a place such as Saddam's Iraq, undetected by intelligence—including Cheney's comment that "intelligence is an uncertain business" and Bush's observation in Cincinnati that "we don't know exactly [how close Saddam is to developing a nuclear weapon], and that's the problem."[38]

The hypothetical judgments would have been more than enough to sustain the simplified theme of "Saddam has WMD" that shaped votes in Congress and opinion among the American people. Themes and politics, as we have seen, were much more important than substantive details. Under this scenario, perhaps a few votes in Congress would have gone differently, but it is almost certain that the war resolution would have passed, most likely still with substantial majorities in both houses.

The sort of thinking that led even many intelligent and perceptive Americans to follow Bush and the neoconservatives into the quicksand of Iraq and that would have been largely impervious to even the most critical and insightful analysis about the unconventional weapons issue is exemplified by the work of liberal *Washington Post* columnist Richard Cohen. In a column he published a week before the invasion, Cohen wrote, "In the run-up to this war, the Bush administration has slipped, stumbled and fallen on its face. It has advanced untenable, unproven arguments. It has oscillated from disarmament to regime change to bringing democracy to the Arab world. It has linked Hussein to al Qaeda when no such link has been established. It has warned of an imminent Iraqi nuclear program when, it seems, that's not the case." Nonetheless, Cohen argued, the war was necessary because "sometimes peace is no better, especially if all it does is postpone a war. . . . [I]f the United States now pulled back . . . Hussein would wait us out. . . . If, at the moment, he does not have nuclear weapons, it's not for lack of trying. He had such a program once and he will have one again—just as soon as the world loses interest and the pressure on him is relaxed."[39] Cohen's empirical observations were right on the mark. He also picked up on what the intelligence community was correctly saying about Iraq and al-Qa'ida not being allied and about an Iraqi nuclear weapon not being imminent. What he wrote was also entirely consistent not only with the best-possible-analysis scenario, but even with the omniscience scenario—the one in which the intelligence community gets everything right. Yet he still backed the war.

MISPLACED HOPES FOR DISSENT

A frequent theme in retrospective examinations about who should have done what on Iraq is that intelligence officers had access to information that might have headed off the war if the officers had made it public. Cohen wrote a pro-leak piece in February 2006 that bemoaned intelligence officers who had "kept their mouths shut" about the administration's misuse of intelligence. I figured prominently in the column as someone who, if only I had picked up the phone and called a reporter to leak something, might have changed history. "The consensus at the CIA," wrote Cohen, "was that there was no link between Saddam Hussein and al Qaeda. And while the spooks of Langley more or less concurred that Hussein had weapons of mass destruction, they also thought his nuclear program was years away from fruition. In short, there was no urgent reason to go to war. I wish I had known that."[40] This comment is odd in light of Cohen's column from three years earlier showing that he *did* realize that an Iraqi nuclear weapon was not imminent and that there was no connection between Iraq and al-Qa'ida (but that he supported going to war anyway).

Americans did not need intelligence officers to point out such gaping holes in the war makers' case, even in the parts ostensibly based on intelligence. Consider what was said about terrorist links in Secretary Powell's presentation at the United Nations. Although that speech was later noted for containing invalid reporting about weapons programs, it was the most thoroughly scrubbed (at Powell's insistence) of the administration's public statements on Iraq and omitted some of the excesses in other administration statements. It said nothing about purchases of uranium in Africa, for example, and it did not repeat the administration's assertions elsewhere—based on an expansive reading of fraudulent statements by a detainee—that Iraq had given chemical or biological weapons assistance to al-Qa'ida. Later in 2003 I published a book in which I noted that 9/11 had confirmed the previously established trend away from state sponsorship and toward terrorism fomented by independent groups such as al-Qa'ida. Focusing specifically on Iraq, I reviewed Powell's presentation at the Security Council and pointed out that nothing in it said the Iraqi regime had ever assisted al-Qa'ida.[41] Scrubbed and stripped of the administration's exaggerations, it had no case for invasion. Any careful reader of the presentation could have made the same observation without being either an intelligence officer or an expert on terrorism.

I scratched my head while reading Cohen's praise of leaks, wondering just what I would have leaked had I been inclined to leak. The only possibilities that come to mind are the intelligence community assessments on postwar challenges and regional repercussions. But if someone were to leak these widely disseminated assessments (and eventually someone did leak them in part), it did not need to be anyone in the intelligence community. Indeed, leaking per se was not even necessary. Any member of the congressional intelligence committees could have issued a statement—without divulging classified information—declaring that the intelligence community had issued assessments about the consequences of invading Iraq that were sharply at variance with the administration's optimistic vision. That person could have called for declassified versions of the assessments to be released promptly and for debate on the issues the assessments raised. The member also could have complained mightily about not having the assessments in hand when he voted on the Iraq resolution in October 2002, and with the invasion still two months away he could have urged his colleagues in Congress to look more carefully at whether the whole Iraq adventure made sense.

Even if the assessments had become public earlier, the politics surrounding the Iraq War (which explain why no member of Congress took the hypothetical action just described) and the way the issue was in fact handled give little room for optimism that history would have been different. Members of Congress already skeptical of the war did pry loose the intelligence community's important judgment about Saddam's being unlikely to use WMD or give them to terrorists, but that information made no discernible difference in the congressional vote or in the wider public debate. The assessments were exactly that—assessments—and they could have been wrong. I wish for the sake of U.S. interests in Iraq and the Middle East that the assessments anticipating a violent mess in Iraq had been wrong. Policymakers, who are entitled to make and promote their own assessments, would have argued that the intelligence assessments were wrong. President Bush, who later would publicly dismiss as "just guessing" a pessimistic intelligence assessment grounded in more than a year of increasing turmoil in

Iraq,[42] would have been even more comfortable dismissing in the same way any intelligence assessments issued before the war began.

EXPECTATIONS WITHOUT INFLUENCE

None of the foregoing discussion about Iraqi unconventional weapons excuses or justifies the now famous intelligence errors on that subject. Although adding to the shelf-straining corpus of commentary on that subject is not the purpose of this book, the errors raised useful lessons. The intelligence community learned and applied such lessons—on its own, before any committees or commissions pronounced on the subject—particularly relating to the error of insufficiently double- and triple-checking the credibility of some sources. Although weapons programs were not part of my account, as the political person for the Middle East on the NIC I shared responsibility for another error, which was insufficient attention to alternative explanations for Saddam Hussein's evasive behavior on the weapons issue. In this case, truth was stranger than fiction, and it would have been extremely difficult to assemble a persuasive case that the evasion was intended only to preserve impressions that did not reflect actual programs. But even the stranger possibilities should have been considered more than they were. For those who derive whatever satisfaction is to be derived from pointing fingers of blame wherever they can be pointed, blame away. But those who instead want to understand why the United States went to war in Iraq, what images guided the decision to go to war, and what all this implies for the chances of avoiding similarly misguided policies in the future need to look elsewhere. That understanding is not to be found in what the intelligence community said about Iraqi weapons and certainly not in the entire corpus of what it said about Iraq.

An enormous load was placed on the intelligence community during this episode, a load that seems to have become even greater in retrospect. The community was expected to uncover truths that others could not uncover, to make judgments that others would use as a politically convenient substitute for making their own judgments about policy, to articulate details about those judgments that others did not make time to absorb, to resist the excesses of a propagandizing administration that others did not resist, to convey politically inconvenient truths to the public even while others who were much better positioned to speak publicly did not convey them, to force water down the throat of a policymaking horse that not only did not want to drink but did not even want to be led to the water, and to call the horse to account while it was stomping on the community's chest with its hoof. The Iraq War was one of the most vivid cases of a recurring pattern: to look to intelligence as a savior expected to rescue Americans and their elected decision makers from their own folly.[43]

CHAPTER FIVE

GREAT DECISIONS AND THE IRRELEVANCE
OF INTELLIGENCE

The George W. Bush administration's launching of the Iraq War was an especially strong example of a major departure in U.S. foreign policy that was not guided, much less stimulated or instigated, by intelligence. This aspect of decision making on the Iraq War differed from other major departures only in degree and not in kind, however. The pattern has persisted despite much variation from one administration to another in the relationship between policymakers and intelligence officers. Intelligence has had almost no guiding role in great decisions—the ones that shape long-standing perceptions of success and failure in foreign policy—such as entries into war or major redirections of U.S. grand strategy. Intelligence has played an important supporting role in many lesser decisions and in implementing the great ones. It also has had important things to say on the subjects about which the great decisions were made. But it has been virtually irrelevant to how those decisions came out, as shown by American decision making throughout the Cold War from the first major confrontation in Korea to the crumbling of the Soviet Empire in Europe and the USSR itself.

Jumping Into the Breach in Korea

On Sunday, June 25, 1950, President Harry S. Truman cut short a stay at his home in Independence, Missouri, and returned to Washington to handle a crisis. Communist North Korea had invaded South Korea. When the president's plane landed at National Airport, Truman had received only fragmentary reports about the invasion, which Secretary of State Dean Acheson had relayed to him by telephone when Truman was still in Independence. There had been no other conversations with his advisers. He had received no assessments about what lay behind the attack and no options paper about what to consider when deciding upon a response. He had mostly just his own private thoughts during the three-hour flight. For Truman, those thoughts were enough. As his limousine met him at planeside, Truman's first remark (to Secretary of Defense Louis Johnson) was that he would not let the attack succeed and that he was going to "hit them hard." [1]

When Truman did meet with senior civilian and military officials that evening, he heard nothing to dissuade him from the decision he had in effect already made. One of Truman's main impressions from that meeting, he later wrote, was "the complete, almost unspoken acceptance on the part of everyone that whatever had to be done to meet this aggression had to be done."[2] Further meetings over the next several days, as the North Korean forces sped southward, gave shape to what became the U.S.-led military intervention we know as the Korean War. During these further deliberations, the initial resolve to respond forcefully never wavered.

The dominant image in the minds of Truman and his advisers was of a worldwide competition between a camp led by the Soviet Union, which sought to expand Communist power and influence, and one led by the United States, which sought to check that expansion. A related component of the image was the belief that the Soviets had ordered the attack in Korea.[3] The decision makers believed that failure to intervene in Korea would encourage further Communist aggression elsewhere in the world. The policymakers saw the invasion as important not so much because of the significance of Korea itself, which the administration earlier had excluded from areas it considered strategically vital—most famously in a speech by Acheson in January 1950.[4] The significance instead lay in what would come next. Truman later wrote of how Communist success in Korea "would put Red troops and planes within easy striking distance of Japan, and Okinawa and Formosa would be open to attack from two sides."[5] Even more important, the American decision makers saw the invasion as a test of will between Moscow and Washington. "The Reds were probing for weaknesses in our armor," wrote Truman. "Firmness now would be the only way to deter new actions in other portions of the world."[6]

The images and beliefs that guided the decision makers came mainly from their reading of history. This was conspicuously true of President Truman, who took pride in his "endless reading of history" and drawing lessons from the experiences of earlier presidents.[7] The particular historical lesson that most inspired the decision on Korea was that of Axis aggression and imperialism leading up to World War II,[8] an experience especially significant to leaders of Truman's generation because it unfolded as they were maturing and assuming positions of responsibility.[9] Also influential was the more recent history of resolute responses by the U.S.-led West that had contributed to the withdrawal of Soviet troops from northern Iran in 1946, defeat of the Communist side in the Greek civil war in 1949, and the overcoming of a blockade of Berlin through the airlift of 1948–1949.[10]

Except for some reports from the front line during the first couple of days of the crisis (as relayed by the embassy and military command), almost none of the information that formed the basis for the decisions the Truman administration made during the first week of the Korean crisis can be called intelligence. It was not the substantive product of any government department. The sources of information and insight instead included the perspectives of key figures such as Acheson and Douglas MacArthur, assumptions about Soviet behavior that senior advisers voiced among themselves in their closed-door meetings, responses from other delegations at the United Nations, and the historical analogies, especially analogies to pre–World War II events.[11]

The decisions on Korea during that week in June grew out of the deliberations and inclinations of a very small number of men. To the extent the policy was not the product of one man—the president—it was the product of a handful of his senior advisers, whose most important interactions were with each other. To the extent expert knowledge was injected, such as expertise on the Soviet Union, it was coming from the few senior experts (in this case George Kennan and another senior diplomat experienced in Soviet affairs, Charles "Chip" Bohlen) who were admitted to the decision-making circle. The bureaucracy was largely irrelevant.

Missiles in Cuba and a Committee of Legend

Intelligence played somewhat more of a role in the legendary superpower showdown in 1962 caused by another major Soviet challenge—the placement of nuclear-armed missiles in Cuba—but not nearly as much as memories of Adlai Stevenson displaying U-2 photography to the United Nations Security Council would suggest. As with the Korean crisis, the deliberations that mattered were confined to a small number of men—in this case the ExComm, the ad hoc NSC Executive Committee, which President John F. Kennedy established to manage the Cuban Missile Crisis and which comprised a dozen of his senior advisers. Also like Korea, historical analogies shaped the decision makers' perceptions.[12] The European powers stumbling into World War I was the analogy that seemed to weigh most heavily on President Kennedy, who instructed his subordinates to read Barbara Tuchman's then-new book on the subject, *The Guns of August*.[13]

Besides historical analogies, the most important sources of images that influenced the formulation of policy were the individual conceptions that members of the ExComm brought with them about human behavior and thus about Soviet behavior as well as about threats, deterrence, bluffing, signal sending, and all the other ways in which different moves might lead to different outcomes of the crisis. The images that were bounced around within the ExComm were not vetted with a bureaucracy. The closest thing to such vetting was the inclusion of Llewellyn Thompson, ambassador-at-large at the State Department and a former ambassador to Moscow, who assumed a role as expert on Soviet affairs similar to that of Kennan and Bohlen at the beginning of the Korean War.

The outcome of U.S decision making in the missile crisis depended at least as much on the dynamics of the decision-making process itself as on information made available to the decision makers, be it from the intelligence community or anyone else. That is why Graham Allison's analysis of the crisis, *Essence of Decision*, deservedly has acquired the status of a classic.[14] Allison showed that what he called the rational actor model—which incorporates the ideal model of intelligence–policy relations—cannot explain all or even most of what happened. The individual decision makers' political standing and the competition among them as well as the proclivities of organizations they led explain at least as much. The ebb and flow of sentiment within the ExComm reflected less the availability of new information than the skill with which arguments were advanced and the influence of those advancing them. Kennedy eventually rejected an air strike in part because those supporting the option, such as the Joint Chiefs, were not his natural allies and thus counted less than other members of the ExComm who were, such as his brother Robert.[15]

As with many other episodes in American foreign policy, domestic political considerations played at least as big a role as any images of overseas reality. The young president's previous brush with Cuba had been the embarrassing Bay of Pigs operation. He also was perceived as having gotten bullied by Soviet leader Nikita Khrushchev when they met in Vienna in June 1961. Kennedy felt compelled to take forceful action to remove the missiles lest public doubts about him increase.[16]

Intelligence about the entry of missiles into Cuba touched off the deliberations in the first place. But the impact of intelligence on the deliberations was far less than that of the images of Soviet behavior that percolated up within the minds of the ExComm membership. Intelligence about Soviet military assets in Cuba was seriously faulty or incomplete in ways that nonetheless did not shape the decisions. The Soviet military presence in Cuba was grossly underestimated (it in fact included about forty-three thousand heavily armed troops), and U.S. intelligence missed altogether a force of nuclear-armed cruise missiles aimed at the U.S. base at Guantanamo Bay.[17] If the intelligence on these subjects had been more complete and accurate, it probably would only have reinforced the eventual decision not to use military force in Cuba.

FATALISM IN VIETNAM

The decision making that in the 1960s led to the intervention in Vietnam— the largest and deadliest U.S. military expedition since World War II— resembled in some respects the thinking that would lead the United States into Iraq forty years later. The process for making the decision, however, was vastly different. There not only *was* a decision-making process, which there was not with the Iraq War, but a seemingly thorough one at that. The bureaucracy was engaged, and centers of expertise within it were repeatedly tapped. Policymakers exposed themselves to extensive relevant information. They agonized at length over many of the implications. For the most part, policymakers did not harbor illusions about what they were getting into. Their policy reflected opinion broadly held inside and outside government. In these respects, the policymaking system worked.[18]

Despite the apparent thoroughness of the process, however, insights and judgments that the intelligence community provided to the policymakers did not guide the policy. The disjunction between intelligence input and policy output began as soon as Vietnam presented itself as a problem for U.S. policy, when France extracted itself from Indochina with a compromise agreement at Geneva in 1954 that left Vietnam split between a Communist North and a non-Communist South. A series of U.S. intelligence estimates painted a pessimistic picture of a South Vietnam unlikely ever to become stable and secure. An NIE produced shortly after the Geneva Accord rated the chances that a strong South Vietnam would emerge from the agreement as "poor." Nonetheless, the Eisenhower administration embraced the security of the South as a goal and placed it under the umbrella of the newly created Southeast Asia Treaty Organization. In an estimate the following year, the intelligence community stated, "[W]e believe that it would be extremely difficult, at best, for a Vietnamese government, regardless of its composition, to make progress towards developing a strong, stable, anti-Communist government capable of resolving the basic social, economic, and political problems of Vietnam, the special problems arising from the Geneva Agreement and capable of meeting the long-range challenge of the Communists." But within a few weeks the United States firmly committed itself to supporting South Vietnamese strongman Ngo Dinh Diem and acquiesced in his noncompliance with political terms of the Geneva settlement. An intelligence estimate in 1959 rated Diem's political and military prospects as poor and assessed that his internal security forces "will not be able to eradicate DRV [Democratic Republic of Vietnam—the Communist regime in the North] supported guerrilla or subversive activity in the foreseeable future." U.S. support for Diem would not waver, however, until after a couple more years of growing violence and unrest.[19]

The intelligence estimates of the 1950s miscalculated the numerical strength of the Viet Cong and—notwithstanding their general pessimism—overrated the military capabilities of the South Vietnamese government. "But as strategic intelligence," the authors of the *Pentagon Papers* conclude, "they were remarkably sound." Given the paucity of information, the authors continue, "U.S. intelligence served policy makers of the day surprisingly well" in warning of troubles that would follow. But these assessments had no apparent effect on two major reviews of policy toward Vietnam by the

NSC between 1954 and 1960. Public statements on the subject diverged even more from the intelligence assessments, with administration spokesmen consistently touting major progress.[20]

The imperative that policymakers felt to go to war in Vietnam derived from another set of images: of monolithic communism, falling dominoes, and the need to maintain the credibility of U.S. commitments. The failure to question most of these images was the most important respect in which the U.S. decision-making process on Vietnam did *not* work. In the few instances in which the intelligence community was asked to assess any of those images, the impact was minimal because the images were firmly rooted and almost impervious to change. The domino theory—the belief that the fall of South Vietnam to communism would lead to the successive fall of neighboring states as well—was widely and unquestioningly accepted and explicitly endorsed by Dwight Eisenhower,[21] John Kennedy,[22] and Lyndon Johnson.[23] At the core of this belief was the image of a single, undifferentiated, worldwide Communist threat.

On the rare occasions when the central images of the domino theory were questioned, the answers were liable to be overlooked, misinterpreted, or viewed through thick lenses colored by the context of the Cold War. The *Pentagon Papers* identify a special intelligence estimate in November 1961 as "the only staff paper found in the available record" that treated Communist policies and reactions in terms of the separate national interests of Hanoi, Beijing, and Moscow rather than in terms of a single Communist strategy for which North Vietnam was acting as an agent.[24] So it seemed that at least the intelligence community had a more differentiated perspective that might call into question the images at the core of the domino theory. The community had an opportunity to pronounce more directly on the theory when President Johnson asked the CIA's Board of National Estimates in June 1964 to assess whether the rest of Southeast Asia would fall if North Vietnam gained control over South Vietnam and Laos. The central judgment of the board's resulting assessment was: "With the possible exception of Cambodia, it is likely that no nation in the area would quickly succumb to communism as a result of the fall of Laos and South Vietnam. Furthermore, a continuation of the spread of communism in the area would not be inexorable, and any spread which did occur would take time—time in which the total situation might change in any of a number of ways unfavorable to the communist cause." The assessment did state that loss of Laos and South Vietnam "would be profoundly damaging to the U.S. position in the Far East" and boost the confidence of China for reasons of prestige and credibility. The wider U.S. interest in deterring military attacks would not be affected, however, and island bases would give the United States the ability to deploy enough power to do so. Even the pessimistic side of the assessment was qualified by two major caveats. One was that the scenario being assessed was a "clear-cut communist victory"; the effects of "fuzzier" outcomes such as neutralization would be less sharp and severe. The other was that even under the worst scenarios the United States would retain substantial leverage if it played its cards right. As the assessment explained, "The extent to which individual countries would move away from the U.S. towards the communists would be significantly affected by the substance and manner of U.S. policy in the period following the loss of Laos and South Vietnam."[25]

One retrospective commentary on this assessment comes from Harold Ford, who, as the principal officer responsible for Southeast Asia within the CIA's Office of National Estimates, was heavily involved in many intelligence assessments on Vietnam during this era. (Hal was my boss in the early 1980s at the NIC when, in his last assignment before retirement, he served as the council's vice chairman.) Ford notes there was some disagreement within the CIA on the subject, which would help to account for the downside-as-well-as-upside quality of the assessment. But he says that the proper one-sentence interpretation of the paper is that although the fall of South Vietnam of course would be a shock, the scenario of rapidly falling dominoes was, except possibly with respect to Cambodia, invalid. Ford sadly points out that the assessment had no apparent influence on policy, then or later. Three months before President Johnson requested it, National Security Action Memorandum 288 already had formally incorporated the domino theory as one of its premises.[26] The intelligence community was a Martin Luther nailing theses to the barn door after the horses had escaped.

The idea that the United States had to take a forceful stand in South Vietnam to preserve its worldwide credibility was the single most prominent theme in the decision making on the war. It was the chief reason repeatedly invoked in policy memoranda.[27] President Johnson said that pulling out of Vietnam would lead U.S. allies to "conclude that our word was worth little or nothing." He was "as sure as a man could be" that Moscow and Beijing would exploit disarray in the United States and within Western alliances through subversion, nuclear blackmail, conventional aggression, or something else.[28] The intelligence community was never asked to assess these beliefs. The beliefs were never questioned, even though later research has shown that backing out of losing or nonessential commitments does not cause governments to lose credibility in the eyes of other governments.[29]

A succession of intelligence estimates in 1964 and 1965—when the Johnson administration was reaching its key decisions to embark on the war—continued a theme of intelligence assessments in the 1950s: the prospects that South Vietnam would become a stable and secure country were poor. An estimate in October 1964 predicted "a further decay of GVN [Government of Vietnam—the South Vietnamese regime] will and effectiveness. The likely pattern of this decay will be increasing defeatism, paralysis of leadership, friction with Americans, exploration of possible lines of accommodation with the other side, and a general petering out of the war effort."[30] Another assessment in February 1965 rated as "considerably less than even" the odds that "the spring and summer might see the evolution of a stronger base for prosecuting the counter-insurgency effort than has heretofore existed."[31] These and other assessments from the intelligence community were more pessimistic than reports from the commander of the U.S. Military Assistance Command Vietnam (MACV), General William C. Westmoreland, on the same subjects.[32] The community's assessments were based in part on gloomy appraisals from the CIA's Saigon station, which then-ambassador Maxwell Taylor filtered out of consolidated reporting from the U.S. mission but which were transmitted separately to analysts in Washington.[33]

The intelligence community expressed similar pessimism about the likely impact of the bombing campaign against North Vietnam, Operation Rolling Thunder (which began in March 1965), while offering just enough hope of affecting Hanoi's policies that U.S. policymakers had a rationale to grasp in deciding to embark on the campaign. An intelligence estimate in May 1964 suggested that U.S. airstrikes would lead North Vietnamese leaders to lower their negotiating terms in the interest of preserving their regime while retaining the strength to renew later the insurrections in South Vietnam and Laos. Even so, there was, in the words of the estimate, a "significant danger that they would fight, believing that the United States would still not be willing to undertake a major ground war, or that if it was, it could ultimately be defeated by the methods which were successful against the French."[34] A further estimate in February 1965 offered similar views and assessed that Viet Cong attacks against U.S. bases in South Vietnam would continue at the existing level of intensity despite an air campaign against the north.[35] Secretary of Defense Robert McNamara later admitted that a presentation on the proposed bombing campaign by himself and other senior policymakers to Johnson in December 1964 was "full of holes" in failing to address not only the intelligence community's views, but even the central conclusions of an interagency working group (in which the community participated) that a bombing campaign was unlikely to impede the Communist war effort by either demoralizing or disabling North Vietnam.[36]

Vietnam in the 1960s was an especially fecund time and topic for intelligence estimation and analysis. It was marked by a steady flow of requests from the policymakers, including the White House and McNamara's Pentagon, for assessment after assessment on trends in political and military developments in Vietnam and on the likely consequences of possible policy initiatives and other future contingencies. On the issues that in retrospect were most important—the poor prospects for stabilizing South Vietnam and for persuading the leaders of North Vietnam that they could not win as well as the limited effectiveness of measures the United States would use to try to achieve those goals—the overall record of the assessments was very good. They were coupled with equally good assessments by some senior U.S. military leaders on another critical issue: the immense cost, as measured in time and troops, of a war required to have even a chance of stabilizing South Vietnam.[37]

Inadequate information or bad intelligence was not the reason the United States embarked on the Vietnam War. The policymakers never claimed that they had been misled or ill informed, and it would have been disingenuous for them to do so. Lyndon Johnson later wrote, "There was no shortage of information at any time. The information I received was more complete and balanced than anyone outside the mainstream of official reporting could possibly realize."[38] McNamara praised the analytical work of the CIA's Office of National Estimates, which he said "influenced me immensely" and on which he "relied heavily."[39] He relied on it especially heavily during his last year or so as secretary—as he became the most significant skeptic about the course of events in Vietnam—before Johnson pushed him out of office in February 1968.

The reasons that the United States nonetheless undertook the tragic misadventure in Vietnam included President Lyndon Johnson's personal and political needs. An unrivaled master of domestic politics, he was a tyro in foreign policy who saw staying the already established course of supporting South Vietnam as the best way to avoid mistakes that would be blamed on his own inexperience. His most prominent political opposition at the time was coming from the right and would materialize in the presidential candidacy in 1964 of the conservative Republican Barry Goldwater. He feared even more that a loss of South Vietnam would let another rival, Robert Kennedy, charge that Johnson's unmanly policies had betrayed the Kennedy legacy. And Johnson's years of politics in Texas and deal making on Capitol Hill had led him to believe that reaching a favorable outcome is all a matter of bargaining, using one's strength, and finding the price that every political leader has, Ho Chi Minh included.[40]

The reasons behind the U.S. entry into the war also included Johnson's decision-making style, which—notwithstanding the other respects in which the larger machinery of government was involved—confined the most important decisions to a small circle of advisers in which loyalty counted more than the free exchange and criticism of ideas. This style was institutionalized in what became known as the Tuesday lunch, an exclusive weekly gathering at the White House that began in early 1965 and in which most of the important decisions on the war were made.[41] The very congeniality and mutual respect that characterized members of the Tuesday lunch and that helped to preserve cohesion and harmony among them also stifled any inclination to express misgivings or doubts.[42]

This pattern of decision making exacerbated one of the biggest reasons for the Vietnam War: the failure to question the dominant beliefs and images—the domino theory and the idea that the United States had to take a stand to maintain its credibility—that guided the decision to go to war. This war resembled the Korean War and many other major policy decisions in that the decisive, guiding images and beliefs were not served up by the intelligence community or by any other part of the bureaucracy but instead were part of a larger, broadly held common wisdom. Because they were so widely held and taken for granted, seldom did anyone think to question them. Only the passage of time makes the gravity of this failure clear. The anguished Robert McNamara, in the memoir of self-flagellation he penned three decades later, said, "It seems beyond understanding, incredible, that we did not force ourselves to confront such issues head-on."[43]

Because of a fatalistic sense that the United States had to try to preserve its much-treasured credibility, the policymakers of the 1960s dived into the abyss of Vietnam despite assessments from the intelligence community that the chance of success was low and from the military leadership that the cost would be high. A remarkable feature of the decision-making record on the Vietnam War is that policymakers realized that the war would be a very costly and maybe ultimately losing effort, but that they saw the *attempt*, even if unsuccessful, to save South Vietnam from communism as what mattered. National Security Adviser McGeorge Bundy came back from a trip to South Vietnam in February 1965 with a sober view of the chances for success (which he assessed "may be somewhere between 25% and 75%"), but also with the belief that "even if it fails, the policy will be worth it." Such an effort, he argued, would "damp down the charge that we did not do all that we could have done, and this charge will be important in many countries, including our own."[44] This perspective parallels assertive nationalists' indifference four decades later to many of the consequences of the United States exerting its might in Iraq in the belief that the exertion itself would have value elsewhere around the globe. Even the most accurate and prescient intelligence analysis about a Vietnam or an Iraq cannot deflect policymakers from a course set for such reasons.

An Exclusive Partnership

The making of U.S. foreign policy and the formation of images that underlie it became more concentrated than ever under the president who extracted the United States from Vietnam, Richard Nixon, and his national security adviser and later secretary of state, Henry Kissinger. The duo shared a flair for intrigue and a penchant for holding business extremely close to the vest. The result was a partnership that reduced the rest of the national security apparatus to at best a tool for these two statesmen to manipulate and at worst an annoying impediment to accomplishment of their plans. Most of the time the apparatus was simply irrelevant. To the extent the triumphs as well as the setbacks of U.S. foreign relations during their time in power can be connected to U.S. policy, they can be attributed specifically to Nixon and Kissinger. The images that mattered to policy resided in the heads of those two men.

The main source of images in Kissinger's head was his scholarly study of classical balance-of-power diplomacy, especially of nineteenth-century Europe.[45] Nixon's path to power gave him a different but comparably influential basis for a well-formed worldview before entering office. That path included his early career as a Communist-hunting member of Congress, eight years as Dwight Eisenhower's vice president, world travel as both an official and private citizen, and, after his electoral defeats in 1960 and 1962, more brooding in the political wilderness about how the world works and what his role in that world might be. By the time a tanned, rested, and ready Richard Nixon took office in 1969, he had ideas about foreign policy that probably were at least as firm and extensive as those of anyone else who has entered the U.S. presidency.

The solidity of Nixon and Kissinger's prior conceptions of international politics made them relatively impervious to insights they received once in office, at least as far as strategy, relationships with other major powers, and the maintenance of world order were concerned.[46] Nixon made clear his view of the foreign-affairs bureaucracy when he gave Kissinger a job interview at a New York hotel three weeks after the 1968 presidential election. The president-elect indicated that he had very little confidence in the State Department, that its officers had no loyalty to him, that the Foreign Service had disdained him as vice president and ignored him once he was out of office, and that as a consequence he was determined to run foreign policy out of the White House. As for the intelligence community, Nixon "felt it imperative," in Kissinger's recollection, "to exclude the CIA from the formulation of policy; it was staffed by Ivy League liberals who behind the façade of analytical objectivity were usually pushing their own preferences. They had always opposed him politically."[47]

The latter belief about political opposition may have had its roots, according to one explanation, in Nixon's losing the 1960 presidential campaign and in the CIA's failure to prevent John Kennedy from exploiting a supposed "missile gap" between the United States and the USSR.[48] In any event, Nixon's antipathy toward the intelligence community was reflected in his effort (still during the transition) to boot DCI Richard Helms out of his seat at NSC meetings. After secretary of defense designate Melvin Laird interceded on Helms's behalf, Nixon agreed to let the DCI attend NSC meetings long enough to present an intelligence briefing and answer questions. That awkward arrangement lasted for six weeks, after which Nixon permitted Helms to participate in entire meetings. But Helms never won Nixon's confidence.[49]

The intelligence Nixon wanted was not what the intelligence community could provide in the way of analysis about the outside world. As Kissinger recalled, "If the NSC system of elaborating options interested him [Nixon] for anything, it was for the intelligence it supplied about the views of a bureaucracy he distrusted and for the opportunity it provided to camouflage his own aims."[50] Kissinger added his own manipulative gloss to the system. He would introduce as "planning" topics issues that already were being secretly negotiated. The papers he commissioned would keep the bureaucracy busy and distracted while he obtained background information and agencies' views without having to clear what he was doing with any of them. The whole system was such a bizarre and hazardous way of making foreign policy that even Kissinger recommends against repeating it.[51]

Under such a policymaking system, how intelligence—or any other source of expertise in the bureaucracy—guided policy can be described very simply: it didn't. The great departures in U.S. diplomacy that became monuments in Nixon and Kissinger's legacy—notably détente with the Soviet Union and the establishment of a relationship with China—flowed exclusively from those two men's strategic sense and the vision of great-power politics they brought with them to office.

The highly secretive opening to China carried close-hold diplomacy to an extreme, embracing tactics as well as strategy. Nixon and Kissinger's strategic concept that cultivating a relationship with China would induce increased cooperation from the Soviets ran counter to the views of the State Department's experts on the USSR, including such veterans as Bohlen and Thompson. When those experts met with the president, Kissinger writes, "Nixon performed in classic fashion—implying sympathy in their presence and then mocking what he considered the incorrigible softheadedness of the Foreign Service as soon as they left the room."[52] The State Department's experts on East Asia also were skeptical about sending an envoy to China, questioning how much China would be willing to concede on matters important to the United States and expressing concern about other Asian countries' reaction to the China visit.[53] The intelligence community had no role either in answering these questions or in interpreting the tea leaves that indicated Beijing's readiness for a relationship; Kissinger performed that task himself, aided only by his assistant Winston Lord (and they missed some of the leaves).[54]

When Kissinger made his secret preparatory trip to China in July 1971, Secretary of State William Rogers was not informed until the national security adviser was in Pakistan and about to fly across the Himalayas. Even then, Nixon lied to Rogers in saying that Kissinger had received a last-minute invitation from China.[55] When Nixon himself made his historic trip in February 1972, his principal notes about what the Chinese probably wanted out of the visit and where there was common ground with the United States were ones he had jotted down himself.[56] His perceptions were largely accurate, and the opening to China unquestionably was a major achievement for him, despite not getting hoped-for help from the Chinese in ending the Vietnam War. Apart from the roles played by Kissinger and a few other trusted officials, the credit for this triumph was the president's alone. The despised bureaucracy had no claim on any of it.

Viewing South Asia Through Cold War–Colored Lenses

The conception of international politics that Nixon and Kissinger brought to office served less well when applied to other problems, such as regional conflicts, that involved much more than the maneuvering of great powers. The Indo–Pakistani war of 1971, which Kissinger aptly describes as "perhaps the most complex issue of Nixon's first term," was such a problem.[57] The images that counted were once again almost exclusively those of the White House, and any conflicting images from the intelligence community or from the rest of the national security bureaucracy were rejected, usually disdainfully. In this case, however, the images that shaped the policy were mostly wrong.

The South Asian crisis of 1971 stemmed from the restiveness of a subjugated Bengali population in what was then the eastern portion of Pakistan. Demands for Bengali autonomy, a Pakistani military crackdown, bloodshed in the East, and flows of refugees into India led to war between India and Pakistan. Most of the outside world viewed the crisis in terms of Bengali self-determination, humanitarian needs, and the search for a way to convert East Pakistan into the independent country of Bangladesh while keeping the Indo–Pakistani conflict from escalating further. The relevant parts of the State Department and intelligence community viewed it in similar terms. Nixon and Kissinger, however, perceived it as primarily a proxy conflict of the Cold War, with India, supported and instigated by the USSR, exploiting the crisis to try to smash Pakistan.[58] The sources of their interpretation were their overall inclination to view international politics as a competition among great powers, their need for Pakistan's support in facilitating the China initiative, and awful personal chemistry between Nixon and Indian prime minister Indira Gandhi.[59]

Nixon and Kissinger's use—or, rather, nonuse—of intelligence was high-lighted by two reports they interpreted much differently than the intelligence community and the State Department. One offered the news that in August 1971 the Soviet Union and India had signed a friendship treaty. The intelligence community produced an assessment that interpreted the pact as partly an effort by Moscow to restrain the Gandhi government. The agreement gave Mrs. Gandhi a diplomatic success that would help her to resist domestic pressures to recognize an independent Bangladesh and trigger a Pakistani declaration of war. Kissinger heaped scorn on the assessment. "In retrospect," he said, "it would have been nearly impossible to concoct a more fatuous estimate. It was a classic example of how preconceptions shape intelligence assessments."[60] He and Nixon instead saw the treaty as a Soviet effort to reassure India about its arms pipeline, to encourage it to deliver a blow to Pakistan, and in so doing to damage the U.S. system of alliances and to demonstrate China's impotence.

DCI Helms provided the other report in December, a few days after full-scale war broke out between India and Pakistan. Nixon described this report as one of the few timely pieces of intelligence the CIA had ever given him.[61] It indicated that Mrs. Gandhi, before agreeing to a cease-fire, intended to straighten the southern part of the line of control in the disputed state of Kashmir and "to eliminate Pakistan's armor and air force capabilities." Nixon and Kissinger interpreted the report as meaning that India intended to expand the war in the West and to reduce Pakistan to impotence.[62] They were virtually alone in that interpretation. The analysis in the intelligence community and State Department was that the report referred specifically to action in Kashmir. The Pakistanis had attacked with armor and aircraft across the line of control a few days earlier. It made sense for India to want to reverse the Pakistani gains in that sector while destroying some of the responsible Pakistani forces in the process.[63]

Amid starkly different images of the South Asian crisis, it was Nixon and Kissinger's image that shaped policy. The main feature of that policy was the saber-rattling deployment of a nuclear-armed U.S. carrier task force into the Bay of Bengal. There is no indication in retrospect that this deployment hastened a cease-fire or increased Soviet pressure on India to exercise restraint, but the U.S policy did have other consequences. It allowed the Soviet Union not only to preserve its friendship with the now unquestioned dominant power on the subcontinent, but also to score points more broadly by being the only superpower to align itself with the cause of Bangladeshi independence. It also helped to tip opinion in India toward favoring the development of nuclear weapons.[64]

Today's slogans about the hazards of being stuck in a Cold War way of thinking can apply to U.S. policy toward the South Asian crisis of 1971. The policy reduced the conflict to a mere appendage of great-power politics and was largely insensitive to issues of nationalism, religion, and the motives behind proliferation of unconventional weapons. The Cold War thinking involved did not come from an unreformed intelligence community, but instead from the tiny number of people—two in particular—who shaped the policy.

Afghanistan and the Imperative to Get Tough

U.S.–Soviet détente survived the South Asian crisis but deteriorated later in the 1970s, largely over accumulating conflicts in such Third World locations as Angola, Cambodia, and the Horn of Africa. The deathblow to détente came during the presidency of Jimmy Carter in the form of large-scale Soviet military intervention in Afghanistan in December 1979 and the hard-line U.S. response to it. The key question in guiding the U.S. response to the intervention concerned the Soviets' purpose in undertaking the operation. Carter's secretary of state, Cyrus Vance, later described two theories about Soviet motives that were voiced within the administration. One was that those motives were primarily local and, insofar as they extended beyond Afghanistan, had to do with fears of restiveness among Muslims in the Central Asian republics of the USSR itself. The other theory was that the Soviets had concluded that relations with the United States had already sufficiently deteriorated that they had little to lose by moving decisively not only to quell their Afghan problem, but also to improve their strategic position in South and Southwest Asia.[65]

The differing interpretations had significantly different policy implications. If the intervention were only one step in a more expansive Soviet strategy to make trouble in the region, then the sensible response would be to impede the Soviet advance by making Afghanistan even more unstable, particularly through assistance to the mujahideen waging the insurgency. If the Soviets were instead focused on the local goal of stabilizing Afghanistan—with the intention of withdrawing once that goal was accomplished—fomenting the insurgency would only prolong the Red Army's stay and would encourage the Soviets to view U.S. motives as hostile, to help kill a détente that was not already dead, and perhaps to make other countermoves that would start turning a Soviet threat to Pakistan from a fear into a reality.

The expansionist interpretation became the implicit basis for the Carter administration's policy. This result did not stem from any thorough analysis of Moscow's motives—even though, as Vance noted, there were other views inside the government. Policymakers hardly debated the motives at all. They dismissed as unimportant any analysis of what the Soviets were really up to. National Security Adviser Zbigniew Brzezinski, whose thinking formed the strategic basis for the Carter administration's policy toward the Soviet Union, later contended that "the issue was not what might have been Brezhnev's subjective motives in going into Afghanistan but the objective consequences of a Soviet military presence so much closer to the Persian Gulf." [66]

One of the main drivers of the policy was Carter's political need to get tough with the Soviets—or, more precisely, to be seen as getting tough. The president added to his vulnerability on this score with an impromptu comment in a televised interview a few days after the intervention in which he said the invasion "has made a more dramatic change in my own opinion of what the Soviets' ultimate goals are than anything they've done in the previous time I've been in office." [67] Carter's political opponents immediately jumped on this comment and labeled it as a sign of naïveté. The administration's apparent helplessness in the face of another ongoing and high-profile crisis in the same part of the world—the seizure a few weeks earlier of fifty American hostages at the embassy in Tehran—added to the pressure on the president to show moxie against Moscow.

The other main driver of the policy was the strategic thinking of Brzezinski, who had brought to the job of national security adviser a view of international politics just as strongly held and thoroughly mapped out as what Kissinger had brought to it eight years earlier. The centerpiece of Brzezinski's worldview was a concern about the Soviet Union's growing power and the need for the United States to do something about it. The Soviet move into Afghanistan fit neatly into his preexisting and thoroughly crafted image of an expansionist USSR, in which domination of Afghanistan would put the Soviets in position to gain long-coveted warm-water ports along the Indian Ocean while dismembering Pakistan and Iran in the process.[68] Brzezinski saw the Soviet move as an opportunity—both for Carter to demonstrate toughness and for the United States to use the tense political climate to embark on a needed military buildup.[69]

The United States thus responded to the Soviet intervention with an array of sanctions, the most significant of which was an embargo on any new sales of grain to the USSR. Others included prohibiting sales of high-technology equipment to the Soviets, restricting fishing in U.S. waters, postponing the establishment of new consulates in Kiev and New York, canceling several cultural and technical exchanges, and withdrawing from the 1980 Olympic Games in Moscow. Another response was what became known as the Carter Doctrine—a bellicose enunciation in the State of the Union Address in January of willingness to use military force in the Persian Gulf region.[70] Yet another response, the one with perhaps the most profound lasting effect, was a program of increasing material aid to the Afghan insurgents.

All of these responses were based implicitly on an image of Soviet behavior and strategy that the policymakers never seriously examined or questioned and that may have been wrong. A cogent case can be made that the Soviet intervention was not about attempting strategic gains by getting closer to oil and sea lanes, but instead about avoiding what would have been a substantial loss: the overthrow of an existing Communist government in a country bordering the Soviet Union by an insurgency that could spell trouble among Central Asian residents of the USSR itself.[71]

Whatever analysis the intelligence community might have offered about Soviet motives and intentions was not requested and not used. The same was true of any analysis about the consequences of using the mujahideen as a vehicle for inflicting pain on the Soviets. In the short term, these consequences included dependence on Pakistan as a channel for aiding the mujahideen, which in turn meant a decision not to pressure the Pakistanis to stop their nuclear weapons program (led by A. Q. Khan), which, as U.S. intelligence had learned, was then getting under way. The longer-term consequences were part of a story whose later chapters would involve Afghanistan's becoming the prime home of international terrorists. There would have been an anti-Soviet jihad in Afghanistan with or without U.S aid, and the details of those later chapters would have been impossible to forecast in 1979 or 1980. But U.S. policymakers never even seem to have asked the relevant questions about consequences beyond the Cold War.

Policymaking in the Carter administration was more regular and transparent than the sham system that Nixon and Kissinger had constructed, but there was some of the same tendency to limit deliberations on important issues solely to the White House while keeping other components such as the intelligence community out of the action. The role of intelligence had arisen in the first day of the Carter administration, when DCI Stansfield Turner questioned Brzezinski about the propriety of the national security adviser rather than the DCI—who was supposed to be the president's principal intelligence adviser—giving Carter his daily morning intelligence briefing. Brzezinski responded by having the president's appointments secretary change the regular entry in the presidential calendar from "intelligence briefing" to "national security briefing." Brzezinski called Turner the next day to point out the change, said he considered the matter resolved, and continued to brief Carter alone for the next four years.[72]

A SIMPLE FAITH

Among the most significant U.S. decisions of the Cold War was Ronald Reagan's decision to embark on an arms race with the USSR to help drive the Evil Empire into the ground during what would be its last decade of existence. Much commentary in later years has mulled over what U.S. intelligence got right or wrong about the Soviet Union during this period—what Soviet defense spending was, what the burden of that spending was on the USSR's economy, and in particular whether the perestroika that Mikhail Gorbachev set in motion after coming to power in 1985 represented fundamental change or tactical expediency. It hardly mattered, however, to the basic course of U.S. policy. That course was set by the ideology of the man at the top, and nothing the intelligence community had to say swayed him.

Ronald Reagan entered the presidency with ideas about the USSR and America's place in the world that were every bit as firm as Nixon's, except that Reagan's ideas were the product of simple ideological faith more than rumination about geopolitics and strategy. His worldview included a dark image of the Soviet Union as responsible for most of the unrest throughout the world[73] and a sunny image of the United States, which he was confident would ultimately prevail because of the superiority of capitalism and freedom over communism and dictatorship. This basic belief—far more than anything Reagan learned in office about Soviet force modernization or anything else—served as the cornerstone of his security policy: the duel with the USSR in building up military forces. He saw the American advantage in this duel quite simply: "The Russians could never win the arms race; we could outspend them forever."[74]

Early personal experience, such as in negotiating with film studio executives as president of the Screen Actors Guild, was more important in shaping Reagan's thinking about dealing with the Soviets than anything he heard inside the government. He said he "never put much faith in bureaucracies" and chafed at attempts by "some members of the State Department's Striped Pants Set" to water down his messages to foreign audiences. Because of that view, he confined consultations about relations with the Soviet Union to a small group of advisers.[75] Apart from some evolution of his perception of Gorbachev based on his own interaction with the Soviet leader, Reagan absorbed little information to add to his preexisting images and beliefs. George Shultz, who was secretary of state for most of Reagan's presidency, observed, "Sometimes President Reagan simply did not seem to care that much about facts and details."[76]

This incuriosity about facts and details and the jaundiced view of the bureaucracy meant almost no opportunity for the intelligence community—or for the State Department or most other parts of the national security apparatus—to influence the president's thinking, except occasionally in supplying some piece of information that buttressed his existing beliefs. For most of his administration, Reagan and the harder-line members of his cabinet, such as Secretary of Defense Caspar Weinberger, brushed aside as irrelevant any careful analysis of Soviet intentions, just as Carter and Brzezinski had brushed aside the question of the Soviets' reasons for intervening in Afghanistan.[77] Data on Soviet military forces or spending, which made Reagan's head swim, did not have any better chance of guiding policy. When, as he put it later, officials "tossed around macabre jargon about 'throw weights' and 'kill ratios' as if they were talking about baseball scores," it had no impact on him.[78]

Shultz, who understood Reagan's aspirations (including the eventual negotiation—from strength—of the abolition of nuclear weapons) better than other senior officials did and who increasingly came to prevail in intra-administration contests for influence, was an active and interested consumer of intelligence. But on important issues involving the Soviet Union he was a highly critical consumer who ultimately rejected most of the

analysis the intelligence community offered. "Our knowledge of the Krem-
lin was thin," he later wrote, "and the CIA, I found, was usually wrong about
it."[79] Shultz was repelled by what he regarded as the politicization of intelligence under the Cold Warrior and campaign manager whom Reagan had
appointed as DCI: William J. Casey. Shortly after Casey's death in January
1987, Shultz told Acting DCI Robert Gates, "I feel you try to manipulate
me. So you have a very dissatisfied customer. If this were a business, I'd find
myself another supplier."[80]

The secretary of state repeatedly engaged with and disagreed with the
CIA on the subject of change in the USSR. He summarized that contentious dialogue to Frank Carlucci when the latter became national security
adviser in early 1987: "The CIA, I told Carlucci, had been unable to perceive that change was coming in the Soviet Union. When Gorbachev first
appeared at the helm, the CIA said he was 'just talk,' just another attempt
to deceive us. As that line became increasingly untenable, the CIA changed
its tune: Gorbachev was serious about change, but the Soviet Union had a
powerfully entrenched and largely successful system that was incapable of
being changed; so Gorbachev would fail in his attempt to change it. When
it became evident that the Soviet Union was, in fact, changing, the CIA
line was that the changes wouldn't really make a difference."[81]

Gates—who was the most influential voice in determining the "CIA
line" on the subject—concedes that he shared with Casey, Weinberger,
and others a mistaken view of Gorbachev as just a friendlier face for the same
old Soviet imperialism abroad and communism at home. He acknowledges
that after 1986 the CIA "more often than not failed to anticipate how far
[Gorbachev] would go" in foreign and defense policy. He also admits personally underestimating how extensive the internal political reforms Gorbachev began in 1988 would be.[82] A later appraisal by a former deputy DCI
(and former boss of mine), Richard Kerr, concluded that the CIA had been
overly preoccupied with the Soviets' investment in strategic military forces
and troublemaking throughout the world—two of the biggest hobbyhorses
of the policymakers—while being too quick to dismiss the significance of
signs of unrest within the USSR.[83]

Whatever success U.S. policy toward the Soviet Union enjoyed during
the Reagan years was not attributable to intelligence analysis. Much of the
analysis was wrong, but it didn't matter because that analysis did not shape
the policy. The images that mattered were the ones contained in the bed-
rock beliefs of the old actor in the White House. Gates notes that Reagan

was "nearly alone" in believing, from the start of his administration in 1981, in the immediate vulnerability of the Soviet system.[84] Fortunately for the success of the policy and the national interest, the presidential instincts turned out to be largely right. In a different time or place, Ronald Reagan's instincts might have turned out badly wrong. But there was a happy coincidence of the man and the moment, and that is why many Americans revere Reagan today.

THE DENOUEMENT

After Reagan's vice president George H. W. Bush succeeded him in 1989, all of the senior policymakers in the new administration were skeptical about Gorbachev's chances of successfully changing the Soviet system in the directions he wanted. The president, Secretary of State James Baker, and National Security Adviser Brent Scowcroft were at least hopeful the Soviet leader would succeed. Others, including Secretary of Defense Dick Cheney, Deputy Secretary of State Lawrence Eagleburger, and Gates (who had become deputy to Scowcroft), were more skeptical. Outside experts whom the policymakers consulted waged their own debate about whether Gorbachev's reforms under the label of perestroika were intended to obtain breathing space (*peredyshka*) or to accomplish a more fundamental redirection (*perekhod*). To Baker, this debate was "academic theology" and almost useless.[85] None of it really mattered in crafting a prudent policy.

It did not matter because the prevailing view among the Bush administration seniors was that it made sense to deal energetically with Gorbachev regardless of the prognosis for perestroika. (Only Cheney and a few others within the Defense Department and the NSC staff appeared to have a different view.) If Gorbachev were to succeed, then it would be advantageous to cement relations with him. If he were destined to fail, it would be sensible to lock in as much change favorable to U.S. interests as possible while he was still around, given the uncertainties of whatever would follow him. When two senior intelligence community Sovietologists gave Baker a pessimistic briefing in January 1991—less than a year before the USSR's dissolution—he said to them, "What you're telling us, fellas, is that the stock market is heading south. We need to sell." But in U.S.–Soviet relations, Baker hastened to point out, "'selling' meant trying to get as much as we could out of the Soviets before there was an even greater turn to the right or shift into disintegration. And the way to do that was to maintain our relations with Mikhail Gorbachev."[86]

When the final disintegration came—beginning with the unsuccessful coup by hard-liners in August 1991—prognoses in Washington still did not matter much. There was little the United States could do anyway. Gates notes that U.S. policymakers watched events in the dissolving USSR mainly "from the sidelines. We didn't have much choice or many options."[87] The same was true of the astoundingly rapid crumbling of Communist control in eastern Europe, which no one, including the U.S. intelligence community, anticipated in early 1989 when it was about to begin. Again, there was very little the United States could have done anyway to promote, hasten, or smooth the transfers of power in eastern European countries. (The United States was later to play an important part in the multilateral diplomacy leading to the reunification of Germany, but only after both the Berlin Wall and the Communist hold in East Germany fell apart.) President Bush's prudent contribution to the process was mostly not to try to contribute anything and simply, in Gates's words, to "play it cool."[88]

In short, images of any sort of events in the Communist world did not drive U.S. policy during the final act of the Cold War drama. This was at least as true of images offered by the intelligence community as of images from other sources. Deputy Secretary of State Eagleburger (who replaced Baker as secretary in the last year of the Bush administration) recalled, "Intelligence never influenced my judgment. It didn't matter what they said. Our ideas were clear and no information or assessments could have made us change them, unless of course they had indicated the other side's intention to start a nuclear war."[89]

IDEOLOGY OVER INTELLIGENCE

The processes by which the United States determined its major strategies, policies, and initiatives during the Cold War bear almost no resemblance to the ideal model in which decision makers consider facts and analysis from the intelligence community and other relevant parts of the government, weigh all alternatives, and select a policy most likely to advance the national interest. The images that mattered were ones generated mostly inside the minds of a few senior policymakers, reflecting their sense of history, their personal experiences, and the political and strategic perspectives that they had brought with them into office. Policy preferences often helped to shape the images. Political necessity sometimes eclipsed images of any sort. And the thoughts and perspectives of the very few men involved in the decision making always eclipsed any contribution from the intelligence community or from any other part of the bureaucracy.

As a shaper of policy, ideology decisively trumps intelligence. However important the contributions of intelligence in executing policy at the tactical and operational levels have been, its contribution to major strategic decisions has been almost nil.[90] Intelligence—whether insightful or inaccurate—has rarely been either the inspiration for successful policies or the cause of failed ones.

CHAPTER SIX

POLITICIZATION

The lack of influence *by* intelligence on major policy decisions is one of the respects in which reality differs from the mythology. Another is the persistent influence of policy *on* intelligence—not just on the questions intelligence investigates, but also on the answers it provides. American foreign policy includes a long history both of the tendentious and sometimes misleading use of intelligence by policymakers and of the shading and bending of intelligence products in response to policy preferences. Here, too, the Iraq War exhibits in acute form patterns that developed with other issues as well.

MISSILES AND CUBA: UNWELCOME NEWS

The U.S. intelligence success in October 1962 in detecting missile sites under construction in Cuba before they were completed had been preceded by an intelligence failure: an estimate the previous month that judged that the Soviets were unlikely to place offensive missiles on the island. The evidence on this issue was ambiguous, including murky reports about Soviet shipments of arms to Cuba. The estimate noted that any such introduction of missiles would alter the strategic balance of power in the Soviets' favor. It accordingly urged a continuous alert to detect any further indications that the Soviets might be trying to accomplish exactly that.[1] Despite the murkiness, intelligence analysts were asked to make a call anyway. The prevailing view as of September 19, when the U.S. Intelligence Board approved the estimate, was that the Soviets probably would not attempt such a strategic coup.

The Kennedy administration's political circumstances and preferences set the context for the analysts' call. With Kennedy on the defensive over Cuba, especially ever since the Bay of Pigs, the introduction of Soviet missiles was not news the administration wanted to hear. In statements earlier in September, the president emphasized the distinction between defensive and offensive missiles, said there was no evidence of the latter in Cuba, and committed himself to firm action in response if the Soviets did introduce offensive missiles. Other administration officials, testifying to congressional committees before the Intelligence Board met, denied there was any evidence whatever of offensive missiles in Cuba. In that environment, as Graham Allison subtly observes, "the implications of a National Intelligence Estimate concluding that the Soviets were introducing offensive missiles into Cuba could not be lost on the men who constituted America's highest intelligence assembly."[2] They also would not be lost on the analysts who worked for them and who knew that a conclusion that the Soviets would attempt such a bold stroke would be both unwelcome and, given the information available at that point, unprovable.

Vietnam: Optimism and Acetate

The long and costly agony of the Vietnam War provided numerous instances of the politicization of intelligence, practiced by the military command as well as by political leaders in Washington. Some of the earliest examples occurred in 1962 and early 1963, when optimism about South Vietnam was a preferred theme in the Kennedy administration. The theme reflected the hope that the U.S. military advisers who had been dispatched to the country could soon be brought home and the even stronger hope that escalation to save the country would not be necessary. MACV, led at that time by William Westmoreland's predecessor, General Paul Harkins, exuded the same spirit, which crept into reports the command conveyed to Washington.[3]

In the spring of 1962, an analytic team from the Defense Intelligence Agency that had been deployed to Saigon assisted the MACV staff in preparing for a conference with a visiting high-level delegation that would include Defense Secretary McNamara, the chairman of the Joint Chiefs of Staff, and the head of the Pacific Command. One of the team's principal products was a carefully prepared map with color-coded acetate overlays that depicted the status of different parts of South Vietnam: red for Viet Cong control, yellow and green for different degrees of tenuous government control, and blue for complete government control. During a rehearsal of the briefing, Harkins and his staff officers were dismayed when they saw the map. Too much red, they said, and not enough blue. The colonel who headed the MACV intelligence staff began stripping off pieces of red acetate, instantly converting areas of Viet Cong control to "status unknown." He also insisted that much of the yellow and green be changed to blue for a more balanced look. Harkins presented an accordingly altered map the next day, nonetheless remarking to his senior visitors that even this more "balanced" version probably was overly generous to the enemy.[4]

Similar collisions with the preferred optimism of the day were occurring in Washington. In late 1962, the CIA's Office of National Estimates initiated a new estimate titled *Prospects in Vietnam*. The draft the analysts prepared was pessimistic—too much so for DCI John McCone, who remanded the paper with instructions to confer with "people who know Vietnam best." He named the people he had in mind, all of whom were senior officials involved in implementing policy in Vietnam, all of whom thought the estimate should be more optimistic, and several of whom were friends of McCone. They included Harkins, Department of Defense counterinsurgency chief General Victor Krulak, and then army chief of staff General Earle Wheeler. The working-level analysts tried to stick to their judgments, citing reports from returning field-grade officers as a basis for their pessimism. But their superiors on the Board of National Estimates—who were one level closer to and bowed to the pressure from the DCI and the senior policy officials—overruled them. The final version of the estimate, which the board produced the following April, struck in the first sentence the optimistic tone the critics of the earlier draft had sought: "We believe that Communist progress has been blunted and that the situation is improving."[5]

Several months later, after continued deterioration of security in South Vietnam had shown the pessimists to be correct, McCone made the extraordinary gesture of admitting he had been wrong, apologizing to the analysts who had worked on the estimate, and promising he would not exert the same kind of pressure again. The draft estimate he remanded had caught McCone—who earlier had expressed to President Kennedy some of his own pessimism about South Vietnam—at a vulnerable moment, given the recent mistaken intelligence estimate that had said the Soviets were unlikely to introduce missiles into Cuba. McCone was in bad odor at the White House as a result and not in a mood to buck policy pressure so soon on another issue.[6]

The episode illustrates two corollaries to the general observation that policy preferences help to shape intelligence estimates. One is that once intelligence estimation becomes in large part a contest—as it often has been—between intelligence officers and policymakers, with the latter having strong preferences about the issue at hand, the former have to pick and choose which contests they will try hard to win. Or, rather, they have to choose not to make a contest of some issues at all as long as there is some path of lesser resistance available, as there almost always is, that at least minimally satisfies the policymakers and at the same time presents a plausible and defensible judgment. The intelligence community has only a limited supply of fuel to burn in bureaucratic battles.

The other corollary is that the intelligence community's reputation from previous successes and failures affects the amount of fuel it has to fight those battles. Recent, salient failures diminish the community's inclination and ability to resist politicizing pressures. An ironic consequence is that failure (or, more precisely, the perception of and response to failure) increases the chance of still more failure.

Phantom Attack in the Gulf of Tonkin

The most consequential instance of politicization related to the Vietnam War concerned a nighttime happening in the sea off North Vietnam in August 1964. The Gulf of Tonkin incident led to retaliatory U.S. air strikes against North Vietnam that set a precedent for what would follow. It also became the rationale for a congressional resolution the Johnson administration relied upon as its authorization for waging a wider war, including combat on the ground in the South.

U.S. and South Vietnamese naval forces had been conducting two separate operations in the Gulf of Tonkin at the time of the incident. One was a series of South Vietnamese raids and infiltrations along the North Vietnamese coast. The other was intelligence gathering by U.S. warships, including the two destroyers involved in the incident, the Maddox and the Turner Joy. There never has been any doubt that on August 2, 1964, North Vietnamese patrol boats fired on the Maddox, which was operating close to North Vietnam's coast. The Maddox quickly retreated to more distant waters in the gulf. Two days later the now keyed-up crews of the Maddox and Turner Joy reported that they were again under attack, citing radar and sonar signals and the efforts of sailors on deck to make sense of glimmers of light on the dark and wind-swept water. The analytical issue was whether such a second attack on August 4 ever occurred. If it did, it would be more significant than the first attack because it would show North Vietnam had aggressive intentions extending beyond protection of its coast.

The Johnson administration had strong political reasons to conclude that the second attack took place and to use it as a rationale for retaliatory strikes. In facing Barry Goldwater in the coming presidential election, Johnson had to couple his posture as the more peace-loving candidate with evidence that he had the backbone to use force when necessary. On August 3, the day after the first attack, Johnson gave this reading of the political environment in a telephone conversation with McNamara: "The people that're calling me up . . . all feel that the Navy responded wonderfully. And that's good. But they want to be damned sure I don't pull 'em out and run. . . . That's what all the country wants because Goldwater is raising so much hell about how he's gonna blow 'em off the moon. And they say that we oughtn't to do anything that the national interest doesn't require, but we sure ought to always leave the impression that if you shoot at us, you're gonna get hit."[7]

A one-time strike in response to a North Vietnamese act of aggression perfectly fit the bill for conveying the requisite impression of toughness without yet pointing to a longer and wider war. Against that background, a prompt press leak on August 4 about reports of a second attack led the administration to reach an equally prompt conclusion about what had happened. The leak made it difficult for the administration to hold back on either a judgment about the reported incident or a military strike in retaliation without being accused of pusillanimously covering up an attack on U.S. forces. Before the day was out, McNamara recommended to the president that, in light of the leak, the Pentagon issue a statement that North Vietnam had attacked the Maddox and the Turner Joy in the open waters of the Gulf of Tonkin.[8]

The presumed attack probably never occurred. That is the conclusion of the most exhaustive study of the subject, completed three decades later and based on meticulous analysis of the technical data and on interviews on both the Vietnamese and U.S. sides.[9] The reports of being under attack likely stemmed from the anxiety of crewmen on the two destroyers and their misreading of what their equipment was telling them. The captain of the *Maddox* had doubts almost from the outset that an attack had taken place. His first message after his initial look at what happened read, "Review of action makes many reported contacts and torpedoes fired appear doubtful. Freak weather effects on radar and overeager sonarmen may have accounted for many reports. No actual visual sightings by *Maddox*. Suggest complete evaluation before any further action taken."[10]

The recommended evaluation was not performed. Washington put out a dragnet for information on the incident—but to support the conclusion already announced, not to conduct a thorough and unbiased evaluation. A message that the Joint Chiefs of Staff disseminated on August 6 made the intention explicit: "An urgent requirement exists for proof and evidence of second attack by DRV naval units against TG 72.1 [i.e., the *Maddox* and *Turner Joy*] on night 4 Aug as well as DRV plans and preparation for the attack, for previous attacks and for any subsequent operations. Material must be of type which will convince United Nations Organization that the attack did in fact occur."[11]

In an atmosphere shaped by a conclusion that senior leaders had already voiced publicly and by a sense of urgency in assembling material to support that conclusion, doubters and dissenters were discouraged from raising their misgivings. The imperative of the moment was to make the case about North Vietnamese aggression and not to focus on deficiencies in the evidence. One CIA officer who attended meetings at the White House on the subject later recalled, "We knew it was bum dope that we were getting from the Seventh Fleet, but we were told to give only the facts with no elaboration on the nature of the evidence. . . . Everyone knew how volatile LBJ was. He didn't like to deal in uncertainties."[12]

Intercepted North Vietnamese communications formed a key part of the case that a second attack took place. A study by an in-house historian at the National Security Agency (NSA), conducted many years later and declassified in 2005, concludes that no attack occurred on August 4 and that NSA analysts and management skewed the handling of the signals intelligence involved. The historian faults NSA personnel for misinterpreting the few intercepts that became major parts of the administration's case and not sending forward a larger amount of material that contradicted the case.[13]

The NSA study depicts a situation—of policymakers strongly favoring certain conclusions—in which other intelligence analysts working on other issues at other times have found themselves. It depicts a typical response to that type of situation. The study itself exemplifies yet another typical pattern: a reluctance to make a clear and explicit call of politicization when it occurs. The NSA historian observes, "That there might have been a lot of pressure on the NSA people to produce 'proof' is quite likely." The NSA analysts' own denials, however, deflect the historian from pronouncing a judgment of politicization. "If the participants are to be believed, and they were adamant in asserting this," he reports, "they did not bend to the desires of administration officials."[14]

Such denials are another recurring—and unsurprising—pattern. For an intelligence officer to admit analytic error may be hard; to admit to succumbing to policy-driven pressure is much harder. Such an admission is a blow not just to the officer's analytic batting average, but to his integrity. Denial is facilitated by the fact that pressure rarely comes in the form of blatant and undeniable arm twisting. Instead, it is more often a pervasive but unmistakable understanding that floats through the corridors and that makes everyone well aware of which sorts of conclusions policymakers would welcome and which sorts they would not. This certainly was true of the atmosphere surrounding the Gulf of Tonkin incident.

The key question for the NSA analysts was whether an intercepted North Vietnamese message on August 4 that mentioned an attack was referring to the firing on the *Maddox* two days earlier or to a new attack on August 4. Arguments could be made either way. The issue was, as the NSA historian aptly describes it, an "analytic coin toss."[15]

Intelligence work is filled with issues that, if they are to be resolved, come down to analytic coin tosses. This does not mean that the associated judgments are merely luck or guessing. Rather, it means that there are reasonable bases for making different inferences based on incomplete and ambiguous reporting and that there is not a preponderance of evidence pointing in one direction over another. In most such cases, the coin is not tossed because analysts do not have to toss it. If policymakers do not have a stake in the outcome of the issue, then analysts can state what they know, what they don't know, and the range of possibilities. But when there is such a stake, analysts are sometimes forced to toss the coin. Once the coin is in the air—and given no preponderant analytic reasons for the toss to come out one way or the other—even a slight political wind is enough to affect the result. It affects the result even if the analysts who toss the coin want to be fair and believe they are being fair. The policy-driven wind blowing after the murky and confusing night in the Gulf of Tonkin was definitely strong enough to affect the coins the NSA analysts were tossing.

THE BATTLE OVER ORDER OF BATTLE

Another politicized issue concerned estimates of Communist troop strength in Vietnam. The underlying problem dated back to the early 1960s, when the U.S. military had only an advisory rather than a direct combat role in South Vietnam. The same imperative to show progress that had led to acetate-ripping instant revisions in estimates of Viet Cong–controlled territory also inflated estimates of how many Communist troops were killed in military engagements. The difficulty in distinguishing the Viet Cong—many of whom wore no uniforms other than black "pajamas"—from civilians invited such inflation, all the more so because civilian casualties from government military operations would not look good for other reasons. Most corpses that could not be identified as government soldiers were counted as enemy dead. The U.S. command frequently elevated the body count further by arbitrarily adjusting it for killed soldiers the enemy was assumed to have carried off the battlefield. The body count was one-half of a numbers game in which the other half was the estimate of enemy troop strength; the usual practice was to subtract the body count from whatever enemy units were known to have engaged in a battle, with no provision for new personnel to replace the losses.[16]

The issue came to a head in 1967, as the Johnson administration and General Westmoreland's command were struggling to show progress amid mounting American casualties and declining public support for the war. MACV had begun conveying to the press the concept that a crossover point had been reached, with the Communists no longer able to replace all of their losses in South Vietnam, let alone add more reinforcements. In this environment, the command and senior U.S. civilian officials in Saigon were jolted by a draft estimate from the CIA that implied—by being comprehensive in counting all Communist forces, including militias—a figure for total Communist forces higher than what U.S. officials had been float-ing. The jolt was not from any sudden awareness about the militias' exis-tence, but rather from fear of how stories about the estimate would play publicly. Both Westmoreland's deputy, General Creighton W. Abrams, and the U.S. pacification chief, Robert Komer, sent messages to Washington in August expressing concern about how the press would react. Komer feared that it would look as if MACV had been omitting the militias to keep the total numbers lower—which, in effect, is exactly what it had been doing. Abrams observed that "we have been projecting an image of success over recent months" and that the press would point to higher estimates of Com-munist strength as refutation of that image. Westmoreland's intelligence chief was blunter in a message he sent to the Defense Intelligence Agency. He said the CIA's figures had "stunned the embassy and this headquarters and has resulted in a scream of protests and denials. . . . In view of this re-action and in view of GEN Westmoreland's conversations, all of which you have heard, I am sure that this headquarters will not accept a figure in excess of the current strength figures carried by the press." The issue was a matter of public relations, not of professional analytical differences. The colonel who headed MACV's section responsible for estimating the Communists' order of battle later privately admitted that he agreed with the CIA's figures but was obligated to resist them.[17]

The showdown came in September when a delegation was dispatched from Washington to hash out the issue, led by the special assistant to DCI Helms for Vietnamese affairs, George Carver. In a cable to Helms, Carver reported that initial discussions convinced him that public-relations consid-erations had led Westmoreland, encouraged by Komer, to dictate a ceiling for Viet Cong troop strength and to order that no one agree to any higher figure. Komer, consistent with his nickname "Blowtorch Bob," had told Carver, "You guys just have to back off, that's all there is to it. You've got to back off."[18]

The CIA, in the person of Carver, backed off. Or to be more precise, it backed off in the way such contests between intelligence officers and policy officials usually are resolved, with the policy team getting the bottom line it wants for public consumption, the intelligence officers getting enough qualifiers and definitional verbiage that they can consider their integrity to have emerged intact, and Carver in this case being able to claim in a subsequent cable to Helms that he had "squared the circle." The agreed formula kept the total estimated Communist strength below the limit that

Westmoreland and Komer had set, but with the addition of qualifying language such as "at least" and "it could be considerably higher." Militias would be mentioned in the body of the estimate, but not in its summary or in any tables.[19] The CIA also insisted that a press briefing that MACV was about to hold on the subject explicitly mention that the figure on troop strength did not include militias.[20]

The formula dissatisfied both sides. Ambassador to South Vietnam Ellsworth Bunker cabled National Security Adviser Walt Rostow at the White House in October that he was uncomfortable with the mere mention that militias had been deleted. That part of the agreement, said Bunker, "still bothers General Westmoreland, Bob Komer, and myself. Given the overriding need to demonstrate progress in grinding down the enemy, it is essential that we do not drag too many red herrings across the trail."[21] On the other side, many in the CIA, including Helms, were at least as uncomfortable with the result. Helms approved the revised estimate in November, but when he sent it to the president, he appended a covering note stating that the figures on Communist strength differed from "our previous holdings" and that he had considered not approving the paper.[22]

So much bureaucratic storm and stress, so much high-level time and attention expended, and none of it had anything to do with informing policy decisions. It was all about mustering public support for policy already being implemented. When a disgruntled CIA analyst raised the matter with Helms, the director accurately replied, "I could have told the White House that there were a million more Viet Cong out there, and it wouldn't have made the slightest difference in our policy."[23]

Selling a Losing War

About the time that Langley and MACV were clashing over the Communist order of battle, the White House initiated additional efforts to bolster dwindling public support for the war by arguing that trends were improving and corners were being turned. Intelligence already had been increasingly and dubiously invoked to support the public case. In a speech in March 1967, for example, Johnson claimed that the bombing of North Vietnam had curbed infiltration into the South. "Our intelligence confirms," he said, "that we have been successful"—an inaccurate characterization of actual intelligence assessments of the impact of Operation Rolling Thunder.[24]

A more concentrated public-relations campaign began that summer, led by Walt Rostow. The campaign was intended to peak in November, when Ambassador Bunker and General Westmoreland were scheduled to visit Washington and testify on Capitol Hill. In September, Rostow turned to the CIA seeking good news about the war. He called Carver's deputy, George Allen, and asked for a paper that would show that pacification was progressing. Allen said anything the agency produced would have to include the bad news along with the good. Rostow replied that with forty-four provinces in South Vietnam, surely ones could be selected that would show progress. Allen balked, commenting that what the national security adviser was seeking was not an intelligence paper but instead a product that he probably should request from the U.S. Information Agency, the Department of Defense, or the Joint Chiefs of Staff.

Rostow then conveyed the same request to the CIA's Directorate of Intelligence, which was organizationally separate from Carver's office and which duly prepared the requested good-news paper. Helms's office sent the paper to the White House with a covering memo explaining that it was written in response to Rostow's one-sided request for indications of progress and should not be construed as a comprehensive assessment of pacification, which would have to discuss many unfavorable trends as well. The covering memo did not slow down the national security adviser; at the White House, the memo was removed and replaced by a routing slip from Rostow that said, "At last, Mr. President, a useful assessment from the CIA."[25]

These attempts to discredit the intelligence community and especially the CIA when their pessimistic assessments clashed with policymakers' needs to sustain public support for the Vietnam War would foreshadow later actions by the George W. Bush administration during the Iraq War (described later in this chapter). Advocates of staying the course, such as Rostow, saw the CIA as a particularly inconvenient contributor to discourse on the subject some three years into the war, as a doubt-ridden Robert McNamara came to rely increasingly on its assessments. On at least one occasion, a report from Carver's office was leaked to a syndicated columnist with the apparent intention of depicting the agency as weak willed and appeasement minded.[26]

Rostow organized and chaired an interagency working group to coordinate the public-relations campaign on the war and to mobilize the entire executive branch to support it. Carver or Allen usually represented the CIA in this group. Allen recalls that as the group performed its functions of manipulating public opinion and altering public perceptions in the administration's desired direction, "there was no consideration of objective truth, honesty, or integrity in performing these tasks, and surprisingly little concern about credibility. . . . On many occasions the truth was grotesquely and deliberately distorted in order to make a point." When Allen pointed out weaknesses in an argument, he usually was met with suggestions that he "get on the team" and questions about "whose side" he was on. The working group meetings were for him "among the most distasteful and depressing sessions" of his career.[27]

Spinning the Soviet Threat

Henry Kissinger's masterly control of the national security apparatus probably made him less troubled than other policymakers by publicly inconvenient intelligence judgments. He was at least as skillful as anyone else at manipulating intelligence to support his and Nixon's policies. An example is an issue that arose in the first round of U.S.–Soviet strategic arms limitation talks (SALT): whether to limit the number of submarine-launched ballistic missile (SLBM) launchers. The U.S. departments and agencies involved wanted such a limit. The Soviets did not, and Kissinger told the Soviets privately that he was willing to omit an SLBM limit. When the U.S. bureaucracy did not budge, Kissinger proposed including a limit but at a level high enough not to constrain the Soviets' likely construction of SLBM launchers. He seized on the Pentagon's worst-case number of what the Soviets might build—which was not the intelligence community's judgment of what they were *likely* to build—against which his proposed figure looked like a meaningful restriction (although the Soviets realized it was not). When selling the eventual SALT agreement, which included this figure, within the executive branch and to Congress and the public, Kissinger made the comparison with what the Soviets *could* rather than *would* do.[28] The tactic paralleled George W. Bush's repeated references to what Saddam Hussein "could" do with WMD despite being at odds with the intelligence community's judgment of what he likely would do.

As the Cold War shifted back into high gear in the late 1970s, the need to build up U.S. military strength to meet an expanding Soviet threat was the dominant theme of national security policy. The roots of that policy had already started growing several years earlier, with conservative intellectuals—some of whom formed a prominent advocacy group called the Committee on the Present Danger—agitating for such a buildup and high-lighting every possible sign of Soviet belligerence and expansionism. Much of the agitation concerned strategic arms and the accusation that the Soviets were in the process of gaining an advantage over the United States. The strategic "window of vulnerability" became an issue that Republicans exploited in the 1980 election, just as John Kennedy had exploited the similar "missile gap" issue twenty years earlier.

The debate ostensibly involved data about what arms the Soviets were procuring, how much the procurement was costing them, what were the trends in procurement and military spending, and what all of it meant in terms of Soviet strategy and objectives. These topics were a priority for the U.S. intelligence community, of course, and the opposition on the right charged that the community and especially the CIA were underestimating the magnitude and significance of what the Soviets were doing. Critics and cognoscenti of intelligence argued then and for many years afterward over costing methods, ruble-to-dollar exchange rates, the boundaries of defense budgets, and a swirl of similar analytical issues. In the end, however, little of that mattered. Intelligence influenced policy far less than ideology influenced both the intelligence and the policy.

A well-publicized episode in that debate was the "Team B" exercise in 1976, the last year of Gerald Ford's administration. The exercise began as a proposal from the President's Foreign Intelligence Advisory Board—which at the time was dominated by conservatives such as William Casey, John Connally, and Edward Teller—to construct an alternative interpretation of the Soviet strategic arms program in competition with the intelligence community's analysis of the subject. The intent and foreordained conclusion of the exercise were clear from the beginning with the selection of members of the alternative study group (Team B, in opposition to the intelligence community analysts, who were Team A). The group consisted largely of Cold Warriors skeptical of détente and the SALT process, such as Richard Pipes, Paul Nitze, William Van Cleave, and Paul Wolfowitz.

The intelligence community's errors in previous years regarding Soviet strategic arms included both underestimations and overestimations. An outside review genuinely intended to improve intelligence analysis on the subject either would have added a Team C to critique the community's analysis from a liberal perspective as well or would have involved a single expert review group not constituted to have any ideological slant at all.[29] But the purpose was not to improve intelligence; it was instead to move U.S. policy in the direction of less détente and arms control and more spending on U.S. strategic arms. The proponents of the exercise would achieve their purpose if they could push intelligence analysis in a direction consistent with their preferred policy or at the very least use intelligence as a foil in their argument that America was failing to recognize the danger of the Soviet arms buildup.

The bias of the exercise reflected the political realities and moods of the time. The accumulating frictions with the USSR over a variety of Third World conflicts were giving traction to the antidétente argument. Gerald Ford, seeking election to the presidency in his own right, was politically vulnerable on the right and had already lost several primary elections to Reagan. The intelligence community also was even more vulnerable than usual to being beaten up politically. The CIA had suffered a black eye the previous year from congressional hearings on covert activities. The community's leadership was unstable, with rapid DCI turnover (the Team B exercise took place during the one-year directorship of George H. W. Bush). Some hard-liners on the right probably also sought payback for the CIA's pessimistic, though realistic assessments of the Vietnam War.[30]

Team B's predictable conclusion was a harsh critique of what it regarded as the intelligence community's failure to perceive and predict a menacing Soviet military buildup. Along with valid criticisms of previous intelligence estimates, the team repeatedly assumed the worst case wherever such assumptions could be made. In retrospect, the team's own assessment was wrong on several counts in overestimating the extent of the Soviet program. Team B also conflated the USSR's military procurement and strategy with its political intentions—even though defense budgets or missile-production rates could not prove whether Moscow's intentions were peaceful or aggressive. (Would increased U.S. defense spending, as the Team B members favored, indicate that the United States intended to commit aggression?) The team's conclusions were remarkably similar to the founding statement of the Committee on the Present Danger, which is unsurprising given that several team members (including Pipes, its chairman) were prominent committee members as well.[31]

The Team B report promptly leaked and became part of the debate over foreign and security policy in the 1976 election campaign. If the leak was intended as an October surprise to defeat Jimmy Carter, it clearly failed. But the report became part of the intellectual foundation in support of the escalation in U.S. defense spending that began in the last part of Carter's presidency and gained steam in the next administration.

The effects of the Team B report and of the policy movement and political environment it represented on the intelligence community's analysis were more subtle but nonetheless apparent in retrospect. Team B members claimed success in substantially redirecting an NIE on Soviet strategic arms that was in preparation at the time and remanded for redrafting at least three times.[32] Whether this claim was valid or not, U.S. intelligence estimates during the remainder of the 1970s and into the early 1980s expressed more alarm than did previous assessments about Soviet military acquisitions.

Those later estimates demonstrated how the political environment, by nudging analysts even a small amount on a technical issue, can mean the difference between an intelligence assessment that seems to confirm a preferred image and one that does not. For example, after 1976 the intelligence community revised its estimate of the accuracy of the first generation of missiles with multiple independently targetable re-entry vehicles that the Soviets were then in the process of deploying. It previously had assessed the missiles' circular error probable—the radius of a circle centered on the target and within which half the warheads would fall—as 470 meters. The new figure was 400 meters—an apparently small change, one small enough for political winds or policy preferences easily to make the difference when analysts are forced to come up with some number amid inconclusive data. The revised figure, however, when applied to calculations of how many ground-based U.S. missiles the Soviets could knock out, suggested the Soviets would soon be alarmingly close to a feared first-strike capability.[33]

Years later it became evident that this alarm was exaggerated. An internal evaluation the CIA conducted in 1989 concluded that every intelligence estimate published on the subject from the mid-1970s to the mid-1980s showed a tendency to "substantially overestimate" the rate at which the Soviets were modernizing their forces.[34] To the extent Team B had influenced intelligence analysis, it was in the direction of making that analysis even more in error than it otherwise would have been. More recent research based in part on Soviet archives confirms that the USSR was not nearly as close to a first-strike capability as the U.S. estimates of the time suggested and that such a capability was not a Soviet objective anyway.[35] The window of vulnerability—the rationale for the major U.S. arms buildup of the time—never existed.

Tracing All Evil Back to Moscow

Reagan's victory in 1980 brought many of the hard-line critics into office. Their perspective became policy. That perspective embraced not just issues of strategic arms, but anything else that involved or could be attributed to the USSR. At the core of their ideology was the belief that the Soviet Union was a serious threat to U.S. interests and an overwhelmingly more serious one than any other. A corollary to this belief was that the Soviets were the prime culprits responsible directly or indirectly for sundry mayhem around the globe.

The anti-Soviet ideology provided a framework for policymakers to judge every activity of governmental departments and agencies pertaining to foreign affairs. For intelligence, it meant that any data and analysis that supported the idea of Soviet culpability were welcomed, while any that pointed in the opposite direction were questioned or dismissed. Intelligence was the handmaiden of policy not in the sense that it guided policy but instead in the sense that pieces of it could be useful in rationalizing and justifying the policy.

This role of intelligence as subservient to policy was personified in Reagan's national campaign chairman, William Casey, who became DCI. Casey, who would have preferred to be secretary of state, intended even as DCI to be fully involved in making, not just informing, policy, as reflected in his insistence on being made part of the cabinet. Casey's protégé Robert Gates later wrote, "Bill Casey came to [the] CIA primarily to wage war against the Soviet Union." Gates further noted that Casey could be "boastfully blunt" about his policy-slanted use of intelligence, as when he told a conference of intelligence community leaders in 1983: "Our estimating program has become a powerful instrument in forcing the pace in the policy area." Gates aptly summarizes, "All in all, there was no line between policy advocacy and intelligence for Bill Casey."[36] The arrival of Casey and of several ideological soul mates from the private sector he installed in senior positions marked the most extensive injection to date of politics into intelligence and specifically the CIA.

The effects of this injection on the daily work of intelligence officers at all levels were substantial. For anyone working on topics that were or could be relevant to the policymakers' preoccupation with Soviet-instigated threats, it was abundantly clear what sort of conclusions would be welcomed and what sort would not. A pronounced asymmetry arose in the questions given priority in allocating analytical and other resources: ones with the potential for uncovering or highlighting Soviet troublemaking would become the focus of spare-no-effort, turn-over-every-stone exercises, whereas many other topics of comparable or greater import for U.S. national interests received little attention. The asymmetry applied not only to the questions examined, but also to the answers expected. Draft assessments that were not consistent with the prevailing tenet that the USSR was behind most of the world's evils would have to pass through a significantly more difficult and sometimes disabling gauntlet of challenges and criticisms than ones that were. For intelligence officers of my generation, this policy-slanted working environment was the most difficult ever encountered—that is, until another one, focused on a different bête noire, would come along two decades later.

A particularly stressful instance of dealing with this difficulty was an intelligence estimate concerning Soviet support to international terror-ism.[37] The stimulus for the estimate was a charge by Alexander Haig, in his first press conference as secretary of state in January 1981, that the USSR as a "conscious policy" was involved in programs that "foster, support and expand" international terrorism.[38] Haig's stimulus in turn had been his reading of an advance copy of a new book on the subject by freelance jour-nalist Claire Sterling.[39] Sterling's book did not provide direct evidence of Soviet involvement in terrorism, but instead only suggestions based on connections to clients such as the Cubans and the Palestinian resistance. She charged that Western governments and intelligence services were sit-ting on harder information about Soviet connections. There was an "offi-cial flight from reality," Sterling wrote. "Western intelligence services may have had pieces of the puzzle in hand for years without matching them up."[40] Immediately after Haig's press conference, the head of the State De-partment's intelligence bureau informed him that available intelligence did not support his contention, and Haig was persuaded to request an intelli-gence community estimate on the subject.

Analysts from the CIA produced a draft that was at odds with Haig's accusation and greatly displeased Casey, who was as enamored of Sterling's book as Haig was. The Defense Intelligence Agency got the next crack and produced a draft that was such an unabashed and ill-supported argument in favor of Sterling's accusation that other community analysts gagged on it. A third drafting attempt, led by a member of the NIC's Senior Review Panel, stimulated additional heated discussion but eventually led to a negotiated compromise based on a manipulation of definitions of terrorism and what constitutes support of it. The final document said that the Soviets were not directly fomenting international terrorism but were deeply engaged in fomenting revolutionary violence and that some of the insurgencies they directly or indirectly supported had used terrorism.

The attempted assassination of Pope John Paul II in May 1981 by a Turkish gunman, Mehmet Ali Ağca, added more flames to this fire (in a later book Sterling promoted the thesis that the Soviets had been behind this attack as well[41]). Casey seized on this thesis and pushed CIA analysts hard to find any possible indication of a Soviet hand. Gates, who was in charge of the agency's analytical directorate, ordered preparation of a paper that would assemble every scrap of evidence that might support the thesis of Soviet responsibility.[42] Casey delivered the analysts' judgment of insufficient evidence to the president but added his own comment: "Of course, Mr. President, you and I know better."[43]

The later substantive verdict of history on all these events is mixed. The opening of the East German Stasi's (secret police) archives revealed support that the East Germans had provided to violent radicals in the West and that was unknown at the time either to the intelligence analysts or their outside critics. But most of Sterling's argument about a Soviet hand, which was more a matter of innuendo and guilt by association, has not been confirmed. Part of that argument—as analysts discovered while they were working on the estimate on terrorism and as Casey was informed at the time—originated, via Italian press sources, in an old CIA propaganda operation. It was a classic case of blowback.[44] As for the still-murky attack on the pope, Ağca appears to have had some ties to the Bulgarian security service. But a quarter-century of investigations and theory mongering have not shown that such ties included a plot against John Paul II, much less that the plot had any direct ties to Moscow.

None of the enormous time, attention, effort, and emotion expended on the issue of the USSR and international terrorism had anything whatsoever to do with guiding U.S. foreign policy. Nothing the intelligence community said on this subject would have changed the policymakers' perceptions regarding the USSR or the policies they intended to pursue toward it. Both the perceptions and the policy were already firmly set.

The taxpayers' expenditure on the salaries of intelligence officers set to work on this set of topics was going not toward informing policy, but rather toward finding anything in the intelligence that could help to justify policy already formed. The whole estimate on the Soviets and terrorism had begun, after all, with the secretary of state's public pronouncement of his own judgment on the topic. Papers were shaped not around questions of importance to U.S. interests (e.g., What are the current sources of international terrorism?), but instead around desired answers to the questions. Analysts were directed not to write an assessment of what lay behind the attempted assassination of the pope, but instead to try to make a case in favor of one particular theory of what was behind it. (No companion paper was written to marshal evidence suggesting that the Soviets were *not* behind the attack on the pope.) The policy-driven shaping of intelligence products was understandably of concern to intelligence analysts, all the more so when products shaped in this way were presented as if they were not. In a move reminiscent of Walt Rostow's tearing Helms's covering memo off the one-sided paper about pacification in Vietnam, the final version of the papal shooting paper that left Gates's office omitted a preface that had explained the paper's purpose, which was not to provide a complete assessment of the incident, but only to muster material that would support one hypothesis.[45]

The process, having no resemblance to the ideal model of intelligence–policy relations, was more like a joust. It was part competition and part ritual. Policymakers (including in this case the DCI) would press intelligence officers—always in one substantive direction, never in the other—and keep pressing as long as sought-after conclusions were not yet forthcoming. They would stop short of blatant arm twisting to maintain the appearance that the analysts were only being healthily challenged, not pressured. Intelligence officers would cope with the pressure while trying to remain consistent with common standards of analytic tradecraft and objectivity. The joust typically would conclude with inventive wordsmithing that met each side's minimum requirements in the competition. For policymakers, whatever caveats or linguistic fine-tuning that were part of the joust's ritualistic conclusion could be cast aside in public selling of the policy. In the case of the USSR and terrorism, a statement of national security strategy that the White House released in 1987 omitted any of the carefully drawn distinctions between types of revolutionary violence and types of support and baldly declared that "the evidence of the relationship between the Soviet Union and the growth of worldwide terrorism is now conclusive" even though "the Soviets attempt to disguise such support by using middle men."[46]

The Extreme Case

Although foreshadowed by earlier episodes under earlier administrations, the politicization of intelligence tested new depths in the George W. Bush administration's selling of the Iraq War. Politicization was blatant and extensive in one meaning of that term: the public use of intelligence to muster support for a policy. It also was a significant factor according to the other sense of the word—policy preferences skewing the work of an intelligence service—even though several interests have combined to mask or downplay that form of politicization.

The bitter relationship that developed between intelligence officers and the Bush administration policymakers who promoted the war had nothing to do with the tensions inherent to a healthy intelligence–policy relationship. None of the policymakers' challenges to the intelligence community about Iraq involved all-azimuths probing of possible weaknesses in intelligence judgments or holding the community accountable for the objectivity and accuracy of its analysis. Policymakers did not challenge the judgments about Iraqi weapons programs that later proved to be incorrect; they were only too happy to pocket any conclusions that appeared consistent with the selling of the war. The policymakers' challenges instead were all in one direction: that of supporting the pro-war campaign. The challenges were aimed at knocking down intelligence judgments that were inconsistent with the campaign, extracting more raw material that could be used in the campaign, and extracting intelligence officers' concurrence, however grudging, to the campaign use of material whose validity was questionable.

The politicization covered various parts of the WMD issue, but the intelligence–policy relationship was turned most vividly upside down regarding the fanciful alliance between the Iraqi regime and al-Qa'ida. The war makers labored more extensively on this subject than on any other in stitching together their own tale from the scraps of reporting through which they sifted. They did so because the intelligence community's judgment was at odds with their message. And they did so because that message was critical in leveraging post-9/11 public anger and anguish into support for the Iraq War.

Spinning a Public Yarn

The Bush administration's public use of intelligence about Iraq was part of its enormous yearlong effort to condition public opinion, which involved more than just the misuse of intelligence. It mostly involved misleading rhetorical artifice. The duplicity in the administration's pro-war campaign has been well cataloged elsewhere;[47] here it will suffice to describe the principal characteristics of the administration's public misuse of intelligence.

That misuse was not primarily a straightforward matter of telling falsehoods rather than the truth. Seldom did an administration official utter a specific factual assertion that would give anyone, inside or outside government, a strong basis for standing up and declaring, "That's a lie." Much more common was the manipulation of the widely varying credibility of the raw intelligence reporting that the administration mined for its public campaign. Tenuous and unverified reports were cited as if they were solid evidence. Firmly stated allegations were extruded from ambiguous statements by unproven sources. Evidence that was questioned and doubted within the intelligence community was mentioned as if it were undoubted and unchallenged.

The administration was exploiting a fact of life in the profession of intelligence: on most issues the intelligence community addresses (and this certainly was true of Iraq), analysts receive both questionable reports, some of which later prove to be invalid, and valid reports, many of which are not easily confirmable as such. A few reports are so incredible that analysts can confidently and quickly discard them. A few others come directly from sources so well tested that the information can quickly be accepted as valid. Much more numerous are reports that cannot readily be either discarded or accepted. Intelligence analysts and reports officers are trained to keep an open mind about the reporting that comes to them and not to discard even dubious reports too quickly. They may even mention such reports on a "for what it's worth" basis in their own finished analysis, while indicating what they have and have not been able to confirm. Intelligence analysis is an unending process in which the analyst is continuously reassessing the validity of earlier reports in light of later ones, eventually discarding some while retaining others as a partial picture of the subject under study slowly emerges.

The process is similar to paleontologists' arranging of fossilized bone fragments on a table to reconstruct the skeleton of an animal that died eons ago. The painstaking task involves slowly unearthing many fragments whose place in the skeleton, if they belong there at all, is uncertain. Placing newly dug up fragments on the table helps to determine whether the placement of previously recovered pieces was correct. The later fragments may show that some of those earlier pieces were not even part of the same skeleton and should be discarded.

The Bush administration war makers came into the paleontologists'—that is, the intelligence analysts'—room and overturned the table. They had no use for any skeletal picture the analysts were constructing because they already were purveying their own picture of the animal. To the extent the picture the analysts were constructing differed from the war makers' own, it was in the latter's interest to trash the analysts' work anyway. The war makers then grabbed whichever fossil pieces (even ones headed for the discard pile) seemed to have the most potential for making an impression on the public and took them outside. They held them before the cameras and proclaimed them to be evidence that the Iraqi beast was the kind of animal they had been describing all along. Then the war makers repeatedly returned to the analysts to urge them to dig up more pieces that could be publicly displayed in the same way.

Vice President Cheney was perhaps the leading practitioner, as Colin Powell would later observe,[48] of referring to uncertain and ambiguous intelligence reporting as if it were fact. On Meet the Press in September 2002, Cheney said of Saddam Hussein, "We do know, with absolute certainty, that he is using his procurement system to acquire the equipment he needs in order to enrich uranium to build a nuclear weapon." Aluminum tubes suspected of being parts for enrichment centrifuges were the specific equipment highlighted in this interview. "It's now public," said Cheney, "that, in fact, he has been seeking to acquire, and we have been able to intercept and prevent him from acquiring through this particular channel, the kinds of tubes that are necessary to build a centrifuge."[49] At the time Cheney was speaking with "absolute certainty," though, the intelligence community was beginning work on an estimate that would reveal substantial disagreement among experts about the purpose of the intercepted tubes.

One of Cheney's favorite bits of reporting was about the supposed meeting between Mohammed Atta and an Iraqi official in Prague. He referred to it as credible even after the Federal Bureau of Investigation (FBI) and CIA had concluded that probably no such meeting had occurred.[50] As late as September 2003—six months after the invasion and well after the investigating agencies had determined that the meeting was fiction—the vice president was still referring to it in reciting reports to support his contention that Saddam Hussein was collaborating with al-Qa'ida.[51]

Another favorite piece of reporting was the interrogation of an Islamist detainee who went by the name Ibn al-Shaykh al-Libi. Almost everything that Cheney and other administration officials said publicly—with certainty and sometimes with considerable embellishment—about supposed cooperation between Iraq and al-Qa'ida on biological or chemical weapons came from the turbid statements made by this one prisoner. Condoleezza Rice's remark in September 2002 that Iraq had provided al-Qa'ida with training in "chemical weapons development" was supposedly based on the interrogation of al-Libi, although the notion of weapons development went beyond even the most generous possible interpretation of the detainee's words.[52] People familiar with the case in the intelligence agencies had already expressed skepticism about what al-Libi was saying. The Defense Intelligence Agency had noticed the lack of detail in his statements and assessed in February 2002 that the prisoner probably was "intentionally misleading the debriefers." The CIA also had reservations, noting that al-Libi had not occupied a position that would have given him knowledge of the kind of training of which he spoke. In January 2004, al-Libi recanted all of his statements about Iraq and admitted they were fabrications offered under the duress of interrogation.[53]

FECKLESS COORDINATION

A consequence of the assertion in the State of the Union Address about supposed purchases of Nigerien uranium ore was that George Tenet's office established a more centralized and tightly controlled procedure for reviewing draft statements from the administration. Someone in that office would log in all such drafts, disseminate copies to all offices in the CIA or elsewhere in the intelligence community whose responsibilities gave them a basis for commenting on the draft, and collect comments to send back to the White House. The purpose was to avoid a repetition of something like the Joseph–Foley conversation substituting for more formal and complete clearance. Following this procedural change, many more administration drafts started coming to my desk for review than I had ever seen before.

They included presidential speeches as well as testimony and statements from other senior officials.

Almost all the statements and speeches on Iraq (which constituted a large proportion of the drafts I saw) came to us very late in the process, with the themes already well established, delivery scheduled for the next day or two, and the deadline for comments extremely short. Only occasionally would I find a specific factual assertion that was wholly or partly wrong and required a corrective comment. Many drafts, however, contained passages that were misleading in the same ways that so many of the Bush administration's public statements on Iraq were misleading. Erroneous messages were conveyed because of the way facts were couched; because certain facts were adduced, and others were not mentioned; or because the rhetoric was crafted to leave an incorrect impression.

My typical comment was that the draft at hand contained no specific factual errors (and no factual assertions based on questionable sources), but that certain paragraphs conveyed messages that were misleading in ways that I spelled out. One of the first drafts to come my way under the new arrangement, for example, stated that the Islamist terrorist Abu Musab al-Zarqawi had in May 2002 "received medical treatment in Baghdad under the Saddam regime." I said the last four words should be deleted because they mistakenly implied that the regime had sanctioned or supervised the treatment, and there was no information to support that implication. (Later information suggests that the regime did not even know where Zarqawi was.)

Another draft presidential statement, which came to me in April 2004, described the burgeoning violence in Iraq as the work of "some remnants of Saddam Hussein's regime," "terrorists from other countries," and the Shia cleric Muqtada al-Sadr. By then, we had enough experience with the new procedure for me to observe in my comment that this was "another example of the fecklessness of a process that pretends the intelligence community is helping to shape administration statements. As with many other drafts that are sent over, this gives a badly misleading portrayal of an external reality even if there may not be a single, uranium-in-Niger, take-this-report-out type of error." But I nevertheless offered the comment that "the depiction of the violence in Iraq as being solely due to remnants of the old regime, foreign terrorists, and Sadr is badly distorted and incomplete." I noted the intelligence community had recently produced an assessment "that presented a far more complex picture of the insurgency, including various other nationalists and with several dimensions of popular dissatisfaction with the occupation."

I dutifully sent my comments each time to the person in the director's office compiling them. I had no expectation they would make any difference in the final version, and when a couple of days later I checked the text of the speech as delivered, there rarely was any indication that they had.[54] This disregard was ground for me as a citizen to be disappointed but not ground for me as an intelligence officer to complain. Intelligence officers are not presidential speechwriters, nor should they pretend to be. The work of the rhetorician is different from the work of the analyst. The line between the two is not clear, but in this instance the rhetorician got the last word in deciding where to draw the line and in determining what images to convey to the public.

PICKING THE CHERRIES

Another fact of life in intelligence that the administration exploited in its selling of the war is that information inevitably is fragmentary. Only small parts of the picture the analyst presents are typically based directly on intelligence reporting; the rest of the picture is analytical inference. A corollary is that policymakers can create the picture they want by highlighting fragments that conform to that picture while not mentioning other fragments that do not. And they can do so while seeming to be making the same type of inferences as proper intelligence analysis.

The Bush administration's campaign for war was largely about selective adducing of fragments. If the intelligence community did not produce attractive enough fragments for public use or if the community balked at misleading public use of certain bits (and the balking could not eventually be overcome, as it had been regarding the false report on purchases of uranium ore), then the war makers relied on leaks. A leak about aluminum tubes became fodder not only for Cheney's comments on *Meet the Press* in September 2002, but also for the administration's biggest written indictment of Saddam's regime, a white paper the White House released about the same time.[55]

Much of the manufactured case about a relationship between Saddam's regime and al-Qa'ida relied on leaks. The case was fabricated during the year-long prewar sales campaign but reached a climax several months into the war, when the *Weekly Standard* published a list, compiled by the unit Douglas Feith had created in the Pentagon, of alleged contacts between Iraq and al-Qa'ida.[56] Cheney completed the circle in this circular sourcing in an interview a few weeks later when he commended the leaked compilation in the *Weekly Standard* as the "best source of information" on the subject.[57]

To conjure up the chimerical alliance between the Iraqi regime and al-Qa'ida, the administration relied in part on the inherent difficulty of proving a negative. In making public whatever reporting it could find about past (even distant past) contacts or other "links," the war makers were daring their opponents to demonstrate there was not a worrisome relationship. Doing so would have been hard enough in any case, but it was next to impossible given that those outside government who had the most freedom to make an alternative case could never know what other information they were not seeing outside of the one-sided selection the administration made public and that those inside the executive branch (including the intelligence community) had no way to make such a public case on their own initiative.

The war makers also relied on the ambiguous and indeterminate nature of "links" (or "ties" or "connections"), which became their standard way to refer to Iraq and al-Qa'ida. A link need not imply anything about assistance, cooperation, or convergence of interests. Even adversaries can be linked, as they are in meeting or negotiating with each other. Many who are neither adversaries nor allies are linked in innumerable ways, most of which are no more substantial than being in the same place at the same time. The only way in which a blow against Saddam Hussein's regime would have been a blow against al-Qa'ida was if the former were rendering assistance or cooperation to the latter. That fact went largely unmentioned in the administration's recitations of "links" between the two. Compilations such as the one leaked to the *Weekly Standard* and touted by Cheney, even if the significant amount of invalid reporting had been weeded out, contained entry after entry that said nothing about assistance, cooperation, or an alliance. But in the campaign to sell the war, mere "links" seemed to be all that was required to make an impact on the public. This usage of reporting was the perfect complement to the rhetorical technique of repeatedly uttering "Iraq" or "Saddam" in the same breath as "al-Qa'ida" or "9/11."

The war makers who strung together lists of links were mimicking one aspect of genuine analytical work on counterterrorism and in doing so could fool some people into believing that they were making a legitimate use of intelligence. Intelligence analysts routinely use various forms of link analysis to try to identify possible terrorists. The arrest or monitoring of one known or suspected terrorist often leads analysts to other individuals with whom he has had contact. This connection does not necessarily mean the other people are terrorists. But it is potentially useful lead information—one technique for trying to identify terrorist needles in a haystack of possibilities. The link analysis may continue through several iterations: suspect A's contacts lead analysts to suspect B, whose further contacts lead to suspect C, and so on.

The limitation and potential abuse of the technique are suggested by the concept of six degrees of separation—the idea that anyone in the world can be connected to anyone else in the world through a chain of acquaintance with no more than six links. This hypothesis is probably not altogether true (especially as applied to isolated denizens of, say, rain forests in the Amazon basin or New Guinea), but some research suggests it applies to most of the world's population.[58] And probably any Middle Easterner with an anti-American bent can be connected to almost any other member of that same population with fewer than six links and in many cases with only one or two. The counterterrorist analyst thus has to go beyond mere links and connections and to examine critically all other information about what a relationship really does or does not entail. The link mongering that was part of the campaign to sell the Iraq War never did that.

HAMMERING INTELLIGENCE

Understanding how politicization infected the intelligence community's own work requires understanding the environment that the Bush administration's push for war created and in which intelligence officers functioned. Such understanding is difficult for anyone who did not experience the environment firsthand. The political masters' intense desire to make the case for war—their *need* to make the case to muster sufficient support for the war they already had decided to launch—pervaded every interaction between policymakers and intelligence officers that had anything to do with Iraq. It thus pervaded thinking by intelligence officers about Iraq. The welcome that awaited any material and any judgments that supported the public case for war and the disfavor that met anything inconsistent with the case were all too obvious. The pro-war wind that the Bush administration policymakers had generated blew through all the corridors of government, including the ones in which intelligence officers worked. That wind was strong, unrelenting, and inescapable.

Among the more outwardly apparent ways in which the policymakers shaped this highly tendentious environment were their own public statements. By preemptively and confidently declaring certain judgments, they skewed the balance of considerations being weighed by intelligence analysts who faced much uncertainty and who were trying to answer questions without provable answers. In addition to whatever other logical and evidentiary reasons kept the analysts from offering judgments at odds with the war makers' case, there was now the added consideration that doing so would contradict conclusions on which the political masters had already publicly staked their prestige and credibility. Cheney's speech to the VFW in August 2002 was the leading example of this kind of preemption. One senior military intelligence official later commented about the speech, "When the vice president stood up and said 'we are sure'—well, who are we to argue?"[59] The following month, as intelligence community analysts were preparing their estimate on the subject, Donald Rumsfeld publicly declared to a Senate committee that Saddam's regime "has an active program to acquire and develop nuclear weapons" and "has amassed large, clandestine stockpiles of chemical weapons." He pronounced in similarly certain, unqualified tones several other aspects of Iraqi weapons programs—at the very moment that intelligence community analysts were deliberating about their differences and preparing their estimate on the subject.[60]

A less visible (to those outside the government) way in which policymakers shaped this environment was their direct, relentless pushing of intelligence officers for more and more support for the public case—for more material, more willingness to use questionable material publicly, and more conclusions that were more congenial to their case. This was particularly true of the part of the case that was most contrived: the supposed alliance between Baghdad and al-Qa'ida. The chief of the CIA's analytical directorate at the time, Jami Miscik, later recalled, "What became apparent is that some questions kept getting asked over and over and over again . . . as if, somehow, the answer would change, even without any good reason for it to change—like any new information coming it."[61] The constant pushing served to glean any usable scraps of reporting that may have earlier been missed, to probe for weak spots in the intelligence community's defenses against improper public use of information (as in the uranium ore matter), and generally to wear down intelligence officers. Like guerilla warfare, it was a means of sapping the adversary's will (and the makers of the Iraq War very much viewed the intelligence community as an adversary) to continue to resist.

The chief shaper of the environment was simply the administration's obvious determination—which by late summer 2002 should have been clear to any perceptive person inside or outside government—to get public support to go to war in Iraq. That determination was a force dominating the professional lives of intelligence analysts working on anything having to do with Iraq. An inconsistency in what is commonly expected of analysts is that they should be sensitive to the subtlest clues of what a foreign government is up to while being totally insensitive to the most glaring indications of what their own government would like them to say. As a robotic ideal, this combination is logical; as a human reality, it is unachievable. Intelligence officers working on Iraq were like detectives charged with figuring out what was going on in the next room but straining to pick up whatever faint sounds and other indications they could while ear-splitting music blared away in their own room (including songs about what was happening in the next room). Of course, the music would affect their work.

The period in my own intelligence career most reminiscent of the environment leading up to the Iraq War was in the 1980s (especially the first part of that decade), when the clear and strong preference of policymakers in the Reagan administration was to find the Soviet Union's hand behind every bit of trouble around the world. There were some of the same preemptive public conclusions by policymakers, the same repeated pushing of favored hypotheses, and the same clear understanding of which judgments would be welcome and which ones would not. I once discussed this view of things with the ombudsman for the CIA's Directorate of Intelligence, who is charged with receiving and investigating internal complaints of politicization (although with little power to do anything about what he finds except to convey those findings to the head of the directorate). The ombudsman, who was part of my generation of intelligence officers, saw the situation similarly.

Even the anti-Soviet slant of the early Reagan years, however, was not as severe for intelligence officers as the George W. Bush administration's anti-Saddam, pro-war drive. The administration had to muster support for a major offensive war, a more extreme step than anything the Reagan administration ever took. My colleague the ombudsman, having inter-viewed numerous analysts and managers within the CIA, told the Senate Intelligence Committee that the "hammering" by the Bush administration on intelligence regarding Iraq was harder than anything else he had wit-nessed during his thirty-two-year career with the agency.[62]

Some perspective on how this environment affected the outlook and work of analysts inside government can be gained from how the broader version of the same environment affected the American press. Some mem-bers of the media were discouraged from raising doubt about the war and the administration's case for it not only because they were co-opted, but because they were intimidated.[63] The *Washington Post's* ombudsman believed this may have been so.[64] He thought his own newspaper had not been in-timidated, but one of the *Post's* principal national security reporters, Dana Priest, told of how public support for the Bush administration's policies cre-ated a climate in which any stories that began to sound skeptical generated threatening hate mail to the journalists.[65] Katie Couric said that while she was still host of NBC's *Today* program, she had felt pressure from govern-ment officials and corporate executives to portray the Iraq War positively.[66] The head of Couric's later employer, CBS News, acknowledged that the trauma of 9/11 and the subsequent surge in patriotic fervor may have con-strained any skepticism the media otherwise would have expressed about the administration's policies on Iraq.[67] Phil Donahue's talk show on MS-NBC, one of the few places on the airwaves where such skepticism was expressed during the run-up to the war, was cancelled three weeks before the invasion. A subsequently leaked internal memo at the network said Dona-hue was fired because he represented "a difficult public face for NBC in a time of war," especially when "our competitors are waving the flag at every opportunity."[68]

The press admittedly is somewhat dependent on the government of the day—directly for access and indirectly for how the government shapes opinion among the public that is the press's market. But the press is still free, not on the government payroll, and thus has a presumed willingness and ability to criticize national leaders and their policies. That this free press was nonetheless intimidated and co-opted as much as it was with regard to the Iraq War should give some sense of the impact the administration's drive for war had on officers who *were* on the government payroll as part of the executive branch, who worked for people who worked directly for the policymakers who were creating the oppressive pro-war environment, and for whom criticism of policy is *not* part of their professional role. Given these circumstances and the war makers' hammering of intelligence on Iraq, it would have been astounding if politicization had not infected the intelligence community's work.

POLITICIZATION UNRECOGNIZED

And yet this type of politicization is seldom acknowledged. There still is no official acknowledgment in the United States that it occurred on the issue of Iraq. One reason for this lack is intelligence officers' reluctance to admit they were bent by the policy wind. Even those who have felt pressure and may speak of it to ombudsmen and others find it hard to say they succumbed to it. Moreover, many of the ways of succumbing to it (which I discuss later) are sufficiently indirect and subtle that it is easy for the officer to convince himself as well as others that he did not bend at all.

Another reason involves the political equities outside the intelligence community. This point applies most clearly to the policymakers who created the politicizing environment—in this case the Bush administration, which had a strong interest in dispelling accusations that it had influenced intelligence work and in fostering the idea that any errors about Iraqi weapons programs were solely due to faults within the intelligence community. Supporters of the administration in Congress and the commentariat accordingly echoed the same line.

The interests of the administration's political opponents were more complex, even though some Democrats in Congress did raise the politicizing influence of what the Bush administration was saying and doing on Iraq.[69] For Democrats (especially those who had supported the war resolution) as well as Republicans, the simple "intelligence screwed up" explanation for how the United States got into Iraq continued to have much appeal. Any findings that went beyond the intelligence community would muddy that explanation. The explanation would be the basis for expiation through intelligence "reform." To acknowledge political influence as contributing to error would raise the question of why the politicians in Congress did not do more at the time to counteract that influence. A desire to maintain at least the appearance of bipartisanship on bodies such as ad hoc commissions was an additional incentive for both Republicans and Democrats to focus on faults in the intelligence community and to brush aside the unavoidably partisan issue of administration influence.

Politicization of intelligence generally tends to be conceived quite narrowly. The common, simplistic concept refers to direct, overt pressure by policymakers on intelligence officers—in other words, arm twisting. This narrow conception has underlain past reluctance to label politicization as such. The NSA historian who examined the work of his agency's analysts on the Gulf of Tonkin incident shied away from using the P word because the analysts denied they had been coerced, even though the Johnson administration's clear preferences almost certainly affected their judgments.

In the case of Iraq, the Bush administration's own rampantly politicized public use of intelligence inured the public, press, and Congress to much of what the administration was doing that affected the intelligence community. The concept of political influencing of intelligence became narrower than ever. In the football game that pitted the policymakers against the intelligence community, the offense's pushing and stiff-arming of the defense were considered proper play. Only a flagrant foul, something equivalent to grabbing a face mask and twisting the defensive player down, would be deemed improper. In the absence of such a foul, the policymakers' pushing did not draw any referee's whistle even though it affected not only the case that the administration presented publicly, but also the intelligence community's own work.

For all these reasons, official inquiries have failed to address adequately the influence of the policy climate on the intelligence community's work on Iraq. The long Senate Intelligence Committee report of 2004 included a section narrowly focused on possible pressure on intelligence analysts regarding the issue of Iraq's terrorist links. The report said that the committee had issued calls to any analysts who had been pressured to change their judgments to step forward and tell their stories and that the committee had heard no such stories.[70] The Commission on the Intelligence Capabilities of the United States Regarding Weapons of Mass Destruction (otherwise known as the Silberman–Robb Commission), the White House–appointed body charged with investigating intelligence work on WMD, similarly concluded in the report it issued in 2005, "The Intelligence Community did not make or change any analytic judgments in response to political pressure to reach a particular conclusion."[71] This blind spot was a rare one in the commission's report, which otherwise was a thorough and carefully prepared document that accurately described weaknesses in the community's work on unconventional weapons.

The Silberman–Robb report conceded that "there is no doubt that analysts operated in an environment shaped by intense policymaker interest in Iraq."[72] That observation did not even begin to describe the nature of the environment in which the analysts worked. "Intense policymaker interest in Iraq"—but without the bias and without the policy imperative to push conclusions in one direction—would have produced a far different environment. It would have had policymakers saying to intelligence officers, "Iraq is so important that we want you to examine all the relevant issues as carefully and comprehensively as possible. We want you to strive as hard as possible to get your judgments correct. That means thoroughly questioning all of your assumptions and all of your evidence. It means taking your time to get it right. It means going wherever the evidence takes you without regard to what others, including we policymakers, may think." The actual environment—one of unrequested and unread estimates, ignored intelligence judgments, preemptive policymaker statements, and repeated pushing to use flaky evidence publicly—was quite the opposite. The intense interest was less in Iraq than in getting support for the administration's public assertions about Iraq.

Subtle and Unsubtle Influence

The focus on pressure to change judgments is a poor approach to assessing political influence because most politicization does not take that form. Arm twisting is rare, and successful instances of it rarer still. Such pressure clearly violates the proper roles of intelligence officer and policymaker, and thus only the most bullheaded policymakers attempt to use it. If attempted, it is easier to resist than other forms of politicization because intelligence officers know they have propriety on their side, and any reasonably objective observer would agree with them.

The most egregious recent instances of arm twisting arose in George W. Bush's administration but did not involve Iraq. The twister was Undersecretary of State for Arms Control and International Security John Bolton, who pressured intelligence officers to endorse his views of other rogue states, especially Syria and Cuba. Bolton wrote his own public statements on the issues and then tried to get intelligence officers to endorse them. According to what later came to light when Bolton was nominated to become ambassador to the United Nations, the biggest altercation involved Bolton's statements about Cuba's allegedly pursuing a biological weapons program. When the relevant analyst in the State Department's Bureau of Intelligence and Research (INR) refused to agree with Bolton's language, the undersecretary summoned the analyst and scolded him in a red-faced, finger-waving rage.[73] The director of INR at the time, Carl Ford, told the congressional committee considering Bolton's nomination that he had never before seen such abuse of a subordinate—and this comment came from someone who described himself as a conservative Republican who supported the Bush administration's policies—an orientation I can verify, having testified alongside him in later appearances on Capitol Hill.[74]

When Bolton's angry tirade failed to get the INR analyst to cave, the undersecretary demanded that the analyst be removed. Ford refused. Bolton attempted similar pressure on the national intelligence officer for Latin America, who also inconveniently did not endorse Bolton's views on Cuba. Bolton came across the river one day to our NIC offices and demanded to the council's acting chairman that my Latin America colleague be removed. Again, the demand was refused—a further example of how such ham-fisted attempts at pressure seldom succeed. There was even more to the intimidation than has yet been made public, but I leave it to those directly targeted to tell the fuller story when they are free to do so.

The makers of the Iraq War were less crude and more skillful in exerting influence than the bullheaded Bolton, but on at least one occasion they attempted what clearly was direct pressure on the intelligence community to change its judgments and which no amount of rationalization or dressing up of policymaker behavior could portray as anything else. George Tenet directed that a draft CIA paper on Iraqi support to terrorism be sent to the White House in December 2002, when it was close to publication. An accompanying message said the agency was sending the paper not to solicit proposed changes but instead as a courtesy, so policymakers would not be surprised when it was disseminated. Despite that message, calls from the White House began to "pour in," according to Tenet, urging the agency to revise the paper or to withdraw it altogether. Deputy DCI John McLaughlin fielded one such call from a "testy" Lewis Libby in the vice president's office with more revisions he wanted made. The CIA officials declined to change the paper.[75]

This episode was exactly the kind of pressure the Senate Intelligence Committee said it had invited intelligence officers to talk about but got no takers. The episode says something about why there were not more takers. The pressure in this case—as in many cases—was exerted at a senior level. If anyone was going to run to the committee and tell stories, it had to be Tenet and McLaughlin, who were still in office while the committee was performing its inquiry and still having to interact every day face to face with the policymakers. More junior people would be no more inclined to stir up controversies that they knew would cause huge problems for their bosses.

The attempt to get the CIA to change the paper about support to terrorism and Bolton's cruder efforts at intimidation are less important as events in their own right—because such blatant attempts are the exceptions rather than the norm and unlikely to be successful—than as indicators of the ruthlessness that fostered the environment in which intelligence officers worked at this time and that led to countless less obvious opportunities for politicization. Intelligence officers hardly needed finger-waving tirades to know what policymakers wanted and how strongly they wanted it. They knew it from everything they were hearing from the policymakers inside the councils of government. They knew it from other aspects of the policymakers' behavior even without the desires being made explicit. When the vice president of the United States made extraordinary visits to Langley to discuss alleged connections between the Iraqi regime and al-Qa'ida, he did not need to say to the analysts, "I want you to find connections, and I will be pleased to the extent you find them and displeased to the extent you don't." The visits spoke for themselves. Intelligence officers for the most part knew what the policymakers wanted in the same way that any observant citizen would know it: from the voluminous public indications of the administration's intention to go to war in Iraq and of the arguments the administration was using to win support for the war.

Intelligence officers also did not need explicit threats or pressure to be all too aware of the ways in which producing what policymakers did not want to hear would make the officers' professional lives unpleasant but producing what was wanted would reduce the unpleasantness. They did not need to be reminded they were members of an executive branch in which the president was everyone's boss. They did not need to be reminded that policymakers were their market—the customers whose support was their professional raison d'être.

Displeased policymakers can spoil an intelligence officer's day in numerous ways. The spoilage can be as simple as a cutting remark or a sneer—which, if coming from a powerful person, can be a major blow to a relatively powerless one (especially if the latter's immediate bosses are present). Under the Bush administration, an additional sanction for unhelpful intelligence was to be accused of not being a team player and, even worse, of trying to undermine the policy.

Intelligence analysts, probably more than any other type of civil servant, hang anxiously on policymakers' reactions to their work. With no other programs of their own as a measure of achievement and with usefulness to the policymaker as the rationale for their jobs, those reactions are taken as immensely important in the corridors of intelligence agencies. One of the brightest feathers in any intelligence officer's cap is a compliment from a senior policymaker about something the officer produced. Such favorable comments are fodder for positive performance reports and input to promotion decisions. In a perfect world, the compliments would reflect the quality and insightfulness of intelligence products regardless of whether they imply support for current policies or not. In the real world of intelligence–policy relations, however, the compliments often correlate with implied support for the policies. In the world of working on Iraq under the Bush administration—which had no use for any intelligence analysis inconsistent with the selling of the war—the correlation was close to 100 percent.

At the most senior levels, intelligence officials have the added vulnerability and susceptibility to politicization that comes from regular, face-to-face interactions with policymakers. Anything inconsistent with the selling of the war would mean the additional pain and strain that comes from displeasing powerful people with whom the official knows he will have to meet again the next morning. A senior intelligence official such as Tenet believed he could do his job only by having the kind of entrée that comes from functioning as part of the policy team. This entrée meant, although Tenet would not use this term, co-optation. The implied sanctions of not being seen as a team player include exclusion from the policymaking circle, a resulting slide into the kind of irrelevance and ineffectiveness that characterized James Woolsey's place in the Clinton administration, and ultimately possible loss of one's position altogether.

The costs that intelligence officers, senior and junior, feel from any such exclusion is very high. It is hard to overestimate the value that intelligence officers place on face time with policymakers. Director of National Intelligence (DNI) Mike McConnell told the intelligence agencies shortly after the 2008 presidential election, "Under the current Administration, we have enjoyed unprecedented access." McConnell highlighted that observation in a puffery-filled message to the workforce because—despite the same administration's abuse, exploitation, and ignoring of intelligence on Iraq—he still was getting face time.[76]

Whatever the impact of cooptation on seniors, junior officers feel the effects that waft throughout the organizations the seniors lead. From the questions that bosses ask their subordinates to the way the seniors review draft papers, the policy wind blows on everyone.

Continua and Complexity

Another common misconception is that politicization consists only of intelligence officers' being pushed in one (incorrect) direction rather than the opposite (correct) direction, which they would have taken had they not been pushed. This simplistic, binary view of politicization melded nicely with the simplistic, binary view of the Iraqi unconventional weapons issue as one of whether Saddam Hussein did or did not have WMD. Conceiving the issue this way made it easy for retrospective inquiries to find a mistake-filled path down which the intelligence community walked to arrive at an erroneous conclusion about Iraqi WMD and down which it probably would have walked without any pushing or politicization. Ergo, concluded the inquiries, politicization was not a factor. Such was the approach of the Senate Intelligence Committee and the Silberman–Robb Commission.

But the Iraqi weapons issue was far more complex than that. The familiar WMD label embraced a variety of programs or suspected programs, including nuclear, chemical, and biological weapons as well as delivery systems. The intelligence community was called on to make multiple judgments about multiple programs, with some judgments turning out to be largely accurate (such as on ballistic missiles) and others largely inaccurate. Each program presented multiple subissues, such as the regime's intent to pursue the program, the current state of development work, the status of production of weapons, the number or amount of any weapons already in existence, and the timetable for producing weapons not yet made. Many of these issues were themselves nonbinary questions with a continuum of possible answers, such as how long it would take to produce enough fissile material for a nuclear weapon. Within many of these issues were also multiple analytic tasks that were inputs to larger judgments—tasks that included the assessment of particular sources and the interpretation of particular pieces of information.

The complexity was all the greater because the analysts were not just stitching facts together but were instead—as with all intelligence work—dealing with uncertainty. Their judgments involved not up-or-down, yes-or-no propositions, but rather degrees of likelihood or unlikelihood. The analysts also had to express their own degree of confidence or lack of confidence in making those judgments, and they had to choose language to convey the degrees of likelihood and degrees of confidence.

Further complexity stemmed from the fact that the analysis was a collective enterprise involving many dozens of analysts spread through multiple offices in multiple agencies. Anything that affected the thinking of even a few of those analysts, not necessarily all of them, affected the final product. Anything wafting through the conference rooms in which the analysts met to discuss their differences and coordinate their assessment also affected the product.

This entire picture—of many analysts selecting degrees of likelihood and confidence from continua of infinite possibilities, choosing from countless possible formulations to convey their selections, and addressing multiple issues with multiple subissues, many of which were also matters of degree and had infinite possible answers—added up to enormous opportunities for any outside influence, including policy influence, to affect the analysts' work. Considering both this picture and the strength of the Bush administration's push to sell the Iraq War and to hammer intelligence to help sell it, it is inconceivable that politicization did not help to shape the intelligence community's output on Iraqi weapons programs.

Amid the uncertainty that intelligence analysts routinely face and that the analysts working on the Iraqi weapons assuredly faced, even policy influence much weaker than the one associated with the Bush administration's drive toward war would have been sufficient to affect the product. Many of the questions about Iraqi programs, like the Gulf of Tonkin incident that NSA analysts had to assess nearly four decades earlier, were analytic coin tosses. The policy wind blowing on Iraq was easily strong enough to affect the direction of the coins that analysts were tossing in 2002.

To acknowledge politicization—however difficult that may be for intelligence officers, politicians, and commissions alike—is not to deny other sources of analytic error, including ones the Silberman–Robb Commission correctly identified. The intelligence work on Iraqi weapons did not involve only one judgment, and errors in that work did not have only one cause. To contend that politicization was not a factor is to argue—implausibly—that the Bush administration's huge push for war had no effect on the huge number of opportunities for the intelligence work to be affected. Any such argument also would have to explain how the intelligence community got from where it was in the first year of the Bush administration—when its statement of worldwide threats did not even mention the possibility of Iraqi nuclear weapons, or stockpiles of unconventional weapons—to where it was when it produced the notorious estimate of October 2002. It is highly improbable that the community somehow picked up on its own whatever bad analytic habits were reflected in that estimate in the space of less than two years. The one big change that had occurred in the interim was the administration's launching of its campaign for war.

Denial of politicization is facilitated by the admitted difficulty of drawing any direct connection between a politicized thought in an analyst's head and a judgment in an intelligence assessment. One whose longtime study of the analytic process has brought him as close as anyone to being able to make such a connection is my first boss when I joined the CIA in the 1970s, Jack Davis. Jack, who later in his career was the national intelligence officer for Latin America, became in retirement a widely respected guru of the methodology of intelligence analysis. His study of many cases of intelligence failure led him to the same observation I noted earlier about how even intelligence analysts who admit feeling policy pressure do not admit that the pressure affected their judgments. But he found, as he put it in one of his more recent essays, that knowing the policy preferences of the administration or Congress or both often influences analysts "at a subconscious level." Awareness of those policy preferences "can subtly influence the analytic process" and "can explain estimative malfunctions by experienced analysts."[77]

The impact of politicization often includes what intelligence officers do *not* do. On Iraqi unconventional weapons, the inaction included not making extra effort to ask probing questions about assumptions and evidence that were parts of both the intelligence community's judgments and the administration's case for war. It included supervisors of analysis not subjecting draft assessments that contained such judgments supporting the case for war to as much scrutiny and questioning as assessments that would discomfit policymakers. Another longtime student of intelligence analysis, Greg Treverton, observes about the Iraq case that whatever fault for these oversights can be placed on the shoulders of intelligence officers, it was "compounded by having policy-makers who share, even praise, flawed analysis." Pressure was applied to forge ahead with the judgments rather than to rethink them, and any would-be dissenters were destined to be "lost in the wilderness."[78]

Among the Middle East specialists within the intelligence community with whom I worked closely as the national intelligence officer for the region, those in the Defense Intelligence Agency probably felt the pressures most acutely. They had to deal regularly with the Defense Department civilian policy apparatus led by Wolfowitz and Feith. The defense intelligence officer for the region and, as such, my principal colleague in that agency, Bruce Hardcastle, later recalled, "You were never told what to write, but you knew what assessments administration officials would be receptive to—and what they would not be receptive to." In that environment, he found it hard to envision any analyst standing up and saying "I don't think Saddam has any of these weapons." Bruce himself clashed sufficiently with Feith's deputies for him to be consigned to the wilderness and not invited to meetings someone in his position normally would be expected to attend.[79]

The Silberman–Robb report mentions that I described to the commission a "zeitgeist" generated by the administration's strong sales pitch regarding Iraqi WMD that permeated the atmosphere in which intelligence officers worked. The report hastens to add my further observation that the zeitgeist did not "dictate" the intelligence community's judgments about Iraqi possession of biological and chemical weapons and reconstitution of a nuclear program and that it would have been hard for analysts to come up with different judgments given the information available.[80] That latter observation was the same as Richard Betts's aforementioned statement that no responsible analyst could have said in 2002 that Iraq did not have the feared WMD. But recall that Betts nonetheless concluded that the best possible judgments, given the information available, would have been different from the judgments the intelligence community actually offered. In particular, they would have expressed more caution about the evidence and been more explicit about the inferential nature of the community's conclusions. Dictating is not the same as influencing. And much of what the policy-generated zeitgeist influenced were the couched terminology and

qualifications—or the insufficiency of qualifications—that made the difference between the best-possible analytic product and the product that was
produced and has been justly criticized.

The Silberman–Robb report itself contains numerous indications that
the policy environment politicized the intelligence community's work,
notwithstanding the commission's striving to send the opposite message.[81]
CIA analysts told the commission, for example, that they were reluctant to
back away from information provided by Curveball, the human source who
spoke fraudulently of biological weapons production, because of "political
concerns" over how doing so would look not only to agency management,
but also to "downtown."[82] Another indication is how agencies stuck to
their guns on technical issues most pertinent to their expertise but conformed to the policy-preferred consensus on the broader question of whether
there were active weapons programs. The Department of Energy dissented—
correctly, as it turned out—from the judgment that Iraq intended to use the
captured aluminum tubes as centrifuges to enrich uranium but nevertheless
concurred that Iraq was reconstituting its nuclear program. Department officers never explained the logic of their position. As a former senior officer
said to the commission, the position "made sense politically but not substan-
tively." One of the Energy Department intelligence analysts admitted to the
Silberman–Robb Commission that the department "didn't want to come out
before the war and say [Iraq] was not reconstituting."[83] Air force intelligence
similarly dissented—also correctly—from a judgment that Iraq was developing unmanned aerial vehicles as platforms to deliver chemical or biological
agents (possibly against the U.S. homeland), but the air force concurred with
the majority judgments that Iraq had active chemical and biological warfare
programs.

Reluctantly Taking a Stand

The State Department's INR agreed with the Energy Department about
the aluminum tubes but considered the tubes to be central enough to the
case about a nuclear program that it dissented from the judgment that Iraq
was reconstituting such a program. INR wanted to be more agnostic. Although it believed that Iraq was pursuing at least a "limited effort" to acquire nuclear weapons, it did not see a "compelling case" that Baghdad was
pursuing an "integrated and comprehensive approach" to acquire them.

Although Iraq "may" have begun such a program, INR was "unwilling to speculate" that it had done so.[84]

INR later won plaudits for its meandering agnosticism. But what worked (especially in hindsight) as a dissent would not have worked at the time as the main judgment. The intelligence community could not just claim ignorance to wriggle out of the bind in which the administration's WMD-based campaign had placed it—especially not after the administration's opponents in Congress had in effect pressed it to take a stand by requesting what became the October 2002 estimate. I have seen enough similar interactions on Capitol Hill to envision how this one would have gone if the community had attempted such an approach:

COMMITTEE MEMBER: Is Iraq reconstituting a nuclear weapons program?

INTELLIGENCE COMMUNITY WITNESS: Some indications suggest that Iraq may be making at least limited efforts in that direction, but we lack persuasive evidence that a full nuclear program is under way.

MEMBER: Yes, I read that language in your statement, but I'm trying to get a clear judgment. Do you or don't you believe the Iraqis have a nuclear weapons program?

WITNESS: We have some reporting that points to possible nuclear activity, but not enough to make a compelling case that the Iraqis have an integrated and comprehensive approach to acquiring a weapon.

MEMBER: All I'm asking is a simple yes or no question. Is that unreasonable? In your judgment, do they or don't they have a nuclear weapons program going?

WITNESS: A simple yes or no answer is not possible. The evidence is unclear.

MEMBER: Of course the evidence is unclear. The evidence on these things is always unclear. Why would we need an intelligence service if we had clear evidence? I'm not asking for clear evidence; I'm asking for your best judgment.

WITNESS: We are unwilling to speculate . . .

MEMBER: [voice rising] "Unwilling?" American taxpayers spend tens of billions of dollars annually on intelligence, and all you can say is you're "unwilling to speculate"? This is one of the most important issues you've had to consider, and that's all you can come up with? What are all those analysts you've got out there doing? They're paid to make judgments, aren't they, even if the evidence is thin? I'll try again. Do you believe Iraq has a nuclear weapons program?

WITNESS: Considering the ambiguities and uncertainties in the information . . .

MEMBER: I'm tired of the waffle language. I'll try one last time, phrasing my question as carefully as I can. While recognizing all those ambiguities and uncertainties, and recognizing that what you will say is a judgment that may not be completely supported by clear evidence, do you believe that Iraq has an active nuclear program—yes or no?

WITNESS: Yes, sir.

MEMBER: At last. It shouldn't be like pulling teeth to get a simple answer out of you intelligence people.

If the Bush administration had not made Iraqi WMD a centerpiece of its pro-war campaign, the intelligence community would have continued to follow the issue the way it had always followed it: as an important subject worthy of significant collection and analytic effort, though not out of proportion to the threat it posed compared with other proliferators such as North Korea. The community would have regularly informed policymakers of what it knew and what it did not know. It would have eschewed speculative judgments that went much beyond what it knew. It would not have volunteered major new assessments in the absence of new information that was reasonably firm or that was not so firm but suggested a possible imminent threat.

In short, when faced with analytic coin tosses, the intelligence community would not have tossed coins if it did not have to. The issue would thus have been comparable to countless other important issues the community follows that also involve untossed coins. But with both the administration and its opponents focusing on the Iraqi WMD issue, the community started tossing.

BENDING TO THE TALE OF TERRORIST LINKS

The issue of terrorist connections was just as major a part of the administration's public case but did not result in an avalanche of recriminations about the intelligence community's performance because, unlike on WMD, the community's central judgment was correct. Precisely because that judgment was correct and clashed with the administration's message, the issue illuminates even better than the WMD issue the full range of ways in which the policy environment politicized the community's work. Although the community did not succumb to heavy policy pressure regarding the central judgment, it bent in other ways.

One way was to go too far with questionable evidence, the major case in point being al-Libi's statements. The problem was not just the possibility that al-Libi was fabricating. It was the ambiguity of the statements themselves. Raw terrorism reporting such as this did not ordinarily come across my screen in the work I did as the regional national intelligence officer, but I once looked up the couple of reports based on this part of al-Libi's interrogation. The statements were incoherent and confusing. The most I could get out of repeated readings was that an Iraqi suggested the possibility of some sort of training related to chemical and biological matters and that a couple of Islamists in Afghanistan may have headed to Iraq in the hope of getting such training. Without major inferential leaps, the statements did not say that Iraq had ever actually provided any training, much less any help in "chemical weapons development," as Condoleezza Rice once put it.

Without something like the huge policy push associated with the Iraq War, a detainee's assertions similar to al-Libi's never would have formed the basis for any finished intelligence analysis, let alone for public statements. The assertions were much too vague and inconclusive. Based on my experience in supervising counterterrorist analysis in the 1990s, analysts would have filed the reports away for reference in case any other information were collected that would verify or clarify what al-Libi was saying. Analysts would probably have asked collectors in the field to seek corroborating information. And that is where things would have stayed until, once al-Libi admitted his fabrications, a burn notice would go out calling for the reports to be destroyed.

I shared my reaction to the interrogation reports with Phil Mudd, who by then headed counterterrorist analysis at the CIA. Phil agreed that without the inferential leaps the reports did not support some of the statements supposedly based on them. By then, however, most of the damage from excessive extrapolation from the reports, mainly in administration statements but also in some intelligence assessments, had already been done. A personal regret is not having seized then on the al-Libi reports in an effort to limit any further misuse of them (i.e., before al-Libi's admission of fabrication ended it all), at least in intelligence agency products.

Playing along with the administration's desire to tout even squirrelly reporting sometimes served as sugarcoating—another way in which the policy environment politicized the intelligence community's work on Iraq, even if it did not change central judgments. With the community's judgment about the nonalliance between Iraq and al-Qa'ida so distasteful to the policymakers, the community lessened the distaste by sprinkling on some of the "links" that seemed to run counter to the judgment. When the unclassified letter containing the community's conclusion that Saddam Hussein was unlikely to give unconventional weapons to terrorists or to use such weapons to attack U.S. interests unless the United States invaded Iraq was sent to the Senate Intelligence Committee, Condoleezza Rice asked Tenet to give a background briefing to a *New York Times* reporter to play down the inconsistency between this judgment and the administration's pro-war message. Tenet did, and he later admitted he shouldn't have. "By making public comments in the middle of a contentious political debate," he wrote in his memoir, "I gave the impression that I was becoming a partisan player."[85]

Politicization also infected the intelligence community's work on Iraq with respect to the questions it investigated and the allocation of resources to investigate them. Directing concentrated attention to the topics of most concern to policymakers is an entirely legitimate response by intelligence agencies. But in this instance the purpose of the enormous amount of work devoted to the policymakers' preferred lines of inquiry was not to help them make better-informed decisions, but instead to help them sell the war decision to the public. This role was not a legitimate one for an intelligence service, and it diverted resources and attention from actual threats.

This role also distorted the intelligence community's substantive message. On many topics, that message is as much a function of the questions posed and the amount of attention devoted to those questions as it is of the specific answers offered. The intelligence community has enough resources to look thoroughly into only a fraction of innumerable topics around the world it can investigate. It faces what amounts to a huge field of stones but has the time and resources to turn over only some of them. It decides which stones to turn over based on prior experience and substantive expertise that lead analysts to conclude where they are most likely to find something threatening or otherwise interesting.

Bias enters when policymakers repeatedly urge intelligence officers to turn over only stones of a certain color, as the war makers in the Bush administration did in urging more and more effort to find links between Saddam's regime and al-Qa'ida. Even when the initial stone turning did not find anything, the community was urged to turn particular stones over again and scratch the dirt to try again to find something. Through sheer quantity of effort, some things of course will be found—disproportionately more things under the favored color of stone than would be found in an unbiased search. The intelligence community's total output thus conveys a biased message. It suggests that what lies under stones of a particular color is a problem more serious than the universe of other problems worth worrying about than it really is. The biased message may thus reinforce the misconceptions of policymakers who are impressed by what is found while forgetting it was their own pressure that shaped the search in the first place. This scenario is probably part of the reason why someone such as Wolfowitz may have really believed in an alliance between Saddam's regime and al-Qa'ida.

The pressures the Bush policymakers exerted regarding terrorist connections indirectly affected the intelligence community's work on WMD. Because the community only bent and did not break regarding its principal judgment about the nonalliance between Iraq and al-Qa'ida, the struggle between intelligence officers and policymakers on this issue was intense and debilitating. It was an energy-draining, wound-inflicting, morale-sapping battle. Fighting that battle felt to anyone in the community who was part of it to be already above and beyond the call of duty. There was little stomach left for an additional battle on an issue that—unlike the one about connections with al-Qa'ida—was not contrived, involved a broad (even if mistaken) consensus about ongoing programs, and lacked a good basis for conclusions contrary to the ones the policymakers favored. With intelligence officers being accused of trying to undermine policy, it is easy to envision the accusations that would fly if the WMD part of the administration's case had been resisted as much as the terrorism part was. In light of the prevailing consensus about weapons programs, the community's much-publicized underestimation of the progress of Iraqi weapons programs prior to 1991, and the battle over terrorist connections, such resistance would have been taken as proof positive that intelligence officers were determined to subvert the administration's policy on Iraq and to substitute their own.

As with other facets of policy pressure on the intelligence community, the effects of the terrorism-related battle did not solely determine the community's core judgments about WMD. There were sufficient other reasons for those judgments, and there were other causes of analytic error. But these effects contributed to failures to raise any more questions about the validity of assumptions and credibility of evidence than were raised, and they certainly were a disincentive to raising doubts serious enough to imperil the judgments.

Intelligence in a Trap

Among the recriminations ensuing from the Iraq War has been criticism that intelligence officers did not do enough to frustrate the administration's drive toward war. Much of that criticism is unspecific, grounded in a vague sense that with a pro-war campaign that used intelligence so much and that proved to be wrong in important respects, surely there was much more that the intelligence community could and should have done to head off the war. Some of the criticism has included the charge that the intelligence community's work on Iraq became politicized; in the respects I have described, that charge is correct. But what the intelligence community as a whole or individual intelligence officers, both trapped in a subordinate relationship to the White House, could have done about this politicization is a different issue.

Opposing politicization in general is one thing; finding ways to deal with specific demands, requests, and pressures is something else. Exactly where should intelligence officers have said "no" to policymakers, and on what grounds could they have said it? Consider, for example, the visual image that perhaps best represents the co-optation of the intelligence community in the war-selling effort: the seating of the DCI prominently in the camera frame behind Secretary of State Colin Powell as Powell made his presentation on Iraq at the United Nations Security Council in February 2003. Not an image for anyone in the intelligence community to be proud of. But for the director not to have been there would have amounted to saying the intelligence community was unwilling to stand publicly by its material and that it was just as callously willing as the White House to let Powell hang out to dry by himself. Or consider Rice's intercession with the DCI to brief reporters as a counterpoint to the letter to the Senate Intelligence Committee about Saddam's intentions. If Tenet had said (as politely as he could) that this intercession was politicization and out of bounds for the intelligence community, the reply would have been: "Let me get this straight. When some Democratic senators ask you to release publicly a judgment that goes against our message you agree. But when the White House asks you to discuss information—from your own sources—that goes in the other direction you refuse. For whom did you say you're working?"

With no policy process for arriving at the decision to go to war, there was no identifiable line between predecision and postdecision phases. Candid input about Iraq to decisions ostensibly not yet taken thus could not be clearly distinguished from insubordinate opposition to policy already made. It was extremely difficult to attempt the former without appearing to commit the latter. Almost none of the retrospective criticism of intelligence concerning Iraq has reflected a full appreciation of how powerful and pervasive the policy-generated wind was during the run-up to the Iraq War. And almost none has addressed why the intelligence community should have been expected to resist that wind better than others who did not resist it even though they were less vulnerable to it.

Consider the response of Judge Laurence Silberman, cochairman of the 2004 WMD commission, when asked why the commission did not address how the Bush administration used intelligence about Iraq. It was a reasonable question given the broad interpretation the commission otherwise applied to its mandate and given the enormous role the administration's public use of intelligence about WMD played in mustering support for the war that caused the commission to be created. Silberman replied: "It was clear and understood that we would not be asked to evaluate the administration's use of the intelligence. And frankly, if that had been the charge I wouldn't have wanted the position. It was too political. Everybody knew what the president and the vice president had said about the intelligence. They can make their own judgments as to whether that was appropriate or fair or whatever."[86]

The White House appointed the commission, so Silberman's position here is not surprising. But Silberman was (and is) an appellate judge with senior status, guaranteed a full salary for life even if he were to retire fully and never hear another case. That job is about as secure a position as anyone who has been on the federal payroll can enjoy. The other commissioners, including university presidents and former officials, were similarly invulnerable. The one active politician on the commission was Senator John McCain (R–Ariz.), who touted his maverick status and whose presidential campaign in 2008 would strive to distinguish him from President Bush almost as much as from his Democratic opponent.

And yet this group's posture toward the administration's misuse of intelligence on Iraq was, "Oh, no, we don't want to touch that—too political." This posture puts into perspective the retrospective expectation of intelligence officers that they should have found ways to tell their demonstrably merciless political masters that those masters were deluding the American people—and even better, that they should have found ways to tell the American people that they were being deluded. This expectation was held even though intelligence officers, quite unlike the comfortably independent commissioners, were serving inside the executive branch as part of a hierarchy commanded by the president. And they were serving there before the war went sour and became unpopular.

The retrospective expectations of intelligence pay scant attention to the effect, if any, that different actions by the intelligence community would have had on the policy story. In the highly politicized environment in which the war was made—and in which the Bush administration policymakers not only rejected but strove to undermine important intelligence judgments—additional efforts at resistance would have been swatted aside.

I witnessed some of this byplay in the fall of 2002, when John McLaughlin instructed me to attend a Saturday morning meeting in the White House Situation Room. The subject was impending testimony about Iraq by administration seniors, including Powell, Rumsfeld, and Tenet, to several congressional committees. The purpose was to ensure that the messages conveyed in these separate appearances were consistent. I was attending because I was preparing one portion of Tenet's testimony. Ben Bonk and Bob Walpole also were there. Among the other attendees were General George Casey of the Joint Staff, later to be the top commander in Iraq, and Ryan Crocker of State, later to be ambassador in Baghdad. Stephen Hadley chaired the meeting, but Douglas Feith did most of the talking.

The whole experience was disturbing because of the implied assumption that a statement from the intelligence community should be no different from policy statements in being subject to centralized control of the message.

It also was disturbing because of some of the ingredients going into that message and the war makers' approach toward constructing the message. At one point in the meeting, Ben corrected an assertion by Feith that was related to the supposed connection between the Iraqi regime and al-Qa'ida. The intelligence doesn't support that assertion, Ben said. Feith responded loudly and dismissively, "Well, if some Congressman decides to nitpick about that, he's going to look pretty stupid!" and quickly moved on to the next topic. It was a "don't bother us with facts, we have a war to sell" attitude, and what was dismissed was by no means a nitpick.

My only contribution to the discussion was to mention that if anyone wanted to talk about what Iraq really was doing in supporting terrorism, there were Baghdad's activities with the Palestinians. Those activities were noted but clearly did not have nearly as much rhetorical appeal and thus did not catch as much of the war makers' interest as the fanciful alliance with al-Qa'ida.

Thinking about that Saturday morning in the Situation Room brings to mind George Allen's observation about his participation in sessions Walt Rostow held to discuss ways to bolster public support for the Vietnam War—that they were "the most distasteful and depressing meetings" of his bureaucratic career.

Discrediting Intelligence

Politicization does not necessarily imply a cozy and cordial relationship between intelligence officers and policymakers. In a severe instance of it, such as with the Iraq War, policymakers' determination to prevent intelligence from impeding their preferred message may make the relationship more acrimonious than ever. The machinations by Cheney's office over the Nigerien uranium ore issue are an illustration. Amid all the delicious details of that affair, including who leaked what to whom, Valerie Plame's cover status, and the legal issues in Libby's perjury trial, it is easy to lose sight of why it became an affair in the first place. The office of the vice president sought to discredit the CIA and the retired diplomat it had hired to help investigate the subject (and who had the temerity later to write an op-ed on the subject),[87] for concluding—correctly—that a report the administration was gung-ho on using in its public case was not credible enough for public consumption. The prior history of the CIA's repeatedly warning the administration not to use the report gave the vice president's office additional incentive to seek ways to discredit the CIA's handling of the matter and to neutralize any impact if the story of these warnings became public.[88]

Several of the conservative and neoconservative policymakers who came into power with the younger Bush entered the scene with an already jaundiced view of the intelligence community. The roots of that view extend back to the Reagan years or even earlier and involve the sorts of strategic Cold War issues that led to the Team B exercise. But the principal reason that policymakers' discrediting of the intelligence community became more ferocious before and during the Iraq War than probably in any other recent period is that inconvenient truths from the community complicated and threatened to torpedo the campaign to build and maintain support for the war. The job of selling an offensive war was already a big challenge, even with the conveniently mistaken intelligence judgments about ongoing Iraqi weapons programs. Anything that complicated the job further was a source not just of frustration, but also of anger and animosity.

I have little doubt that war makers who accused intelligence officers of willfully subverting the administration's policies sincerely believed their accusations. I heard enough such charges in private hearsay (including accusations directed against me) and saw enough reporting of other private comments along the same line to believe that this frequently voiced allegation was not just being flung for public effect. Hostility toward intelligence officers rested on perceived hostility *from* intelligence officers, as reflected in a comment from a conversation among White House speechwriters: "The CIA's job is to screw you. . . . Why can't we get the CIA to stop regarding the White House like a foreign government?"[89]

My own involuntary role as a target to be discredited goes back to some of my earlier scholarly work on terrorism, which analyzed the shift in relative importance from states to nonstate actors such as al-Qa'ida.[90] There was nothing controversial about this analysis among the great majority of experts on terrorism, but it was unwelcome to anyone wanting to play up the dangers of rogue states, including Iraq, in fomenting terrorism. Another unwelcome subject of my earlier writing on terrorism concerned the need (as would be borne out by the 9/11 attack) to maintain analytical clarity in not mashing together weapons proliferation and terrorism as if they were one subject and one threat. In February 2002, I gave a guest lecture to a class at Johns Hopkins University that touched on these and other aspects of thinking about terrorism. In response to a student's question, I expanded on the issue of unconventional weapons and terrorism by alluding to the just-delivered "axis of evil" State of the Union Address as an example of the kind of conflation of these two issues that I preferred to avoid. A garbled leak of my response became the subject of an item in *Insight*, a now-defunct conservative newsmagazine, with the eye-grabbing headline, "Senior Intelligence Officer Blasts President's Speech."[91] This article in turn became fodder for repeated replays by editorialists on the right, particularly at the *Wall Street Journal*, who embellished the story in the retelling to one in which I had "assailed Mr. Bush's Iraq policy in a public appearance."[92]

The incentive to disparage the intelligence community strengthened once the war was under way because the Bush administration faced not only decreasing public support for an increasing mess in Iraq, but also a mess that had largely been anticipated by prewar intelligence analysis the administration had ignored. The community, moreover, was producing new assessments that confirmed what much of the earlier ones had anticipated.

By the autumn of 2003, the administration was already on the defensive regarding the war and not just because of the nondiscovery of WMD. The notion of an alliance between Iraq and al-Qa'ida was being subjected to increased public questioning, and a flow of news stories addressed the role of the vice president's office in the Nigerien uranium affair.

An even more sensitive period for the administration came the following autumn as President Bush was campaigning for reelection. By then, another intelligence product on Iraq had become part of the mix. In July 2004, my office completed an NIE on the prospects for Iraq over the following eighteen months. Much of what the estimate described concerned the sectarian conflict and undemocratic habits that the intelligence community's prewar assessments (which by the autumn of 2004 had partially leaked)[93] had anticipated would characterize post-Saddam Iraq.[94] A portion of the estimate itself was leaked in September, leading to Bush's dismissive "just guessing" comment.[95]

With the presidential election just weeks away, the incentive was strong to portray the purveyors of such inconveniently downbeat intelligence assessments as politically motivated. The intelligence officers involved are out to undermine the president and his policies, went the narrative, and so what they say about Iraq and the effects of the war is not to be believed. The narrative was aided by a column from syndicated columnist Robert Novak focusing on another garbled leak from another long-scheduled private talk I had given to a small group, this one focused on Middle Eastern affairs. Novak portrayed my talk as part of a calculated effort by the CIA to wage "war" with the White House, as an extension of the recent leak of the pessimistic intelligence estimate on Iraq, and as an "unprecedented but shocking" instance of the CIA's going "semipublic," reminding Novak of how "history is filled with intelligence bureaus turning against their own governments."[96] The *Wall Street Journal* went into overdrive with an editorial titled "The CIA's Insurgency."[97] The themes in the *Journal*'s editorials also appeared in other commentaries from the right.[98] A few days later, taking part in a briefing for the Senate Intelligence Committee on a different topic, I spent part of the afternoon getting grilled by Republican committee members about the "insurgency" I supposedly was leading against the Bush administration.

This incident is just a sample of the larger assault that the administration and its supporters were mounting against an intelligence community that had been producing judgments that were inconvenient for sustaining support for the war and by implication for the president for whom the war was by far the biggest initiative of his presidency. The assault constituted more hammering of the community and, as such, more of the pressure that encouraged politicization of the intelligence product. The charge of insubordination made intelligence officers all the more disinclined to offer judgments at odds with the policymakers' wishes or to question judgments that supported those wishes.

It is ironic, to say the least, to hear criticism that intelligence officers facilitated a tragic policy when the policymakers themselves felt so frustrated by inconvenient (and for the most part correct) intelligence judgments that they thought intelligence officers were trying to undermine the same policy. In that regard, the castigation of the intelligence community by the pro-war Right involves one of the bigger ironies of the Iraq War. Not only was a misadventure that has become closely associated in the public mind with intelligence failure *not* guided by intelligence judgments, but the makers of the war despised and distrusted intelligence officers, regarded them as adversaries, discredited their integrity, disparaged some of their most important judgments, and strenuously opposed the influence of those judgments.

The basis for any politicization, including instances less severe than with the Iraq War, is institutional and systemic. Politicization occurs less because of weak knees or lily livers than because intelligence officers are subordinate to policymakers. It is a matter of power. Policymakers have it, and intelligence officers don't, which is why policy shapes intelligence more than the other way around.

CHAPTER SEVEN

SCAPEGOATS AND SPECTATOR SPORT

A common response by nations (and other groups) to failure is to search for scapegoats. It is always less discomfiting to believe that trauma and tragedy have resulted not from our own mistakes or weaknesses or failures by leaders we admire or unavoidable consequences of the circumstances we faced, but instead from the actions of people or institutions we feel comfortable blaming. Notorious instances of scapegoating litter the history of foreign countries that have endured failure, such as the "stab in the back" legend that attributed Germany's defeat in World War I to subversion from within by socialists, Jews, and others.

The United States does not seem to have shared in much of this history, but only because it has not had as many defeats to explain away. When faced with failure, Americans are at least as prone as other people to scapegoat because of their historically grounded expectation of success. They resist accepting that there may be problems that the United States, no matter how well it uses its available resources, is simply not able to solve. Americans' outlook is the opposite of the inclination in some other cultures to attribute bad outcomes to fate or the will of God. Americans always need to find someone to blame; for them, it is the least disturbing way to cope with failure.

That the United States has been spared many of the ethnic and religious tensions that have wracked other societies has meant it also has been spared the ugliest forms of scapegoating. The United States has experienced nothing comparable (except to a limited degree with some anti-immigrant beliefs) to how the "stab in the back" notion contributed to anti-Semitism in Germany as the Nazis were rising to power. Instead, political parties or movements, individual officeholders, or mere strains of opinion have at various times served as scapegoats for Americans. A lingering minority view still blames the U.S. failure in Vietnam, for example, on end-the-war sentiment that resulted in what is believed was a premature withdrawal of resources to fight the war. A similar version of that view will arise in response to any upsurge of violence in Iraq as U.S. troops withdraw or any lasting outcome in Iraq that is seen as unsatisfactory.

Secretary of Defense Donald Rumsfeld served as a scapegoat for troubles in Iraq as he was forced from office in late 2006. He became a symbol of much of what had gone wrong in the war, well beyond his own undeniable mistakes. Cashiering Rumsfeld helped to divert blame away from President Bush and his policies and from the advisability of going to war in the first place as distinct from the execution of the war.

The entire Bush administration similarly became a scapegoat for some of the most fervent neoconservative supporters of the war, at least ones who did not occupy positions within the administration itself. As the war went sour, a marked correlation became apparent between the strength of an individual's original support for launching the expedition and the subsequent ferocity of the same individual's criticism of how the administration was executing it. Former Reagan administration official Kenneth Adelman, who had earlier forecast that the Iraq War would be a "cakewalk"[1] and who in the flush of the war's first days was singing the praises of the Bush administration officials who were leading it,[2] was by 2006 lambasting the same officials as "among the most incompetent teams in the post-war era." "The problem," said Adelman, "is not a selling job. The problem is a performance job."[3] Richard Perle, another early and prominent neoconservative promoter of the war, became similarly vituperative in his denunciation of the Bush administration's execution of it. "Huge mistakes were made," said Perle in 2006, "and I want to be very clear on this: They were not made by neoconservatives, who had almost no voice in what happened, and certainly almost no voice in what happened after the downfall of the regime in Baghdad." Perle injected the traditional scapegoating theme of subversion from within: "At the end of the day, you have to hold the president responsible. . . . I don't think he realized the extent of the opposition within his own administration, and the disloyalty."[4]

THE PERFECT FOIL

No institution or individual has served better as a scapegoat for Americans than the U.S. intelligence community. Repeatedly throughout the seven decades since Pearl Harbor, the finger of blame for trauma that Americans have suffered at the hands of foreigners has quickly and reflexively pointed at intelligence. And the blame finger has always been one of the first fingers to move. When Secretary of State Dean Acheson and Secretary of Defense Louis Johnson appeared before the Senate Appropriations Committee the day after North Korea's invasion of the South to appeal for quick approval of additional military assistance funds for Korea and the Philippines, the senators' main interest was not the requested appropriation. It was not the other measures the Truman administration was scrambling to take in response to the invasion. What the committee members most wanted to know was why the nation had not been warned of the invasion. Acheson and Johnson said they should direct the question to DCI Roscoe Hillenkoetter, whom the committee summoned to appear later the same afternoon.[5]

The attraction of using intelligence as a scapegoat rests on its traditional lack of attraction as an American institution. Americans are less comfortable than citizens of most other democracies with standing intelligence services and more likely to be distrustful of them. They have considered intelligence to be at best a necessary evil and sometimes not even necessary. These attitudes are based in part on Americans' relative lack of long-term familiarity with intelligence. That unfamiliarity in turn is based on America's splendid geographic isolation and episodic interaction with the outside world that long made a permanent intelligence service seem superfluous. The necessary evil, like some other necessary evils Americans have tolerated, has been associated with war, not with peacetime. Once the British on whom Nathan Hale was spying were pushed out, the need for intelligence was no longer seen.

As late as 1929, Secretary of State Henry L. Stimson withdrew funds from a cryptologic operation jointly funded by the State Department and the army (resulting shortly afterward in termination of the operation) on grounds that "gentlemen do not read each other's mail."[6] As a result of such attitudes, the United States, of all countries that have been major powers during the past century, has had the briefest continuous experience with intelligence.[7] Apart from some military and naval intelligence units, that experience did not begin until five months before the attack on Pearl Harbor, when President Franklin Roosevelt created under William J. Donovan the Office of the Coordinator of Information, which after American entry into World War II evolved into the Office of Strategic Services. After the war, President Truman's initial inclination was to forgo a peacetime civilian intelligence service as being too redolent of a secret police and subject to abuse. Only the lobbying of Donovan and other officials led to the establishment of the Central Intelligence Group, the forerunner of the CIA, a few months later.

The secrecy inherent to intelligence is anathema to the value Americans place on openness in the working of their government institutions—the value reflected in Woodrow Wilson's call for open covenants openly arrived at. The duplicity (i.e., the lying) inherent to some intelligence operations makes Americans uncomfortable for similar reasons. The association of intelligence with covert action compounds the discomfort. Although Americans do not value secrecy in their government institutions, they value it highly in their individual lives under the label of privacy. And so intelligence by its very nature starts with two strikes against it in winning any favor with the American public. Americans want their government institutions to be open and their individual lives to be closed; intelligence is associated with the opposite of both.

Sustaining the Lore

Each well-publicized scandal or controversy that relates to intelligence in any way, even if indirectly, builds on all the previous ones to bolster popular distrust and dislike of intelligence institutions. The high (or low) point of this process in the intelligence community's history was marked in the 1970s by the congressional inquiries into abuses by intelligence agencies. There were real abuses, but the American public already had been primed to be disillusioned with government agencies by other national traumas of the time, most notably the Vietnam War and the Watergate affair. More recent controversies such as warrantless intercepts of communications or the coercive interrogation of detainees, both involving intelligence agencies, have added to popular distrust and dislike, even if the practices in question were conducted at the behest of political authorities and did not represent the initiative or even the preference of the intelligence agencies themselves.

In view of all these factors, it is unsurprising that polling of American opinion has shown intelligence agencies to be among the less popular government institutions, although opinion naturally has varied with events of the day. An intelligence agency such as the CIA enjoys less esteem than other security-related agencies and institutions. A poll in 2001 (before both 9/11 and the Iraq War), revealed substantially less confidence in the CIA than in either the FBI or the state or local police.[8] A poll two years later that asked how well a job each of eight well-known federal agencies was doing put the CIA on the lower rungs, barely ahead of the Internal Revenue Service and behind even the much-maligned Department of Homeland Security.[9] Attitudinal consistency working the way it does, different types of negative perceptions and sentiments go together. The same institutions that are not popular also tend not to be respected or trusted. And they also tend to be seen as not performing their mission well.

As with so much else that is said or felt about U.S. intelligence today, little of this opinion about it is new. The Hoover Commission called attention in the mid-1950s to the American public's insufficient appreciation for the intelligence community's work.[10] In 1957, Congressman Daniel Flood summarized the popular lack of respect for the community: "The average American thinks . . . that our intelligence is a laughing stock . . . that the British are the finest intelligence people in the world, that the Germans are great, but that we do not have anybody on this intelligence business."[11] Nearly all of the failures that enter into commentary about intelligence today were then still in the future. They would of course enrich and bolster the negative American lore about intelligence, but they are not the cause of it.

Intelligence lacks a constituency that will push back when blame gets pushed onto it, whether fairly or unfairly. DCI Richard Helms once remarked, "I am the easiest man in Washington to fire. I have no political, military or industrial base."[12] Although institutions do not get fired, the same principle of lacking a base and thus of lacking support when under fire applies to the institution as well as to the individual who leads it. No politically significant interest gets offended when intelligence is made a scapegoat.

The intelligence agencies themselves also provide little pushback. They have been ineffective—or, to be more charitable, relatively inactive—in getting a message of their own out to the American public.[13] This inactivity may be due in part to an admirable trepidation within such agencies about doing anything that smacks of domestic influence operations. Whatever the reason, the intelligence community's public relations contrast sharply with the image polishing of, say, the U.S. military, which leverages its own recruitment activities as well as countless facets of popular culture to enhance its standing with the American public.

The best scapegoats provide an explanation for trauma and failure that not only is psychologically satisfying but also lifts responsibility from those seeking the explanation. An unelected, apolitical bureaucracy serves that purpose well both for political leaders and the public that elects them. The more that failure in foreign or security policy can be attributed to inattention or misjudgment in the intelligence community, the less that the leaders or the American people themselves need to shoulder responsibility for their own inattention or misjudgment.

An Unchallenged Consensus

Rooted in American history and culture as well as in human nature, boosted and legitimized by periodic official inquiries, and further amplified by circularly self-reinforcing unofficial commentary, the American mythology of intelligence is as strong as ever. Because most of what is said and written about U.S. intelligence stays within limits set by the same basic narrative about intelligence failing, misguiding policy, and needing to be fixed, the flaws in the inquiries into and commentary about intelligence seldom get exposed. Or if they do, the exposures do not gain traction. The homogeneity of the commentary means most errors in it go unchallenged. There is not an effective marketplace of ideas about U.S. intelligence because most consumers of ideas on this subject are more interested in getting reassuring explanations about supposedly fixable problems than in dispassionately learning about how intelligence really has functioned.[14]

The few commentators who begin to depart from the mythology make themselves vulnerable to accusations that they are co-opted apologists for the intelligence community. Those who have been part of the community are dismissed even more readily as having obvious bias and self-interest. If they defend any criticized portion of what the community has done, they are disparaged as being defensive. If they deny that a supposed problem with intelligence is not as much of a problem as generally perceived, they are met with the undeniable charge of being "in denial." And so whatever insights and truths they may have to offer never really make it into the marketplace.

The tendency to dismiss insiders' perspectives as biased can arise with regard to any business, of course, but for two reasons it is especially a problem with intelligence. First, the very strength and homogeneity of the mythology make it invulnerable to most challenges from any source, insider or outsider. Second, secrecy cloaks so much of the intelligence business that the public has no way of obtaining direct knowledge of most of the business, and insiders who do have direct knowledge are constrained in what they can say. Most of the peeks behind the curtain of secrecy are offered by the official inquiries that are themselves conveyors of the consensus mythology. The result is a public discourse about intelligence that in significant ways is either ill informed or misinformed.

Against the backdrop of this discourse, U.S. intelligence serves for most Americans a function that is a combination of hope chest, voodoo doll, and the portrait of Dorian Gray. Intelligence is the object of a naive expectation that if it can be constituted properly, it will lead to a happier tomorrow. It can be skewered in frustration when the tomorrows turn out to be unhappy. And the misjudgment, inattention, or other faults that underlie national failures can be projected onto intelligence so that Americans can maintain a more positive image of their other institutions, their leaders, and themselves.

SCOREKEEPING

Keeping score—more specifically, counting failures—is a big part of sustaining the American mythology of intelligence. The scorekeeping is inherent to the scapegoating. Litanies of what the intelligence community failed to do through the years reinforce the idea that it is the source of misguided policies and is what needs to be fixed.

Scorekeeping on intelligence, even if conducted with attempted objectivity, unavoidably involves a truncated and biased sample. Only some of the things intelligence addresses can readily be scored. The items that show up on the scorecards are discrete, one-off events rather than patterns that are broad, fuzzy, or indeterminate. They are items that can be expressed in binary, yes-or-no terms and not just as matters of emphasis or degree. They are visible matters of public knowledge. Among the types of events that most often exhibit these characteristics are coups, revolutions, wars, election results, terrorist attacks, and nuclear tests.

Such events represent only a small proportion of the intelligence community's work, however. Making calls on them constitutes an evaluation of only a small proportion of the community's contribution to national security. Yet the scorecards exclude everything that does not become publicly visible. They exclude every trend, pattern, or threat that cannot be expressed in discrete yes-or-no terms. They exclude all nonevents, including ones that did not occur because of successful responses to accurate intelligence. These exclusions add to the distortions introduced by stripping complications and qualifications from much of the intelligence community's output and reducing it—in memory and in public perceptions—to the kind of simple, yes-or-no judgments that can be more readily scored.

Disconnect from Policy

An even more fundamental shortcoming of the American scorekeeping habit is that it has become divorced from any sense of importance or relevance to U.S. policy and U.S. national interests. Scorekeepers keep marking their scorecards without stopping to consider how much any of this matters to U.S. foreign and security policy. Items get entered on the cards because they are easily scored, not because they have made any difference to U.S. interests.

Several conditions must be met for good intelligence to make any difference for the better or for bad intelligence to make any difference for the worse. The specific subject of intelligence scrutiny must have an impact on U.S. national interests. The United States must have policy options that will prevent, deflect, or otherwise affect the events in question or that will enable it to prepare or position itself so that the impact of those events on U.S. interests will be more favorable or less unfavorable than it otherwise would be. The information or insights that intelligence provides must make those policy options appear more attractive to the decision maker—and sufficiently more attractive to affect decisions—than they would without the intelligence. The policymaker must accept the intelligence as sound and be willing to be influenced by it. He must be more influenced by intelligence than by other, different inputs to the image he holds of the overseas situation he faces. And the policymaker must not feel so constrained by other considerations—including resource limitations, domestic politics, or competing foreign-policy objectives—that he otherwise fails to act in a way that the intelligence implies would be prudent.

That is a long and demanding set of requirements. It should not be surprising, as earlier chapters in this book have shown, that intelligence has seldom made the difference in guiding the most important U.S. foreign-policy decisions. This was so even with something as momentous as the collapse of the Soviet Union. As Lawrence Eagleburger recalled, "Even if the CIA had told us at an early stage that the USSR was on the way out, it would not have had much effect on our policy."[15] But scorecards on intelligence pay no heed to any of these realities. The scorekeeping is part of a spectator sport, which the spectators watch without worrying about the game's possible larger significance. They cheer or jeer—mostly jeer—the part of the intelligence team's performance that they can see because doing so makes them feel good or because it is in their political interest to do so, not because they have analyzed how that performance affects their nation's security or welfare.

PREDICTION

The most common type of entry on the scorecards concerns predictions. The intelligence community is repeatedly criticized for not predicting certain events or, much less frequently, given credit for accurate predictions. Besides being susceptible to scoring, predictions (or nonpredictions, which then are scored as a failure to predict) do seem on the surface to be important to policymakers. No policymaker—or any other type of leader, for that matter—likes to be surprised. "No surprises" is usually a cardinal rule for getting along with the boss in any organization, public or private. It is understandable that U.S. policymakers express annoyance and disapproval when they are surprised about events overseas. But avoiding annoyance among officeholders is not a U.S. national interest, and it is not a valid justification for spending billions on intelligence.

A focus on predictions fits well with scapegoating. Because it is assumed that problems are solvable with the right advance information, it is easy to affix blame to whoever has responsibility for doing the predicting. Making this assumption is somewhat like shooting the messenger, except in this case the person who supposedly failed to deliver a message is the one who is shot. An extreme example of this phenomenon was Senator Rick Santorum's (R–Pa.) criticism of the National Weather Service for a forecast of the highly destructive Hurricane Katrina in 2005 that he said was "not sufficient." Even Santorum's Republican colleagues apparently realized that the criticism had no basis. The weather service's forecasts regarding the hurricane actually had been quite good, and Santorum's charge probably had more to do with his interest in privatizing part of the service.[16] The charge demonstrated, however, how strong can be the urge to use predictors as scapegoats.

Some predictions are self-negating, which make them a poor measure of the intelligence community's performance. The point is perhaps clearest with regard to terrorist attacks. Common references to "predicting" terrorist attacks or failing to do so are illogical in that the only possible purpose of such "prediction" is to roll up the plot and prevent the attack from occurring. Either an attack occurs and the public scores it as an intelligence failure, or an attack is preempted and (except for the few instances in which such preemption has been made public) it does not get scored as either a success or a failure. Intelligence officers will never have the satisfaction of successfully predicting a terrorist attack—in the sense of providing tactical information about a specific attack rather than a strategic assessment of a more general threat—because it would be a shockingly irresponsible policy response to allow such a prediction to come true.

Even other types of predictions, which do not exhibit this paradox to the same degree, leave open the question of how useful they are in facilitating beneficial policy responses. Two of the wars between Israel and its Arab neighbors—those in 1967 and 1973—provide a useful way of approaching this question because they involved different predictions, or nonpredictions, by U.S. intelligence.

The Six-Day War of 1967 was well anticipated. U.S. intelligence gave good warning, weeks ahead of the event, to policymakers. Accurate analysis about the impending outbreak and military outcome of the war was reportedly what earned DCI Richard Helms a seat at Lyndon Johnson's Tuesday lunch table. Johnson made it clear that he was not at all surprised by the conflict and that he had utilized the warning to try to avert it. "During those trying days," Johnson later wrote, "I used all the energy and experience I could muster to prevent war."[17]

In contrast, the Yom Kippur War of 1973 is one of the most common entries on scorecards of intelligence failure. Given the extremely close-hold manner in which Richard Nixon and Henry Kissinger managed foreign policy, as demonstrated in their China initiative, it is fair to ask whether they share responsibility for not anticipating the Arab attack, especially in dismissing warnings that Soviet leaders had given directly to them earlier in the year.[18] In any event, Nixon later wrote that news of the impending attack, which Israel conveyed only hours before the war began, took him "completely by surprise." He said he was "disappointed by our own intelligence shortcomings" and "stunned" by a parallel failure of Israeli intelligence.[19]

The United States was unable to prevent war in 1967 despite ample warning and subsequent efforts by policymakers. We do not know what the U.S. policy response would have been in 1973 if U.S. (or Israeli) intelligence had provided weeks rather than hours of warning. We also do not know whether U.S. policymakers would have had any more success than their counterparts in 1967 did if they had responded to such warning with efforts to avert the conflict. Quite possibly they would have; the situations had important differences, and the Arab strategy in 1973 depended on achieving initial battlefield success through surprise and by attacking Israel on a Jewish holiday. The more fundamental observation, however—not dependent on speculation—is that war broke out in both years despite warning (or "prediction") in one case but not in the other.

The consequences of these two wars in the Middle East provide a further basis for assessing the importance and usefulness of prediction. Taking a broad view—bearing in mind all relevant U.S. interests and four decades of perspective—the war in 1967 was the far more damaging of the two. It began the Israeli occupation of Arab territory that continues to this day in the West Bank and Golan Heights and that underlies the painful and seemingly intractable issues of land, settlements, and violent relations between occupier and occupied that have helped to poison the politics of the Middle East and have frustrated a series of would-be peacemakers. The occupation engendered Palestinian uprisings, which in turn stimulated the emergence and growth of radical movements that have inflicted damage and insecurity on Israelis greater than anything that earlier movements or Arab armies were able to inflict before 1967. And not least important for the current comparison, the Six-Day War led directly to the Yom Kippur War. The conflict in 1973 was an attempt to reverse some of the results of the conflict in 1967; without the earlier war, the later one would not have happened.

The Yom Kippur War was challenging to U.S. policymakers in other ways, but the balance sheet of its consequences for U.S. interests looks far more favorable. Nixon and Kissinger's adept diplomacy (and airlift of military equipment and supplies to Israel) cemented the alliance with Israel, foiled Soviet ambitions to make inroads in the Middle East, and lay the groundwork for improved relations with Arab states. Because the Egyptian army did well enough on the battlefield (despite later losing ground to an Israeli counterattack) to redeem its honor and reputation, the war was a critical prerequisite to Egyptian president Anwar Sadat's historic trip to Jerusalem, leading to the first Arab–Israeli peace treaty. Sadat's dramatic redirection of policy, of which the October 1973 war was an integral part, also included his break with the Soviet Union and the establishment of a de facto U.S. alliance with Egypt, the most populous Arab state. Nixon could state with pride in his memoirs that "for the first time in an Arab–Israeli conflict the United States conducted itself in a manner that not only preserved but greatly enhanced our relations with the Arabs—even while we were massively resupplying the Israelis."[20]

In short, prediction in 1967 did nothing to stop either a war or its severe and long-lasting damage; lack of prediction in 1973 did nothing to stop U.S. policymakers from turning a crisis into a U.S. success.

PREDICTIONS AND POLICIES

Several possible factors keep prediction or a failure to predict from spelling the difference between successful and unsuccessful foreign policy. The 1973 Middle East war illustrates one factor, which is that even if a U.S. policy response can make a difference, the response may not be feasible until after the contingency or crisis in question occurs. The best actions the United States could have taken in the 1973 crisis were the ones the Nixon administration actually took. But it could not have taken them, at least not with good effect, until after the war broke out.

The same crisis illustrates another factor, which is that unpredicted events can have beneficial as well as deleterious consequences. If the former outweigh the latter, the best course of action may be to let the event occur rather than to try to head it off. This is true even of wars. From the hard-boiled realist perspective that characterized Nixon and Kissinger's foreign policy, the Yom Kippur War was not a bad thing. If the intelligence community or anyone else somehow could have furnished U.S. policymakers an extremely prescient and detailed set of predictions—anticipating not only the war but also its principal consequences, including Sadat's strategic reversal and the effects on U.S.–Arab relations, it might not have been in U.S. interests to try to prevent the conflict.

Warning from an intelligence service (or from anyone else) is one thing; having sufficient domestic or foreign support or both to act on the warning is quite another. Policymakers have repeatedly been constrained by the insufficiency of such support, more so than any insufficiency of predictions. The difficulty is in persuading larger audiences. No matter how much an intelligence service's analysis may convince policymakers of an impending event, the American public as well as foreign governments and their publics almost always require something more. This is why it is unlikely that more prescient analysis by the intelligence community about Soviet activity in Cuba in the autumn of 1962 would appreciably have changed the U.S. response. In his memoir of the missile crisis, Robert Kennedy referred to a postmortem study (an example of the usual application of hindsight to such failures) that pointed to reports that might have tipped U.S. officials off sooner to the presence of Soviet missiles. But Kennedy rightly said that such reports had to be checked and rechecked. Even more important, he noted, the same postmortem study also stated that "there was no action the United States could have taken before the time we actually did act" because even overhead photography available before then "would not have been substantial enough to convince the governments and peoples of the world of the presence of offensive missiles in Cuba. Certainly, unsubstantiated refugee reports would not have been sufficient."[21]

Actual, graphic events—a war, a surprise attack, or whatever else leads to later recriminations about its not being predicted—have far more power to move publics and governments and to generate support for a vigorous response than even the most pointed and prescient predictions. They have far more impact than even the most elegant and well-documented analysis any intelligence service can ever offer. This point was illustrated in 1979, when to Zbigniew Brzezinski's pleasant surprise the Soviet invasion of Afghanistan instantly generated public support for tougher measures against the Soviet Union.[22] Short of Red Army tanks rolling into Afghanistan en masse, Americans would not have accepted keeping their athletes out of the Olympics. This pattern is common. Strong measures follow rather than precede dramatic events such as military invasions or major terrorist attacks not because the event is a revelatory, scales-dropping-from-eyes lesson to policymakers who previously were unaware of a danger, but instead because the event—as a matter of public mood and emotion—generates the necessary political support for the measures.

A similar pattern arose with Iraq's invasion of Kuwait in 1990. The George H. W. Bush administration was so far away from having sufficient political support for tough preemptive measures against Iraq that it is unlikely any better warning about the invasion would have mattered. Bush's secretary of state, James Baker, believes that nothing short of moving U.S. armed forces to the region would have deterred Saddam Hussein from his invasion, but the administration lacked support even for measures short of that. Any preinvasion attempt to alter U.S. policy toward Iraq, he recalls, "would have prompted a considerable outcry from many who later criticized us for not changing our policy sooner. Key members of Congress would have fought us tooth and nail if we'd threatened to cut off grain credits. Similarly, many skeptics who in hindsight criticized us for not being more assertive with Iraq also chastised us for threatening use of force when we did. I continue to believe that if the President had said prior to August 1990 that we were willing to go to war to protect Kuwait, many members of Congress would have been muttering impeachment."[23]

TESTS AND TIMING

Another event entered as "failure to predict" on intelligence scorecards is the series of nuclear tests that India and Pakistan conducted in 1998. "A colossal failure of U.S. intelligence!" thundered Richard Shelby, chairman of the Senate Intelligence Committee, who promptly convened a hearing on the subject.[24] But the posturing by Shelby and many others did not address in detail exactly what U.S. intelligence predicted or should have been expected to predict, nor did they address at all what difference any prediction might have made. The episode raises several issues about the common fixation on prediction and on easily scored events such as nuclear tests.

The first issue concerns what aspects of India and Pakistan's nuclear activities really matter to U.S. interests. The nuclear weapons that the two South Asian rivals possess are unquestionably of major importance to international security both because of the risk that a South Asian war will escalate out of control and because of the possible effects of the Indian and Pakistani programs on broader nuclear proliferation. For these reasons, the U.S. intelligence community had devoted concentrated attention to these programs for many years. The Pakistani program had long been the single most closely followed nuclear program in the world. And based on what is publicly known, the assessments the intelligence community offered of the two programs—their purposes, their progress through the years, and the size and existence of the nuclear arsenals, which predated by many years the tests in 1998—were generally accurate. There were no strategic surprises. The tests gave technical experts in the community data to analyze regarding such details as the yield of the detonated devices, but they did not change the overall picture that the community and U.S. policymakers already had of the nuclear weapons capabilities of the two South Asian powers.

Those capabilities are far more important than any tests. The tests in 1998—initiated by India, after which it was certain that Pakistan would follow suit—were not even the first such event in South Asia. India had accomplished that feat twenty-four years earlier, although New Delhi sanctimoniously described its test in 1974 as a "peaceful nuclear explosion." Tests are not necessary to build a nuclear weapons arsenal, as Pakistan and Israel had already demonstrated.[25]

Dueling nuclear tests obviously did not improve the tone of Indo–Pakistani relations. But the two sides had long been well aware of each other's nuclear weapons capabilities, so the weapons were already having effects on strategy and diplomacy in South Asia, tests or no tests. Deployments of conventional forces, both before and after each side acquired nuclear capabilities, have repeatedly brought the two countries closer to the brink of war than anything that happened in 1998. Military exercises in the winter of 1986–1987, for example, led the two sides to mobilizing more than one-quarter of a million troops and staring each other down across their common border. The nuclear tests caused no comparable crisis.

Nuclear tests are more easily scored than subwar crises, however, so the tests were the focus of criticism of the U.S. intelligence community's

performance. Because the intelligence community has to be, for this political reason, in the business of predicting tests, the next question is, What
constitutes a prediction? Does it have to be a precise and certain forecast,
with date and time specified, for it to count? It would be foolhardy for any
intelligence service, no matter how well placed its sources, to offer such a
prediction because problems often arise in testing programs, and delays
may occur before the button finally is pushed. If a prediction cannot be
that precise, then just how much does it have to narrow the time frame to
avoid being labeled an intelligence failure, let alone a colossal one? Is it a
matter of days? Weeks? Months? The question is all the more pertinent in
the case of India in 1998 because U.S. intelligence analysts had acknowledged that India was technically capable of testing at any time and had
warned the Clinton administration accordingly.[26]

Moreover, the administration did not even need to listen to its intelligence analysts; it could have listened to Indian leaders. The Indian decision
to conduct a nuclear test reflected a determination by the rightist Bharatiya
Janata Party (BJP) to flex India's muscle as a reassertion of its dominant
role on the Asian subcontinent and its status as a rising power with aspirations for greater influence beyond its immediate neighborhood. In a national election campaign during the previous several months, the BJP had
made an issue of nuclear weapons and the need, as it saw it, to brandish
this part of India's military power openly.[27] The party's secretary-general
had already declared that if it came to power, it would test a nuclear weapon.[28]
When the BJP won the election and took power in March, no secret intelligence was necessary to realize that such a test in the near future was a
strong possibility.

All that U.S. intelligence could have added was not a judgment about
likelihood, but instead a prediction about timing—and evidently timing
more precise than a matter of weeks; less than eight weeks transpired between the BJP's assumption of power and the first of the tests in May. It is
hard to think of any difference such a forecast about timing would have
made to U.S. interests or the security situation in South Asia. U.S. policymakers had discussed a parallel question thirty-four years earlier as China
was preparing its first nuclear test. When DCI John McCone recommended
that a U-2 aircraft overfly the Chinese test site to get more detailed information about the test preparations, President Johnson's other senior advisers initially resisted the idea, correctly concerned that the cost from an
overflight that went awry would outweigh any benefit from the information

a successful mission would collect. Secretary of State Dean Rusk stated that he knew the test was inevitable and could not envision anything he would do differently if he were informed of the exact timing.[29]

Knowledge of timing would have been similarly inconsequential with India in 1998. It is difficult to see how such knowledge would have improved any chance that U.S. action could have prevented the tests. There is no reason to think the BJP-led government would have been any more likely to back down from its plans at a late stage after test preparations had been made and a date had been set than it would have been in response to an earlier demarche not informed by any information about timing.

There was probably little chance of heading off the tests anyway, especially given the BJP's determination to proclaim a more muscular foreign policy and the role nuclear weapons played in that policy. An additional indication of this outcome is how the right to test became a point of principle for New Delhi in later negotiations, even with the less fervently nationalist Congress Party back in power and even after India received what many observers considered an enormous concession from the United States in the form of a nuclear cooperation agreement.[30] Poor international support also worked against any chance of heading off the tests in 1998. Four months before the tests, French President Jacques Chirac led one hundred French business executives on an economically motivated trip to India during which Chirac told the Indians, "France would fully understand if India conducted nuclear tests. We will be with you."[31] When U.S. admiral David Jeremiah, who chaired the subsequent inevitable inquiry after the "intelligence failure," was asked whether better advance warning could have been used to prevent the tests, he replied, "No, I don't think you were going to turn them around."[32]

The Indian nuclear tests also illustrate a variation on how some predictions can be self-negating. The U.S. intelligence community had detected preparations for a nuclear test in 1995 under an earlier Congress Party–led government—a successful "prediction" that of course is less remembered than the subsequent failure—after which the Clinton administration exerted heavy pressure on India not to test. The Indians stood down that time, but having been tipped off by the demarche about what the United States had been monitoring, they changed their pretest procedures to make them less detectable by U.S. intelligence three years later.[33]

The recriminations over the South Asian nuclear tests are a good example of commentary about intelligence performance being a spectator sport in which Americans watch and score that performance with almost no regard for what difference the game makes for U.S. policy or for U.S. national interests. The topic in question—the tests—was part of a larger subject of unquestionable importance (i.e., nuclear weapons in South Asia), but the focus of failure was only one slice (timing) of another slice (testing) of that subject. The slice was selected not because a different intelligence output would have meant more successful U.S. policy. It was selected because it was easy to score.

What gets scored as surprise and a failure to predict also depends on what policymakers choose to highlight to the public. When U.S. officials were anticipating the Chinese nuclear test in 1964, Secretary Rusk announced publicly that such a test was coming in order to lessen the risk of any panic among Americans once the blast occurred.[34] Rusk still did not know the exact timing—the test was almost three weeks away when he made his announcement—but that did not matter. The first nuclear test by what was then a worrisome enemy of the United States made such a precautionary, opinion-conditioning statement prudent. There was no chance of public panic over a nuclear test in 1998 by India, which was not considered an adversary comparable to China and whose nuclear weapons capabilities had been known for more than two decades. It would therefore not have crossed policymakers' minds to make a similar public statement about India. But they could have done so based on nothing more than the BJP's campaign rhetoric. If they had, the scorekeepers would not have had a failure to mark on their cards.

China also provides a more recent instructive comparison with the Indian and Pakistani tests. In January 2007, China successfully tested an antisatellite (ASAT) weapon, using one of its own aging weather satellites as a target. Three months after the test, press reporting revealed that the U.S. intelligence community had given U.S. policymakers advance warning of the event.[35] As with many other successful predictions by U.S. intelligence, this one is much less likely to appear on scorecards than the unpredicted events. Two other aspects of the Chinese ASAT test also are worth noting against the backdrop of commentary about the South Asian nuclear tests.

One aspect is that in this case the test—as distinct from the military capability that it demonstrated—was far more consequential than what India and Pakistan did in 1998. The ASAT test had the serious and immediate result of creating a huge field of debris in Earth's orbit. As of August 2007, the North American Air Defense Command had cataloged more than two thousand pieces of debris from the test.[36] The National Aeronautics and

Space Administration (NASA) estimated that the test created more than thirty-five thousand pieces of debris larger than one centimeter, most of which are too small to track but still capable of damaging other satellites.[37] The test was the single biggest creator of junk in Earth's orbit in the history of the space age, and it broke a more than twenty-year-old moratorium on debris-creating ASAT tests. The danger that this result of the Chinese test posed to other spacecraft, including the International Space Station and many operational U.S. satellites, should have been reason enough to try hard to dissuade the Chinese from conducting the test.

That makes the other aspect of this test all the more remarkable: the response of U.S. policymakers to the intelligence community's warning was to do nothing. Policymakers reportedly believed that China was determined to proceed with the test, that there were no good options for punishing China if it did proceed, and that a demarche might only educate the Chinese about U.S. intelligence capabilities.[38] Much the same things could have been said about India and its nuclear tests nine years earlier. Such conclusions about China and its ASAT test in 2007 may well have been correct, given Beijing's apparent determination to reduce the gap between it and the United States in space capabilities, although some experts outside the government believe the test could have been prevented.[39] In any event, the successful intelligence prediction, besides going relatively unnoticed in comparison with celebrated nonpredictions, also appears to have gone unused, at least as far as visible U.S. actions were concerned. As with the wars in the Middle East, prediction—successful or not—was largely irrelevant to U.S. interests.

THE IRANIAN REVOLUTION: DESPAIR AND DISAGREEMENT

It is instructive to examine one more prominent "failure to predict" entry on the scorecards of intelligence failure: the political upheaval in Iran that toppled the shah from power in 1979. The Iranian revolution exemplified the sort of complex interplay of social and political forces that is largely and inherently unpredictable. But let us set aside the epistemological issue of how much accuracy in forecasting it would have been reasonable to expect, accept the scoring of the episode as an intelligence failure, and consider the relationship between prediction (or its absence) and policy. The principal policy players certainly believed they were inadequately forewarned—by the intelligence community, the U.S. embassy in Tehran, or anyone else— about the disturbing events in Iran.[40]

Unlike the South Asian nuclear tests, the Iranian revolution is on the scorecards not just because it is easily scored. The consequences of this revolution for U.S. foreign policy have been large and long lasting. Unlike policy departures clearly driven by ideologies that predate the policymakers' terms in office (such as the Iraq War or Reagan's posture toward the Soviet Union), events in Iran forced themselves onto the policy agenda. And given the broad and deep U.S. relationship with the shah's regime, it seems reasonable to think that the United States had levers to pull that might have changed the course of events. For all these reasons, Iran is a good test case; if a lack of prediction has harmful effects on U.S. policymaking and U.S. interests, it should have had them here.

The first discovery one makes from a closer look at the Iran crisis is that ideologies and strategies predating the Carter administration actually did play a major role in shaping U.S. policy. Nixon and Kissinger had firmly set the policy course several years earlier: the United States would rely on the shah to protect U.S. interests in the Persian Gulf region, and the shah would rely on the United States for advanced technology and other assistance as he accelerated his attempt to transform Iran economically and militarily. The mutual dependence and the difficulty either side would have had in extracting itself from it grew through the 1970s. Neither government had a plan B. Gary Sick, who managed Iranian affairs for Jimmy Carter's NSC, observes that the policy of placing U.S. interests in the gulf "almost exclusively" in the hands of the shah came to be "fully absorbed by the bureaucracy and the U.S. power structure."[41] Carter himself said of the shah, "There was no question in my mind that he deserved our unequivocal support."[42] By the time Carter became president, Sick says, U.S. security policy in the gulf region "was in many respects hostage to the social and economic experiment that the shah was conducting in Iran. Whether one liked it or not, Iran was the regional tail wagging the superpower dog."[43]

This meant that anyone in the U.S. government who questioned the shah's staying power would have to face the further question, to which there was no satisfactory answer, of how U.S. interests could be preserved if the shah fell.[44] The situation closely paralleled U.S. perspectives toward Vietnam in the 1960s, where there was a similar burden of previously incurred commitments and a lack of perceived alternatives to them. In-house devil's advocate George Ball (and others) correctly identified the most important problems in the existing policy course regarding Vietnam, but because Ball did not also offer attractive solutions, his questioning did not divert the policy. In the Iran case, this problem tended to discourage even the questioning. "There is no doubt," says Sick, "that the immense responsibility of proclaiming a generation of U.S. policy bankrupt weighed heavily in the minds of those observing the ominous unfolding of events in Iran."[45]

Those nervously watching the drama that began to unfold in Iranian streets in early 1978 were also nervous about how any such pronouncement might be self-fulfilling. Secretary of State Cyrus Vance hesitated recommending that the ambassador, William Sullivan, contact opposition leaders because that might further weaken the shah's confidence. Even after Sullivan submitted a "thinking the unthinkable" cable in November, Vance recalled, "There was a brooding fear that any action that implied we did not expect the shah to survive would contribute to his paralysis of will and stimulate the opposition to increased violence."[46] Anticipation of ill effects of a U.S. response thus shaped assessments of the situation, and the same anticipation discouraged a response even if policymakers held a correct assessment.

Go back in time to before the action in Iranian streets forced itself onto the policymakers' plate as a crisis—back to when any prediction, if it ever had any chance of helping to prevent a crisis, would have done so—and Iran represented not a U.S foreign-policy decision, but instead a nondecision. Policy toward Iran was representative of most of U.S. foreign policy, which at any given moment consists more of continuity than of new departures. Underlying and guiding such a continuing policy are not so much images of a situation overseas but rather inertia and the absence of images—and in cases such as Vietnam in the 1960s and Iran in the 1970s a sense that there are no good alternatives to the current course anyway. If such a policy turns out to be misguided, it is less a matter of faulty images and more a matter of limited time and attention to make new policy. Turning a nondecision into a decision means overcoming those limits and the inertia. As noted earlier, predictions or warnings are far less able to do that than actual, disturbing events.

The senior policymakers in Jimmy Carter's administration did not have the time and attention to make Iran an issue before events forced the issue upon them. Even *after* events in Iran forced the issue on them in 1978, they still lacked time and attention. They were immersed in negotiations on an

Egyptian–Israeli peace treaty and devoting major attention to accelerated strategic arms negotiations with the Soviets, secret talks with China aimed at normalizing relations, and a crisis in Nicaragua. "Our decision-making circuits were heavily overloaded," recalls Brzezinski. "Preoccupied on a daily basis with other major issues, deeply involved particularly in the Camp David process, we simply did not have time to reflect more deeply and from a longer-range perspective on the broader strategic and geopolitical ramifications of the Iranian crisis."[47] Because of these other priorities and distractions, by the end of October 1978—after months of disturbances in Iranian cities—the administration still had not convened any high-level policy meeting on Iran.[48]

An even more fundamental impediment to taking on the Iran issue any earlier or more fully than the Carter administration did was a lack of agreement within the administration over what the U.S. objectives should be if the shah's hold on power weakened, let alone the best way to achieve whatever objectives were chosen. Brzezinski defined the issues in the internal debate as: "(1) What was the nature of our central interest in Iran, and thus what was truly at stake and must be protected as our first priority? And (2) how to maintain (and encourage from outside) political stability in a traditional but rapidly modernizing state."[49] The first question involved values and principles and was impervious to any guidance from policy-neutral analysis or prediction. The second question always has been a puzzle for students of political change and continues to be one in discussions of policy toward other Middle Eastern autocracies.

On one side of the policy conflict over Iran were Brzezinski and Secretary of Defense Harold Brown, who came to favor a military coup as a way to keep the shah on his throne with reduced powers. On the other side were Vance, others in the State Department, and Vice President Walter Mondale, who disparaged the shah as an autocrat and believed that U.S. interests lay in promoting the democratization of Iran. President Carter, as Brzezinski notes, "was thus clearly pulled in opposite directions by his advisers and perhaps even by a conflict between his reason and his emotions."[50]

The images and predictions that the policymakers threw at each other as the crisis intensified were entwined with their competing values and principles. Vance strongly opposed a military coup, for example, not only because he believed the Iranian army could not pull it off, but also because, he later wrote, "support for the iron fist would be antithetical to what I be-

lieved the Carter administration stood for."[51] The disagreements were un-
resolvable, which made the resulting policy appear incoherent. They remain
unresolved today. Differences over democratization were fundamentally
differences over values and ideology, not analysis. Even the analytical differences involved uncertain conjectures about contingencies. Brzezinski
admits to "inner agony" over his realization that a coup might have failed
and thus have led to a civil war that would benefit the Soviets.[52] No policy-
neutral prediction of the sort the intelligence community might have provided, either before or during the crisis, would have enabled the policymakers to overcome these disabling disagreements.

The disagreements generated rancor and distrust and thus more disarray
and dysfunction. Carter and Brzezinski believed the State Department was
insubordinate; at one point, the president summoned the State Department
desk officers to the White House and dressed them down for allegedly not
faithfully executing his orders.[53] Relations between the White House and
Ambassador Sullivan became especially strained. Carter wanted to fire Sullivan. Vance dissuaded him from doing so, but Carter came to rely less on
the ambassador's reports than on those of a special military envoy, General
Robert Huyser, whose perceptions often contradicted Sullivan's.[54] The connection to the military envoy was one of several confusing channels of communication that developed in response to the policymakers' inability to
trust each other. Brzezinski opened up his own channel to the Iranian ambassador in Washington without the State Department's knowledge. When
Vance indirectly got wind of it, he confronted Brzezinski and complained to
the president.[55]

The cauldron of dispute and acrimony that was the Carter administration's policymaking machinery on Iran constituted another very large impediment to making use of any warning that the intelligence community
might have provided about instability in Iran. If the drains on attention
from other issues and the absence of any apparent alternatives to continuing to support the shah were not sufficient to deter the policymakers from
giving concentrated and early attention to Iran, then the prospect of a bruising internal battle over defining objectives and finding alternatives would
have been. Prospective decision-making costs are a major reason many
nondecisions are not replaced by decisions, including on issues where the
costs would not be as high as they were in this case. After events forced the
Carter administration to focus on Iran, the policy battle was not only

bruising but ultimately inconclusive and ineffective. It is very unlikely that even a strongly worded and sharply defined warning about coming upheaval in Iran would have induced the policymakers to wage that battle any earlier than they had to. Yet nonprediction of the Iranian revolution is on scorecards of intelligence performance for the same reasons that other entries are on the cards: it can be scored, and it sustains an American ideology (including the mythology about U.S. intelligence) that offers a reassuring explanation of American success and failure in the world. It is not on the cards because it actually made the difference between success and failure in the Iranian case.[56]

CAUTIOUS WARNINGS AND HESITANT RESPONSES

Most warnings from intelligence—at least most responsibly rendered warnings—are not strongly worded and sharply defined. One reason for these qualities is the previously noted paradox of self-defeating prediction. If a prediction were important to policy decisions and the outcome of policy, that means actions taken by policymakers would cause events to unfold differently than they otherwise would have. So which version of events would be getting predicted? If one believed, like Brzezinski, that different U.S. actions might have saved the shah (or at least the Pahlavi dynasty, given the shah's hidden but eventually fatal illness), then a clarion warning that "the shah will fall" would have been a bad prediction.

Another reason is that any question that is difficult enough for a government to turn to its intelligence service has enough uncertainty for the proper answer to be tentative and laden with caveats. Intelligence services can err not only by failing to warn, but also by warning with unfounded certainty. The latter error was involved in the most validly criticized aspects of the intelligence community's work on Iraqi weapons programs. Appropriately tentative warnings have even less chance of breaking through policy inertia and forcing policymakers to take fresh decisions than do strongly worded and sharply defined ones.

The common equating of intelligence input with policy output is just as fallacious with regard to warnings and predictions as it is with regard to other types of intelligence input. Warning is a function not solely of intelligence, but also of policymaking. It includes determining which, if any, responses to take in the face of typically fragmentary and ambiguous information.[57]

Policymakers frequently hesitate to act on predictions and often do not act on them at all. To point out this inaction is not a knock on policymakers. They *should* hesitate to act. However much confidence they may have in the accuracy of the prediction, and however accurate the prediction really is, they need to consider the costs, complications, and likely effectiveness of actions available to them. In many cases, they may decide (as with the Chinese ASAT test) that no action is the best response, regardless of the importance of the subject at hand.

Moreover, the prediction may be wrong, and the policymaker has to take account of that possibility. A good physician may delay treatment until seeing clearer symptoms of the diagnosed disease because the diagnosis may be wrong and the treatment has serious side effects. A good statesman may delay acting preemptively on even a prediction of an impending attack because the prediction may be wrong and the preemptive action has serious costs and consequences, including perhaps starting the very sort of war he would like to avoid.

The 1968 Tet Offensive in Vietnam illustrates another repeatedly demonstrated limitation of prediction: warning fatigue. Whether officials are spurred to action depends not just on the accuracy of any one prediction, but on how that prediction stands out from all the other warnings, forecasts, suggestions, and expressions of concern they have heard. The CIA station had alerted U.S. installations in Vietnam to the coming offensive (as reflected in one especially prescient memo from the station that Lyndon Johnson and Walt Rostow would later cite in arguing that the offensive had not surprised them).[58] The military command later added its own warnings, but by early 1968 such alerts had begun to seem routine. Responding to them entailed costs and effort. Journalist Don Oberdorfer described the attitude in the U.S. installations this way: "The inertial force of habit and of bureaucracy overpowered the evidence at hand. Belief in a tremendous attack would have required tremendous counterefforts. Personal plans would have to be altered; holidays and furloughs canceled; daily habits of comfort and convenience in previously safe cities abandoned."[59] The difficulty of any one prediction standing out in a crowd of competing stimuli as well as the cost and effort required to respond to the prediction may discourage not only responses to the prediction, but even any awareness of it. The then deputy chief of mission of the U.S. embassy in Saigon told me many years later that regardless of what alerts the record shows were issued prior to the Tet Offensive, he did not recall being warned.

CONSEQUENCES

America's customary treatment of intelligence as a spectator sport, with "accurate" prediction being the principal standard by which the game is scored, has several unfortunate consequences. One is that the perceived performance of U.S. intelligence is further distorted. Correct predictions necessarily are limited to the number of predictions the intelligence community ventures; failures to predict are potentially unlimited. Any happening on the globe can become labeled, depending on how the U.S. public and its leaders subsequently come to define their interests, as an unpredicted event. Intelligence cannot follow everything, but anything can become an intelligence failure. Contestants in this sport are doomed to have a losing score.

Another consequence is to distort the perceived mission of intelligence. Most of what intelligence does and most of how it supports the national interest does not involve prediction. It includes the collection, interpretation, processing, and analysis of information. It includes the pointing out of possibilities without identifying them as certainties or even as probabilities. These and other functions of intelligence support specific endeavors ranging from the breaking up of terrorist cells to the delivery of diplomatic demarches. They do not involve trying to eliminate uncertainty with prediction. Instead, intelligence is a tool for helping policymakers to manage inevitable uncertainty. Failure to understand this distinction means an inability to assess properly the contributions by intelligence. It means inadequate attention to shortcomings of intelligence that do not involve prediction. And it may lead to misguided "reform" of intelligence that hinders rather than helps the performance of its mission.

The most important consequence of the spectator-sport approach to evaluating intelligence is that it moves the spectators ever farther from what ultimately is important to their nation, which is to facilitate more successful U.S. foreign policy. Narrow focus on the sport means inadequate focus on other ingredients of foreign policy, including other sources of images about the world abroad. It means less awareness of how often the world throws inscrutable or unsolvable problems at the United States. And it means inadequate attention to preparing for such problems because of an unrealistic expectation that if only the intelligence sport were played better, all the problems could be figured out and solved.

CHAPTER EIGHT

THE NEVER-ENDING ISSUE

The theme of intelligence failure and reform has persisted through the seven decades since Pearl Harbor and never seems close to going away. Commissions created to examine Iraqi weapons programs and 9/11 are only among the most recent in a long line of official inquiries into intelligence. Official studies on intelligence have become so numerous that official studies on the studies have been written just to keep track of them all.[1] Some of the inquiries made enough of a splash that their names have lingered in memory, such as the Church and Pike committees of the 1970s. Many others seem more obscure today, such as the Dulles–Jackson–Correa report, the Doolittle report, the Bruce–Lovett report, the Murphy Commission, the Taylor Commission, the Kirkpatrick report, the Ogilvie report, the Schlesinger report, the Rockefeller Commission, the Aspin–Brown Commission, or the Scowcroft review. Since 1947, commissions, congressional committees, and elder statesmen acting as consultants have submitted, by one scholar's reckoning, between fifteen and twenty sets of official proposals (depending on how important a proposal has to be to count) for changes in U.S. intelligence.[2] And beyond the official discourse is a huge—and just as old and unending—flow of unofficial commentary on the subject. The editors of one recent compendium of essays on improving intelligence analysis conclude that "fixing analysis seems a perennial and elusive goal."[3] The same might be said about collection and other parts of the intelligence business.

This history raises a question: Given that there has been so much attention for so long on fixing intelligence, why does it never seem to get fixed? Or to phrase the question in its most objective and inclusive form: Why is intelligence failure such a perennial issue? Anyone who wants to add still more commentary and still more proposals for fixing intelligence to what already is straining our shelves and overflowing our in-boxes needs to address that question first. Otherwise, we would be entitled to dismiss the latest demand on our attention as probably a reinvention of wheels already invented several times over, an exploring of dead ends that experience has demonstrated to be dead, or a quixotic attempt to solve unsolvable problems. Or it may all be part of a largely misdirected exercise that misses most of the reasons that inaccurate images form in policymakers' minds and that misguided foreign policies continue to get made.

IDEAS NEW AND OLD

Several possible reasons, not all mutually exclusive, might explain why intelligence failure has been an unending issue.

One of the most popular is that we simply have not yet hit on the right formula for making intelligence work well. The popularity of this explanation is unsurprising. The main selling point of any book or article on the subject is that the author supposedly has better ideas than all who came before. There is no reason to assume, however, that the latest pundits (or commissions or anyone else who holds forth on the topic) are any more insightful or creative than their predecessors. The sheer amount of time the subject has been in play and the large number of proposals and ideas propounded make it unlikely there are undiscovered nuggets of organizational or procedural wisdom that, once found and implemented, would enable Americans finally to stop stewing over the performance of their intelligence agencies.

Abundant ideas for change in the U.S. intelligence community have been not only advanced but also implemented. The community's history is one of continual experimentation and flux. Almost any significant idea about better ways of conducting the intelligence business has been not only hashed over as a subject of critical commentary but also tested in practice.

Take, for example, the favorite staple of reform: reorganization. Organizational charts have been frequently and sometimes sweepingly redrawn at all levels of the community. Whole agencies get created, as with the establishment of the Defense Intelligence Agency in 1961 and the National Geospatial-Intelligence Agency, originally under a different name, in 1996. Reorganizations within agencies are even more frequent and can be just as extensive. When I was a national intelligence officer and had frequent dealings with different parts of the Defense Intelligence Agency, I gave up ever having an up-to-date telephone directory of the agency because any directory that came to my desk had already been superseded by another reorganization. The CIA also has had a long history of molding, merging, mixing, and nixing its directorates, offices, divisions, and staffs. A particularly extensive reorganization, for example, took place in 1981 in which the CIA's Directorate of Intelligence, which performs analysis, was reconstructed beyond recognition when it changed from a functional to primarily a regional organization.

Some of the reorganizations have been bold experiments that have broken bureaucratic crockery to test better ways of doing business. One of the most successful of these experiments was the CIA's creation of the CTC in 1986, which brought together operators, analysts, trainers, technicians, and other specialists to work literally side by side toward the common mission of combating international terrorism. The establishment of the CTC was a bureaucratic revolution that flew in the face of previous practices of compartmenting information more according to occupation than to subject matter. The CTC became a model for similar centers that were established to work on topics such as narcotics and the proliferation of unconventional weapons. It also inspired a more general breaking down of barriers between the CIA's operational and analytical directorates, in which offices were co-located to enhance the flow of information across what previously had been largely impenetrable bureaucratic lines. The CTC itself evolved in subsequent years into a multiagency center with increasing numbers of non-CIA staff. As a reflection of this evolution, its formal name became the "DCI Counterterrorist Center"—referring to the since-divided DCI position, which led not only the CIA but the entire intelligence community.

Other reorganizations within the intelligence community have been less evidently effective; some have undone previous reorganizations. But even the less successful experiments have been experiments nonetheless and constitute more testing of ideas for reform. The FBI's repeated reorganizations of its counterterrorist apparatus are an example. The FBI traditionally lumped counterterrorism with counterintelligence in a single division for national security matters. As counterterrorism became a more prominent task in the 1990s, the bureau gave the subject its own division. The FBI partially undid this change in 2005, when it brought its divisions for counterterrorism, counterintelligence, and intelligence under a single umbrella, the National Security Service.[4] Two years later it announced further organizational changes, which it billed as "the most comprehensive" realignment of its counterterrorism division in the past six years.[5] Which change in this serial reshuffling represents the best way for the FBI to organize its counterterrorist effort? There is no clear answer. Different chapters in this story have reflected emphasis on different worthwhile objectives, including giving a subject its own office to enhance its priority and visibility as well as merging offices to enhance communication and cooperation across different parts of a bureaucracy. The FBI case is typical of countless issues in intelligence reform: an ideal is never achieved not because of a lack of good ideas, but because many good ideas inherently conflict with each other.

Another popular explanation for why intelligence failure is a perennial issue is that good ideas for reforming intelligence have existed for a long time but have not been adopted because of bureaucratic resistance or inertia or because the political stars never were aligned right. Some evidence supports this explanation. Officials sometimes do tend to be quick to see the downside of ideas that others advance for changing their organization. When Senator Pat Roberts (R–Kans.), then chairman of the Senate Select Committee on Intelligence, proposed in August 2004 an extensive reorganization of the intelligence community that, among other things, would have wiped the initials "CIA" off the government's organization chart, he was swiftly shouted down before his idea could get serious scrutiny. Some of that reaction was due to the 9/11 Commission's already having seized control of the playing field with its own reorganization scheme. But some of it was a reflexive reaction from intelligence officers and former officers. Former DCI George Tenet, who was out of office but whose views reflected those of many veteran CIA officers, stated that Roberts's plan was a step toward driving "the security of the American people off a cliff" and "would result in the demoralization of a proud and extremely capable agency." Other intelligence officials were quoted anonymously as calling the proposal "reckless" and charging that it would cause "irreparable damage to U.S. national security."[6]

The concept of political stars needing to be aligned properly also has some validity. The idea of splitting the DCI's job into a DNI and a separate CIA director, which was a major feature of the 9/11 Commission's plan, had been floating around for years. It took a special set of circumstances—the national horror over 9/11, a presidential election campaign, and an aggressive and politically adept commission that skillfully exploited both—to see the enactment of this idea finally into legislation.

This explanation is largely unsatisfactory, however, for the same reason the first explanation fails: the long record of extensive reforms that the intelligence community itself has implemented. Notwithstanding occasional hasty rejections such as the reactions to Senator Roberts's plan, the overall bias within the community has been in favor of change, even to the point of disruption, rather than against it. This bias should not be surprising. Ambitious managers in the intelligence community, like ambitious managers anywhere, make names for themselves by instigating and championing change rather than sitting on the status quo. Officials do not rise rapidly by saying, "I'll take the well-run organization that my predecessors have handed to me and try to manage it as skillfully as possible." They bring attention to themselves and rise to higher office by highlighting shortcomings, promulgating ten-point (or fifteen-point or x-point) "strategic plans" for changing the way the organization conducts its business and generally appearing to shake things up. One of the best-known rapid risers in the intelligence community, former wunderkind Robert Gates, liked to boast of being an "agent of change" and acted accordingly when an official at the CIA. He later applied that label to himself when being interviewed for a university presidency at Texas A&M—which he got.[7] President George W. Bush referred to the same "agent of change" label when he nominated Gates in 2006 to be secretary of defense, stating that his nominee had implemented "wide-ranging reforms" in his university job and would bring the same "transformational spirit" to the Pentagon.[8] Intelligence community managers hoping to emulate Gates's career will take notice.

When intelligence officers do point out the downside of someone else's proposal for changing their business, why should one assume that this criticism is always an instance of bureaucratic resistance to reform? Sometimes it is, but it may sometimes instead be knowledgeable people's assessment of real flaws in a proposal. Yet the cliché that government bureaucracies are inveterate opponents of change is so prevalent that any objection by incumbent (or even former) officials tends to be dismissed as primitive and lamentable resistance to change. A corollary of this tendency is the attitude that most (or even all) good ideas for reform come from outside the intelligence community and that most (or even all) outside ideas for reform are good. Proposals from commissions, committees, and study groups are assumed to represent improvement, whereas changes initiated by the intelligence community itself are not given comparable weight as true reform.[9]

Fresh ideas can help in any business, of course, although most ideas about intelligence have long since ceased to be fresh. Those who know a business best (and are at least as committed as anyone else to making it better) by virtue of having worked on the inside are at least as able as anyone else to discern, once presented with an idea, whether it would make the business perform better or perform worse. This is true in the private sector; a chief executive hires management consultants to offer fresh ideas on how to improve his or her business but does not blindly adopt whatever the consultant recommends. Instead, the executive implements what he or she is convinced are ideas worth trying and rejects the other ideas. The same principle should apply to at least the same degree to the relatively arcane business of intelligence.

CHALLENGES NEW AND OLD

A third popular explanation for why the issue of intelligence failure and intelligence reform never goes away is that the subjects that intelligence is charged with following have changed. Or, more succinctly, the world has changed. Regardless of how well the intelligence community may have followed issues of the past, the argument goes, further changes are required to follow the different issues of the present and future. Intelligence failures occur, according to this explanation, because the intelligence community has not adapted itself rapidly enough to address new and different threats to national security. The most common rhetorical expression of this view is that the intelligence community "must get away from a Cold War way of doing business."

Of course the subjects that intelligence must follow have changed, at least in relative importance. It is true, for example—to cite one of the

common themes in commentary about a changed post–Cold War world—
that nonstate actors have more influence on world events today than they
did two or three decades ago.[10] The intelligence community's list of subjects also changes for reasons that have less to do with what is going on in
the outside world than with changes in the American people's fears and
mood, in their political leaders' priorities, and especially in the leaders
themselves after elections. All these reasons for the intelligence community to alter its own priorities are legitimate. The community is responsible
for telling leaders about both threats they are not worrying about and subjects they already are keenly interested in. The community has experi-
mented with a variety of systems through the years aimed at keeping its
priorities for collection and analysis aligned with these missions.[11]

The theme of inadequate adaptation to changing issues as a reason for
intelligence failure is overstated, however, for two reasons.

The first reason is that the new challenges to national security are not
nearly as new as commonly portrayed. Americans—not uniquely, but more
than most others—expect new things, are fascinated by them, and welcome
many of them. Americans, whose own country's birth marked a break with a
European past, are quick to perceive things as new and different but slow to
recognize patterns rooted in history. Most Americans have scant historical
knowledge, anyway. Newness is a leitmotif of American life, as Madison
Avenue has determined in using "new" as one of the most attractive adjec-
tives it can use to tout a product. Beyond everyday consumerism, newness
becomes a defining characteristic of the bad as well as the good. Television
networks and other mass media continually have to produce "news." The
more that something can be portrayed as shockingly novel rather than an
old familiar problem, the more likely we are to tune in.[12]

The bias toward exaggeration of newness extends beyond the masses to
the intelligentsia and chattering classes. Commentaries and thus the commentators who write them get noticed insofar as they are perceived as conveying new thoughts about new issues, new threats, and new strategies needed
to meet them. Observations about what has *not* changed are less likely to
sell. The theme of newness in international affairs and of how the United
States and its intelligence community must adapt to the new has been repeated so many times that it now sounds very old.

This bias leads to an oversimplified image of the past. Another common
theme about the post–Cold War world is that it is more complicated than
what came before. There is some basis for this theme, particularly as it re-

lates to the increased role of nonstate actors. But the theme usually gets pushed farther than that, to include a simplistic view of the Cold War as an era in which, although the USSR was strong and scary, at least the lines of confrontation were clearly drawn and the United States had only one enemy to worry about. In fact, however, the Communist threat was far more complex and multifaceted than that.[13] This complexity and sometimes a failure to appreciate it fully were involved in some of the most difficult U.S. foreign-policy issues during the Cold War, most notably Vietnam.

International terrorism is one of the issues that apostles of newness most often mention. But it is not new, even in the particular forms that are most worrisome today. Martha Crenshaw, one of the very few American scholars whose study of terrorism stretches back over decades, assesses that "the departure from the past is not as pronounced as many accounts make it out to be. Today's terrorism is not a fundamentally or qualitatively 'new' phenomenon but grounded in an evolving historical context."[14] Even the seemingly newer specter of nuclear terrorism, with its associated issues of rogue regimes and lack of return addresses, received concern and attention during the first half of the Cold War. The CIA was issuing assessments as early as 1950 about the danger of a nuclear device being smuggled into the United States.[15]

Terrorism illustrates how several factors can contribute to the misperception that such a threat is new. Inadequate knowledge of history is one such factor. It inhibits awareness not only of the centuries-old use of terrorism, but also of more recent but pre-9/11 ways it has affected U.S. interests. Americans have remarkably little awareness today, for example, of how much international terrorism—more specifically, Middle Eastern Islamist terrorism in the form of several spectacular attacks by Lebanese Hizballah—seized U.S. attention in the 1980s. Many erroneously believe that America's encounter with the phenomenon started in September 2001.

Look back one more decade to see another factor shaping public perceptions of terrorism. The mid-1970s exhibited what would be regarded today as an alarmingly unrelenting wave of terrorist attacks within the United States, even though the casualties did not approach those of a 9/11. The protagonists included radical leftists, Puerto Rican nationalists, black militants, Croatians, Chileans, and others. The attacks included bombings of Grand Central Station, LaGuardia Airport, and Fraunces Tavern in New York; a car bombing in the streets of Washington and another bomb in the U.S. Capitol; as well as a hijacked airliner and assorted kidnappings, assassinations, and other mayhem from California to New York. But terrorism did not rise to the top of the national agenda. There was little support for giving additional terrorism-fighting authorities to the likes of the FBI or CIA because the greater public concern at the time was with curbing excesses by those same agencies.[16] Hardly anyone today remembers the events of that period or the mood that governed the response to them.

Even the particular targets and objectives of the 9/11 attack were not new. Islamist terrorists had attacked the World Trade Center on February 26, 1993, with the goal of toppling the twin towers and killing thousands or even tens or hundreds of thousands. They killed only six, but if their technique had been more effective, the United States would have had its 9/11 (or 2/26) more than eight years earlier. The difference in the impact of the two attacks came down to technical issues such as the effects of burning jet fuel on steel girders.

The national trauma of the nearly three thousand deaths from the eventual 9/11 attack led to two more reasons that the underlying threat has been misperceived as new. One involves public psychology. Americans want to believe that their government will protect them from any known danger. The least discomforting interpretation of the horrible event of September 2001 is that it must have come from a threat that was so new and so different that no one, the government included, had been fully aware of it. The other reason involves the mustering of public support for new policies—which in the case of the Bush administration then in office involved vast expansions of executive authority and much else under the rubric of the "war on terror." Unprecedented governmental powers and initiatives are easier to sell and to accept if they are presented and viewed as responses to an unprecedented threat.[17]

We tend to think of the latest changes in anything—including international affairs—as more significant than earlier changes. We are more conscious of recent events than of developments in the past. We are more excited to talk and write about things happening now, especially if we perceive them as new and different, than to brood over old problems. But many of the most significant and vexing problems are in fact old.

Our immersion in current rhetoric about new challenges makes us unaware that the rhetoric itself is not new. Consider some observations from a former official in Lyndon Johnson's administration, Townsend Hoopes, in a well-received book published in 1969.[18] Hoopes attributed misguided decision making on the Vietnam War to the decision makers' being trapped inside a Cold War frame of reference and failing to recognize important changes in the world. "By 1965," Hoopes wrote, "many of the major elements of the Cold War mosaic had undergone drastic transformation or had ceased to exist." He cited a lessened threat of military attack in Europe, the loosening of Soviet control over eastern Europe, increased schisms within the Communist world, the decreased role of ideology in East–West relations, and other trends. But the men closest to President Johnson did not appreciate these changes because "the tenets of the Cold War were bred in their bone." Hoopes was writing at the midpoint of the Cold War, but most of his words might have come straight out of the "get beyond the Cold War" commentary written today.

Or consider two American academics' somewhat later observations about how the U.S. government needs to be organized to conduct foreign policy effectively.[19] Their book was published in 1976, when the Cold War still had a decade and a half to run. "Times have changed," the authors declared, and their major theme was the need to "remake" the procedures and especially the organizations for making foreign policy in order to adapt them to new issues and challenges. They referred especially to greater economic and physical interdependence among nations (the term *globalization* was not yet in vogue, but that's what they were talking about). They also wrote about the dispersion of power, which was no longer held just by two superpowers, but also by a variety of other states that were important because of ambition, technical accomplishment, or natural resources.

Move forward to 1989—with the Cold War nearing its end but not quite over. A book by a couple of other academics focusing on the organization and procedures of the intelligence community struck similar notes about the need to adapt to changing issues and needs. They observed that "the intelligence community must analyze more information on a greater range of subjects today than ever before." The community had to cover not only more states, but also important international organizations and groups. "Religious movements can turn back the clock on modernizing societies," they noted. "International terrorist movements threaten people and commerce throughout the world."[20] Besides more targets and more issues, the community also had more customers, such as ones charged with combating narcotics trafficking.

One conclusion from this glance at commentary of the past—besides the fact that the similar commentary of the present is hardly original—is that many of the issues and trends portrayed as new not only have been around for decades but also have been recognized for decades. Another conclusion is that the "need to adapt to a changed world" theme is so prevalent in commentary about intelligence probably less because of the nature or newness of the world than because of the appealing nature of the theme. It is popular because it sounds foresighted, perceptive, and progressive. And that is why writers have used it for so long, during the Cold War as well as after it.

The second reason that inadequate adaptation to changing issues is overstated and does not explain why intelligence failure is such a persistent subject is that the intelligence community in fact has been addressing the "new" issues and adapting to them for a long time. When I started work at the CIA as a junior analyst in 1977—while the Cold War was still going strong—I joined a component that was producing assessments on subjects that today would be considered a potpourri of post–Cold War issues. My own initial projects addressed the global trade in conventional arms and less-developed countries' perspectives regarding regional security. Some of my colleagues were studying international terrorism, despite the scant public attention to the subject at that time in the United States and despite the scarcity of American experts on the topic outside government. Other analysts were scrutinizing the proliferation of nuclear weapons. They were looking most closely at South Asia and especially Pakistan, where the previous year the nuclear entrepreneur A. Q. Khan had returned from the Netherlands with the stolen technology that would make him rich and infamous. Others analyzed the politics of oil markets. Still other colleagues were analyzing ethnic separatism, with a particular focus on Kurdish nationalism. The papers they wrote, if dug out of whatever dusty file in which they now lie, would provide valuable insights on the ethnic conflict that has been part of the instability afflicting Iraq since 2003.

None of this squares with the widespread and mistaken perception that during the Cold War the CIA and the rest of the U.S. intelligence community focused their attention almost exclusively on the Soviet Union. The analytic efforts of the division in which I worked in the 1970s were admittedly modest in scale, but much other work on related topics was going on elsewhere in the agency and the community. The CIA was never close to being all about the USSR all the time. Of the five multidisciplinary regional offices created in the agency's analytic directorate in 1981, for example, the Soviet Union was the focus of only one.

As external realities and policy priorities have evolved, and as small issues have grown into not so small ones, the intelligence community has shifted its own priorities and adapted by searching for better ways to accomplish changing missions. Much of the story of adaptation and response unfolded during the Cold War, even though most of the issues were non–Cold War issues. The creation of the CTC in 1986 and its subsequent evolution into a multiagency component is probably the outstanding example. It is still the single most important and effective organizational innovation in counterterrorist intelligence, notwithstanding the heavy publicity given to reorganization following 9/11. But because the intelligence community itself initiated this adaptation more than two decades ago while the Cold War was still in progress and because this fact is inconsistent with the popular story line of the need to adapt to post–Cold War change and of bureaucratic resistance to adaptation, this adaptation is seldom remembered or mentioned.[21]

Even if one accepts the notion of changed issues and the need to adapt to them, the rhetoric on this theme rarely gets specific in any way that would be useful in explaining intelligence failures or prescribing ways to reduce them. *Exactly how* should the intelligence community change to be more adept at covering new issues rather than old ones? *What specifically* about current intelligence activities is oriented toward old issues, and *how* is it so oriented? *What* alternative arrangements would be better suited to handling new issues, and *how* and *why* would they be better suited? The absence of satisfactory or even unsatisfactory answers to these questions forms a stark contrast to the ubiquity of the general rhetoric. Exhortations about getting beyond a Cold War way of doing business seldom explain what that would mean in practice, particularly with regard to such favorite reform topics as reorganization. How exactly is a particular organization chart any less Cold War–like than a different chart? That question is not posed, much less answered. Getting beyond the Cold War is a slogan, not a strategy.

HUMANS ARE FALLIBLE

Another possible explanation for why the problem of intelligence failure never seems to go away is that intelligence officers keep making avoidable mistakes. The focus is not on institutional shortcomings, but rather on individuals screwing up. This theme appeals to the popular urge for accountability and for heads to roll after disasters and thus is frequently at least a subtext for public discussion of intelligence failures. It does not get used explicitly in commentary about intelligence reform as often as the first three explanations because it is not as compatible with them as the first three are with each other. Attributing failures to avoidable individual errors makes them less attributable to institutional defects and thus might weaken a case for reforming the institutions (although there always seem to be critics of intelligence who are calling simultaneously for heads to roll and for organizations to be overhauled).

Of course intelligence officers, like all government officials and all human beings, sometimes make mistakes. In this trivial sense, the explanation obviously is valid. But a couple of other questions need to be answered if this perspective is to have value in explaining the persistent national preoccupation with intelligence failure. One question concerns standards for success and failure. At what point does a mistake go beyond everyday fallibility and the normal limitations of human beings and become a "failure" worthy of public consternation? In practice, what separates unnoticed everyday errors from spotlighted failures is not the quality of individual performances on the job, but the salience of the events with which they happen to be associated. Errors linked to prominent events such as wars or terrorist incidents may constitute no more serious a deficiency in job performance than countless other errors that go unnoticed because they luckily are not linked to untoward events or because the consequences of those events are of a kind that do not draw public concern and attention.

Even if it can be established that errors associated with well-publicized intelligence failures constitute more egregiously deficient job performance than all the errors that go unnoticed, there would remain another question: If human error is the problem, why should different humans keep making major mistakes in this one line of work? Recall that the pattern to be explained is a decades-long preoccupation with intelligence failure. So there is not just one batch of mistake-prone officers to blame. Why have several generations of intelligence officers supposedly kept screwing up?

The difficulty in answering this question leads some to adopt a variation on the human-error explanation, which is that there is something inherently flawed about the intelligence profession and those who enter it. This variation has the attraction of mitigating some of the tension with the other popular explanations and with arguments in favor of intelligence reform. If the intelligence community as currently constituted does not attract and retain capable people, then one can both blame the incapable people *and* agitate for reconstituting the institutions that employ them.

One version of this variation that usually is not voiced in polite company is that the intelligence profession—which inherently involves deceit—is ignoble and that the profession either attracts ignoble people or corrupts people once they join it. This is more of an attitude or even a prejudice than an explanation. The version that is more often voiced explicitly in the context of intelligence failure is that government service as a whole, the intelligence community included, does not offer lucrative and rewarding careers for the brightest people who might otherwise consider such service. A clear statement of this variant came from Herbert E. Meyer, whom DCI William Casey hired in 1981 as one of his ideologically like-minded aides to ride herd on the CIA. Meyer—who at the time Casey hired him was a thirty-five-year-old associate editor at *Fortune*—commented, "The rewards of professional life in the outside world are greater, so if government only gets second or third rate people, who in turn employ third or fourth rate people, you end up with a system that can't cope with the realities of a rap-idly changing world."[22] Meyer perhaps had a personal reason to think that those who are not capable enough to succeed in the private sector might look to government service. His biggest professional effort before Casey hired him was to write a book (which criticized the limits-of-growth school of economics of the 1970s) that thirty-six publishers rejected before Meyer published it himself.[23]

The limited material rewards of government service have long been a staple of discussion about public administration. Salaries for federal employees have indeed lagged behind what many of the more capable people consider-ing public service might earn in the private sector. The intelligence com-munity faces some additional challenges in attracting and keeping talented people in the form of long waiting times to obtain security clearances and the efforts by corporate employers who value such clearances to lure people out of the community.[24]

Even with regard to monetary incentives and alternative employment possibilities, however, the picture is more complicated. Some argue that if entire compensation packages are considered, then federal employees do not really lag far behind private-sector counterparts and that their job satis-faction is suggested by much lower rates of voluntary resignation than those found in the private sector.[25] Moreover, the extent to which skills associated with public service have private-sector counterparts varies greatly. Military veterans sometimes discover this to their chagrin; the best tank gunner in the U.S. Army probably will have trouble locating a niche for his skills when he leaves the service. Among intelligence occupations, transferability to a well-paying private-sector job is probably greater with, say, the interpersonal skills required of a good case officer than with the talents of a good analyst. In short, performing well in a chosen profession does not necessarily mean forgoing a more lucrative profession in which one can perform equally well. Good philosophers—or good intelligence analysts—do not necessarily make good businessmen or vice versa. To believe otherwise is to buy into the fallacy underlying the question, "If you're so smart, why aren't you rich?"

The largest flaw in the explanation that government does not attract capable people is that many capable people—fortunately for the national interest—are not solely interested in getting rich. The explanation denies the whole concept of public service and the reality that many skilled individuals devote careers to government service in part because of patriotism and a desire to make a difference on behalf of a greater good. And that is not even to mention the other nonpecuniary attractions of a career in intelligence—such as operations officers' finding the recruitment of spies to be much more interesting and exciting work than, say, the recruitment of restaurant franchisees. Many who are focused on seeking material rewards in the private sector may unsurprisingly find all this hard to understand. Many of those same people probably also find it comforting to believe that they have chosen their path because they are more talented, not less public spirited, than their contemporaries who instead pursue careers in government.

This variation of the individual-errors explanation also has other weaknesses. One is that it does not explain why the issue of intelligence failure is so persistent even though the status of public service has varied over the same period—higher, for example, when President John F. Kennedy was appealing to Americans to ask what they can do for their country and lower most of the time since then. The explanation also does not connect errors to the aptitude levels of those who commit them. Postmortems of intelligence failures do not relate mistakes to the IQ scores or college transcripts of the officers involved. Any attempt to find such a pattern would be as fruitless as an attempt to explain blunders in the private sector, such as the introduction of the Edsel or New Coke, in terms of the aptitudes of the businessmen who made those decisions.

The vast majority of comments on intelligence failure and reform of intelligence—in books and articles, on the floors of Congress, in hearing rooms, and in the reports issued from ad hoc inquiries—are based on one or more of the explanations addressed so far. None of these explanations, however, can account for the strong and persistent nature of the issue of intelligence failure. Three other explanations, less often invoked, are better able to do so.

NOT ALL FAILURES ARE CONSIDERED EQUAL

One such valid explanation is that intelligence failures are inevitable. No matter how well an intelligence service is organized, how sound its tradecraft, how extensive its resources, and how skillful the people who staff it, it sometimes will fail. Some of the failures will involve major events and significant national interests.

To understand this point, begin with the basic reason for having an intelligence service, which is to try to find out things that are worth knowing but very difficult to know. If these things were not difficult to know, they would be known either through the normal flow of publicly available information or through the activities of other parts of the bureaucracy. Governments have components that do the extraordinary and sometimes dangerous things intelligence services do—such as espionage—because the information sought is extraordinarily difficult to obtain.

The expectations placed on intelligence for uninterrupted success also are extraordinary, which dulls the senses in thinking about failure. We tend to lose sight of how typical it is in many lines of work for expected success to be less—often much less—than 100 percent and for failure to be seen as a normal part of business rather than a distressing crisis. An inspirational plaque I once saw read, "Babe Ruth struck out 1,330 times." An updated version might say that Barry Bonds struck out 1,539 times.[26] In the sport in which the term *batting average* originated, an average of .300 or so is usually considered good batting. In business, some of the most admired enterprises are ones that take chances in where they invest their resources, hoping for some big winners but understanding that some of their bets will lose. That is what the venture capital business is all about.

The businesses and businesspeople involved are often still admired even after conspicuous and costly mistakes. New Coke is an example. Coca-Cola's changing of the recipe for its signature soft drink in 1985 reflected a badly mistaken analysis of what Coke meant to many customers, for whom it was an institution and not just a source of refreshment. The company received hundreds of thousands of calls and letters, with those who liked the new taste shouted down by those who protested the change. The protests and pressure from bottlers led Coca-Cola to bring back the old recipe.[27] The mistake did not seem to harm the reputation of either the company or its high-profile chief executive officer, Roberto Goizueta. Over the next several years, Goizueta's annual compensation reached $63.5 million before publicity over the size of his package led Coca-Cola's board of directors to reduce it.[28]

Comparable mistakes in government are not forgiven so easily. Public attitudes toward errors by government departments and officials are quite different from attitudes toward failures in baseball or business. Of course, the nature of the activity is different; government is not playing games or seeking a profit. But the dominant attitude does not even admit that some endeavors of government are *like* sports or commerce insofar as they are competitive or for other reasons very difficult and thus inherently likely to have failures amid the successes. Government is instead viewed in simple, absolutist terms in which citizens and taxpayers expect to get full measure of important things they count on government to provide.

This attitude misses how much some endeavors in government constitute taking best shots at small, difficult targets, with some of the shots likely to miss. This point is especially but not uniquely true of intelligence. It is also true of many of NASA's operations in space. NASA literally does rocket science—a term that when used metaphorically in other contexts denotes extremely complicated and difficult tasks. Intrinsic to its mission is to press the limits of the possible in space exploration and to go beyond the limits of what is known and safe.

NASA's two most highly publicized failures in the past quarter-century were the loss, from different causes, of the space shuttles *Challenger* in 1986 and *Columbia* in 2003. Overlooked amid the national anguish and recriminations over those two accidents was the fact that the space shuttle had always been a risky engineering experiment, which engineers recognized as such. NASA computed and periodically revised a "probability risk assessment number," which estimated the odds of any shuttle mission resulting in complete loss of the vehicle and crew. The number was sometimes quoted as one in one hundred, although it fluctuated above and below that figure.

The shortest odds were in the years following the *Challenger* accident, when the risk was estimated at one in seventy-eight.[29] If, as an approximation, the risk of catastrophic failure was one in one hundred for each mission, then there was a 74 percent chance of at least one such failure in the 134 shuttle missions through the scheduled end of the program. The chance of at least two failures was 39 percent.

The dominant public reaction to the accidents, however, was not one of stoic acknowledgment of the inherent risk. It instead involved boards of inquiry, demands for change, calls for accountability, and general abhorrence over what were regarded as avoidable tragedies. NASA can be blamed in part for eliciting such a reaction by publicly coming to portray the shuttle (perhaps in the interest of sustaining appropriations) as less of an engineering experiment and more of a reliable means of transportation into Earth orbit. This portrayal went as far as giving seats on the shuttle to members of Congress and private citizens. The latter included Christa McAuliffe, the likeable schoolteacher whose loss while on *Challenger* made that accident all the more heartbreaking.

THE OPPOSING TEAM

The obstacles and sources of error inherent to intelligence go beyond even those of rocket science. A major source of obstacles is the competition: adversaries always are working hard to thwart our efforts to obtain information. They thwart the efforts in part through denial, which includes any measures to conceal activities and protect secrets. They also do it through deception, which involves dissemination of false information to cause confusion. States are generally very good at denial and deception, but other entities such as terrorist groups can be good at it as well. Al-Qa'ida, for one, has circulated among its members a manual that reveals a remarkably high level of expertise in techniques to frustrate collection of information about the group.[30]

With adversaries taking direct action to impede collection and analysis of information, intelligence is not analogous to a sport such as golf, in which no one other than the course is impeding the golfer and par provides a standard of performance. It is instead like baseball and other sports in which direct confrontation with a competitor is inherent to the game. There is no par in baseball. Every time a batter succeeds, a pitcher fails, and vice versa. We understand this in watching such sports and interpret success and failure accordingly. One does not hear talk after each strikeout about a "batting failure," and the team's management does not convene a board of inquiry to investigate the causes.

The competitive aspects of intelligence seem to be less widely understood or accepted. The United States and its adversaries are pitching and batting simultaneously; each is trying to uncover the other's secrets while protecting its own. When an adversary succeeds in obtaining some of our secrets, especially through a human spy, we treat it as a scandal. And yet that is exactly the sort of breakthrough that U.S. intelligence often is expected to achieve and that leads to talk about intelligence failure when it is not. One side's intelligence success is the other side's counterintelligence failure, and vice versa. There is no reason to expect either side, including our own, to win that contest consistently.

Rather than having a comparative advantage in this competition, the United States more often faces the disadvantage of being an open society confronting closed adversaries such as police states and terrorist groups. The latter is the apotheosis of a hard intelligence target. The details of terrorist plots typically are known only to very small groups of individuals who plan their operations behind closed doors and are highly suspicious of outsiders, fastidious about operational security, and ruthless toward anyone suspected of betraying them. It is fantasy to believe that with enough skill and ingenuity an intelligence service ought to be able to penetrate all such groups, learn the details of their plots, and prevent their attacks. And that does not even consider how to become aware in the first place of a terrorist needle in a haystack of potential terrorists if the terrorists in question have not previously attempted attacks.

Adversaries' actions directly impede collection of information but also indirectly complicate analysis, in part because analysts often have so little good information to interpret. Most of the information they do have on the more difficult intelligence problems is fragmentary and ambiguous. Clichéd references to "connecting dots" ignore the reality that in the typical case the available dots can plausibly be connected in many different ways, most of which would be wrong. Unlike in children's puzzles, the dots that intelligence analysts face do not have numbers. They also do not have a white background and are indistinguishable from many of the meaningless marks also on the paper.[31]

PROPHECY AND COMPLEXITY

Challenges for analysis multiply when intelligence is expected not only to discern present activities, but also to anticipate future ones. The prediction failures that dominate scorecards on intelligence involve these challenges. Such a failure sometimes reflects an inability to obtain a secret, such as a decision by a foreign government to test a weapon or to launch a war. But secrets often have little to do with the unpredictability of events, which stems even more from the nature of the events themselves. Sheer complexity is the chief characteristic that foils prediction. A popular revolution, for example, is commonly the product of innumerable social, political, and economic phenomena that dance together in complicated and constantly evolving ways. Accidental and for all practical purposes unpredictable events sometimes lead the dancing to become revolutionary upheaval. Social scientists have yet to construct a theory that reliably explains the outbreak of revolutions in the past. Intelligence analysts are even less likely to be able to predict reliably the revolutions of the future.

Large events such as revolutions are often unpredictable because extremely small events can determine whether they occur. Mathematicians have studied this pattern as it applies to physical systems; the subject is known as chaos theory. One of the pioneers of the field, Edward Lorenz, whose career moved from mathematics to meteorology, noticed that extremely small differences (rounding error in a computerized model in the case of Lorenz's discovery) in initial atmospheric conditions can lead to major differences in subsequent weather. Lorenz concluded that "prediction of the sufficiently distant future is impossible by any method, unless the present conditions are known exactly"—an exactness that observations of the weather never can achieve.[32] This phenomenon is sometimes known as the "butterfly effect," after Lorenz's suggestion that a butterfly flapping its wings in Brazil might be part of what sets off a tornado in Texas.

Human events, including important ones that interest governments and that intelligence services are expected to monitor and assess, also exhibit butterfly effects. Such effects are expressed in the traditional poem about how a lost nail results in the loss of shoe, horse, rider, battle, and kingdom. They also are the basis for many alternate histories, which spin large consequences out of small diversions from actual history. A well-written alternate history is appealing largely because it is so plausible that such minor details can shape momentous events. The premise of one of the classics of the genre, Robert Sobel's *For Want of a Nail: If Burgoyne Had Won at Saratoga*, is that British reinforcements arrive in time at the Battle of Saratoga in 1777 to enable the British commander John Burgoyne to defeat the colonial forces of Horatio Gates. This defeat leads the tide of the revolutionary war to turn in Britain's favor, the French to withdraw their support from the colonies, the colonial leaders to surrender, the United States never to come into being, and North America's relationship with the rest of the world over the subsequent two centuries to unfold much differently from actual history.[33]

Intelligence analysis does not have to look out over centuries, but the outcomes of many nearer-term events that intelligence is expected to anticipate are determined by small unpredictable details of how those events unfold. The success or failure of many attempted coups d'état has hinged on whether a small unit such as a well-placed element of a palace guard does or does not switch loyalties. Or it may depend on whether a single officer important to the plot gets cold feet—the conspiratorial equivalent of a lost nail.

Very small but critical details often determine not only whether a major event occurs, but also *when* it does. Much of the prediction that is expected from intelligence analysis is a matter of timing. We rightly scoff at a person who predicted each year during the twentieth century that no world war would break out and later brags that he was right most of the time and wrong only twice. Not deserving of scorn is someone who has profound understanding of social forces that make a country combustible and a candidate for revolution but is unable to predict what spark will ignite a revolutionary fire and when ignition will occur. Such potentially revolutionary situations can persist for years and thus be beyond the politically meaningful time frame of most makers of foreign policy. For these situations, not having a prediction about timing may be little different from having no prediction at all. Timing is the major problem for analysts who see combustible material in countries where revolutionary change might present hazards for U.S. interests (e.g., Egypt) as well as ones where it might provide opportunities (e.g., Iran).

Not only does history turn on some very small pivots, but it sometimes jumps as well. It is discontinuous. The discontinuities make for surprises and frustrate attempts to project a future based on a known past and present. Mathematicians have also studied this pattern, under the label *catastrophe theory*.[34] Their models help to explain (in retrospect) some physical catastrophes such as collapses of bridges and capsizing of ships. Even without the mathematics, big discontinuities appear in living systems. The late evolutionary biologist Stephen Jay Gould advanced a theory of "punctuated equilibrium," under which most species are stable most of the time and evolutionary change occurs mostly in spurts.[35] Gould's perspective helps backward-looking intelligent beings understand spurts in the evolution of life forms, such as the one more than half a billion years ago known as the Cambrian explosion. It also helps to explain why if any intelligent beings had existed before such spurts, they would have been unable to predict them.

Discontinuities in human history sometimes emerge as "black swans"—a metaphor referring to events that have major consequences but, because they are rare and beyond normal experience, are difficult to predict. The large impact that black swans have on history accounts for much of the unpredictability of history as a whole. The unfamiliarity of such consequential events also contributes to chronic overestimation of our ability to predict. "What is surprising," observes the leading proponent of the black swan concept, Nassim Nicholas Taleb, "is not the magnitude of our forecast errors, but our absence of awareness of it." Taleb adds, "This is all the more worrisome when we engage in deadly conflicts: wars are fundamentally unpredictable (and we do not know it)."[36]

GREAT MEN AND THE ACCIDENTS OF HISTORY

The unpredictable pivots and jumps of history often involve the actions of very small numbers of people. The immense role that the Soviet Union played in history, including the entire Cold War and other conflicts of the twentieth century, began with the actions of a small but skillfully led group of conspirators. After their coup of 1917, the Bolsheviks clung precariously to power until finally beating back a variety of internal and external adversaries. Even accepting that czarist Russia was ripe for revolution by the early twentieth century, the revolution was not preordained to come out as it did. The subsequent history of Russia and of the world would have been much different without the presence, inclinations, and abilities of Lenin and his comrades. Even with them, the outcome was a close call.

How should analysts and policymakers at the time, particularly in the United States, have viewed the events in Russia? In fact, they viewed them negatively, to the extent that the Woodrow Wilson administration dispatched U.S. troops to the far eastern and northern parts of Russia. The expeditions were justified publicly on other grounds but were intended at least in part to strengthen opposition to the Bolsheviks enough to defeat the new regime. The expeditions were short-lived and ineffective in achieving this purpose. Shouldn't an accurate assessment of where revolutionary Russia was heading have led to an all-out effort to strangle the Communist monster in its infancy? The same kind of question has been asked in hindsight of other unfavorable developments that have affected U.S. interests. The question overlooks the inherent unpredictability of most important future events. It also fails to consider that because even a prescient assessment of the future is inherently uncertain and long term, it loses out in policymaking to more immediate interests and pressures. The Wilson administration withdrew U.S. troops from Russia in the face of poor morale among American soldiers, insufficient willingness by European allies to commit their own troops, and isolationist sentiment at home as expressed in the U.S. Congress.[37]

Fidel Castro and his colleagues offer an example of an even smaller number of people redirecting national history. Fulgencio Batista's regime in Cuba may have been a rotten fruit waiting to fall, but its replacement by a regime that would become a U.S. preoccupation for the next half-century was the result of a few exceptionally willful, skillful revolutionaries' surmounting of long odds. Eighty-two men sailed from Mexico to Cuba on the yacht *Granma* in December 1956. The Cuban army almost eradicated the tiny and underequipped force within its first three weeks after landing. Eleven men—including Castro, his brother Raul, and Che Guevara—escaped to the rugged terrain of the Sierra Maestra.[38] These eleven then began two years of recruiting new followers and attacking government targets, culminating in their defeat of Batista on New Year's Day 1959. Much of this revolution was barely plausible, let alone predictable.

Leaders with the impact of Lenin or Castro illustrate how much single exceptional individuals can redirect human events.[39] This conclusion points to several elements of uncertainty, including such people's being born in the first place and their possibly being diverted into nonpolitical careers before they start shaping history. More relevant to intelligence analysis is whether they stay alive once they already are shaping history. Adolf Hitler, for example, had as much impact on modern history as any single individual, but his survival (until he would kill himself at the end of World War II) was far from assured. The best-known plot to assassinate Hitler, in July 1944, came very close to doing so. There were other plots to kill him earlier, including other near misses.[40] The accuracy of any forecasts at the time about the course of German policy and the war, not to mention the countless events to be shaped by the war in Europe and its outcome, would have rested on the luck of whether any of the attempts on the dictator's life succeeded.

The major implications of a key leader's surviving or dying, especially in wartime, make this another favorite subject of alternate histories. The novelist Mackinlay Kantor wrote such a story about the Civil War in which the key counterfactual event is the death of Ulysses S. Grant after he is thrown from a horse during the Vicksburg campaign in the summer of 1863. (Grant really did have an equine accident at Vicksburg, but he survived.) The death of Grant, along with a bit more aggressiveness by Robert E. Lee on the first day of the Battle of Gettysburg, sets the stage for the Confederacy to win the war and establish its independence.[41] Other alternate histories set in the Civil War also have been premised on whether a particular leader lives or dies—for example, Stonewall Jackson does not get killed at Chancellorsville. The important role that good and bad generalship played in determining the course of the Civil War makes such literary inventions plausible.

Consider the problem that generalship in the war—a variable so fickle because luck kills off some generals but not others—would have posed at the time to analysts or policymakers in other countries, such as Britain. The American Civil War was very important to Britain for economic and other reasons. London considered recognizing the Confederacy, although it never took that step. An accurate and well-grounded assessment of the course of the war and its eventual outcome would have been quite valuable to British policymakers, but it also was unattainable.

The Civil War posed numerous other uncertainties to British leaders, including whether it would break out in the first place. Richard Neustadt and Ernest May had students at Harvard perform an exercise centered on this question. They provided the students with materials about the crisis in the United States in the spring of 1861 that would have been available to British decision makers, such as newspaper articles and dispatches from diplomats. The specific issue for decision was whether to buy options in the B&O Railroad, which would be profitable unless a prolonged war occurred in the mid-Atlantic region. Neustadt and May believed that, based on the material provided, they would have bought the options. Most of the students, knowing what actually happened, struggled to find in the documents a basis for predicting a long and bloody war, and some of them succeeded. "But even those who compose[d] the best such briefs," the professors note, "appreciate better, as a result, how very hard it is to foresee at a given moment what later may seem an inevitable future."[42]

The difficulty posed by the influence individual leaders have for anyone attempting to project future events extends beyond the question of whether key people die or not. It includes as well the unfathomable complexity and thus unpredictability of the decision making of those who live. That complexity, as summarized in one study of human nature in decision making on foreign policy, includes "the role of emotion and memories, testosterone and dominance, stress, and time horizons." A conclusion from such research is that even with more research, a theory that makes good general predictions about human behavior in international relations is out of reach.[43] And as in any field, good specific predictions tend to be even more elusive than general ones.

Beyond the testosterone and other stuff of psychologists and physiologists, there also is the stuff of philosophers: free will. If one believes in it, one necessarily believes in a major handicap to any effort to predict foreign leaders' behavior. We expect to be able to predict an adversary's behavior accurately even though we also expect our own leaders to use such predictions in exercising their free will to outsmart the adversary. The inconsistency between these two expectations seldom is noticed.

The psychologist Philip Tetlock, who has extensively studied expert judgment, assesses that for a variety of reasons political forecasting is never going to be very good. The reasons include not only human beings' cognitive limitations but also characteristics, such as butterfly effects, that are intrinsic to the situations about which forecasts are attempted. Tetlock identifies some approaches to forecasting that tend to work better than others, but the achievable level of accuracy will always be less than what is commonly expected.[44]

Intelligence analysts face an additional challenge in such forecasting, which is trying to predict what their own government will do. The United States is itself one of the biggest influences in most of the situations that its analysts are expected to address. The difficulty goes beyond the technical one of how to draft an intelligence analysis without sounding policy prescriptive. The more fundamental problem is simply not knowing what one of the most important players is going to do and not having a charter for explicitly analyzing what that player will do. Asking the policymakers what they are going to do seldom helps because they cannot predict their own future intentions well. They cannot because events overseas outrun their imaginations and create a context different from what they earlier expected or because events lead them to rethink their own goals and values.[45]

In sum, the analytic work of intelligence—for reasons inherent to the subject matter and the task itself—always will exhibit significant inaccuracies and omissions. This characteristic as well as the inaccessibility of many secrets recurrently produces what are commonly labeled intelligence failures. Just as it is fantasy to believe that every enemy organization can be penetrated and its secrets purloined, so too is it fantasy to believe that with the right ideas, techniques, organizations, and people an intelligence service ought to be able to provide consistently accurate images of the outside world as it is today, not to mention predictions for the future. As an unusually insightful longtime student of intelligence, Richard Betts, puts it, "Intelligence failures are not only inevitable; they are natural." "The awful truth," says Betts—and the awfulness of this truth is why few Americans want to accept it—"is that the best of intelligence systems will have big failures."[46] This truth unquestionably is a major reason why the issue of intelligence failure never goes away.

THE SLANTED SCORECARD

Another explanation for why the issue of intelligence failure is so persistent is that the record of intelligence is commonly perceived to be worse than it really is. Failures outweigh successes in the public mind, much more than in reality, chiefly for three reasons.

First, failures are more likely to become news. This is to some extent true of many lines of work besides intelligence; crises and setbacks tend to make headlines, whereas routinely competent and successful work does not. The special characteristics of intelligence amplify this pattern. The secrecy that is essential to intelligence means that many successes cannot be made public lest adversaries learn more about one's own capabilities, and it thereby becomes harder to score similar successes in the future. By contrast, the failures that tend to be associated with intelligence are highly salient and newsworthy, such as political upheavals or spectacular terrorist attacks.

More fundamentally, many intelligence successes are automatically self-effacing because they produce nonevents, such as wars that are not launched, coup plots that are not executed, or terrorist plots that are rolled up. Good intelligence, properly used, prevents crises from emerging in the first place. Most intelligence successes thus not only get little publicity, but do not make it onto scorecards at all. How things might have been worse if good intelligence instead had been bad never becomes a subject of discussion.

Second, through hindsight the public perceives the performance of intelligence to be much worse than it is. Hindsight, with all the distorting effects of looking through a telescope backwards, has played a huge role in misperceptions about the performance of intelligence because almost everything that is known about an event becomes known only after the fact. The backwards telescope gazing that has most shaped public perceptions of intelligence is that of ad hoc inquiries that are convened to investigate intelligence failures—or, rather, what are preconceived to be intelligence failures. Once convened, the commissions and committees that conduct such inquiries have an enormous advantage over the intelligence agencies whose handling of a story they are investigating: they know how the story ends. And so they proceed like Neustadt and May's students, who, knowing that a civil war broke out in the United States in 1861, comb through their material for anything that could have pointed to such an event. The investigators, like the students, stitch together a hindsight-driven brief in an exercise that is far different from the intelligence officers' task of following the issue in real time. The conclusions that come out of such investigations then become standard fodder for countless other commentaries about how badly intelligence performed.

The ad hoc inquiries also distort public perceptions about intelligence performance because they contribute to the disproportionate attention given to failures rather than successes. Commissions of inquiry are convened only after the former, not the latter. The extra publicity from the inquiries makes the attention to failure even more disproportionate.

The third reason for the mistaken public perceptions is the general assumption that the connection between intelligence input and policy output is much more direct than it really is. Intelligence therefore gets blamed not only for its own failures but also for some policy failures as well.

The assumption that intelligence problems underlie policy problems, although at the core of an American national mythology, is not uniquely American. In the Arab–Israeli war in the Middle East in 1973, Egyptian success in using precision-guided antitank missiles to destroy Israeli armored vehicles shocked the Israeli public and stimulated an outcry over why this tactic had not been anticipated. In fact, Israeli military intelligence had warned well before the war about the threat the Egyptian antitank weapons posed, but Israeli war planners evidently did not sufficiently take such warnings into account.[47]

Thirty-three years later Israel encountered problems in a war against the Lebanese Hizballah in the form of stiff resistance by the Hizballah militia inside Lebanon and retaliatory rocket salvos against civilian targets in Israel. During the war, a broadcast journalist asked to interview me on Israel's "intelligence failure" regarding Hizballah. I declined because I had no information on that subject or on whether there was any intelligence failure at all. At that point, no one who had not been present at discussions between Israeli intelligence officers and the military command and political leadership had the slightest insight about how much the Israelis' difficulties may have been based on poor intelligence. Some indications since then suggest that Israeli intelligence had accurate perceptions at least about Hizballah's rocket capabilities, but that this information did not deter the Israeli government from prosecuting the war.[48]

As indicated in earlier chapters, many other ingredients besides the images that policymakers hold of the outside world go into the making of their decisions. Those ingredients include competing values, competing and shifting policy objectives, strategic considerations as to how best to achieve the objectives, domestic politics, decision makers' inner needs, and much else. Even when an image of the outside world appears to drive a policy decision, the image may not necessarily have come from an intelligence service. It is at least as likely to have come from one or more of the policymaker's many other sources of information, analysis, and belief. My Georgetown colleague Jennifer Sims has emphasized the distinction between intelligence as a function and intelligence as a piece of bureaucracy and notes that "diagnosing intelligence ills by examining only the interaction of those collectors and analysts carrying 'intelligence' in their titles would be a mistake. One flaw of past commissions that have looked into U.S. intelligence problems has been the failure to examine what may be termed the 'nonintelligence' sources of intelligence failure."[49]

The All-Purpose Issue

A final reason that intelligence failure is a perpetual issue is that the issue itself serves other purposes for those who help to perpetuate it. The theme of intelligence failure and reform fills needs that no amount of real reform can fill, and so the theme continues indefinitely.

The public's yearning for reassuring explanations for costly wars, lethal terrorist attacks, and other painful and unpleasant things that hit them is at the foundation of this reason. To be reassuring, an explanation must be direct, simple, and understandable. "Intelligence screwed up" is such an explanation. It is far more satisfying than any explanation that gets the least bit complicated by raising epistemological issues about the limits of forecasting or unavoidable trade-offs among policy objectives or the multitude of reasons that well-intentioned foreign policies can come a cropper. The simplicity that appeals to the yearnings of the general public then colors discussion and debate among even the more sophisticated.

The public longs for explanations that not only are simple and understandable, but also hold out the promise that past tragedies and the problems that underlie them will not recur. The public wants fixes to fixable problems. The idea that intelligence has failed and needs to be fixed appeals to that desire. And the supposed need to inject new ideas and new people into hitherto inflexible intelligence bureaucracies so they can deal with new issues is appealing because it promises such a fix. The views that intelligence failures are inevitable and that past tragedies have occurred even though intelligence is already working better than widely perceived do not offer a fix and thus are not at all appealing. They are disturbing, which is why they are never likely to gain wide currency.

The public also wants explanations that help it to avoid having to face up to its own failures, such as in giving insufficient attention to an issue or unwisely supporting misguided foreign ventures. It is more comfortable to think that we, the public, were just not given the right information. A related tendency is for the public to project its own ignorance or inattention onto the intelligence services. If we in the public were not paying enough attention to a problem (such as international terrorism before 9/11), we believe it must have been because nobody—in particular, nobody official— was paying enough attention to it. And since intelligence services have the most responsibility for paying attention to emerging threats overseas, that is where the public believes the main fault should lie.[50] The public further would prefer to relieve itself of any share in responsibility that comes from having elected leaders who pursue bad policies. Better to shift more of the responsibility to an unelected bureaucracy.

Political leaders themselves are skilled practitioners at shifting responsibility. The process usually does not reach the extreme that it did in the case of the Iraq War, which led to an orgy of blame shifting and finger pointing directed at much more than just intelligence. But whenever there is failure in public policy, there will be political leaders (to include appointees as well as elected leaders) with an interest in assigning blame. Because policymakers shape the public agenda far more than intelligence services do, public discussion is thus apt to be shaped more to protect the policymakers' reputations than those of the services.

Many diverse players have interests in keeping intelligence failure and intelligence reform a prominent issue. Political leaders want to divert attention from other problems or shortcomings. Journalists, academics, and others in the ideas industry earn their livelihood at least in part by writing and commenting on the topic. Foundation grants and the substantial place that the study of intelligence has assumed in universities (including my own) indicate some of the interests involved. Former intelligence officers also help to sustain the issue by weighing in about failure and the need for reform in order to grind old axes, exorcise old demons, or demonstrate that they are open-minded.

As with some other topics that, for whatever reason, achieve prominence, the issue has become self-sustaining. Expressions of concern about intelligence failure and the need for reform expand the market for still more such expressions. The dynamic is similar to the celebrity phenomenon, in which some people are famous mostly for being famous. Intelligence failure has long been a focus of attention in part because it has long been a focus of attention.

The many commissions, committees, panels, and other ad hoc inquiries on the subject have been important intermediaries in this dynamic. Such bodies, once created, have strong needs and interests of their own, in particular the need to appear necessary and useful. No such panel—on any subject, not just intelligence—ever issues a report that says, "The operation we've studied works about as well as can be expected, and we really don't have any significant ideas for change beyond what is already being tried."

Fish have to swim, birds have to fly, and commissions have to identify problems and propose solutions, preferably big ones.

Secrecy and the resulting constraints on scrutiny by outsiders lead to at least as much intellectual inbreeding in discourse about intelligence as about any other subject. Assertions about intelligence shortcomings get repeated again and again, including by countless commentators who have not the slightest basis for knowing whether these assertions are true, until they become common currency. Even the more diligent scholars and journalists have far less to go on than their colleagues who cover topics that offer more opportunities for field research or perusal of archives. Amid slim pickings, the reports of the ad hoc inquiries in particular get seized upon, and lines from them get repeatedly replayed. They are treated as primary sources even though they are not. Mere impressions the panels convey are regarded as truths etched in stone. And any inaccuracies and biases in the panels' reports get replayed and become part of the common currency as well.

Amid the clamor of commentary on intelligence, one has a better chance of getting attention by railing about problems and proposing (supposedly) new solutions than by speaking more mundane truths about the inevitability of problems and the limitations of solutions. And so the issue of intelligence failure and reform rolls on with as much energy as ever.

CHAPTER NINE

CATHARSIS AND 9/11

The terrorist attack against the United States on September 11, 2001, universally known as "9/11," was one of the most severe public traumas in modern American history. Regardless of what the attack did or did not demonstrate about the strength of particular terrorist groups or the state of international terrorism in general, it unquestionably seared the emotions and consciousness of the American public. The response to the event demonstrated vividly the patterns Americans have repeatedly displayed in responding to national tragedy, including patterns described in previous chapters regarding attitudes toward intelligence.

The U.S. government counters or otherwise affects international terrorism in many ways. These ways range from security measures for protecting aviation and other vulnerable targets at home to foreign policies that shape the attitudes of would-be terrorists or their sympathizers toward the United States. But as with previous national shocks and setbacks that involved anything foreign, Americans wanting to find explanations for 9/11 and to assign blame turned immediately and reflexively toward intelligence. The same basic assumptions that have sustained the themes of intelligence failure and reform for so long were present in spades in this episode; that if intelligence services are working properly, they should be able to uncover any such threats; that if they uncover these threats, then policymakers will take the necessary actions to preempt them; and that if the threats are not preempted, then the problem is intelligence failure and the solution is to fix intelligence. The episode warrants extended examination because of the very large influence it has had on discourse about U.S. intelligence and because as a case study it demonstrates how such discourse can go awry.

SLAKING A THIRST

The institution that, much more than any other, shaped Americans' perceptions of 9/11 and why it had happened was the National Commission on Terrorist Attacks Upon the United States, which became known more concisely as the "9/11 Commission." Congress established the commission in the autumn of 2002, despite the Bush administration's initial opposition to the idea, after an earlier inquiry conducted jointly by the House and Senate intelligence committees. (I testified in open session to the joint inquiry, at which, in response to a question, I supported establishing a commission.)[1]

The 9/11 Commission would attain—in part because of the salience of the event it was charged with investigating and in part because of its own prodigious salesmanship—prominence and influence that would make it the envy of ad hoc panels everywhere. It would come to be listened to as the arbiter of all that is good and bad in counterterrorism. Its word would be accepted and replayed again and again as the last word on everything about 9/11, including everything involving intelligence.

After a false start in selecting the commission's leadership, a Republican, former New Jersey governor Thomas Kean, became the chairman. A Democrat, former Indiana Congressman Lee Hamilton, became vice chairman. In a later book about their experiences, Kean and Hamilton made clear what they saw as the commission's function: it would be "cathartic for the nation."[2] The dust jacket blurb accurately expanded on the commission's role: its report "slaked the national thirst for accountability." Kean and Hamilton say their main worries—the criteria according to which they would consider the commission to have failed if any of these things occurred—were splintering of the commission along partisan lines, leaks of classified information, not getting access to relevant material, and alienating the families of 9/11 victims.[3] The commission was a success on these counts and certainly also in terms of how much attention the commission's report and other output received and how widely that output was accepted.

Notably absent from these criteria was accuracy. Whether what the commission said was a true and complete rendering of what the government had done was not going to be the principal standard by which the commission's work would be judged, either by the commission itself or by the American public. The inquiry was not going to be a dispassionate search for the truth because satisfying the passions surrounding the 9/11 tragedy was what the exercise was mostly about. Avoiding failure on two of Kean and Hamilton's criteria—the ones involving partisan divisions and the victims' families—took the commission ever farther from a dispassionate search for the truth.

The commission was frequently on the verge of being torn apart by partisanship. A constant subtext of its deliberations was the passing of judgment on what the Democratic administration of Bill Clinton and the Republican administration of George W. Bush had and had not done about terrorism. In their account, Kean and Hamilton repeatedly write of how they struggled to contain the partisanship and to counter urges to assign blame along party lines. As part of their struggles, they placed great emphasis on achieving unanimity in their report.[4] Because explicit accusations against either administration were out of bounds, that much more attention had to be directed against the bureaucracy and in particular intelligence to achieve catharsis and to slake the national thirst for accountability.

Kean and Hamilton also write at length about the tremendous pressure from the victims' families, who had been among the most energetic proponents of creating the commission. The families later lobbied effectively for increasing the commission's budget from $3 million to $14 million, making them, in effect, some of the commission's most important stockholders. In their meetings with the commission, the families were emotional, intense, and insistent. As in any group that size, there was variation in attitudes and level of understanding. But the overall pressure the families exerted was consistently in the direction of assigning blame and rolling heads. They expressed impatience with any time taken up by experts conveying background information. When Kean stated at the opening hearing that the purpose was not to point fingers, there was a stir in the hall among families angry at such a comment; for them, pointing fingers was the whole purpose of the proceeding. The up-close pressure continued over the remaining hearings. Kean sometimes had to ask the families, who had reserved seats, to refrain from emotional outbursts.[5] The commission did not name as many names and use as much explicitly accusatory language as would have satisfied the families fully, but this source of pressure clearly was a major influence in crafting a report that implicitly achieved the same result.

Given the politically and emotionally supercharged atmosphere and the huge attention that the commission's multi-million-dollar effort received, it would have been unthinkable for it not to produce at the end a major proposal that it could tout as a major improvement in protecting Americans from terrorism. And it would have to produce such a proposal regardless of what its inquiry actually found regarding problems that did or did not exist, mistakes that were or were not made, and events that were or were not avoidable. The commission shrewdly did not resist the pressure but instead turned it to its advantage. Not only would it offer the expected major proposal; it would use the emotion and the politics as fuel to get Congress to approve the proposal. If successful, this process would achieve the objective of catharsis, which no mere proposal that is never enacted into legislation ever could. It also would elevate the 9/11 Commission to the top of the pantheon of blue-ribbon panels, whose reports usually serve as little more than doorstops.

Much of the political fuel would come from the 2004 presidential election campaign, which would be in full swing when the commission released its report. Kean devised the strategy. As he and Hamilton later described their intentions, by releasing the commission's report "in the run-up to the conventions, we could set off a bidding war between the two parties to embrace our recommendations, prompting the Congress to act, and act quickly."[6] The strategy would work splendidly. Of course, a partisan bidding war amid an election campaign would be the worst possible environment for careful consideration of the proposal, critical perusal of the underlying report, and the uncovering of flaws in either the report or the proposal. But if the objective was catharsis rather than either accuracy or effectiveness in future counterterrorist efforts, the strategy was brilliant.

The commission's own part in the strategy was to make its principal recommendation a package with a few easily understood features that could be legislatively enacted and then to push the proposal as hard as it could. Part of the pushing was to portray adoption of the proposal as the litmus test of whether the nation was serious about combating terrorism. Kean declared, in presenting the proposal to Congress, that without a restructuring of intelligence agencies "the American people are going to be less safe."[7] The commission hired a public-relations firm as a supplement to its in-house public-affairs staff to manage the rollout of its report.[8] Thus, the commission became heavily committed—extraordinarily, even uniquely so for a panel of inquiry—to a single proposal. It invested much of its prestige, its sense of accomplishment, and image of success in adoption of the proposal. It accordingly also became committed to a version of the 9/11 story that would help to muster support for the proposal. The extent to which the commission had become more advocate than investigator was highlighted after the commission's official mandate expired, when it morphed into an unofficial pressure group called the 9/11 Public Discourse Project, which continued to operate for another year and a half.[9]

It was not just the commission as a whole that acquired a large stake in the process, but also the people working for it. The tremendous attention to the commission and to the terrorist event that had given rise to it made work on the staff a terrific career opportunity or a defining point in careers that already were in later stages. Members of the staff had an interest not only in enactment of the commission's main proposal as a mark of its success, but also in favorable public reception of the rest of their work. To the extent they were perceived as tough-minded investigators uncovering incompetence or malfeasance in government agencies, they would be applauded—or even considered as, per the caption to a staff photograph in Kean and Hamilton's book, "a national treasure." To the extent they were softer on those same agencies and not contributing to the catharsis, they would be considered something much worse, especially by the 9/11 families.

The individual interests were all the stronger when there was an opportunity for individual time in the klieg lights—so strong that such interests became a subject of discord among the staff. The staff director, Philip Zelikow, wanted to be the only person to read aloud the statements that the staff had prepared for public hearings. As Kean and Hamilton note, this arrangement "did not go over very well" with the rest of the staff. "Having seventy high-quality people working for us also meant that we had seventy egos," they said. "To those doing the reading, it was the culmination of a huge amount of work, and an important moment in their careers." The eventual compromise had Zelikow introducing every statement and reading some of them.[10]

This disagreement was only one of many clashes between Zelikow and the rest of the staff, which involved not only the staff director's autocratic style but also his close ties to the Bush administration and Condoleezza

Rice. According to Kean and Hamilton, Zelikow wanted to monopolize the microphone in part to display toughness in the eyes of the 9/11 families, who thought those ties constituted a conflict of interest. Many staff members viewed those ties the same way. Much of the journalist Philip Shenon's book *The Commission* recounts how Zelikow's conflict of interest repeatedly affected his own work and was the focus of acrimony with commissioners and with other members of the staff. But a shared interest among the staff in maintaining an outward appearance of rectitude deterred them from airing any of this dirty linen. Shenon describes one episode in late 2003 in which several staff members considered protesting to the chairman and vice chairman about Zelikow's continued communication with his friends in the White House but decided against doing so for fear that their initiative would leak and cause a scandal. The staff members "were furious with what Zelikow had done and how his conflicts had threatened the integrity of the investigation," writes Shenon, but they knew "how valuable their affiliation with the 9/11 commission would be to their careers. They wanted its legacy to be untarnished."[11] This episode would hardly be the only time in the commission's work that integrity was subordinated to public relations.

PREJUDGMENT

The careerism, the politics, the emotions, the desire for catharsis, and the yearning for fixes all pushed the commission's inquiry toward the same conclusion: that 9/11 was an avoidable tragedy that occurred because of correctable problems in the U.S. government—not within the political leadership, which was too divisive a topic to address, but in the bureaucracy. The further narrowing of the primary target to intelligence occurred just as swiftly. Kean and Hamilton declared as a conceptual foundation of the commission's work, "There was broad consensus in the country that 9/11 had revealed fundamental problems with U.S. intelligence agencies."[12] This conclusion was not reached as the result of an inquiry, nor was it treated as a popular belief to be considered as only a hypothesis until confirmed by an inquiry. It was instead taken as a foregone conclusion, with the inquiry to provide supporting details.

Zelikow made the prejudgment more starkly obvious. Within a few days of his appointment—before any investigator had opened a file and before almost any of the staff had even been hired—he visited CIA headquarters to meet with two senior deputies of DCI Tenet. The conversation had hardly begun before Zelikow slapped his hand on the conference table and declared, "If you guys had a national intelligence director, none of this would have happened." He said that 9/11 was a "massive failure" of the CIA and that the attack had happened because "you guys weren't connected to the rest of the community."[13] It was the opening shot in what would become a major avenue of attack. As Shenon summarized the situation, "Philip Zelikow had made it clear that he was fixated on George Tenet and the CIA's performance before 9/11, and his obsessions drove the workings of the rest of the staff."[14]

There were other indications of conclusions being reached first, with the supposed basis for those conclusions to be developed only later. Near the beginning of the investigation, with the staff barely even in place, Zelikow prepared a finely elaborated outline of the final report that would be released sixteen months later. It was very detailed, down to second-level subheadings within each chapter. When he showed it to Kean and Hamilton, they were impressed with his energy and diligence but understandably alarmed about this indication that the report's conclusions were precooked. So they agreed to guard the document closely, keeping it to themselves and withholding it from the rest of the staff. When the staff finally got to see it more than a year later and learned when it had been prepared, they were alarmed for the same reason.[15]

With it determined from the beginning that the principal focus of the commission's report would be intelligence failure and that the principal product of the commission's work would be a major, legislative proposal for intelligence "reform," the commission staff needed to look for such a proposal. They did not have to look far. Zelikow's declaration at CIA headquarters pointed to an obvious candidate: the old idea of dividing the DCI job into two, leaving a director of the CIA and a new position of director of national intelligence (DNI) to oversee the entire intelligence community. Because the idea had been in play for years, it offered the advantage that arguments for and against had already been well rehearsed. For the commission's purposes, it offered the additional attraction of appearing to be a kind of punishment of the CIA, with the agency's director being stripped of his community authorities.

The staff also did not need to look far for the other major element in its reorganization proposal: the establishment of a National Counterterrorism

Center (NCTC), which would draw personnel from the CIA and FBI but be independent of those or any other existing agencies. The Bush administration established in early 2003 a Terrorist Threat Integration Center that was similarly designed and later would become the core of the NCTC. Zelikow also had available a proposal that he and two coauthors had made in 1998 for a "national terrorism intelligence center."[16] This proposed center looked much like the future NCTC, except that it would be a solely intelligence element that incorporated rather than duplicated the existing DCI CTC (which Zelikow and his coauthors described in their article as "highly successful") and would be housed in the FBI. To have retained the latter feature in the commission's proposal for the NCTC would have seemed too much a reward for the FBI, which was one of the very agencies the commission was indicting. Besides this factor, creation of the position of DNI would provide a new umbrella under which NCTC could be placed.

These ideas for reorganization did not flow from any investigation into 9/11. They predated 9/11. Even after the commission staff's work assembled the narrative of intelligence failure that would constitute the case for the reorganization scheme, the scheme still did not flow from the investigation—not as a matter of logic. There would always be a disconnect between the commission's conclusions about past performance and its proposal for a future organization. Anything that contributed to the impression of ineffectiveness by the intelligence community, however, would strengthen public support for "reforming" it.

SHAPING THE SCRIPT

The proposal was set. The basic narrative of intelligence failure was set. But the narrative did not necessarily coincide with reality. This potentially posed a difficult challenge for the commission staff, but the staff had several things going for it. One was that at the tactical, plot-specific level, 9/11—like almost every other terrorist attack—was by definition an intelligence failure: if details of the plot could have been obtained, U.S. authorities surely would have preempted it. Given the oversimplified, detail-stripping way in which the public views such matters, this narrative alone would be enough for many Americans. Failure is failure. Questions of whether the plot-specific details were ever obtainable or whether the failure to obtain them denoted a fundamental flaw or whether the intelligence community had an accurate understanding of the terrorist threat manifested by the plot got lost in the noise.

Another major advantage for the staff was the same one any retrospective inquiry enjoys: hindsight—the ability to look backward for anything possibly connected to the now-known end of the story. With its $14 million budget, staff of seventy, and the better part of two years to scour for material, it would have been surprising if the commission had not come up with a significant number of items that the agencies working the problem in real time had missed. If the commission had failed to unearth such items, American taxpayers footing its bill would be entitled to ask why.

Another asset was the great deference that Americans gave to the commission and with it the benefit of any doubt. This deference and the assumption of impartiality were the usual accorded to most ad hoc inquiries. In this case, however, the commission enjoyed extra trust from being the vehicle for the public to achieve its catharsis. Related to this trust was the larger public mood, which was broadly and strongly in favor of the direction the staff was headed: to explain 9/11 mainly in terms of failures by the bureaucracy and especially by intelligence. The public had a large appetite for fault finding and a small one for details. Points of detail where the preferred narrative conflicted with reality would not be a problem.

One of the biggest advantages the commission staff enjoyed was its tight control over the message and over material that would be released. The staff would reveal only a small proportion of the huge amount of material and information available to it. It could make public, as part of its report and other presentations, whatever supported the preferred narrative or could be construed as supporting the narrative but leave unsaid and unreleased whatever material contradicted that story.

The tight control extended to communication within the commission itself. In almost every ad hoc inquiry, the staff does most of the work, and the commissioners serve more as a board of directors. The 9/11 Commission took staff control and more specifically control by the staff director to even greater lengths. At Zelikow's insistence, the commissioners had no personal staff, no permanent presence at the commission's offices, and no charter to look into particular topics on which a commissioner may have had experience or expertise. Zelikow determined the witness lists for hearings. Commissioners were kept in the dark about access arrangements that the staff director had negotiated—as Commissioner Tim Roemer discovered to his anger and embarrassment when he tried to read classified transcripts from the congressional joint inquiry and was turned away. Zelikow even attempted to bar other members of the staff from directly returning commissioners' phone calls but was forced to back down when another commissioner, Jamie Gorelick, became furious upon learning of the arrangement.[17] Most of the commissioners took their responsibility seriously and tried hard to make a contribution. But their good names and the panel's bipartisan composition, which contributed significantly to the aura of impartiality and legitimacy that the commission enjoyed, were for the most part a front for output that was shaped far more by the staff and in particular by the preferences of one strong-willed member of it.

Kean and Hamilton tell of an episode in which Hamilton had to negotiate with Zelikow over the proposal for the NCTC, which Zelikow "strongly advocated." Hamilton was wary of the idea, which as Zelikow then conceived it would combine intelligence and operational planning. The staff director got his way, against the vice chairman's better judgment, with Hamilton winning only some concessions about an additional reporting line to the president and separation of intelligence and operational functions within the center.[18]

The commissioners never were exposed to much material, much information, many witnesses, and many considerations that were highly relevant to their charter. I am an example. From 1993 to 1999, I had been either the chief of analysis of the DCI CTC or deputy chief of the entire center, and I had subsequently written at length about counterterrorism. The commission's report would cite an item from my writings as supposedly being representative of a government-wide pattern of gauging terrorist threats (more on this episode later), but I was never called as a witness, for either open or closed testimony. The staff did not even evince any interest in what I had to say in the less formal venue of a staff interview. I was interviewed, but by a trio led by a low-ranking staffer who had worked on budgets and had never been involved in analysis. Neither Zelikow (who was directly involved in writing the part of the report on performance of the intelligence community) nor Douglas MacEachin (who led the staff team responsible for that part of the report) took part. The interview clearly was a perfunctory box-checking exercise and not an effort to learn or to become informed. Several of my former colleagues had similar impressions of their staff interviews.

This interview was quite different from my experiences with earlier official inquiries, including ones that had no more reason to hear from me than this one. These inquiries included a commission on aviation security supervised by Vice President Gore in 1996, a national commission on terrorism chaired by future Iraq viceroy L. Paul Bremer in 2000, an accountability review board investigating the attacks on U.S. embassies in 1998, and the congressional joint inquiry on 9/11. I was a witness for all of these panels, with ample opportunity to speak directly to the commissioners or members and to be questioned by them. The same would be true of the Silberman–Robb Commission that studied intelligence on Iraq and unconventional weapons later in 2004. That commission's first meeting with witnesses was a long session that included several of my fellow national intelligence officers and myself. The commissioners probed at length and in depth and invited those of us on the other side of the table to address anything else that their questions had not covered but that was important to their inquiry. It was at that session that I spoke of the "zeitgeist" that affected analysis on Iraq and that the commission would mention in its report. Even if the commissioners decided to go in a different direction on an issue such as politicization, they did so knowingly and after being exposed to different perspectives and to all of the relevant and important facts. Nothing like this took place in the tightly controlled and heavily scripted process of the 9/11 Commission.

Televised Drama

The principal forum for acting out the script was a series of twelve carefully staged public hearings between March 2003 and June 2004. The hearings were even more important than the commission's final report in molding public opinion about the background to 9/11 and the performance of government agencies. Far more Americans were exposed to the hearings, either directly on television or through press coverage, than would ever crack open the five-hundred-plus page report. The hearings were a vital part of the strategy for mustering support for the commission's reorganization proposal. Most of the press coverage of government agencies' shortcomings and alleged shortcomings stemmed from the hearings. When the commission finally released the report containing its proposal—at that politically advantageous moment during the 2004 election campaign and after more than a year of conditioning public opinion through the hearings—the media focused on the proposal. Even if the report included adjustments in the commission's earlier accounts of how government agencies had performed, almost no one noticed. The story that those agencies had performed badly was by then already old news and taken for granted.

That the hearings were more about catharsis than about learning how government performed was highlighted by the choice of lead-off witnesses in the first hearing, which was held in southern Manhattan not far from the site of the destroyed towers of the World Trade Center. The witnesses were survivors of the attack and relatives of victims of the attack.[19] Their stories were wrenching and their situations deserving of compassion. But their testimony did nothing to advance understanding of why 9/11 happened or what the government did or did not do to prevent the attack. Instead, the testimony only made the process even more one of emotion and less one of information and analysis.

That the hearings also were more about other political interests and objectives than about government agencies' performance was demonstrated by some of the other witnesses. Particularly noteworthy was the choice of Laurie Mylroie, who in various writings propounded the thesis that Saddam Hussein's regime in Iraq had been responsible not only for 9/11 but also for the earlier attack on the World Trade Center in 1993 and much other mayhem that in fact had nothing to do with Iraq. Possibly Zelikow's choice of Mylroie was part of the staff director's larger effort to bolster the themes the Bush administration used to sell the Iraq War.[20] A more generous interpretation is that Zelikow was only leaning over backward not to exclude any possibilities. Either way, it meant putting at the witness table someone whose theories already had been thoroughly discredited. Peter Bergen, whose work as a journalist and scholar has made him a leading expert on al-Qa'ida and bin Ladin, describes Mylroie as a "crackpot."[21] Mylroie's inclusion on the witness list was one of the most conspicuous indications of a lack of seriousness in educating the public about 9/11.

While the commission was giving airtime to crackpots, it was not hearing from others who could have given the commissioners and the public important insights about the very topics to which the commission would give prominence. Even though intelligence would be the subject of its centerpiece proposal, a remarkably small proportion of the testimony from noncommission witnesses addressed the intelligence community's pre-9/11 performance. That subject was left largely to one unavoidable witness, DCI George Tenet. The result was predictable, especially considering the extra demands on the intelligence director's energy and attention associated with the unraveling of the Iraq War and of the Bush administration's case for it. With too much ground to cover, Tenet came across as rigid and defensive. The impression he left formed a contrast to the crowd-pleasing contrition with which former White House counterterrorist chief Richard Clarke began his appearance before the commission. Tenet's closed testimony did not go any better; his frequent inability to recall details convinced some commissioners he was dissembling.[22]

Except for dramatic moments such as Clarke's disarming apology, most of what the press and the public took away from the hearings came not from the government or outside witnesses, but instead from statements by the commission staff. The attention the statements received helps to explain the bickering between Zelikow and the rest of the staff over who would get to read them before the cameras. The statements were prepared in accordance with Zelikow's preemptive outline, and after revision (much of it minor) most of them became sections or chapters in the final report.

In their later book, Kean and Hamilton were candid about the spirit in which the statements were prepared: "These staff statements functioned like opening statements at a trial, where the prosecution lays out its case."[23] The statements were thus not objective assessments, not the reports of disinterested fact finding, but instead the presentation of a prosecution case. Kean and Hamilton extended the trial analogy to say that subsequent testimony and questioning would "support, refute, or elaborate on" the staff's case, but that is not how the hearings operated. A few pages later in their book the chairman and vice chairman make it clear that the whole process, not just the opening prosecution statement, was tightly controlled. "We wanted to use the public hearings to present our findings," they said. "We did not want witnesses at our hearings presenting information that we were not prepared for."[24] If this inquiry were indeed a trial, it was one in which the prosecution team controlled the proceeding, only the prosecution and not the defense could call witnesses, there were no defense attorneys, and no one associated with the prosecution's case was cross-examined.

Although the staff prepared its statements as a prosecution case, the statements were not portrayed and interpreted in this way at the time. No one at the hearings ever said, "Here's one version of events—the prosecution version—to be subject to critical examination and questioning." The statements were instead presented and taken as definitive findings. Press coverage of the hearings cited assertions in the staff statements as, for example, "The 9/11 commission has found that. . . . " As Kean and Hamilton accurately note elsewhere in their book, "The public widely accepted the staff statements as objective and informative."[25] Rather than the accusatory first word that they were, the staff statements were instead taken as the authoritative last word.

The output of the 9/11 Commission thus was the result of a closed, controlled process, tightly managed by the commission staff, based on predetermined conclusions, with the flaws in that output going mostly unquestioned and uncorrected. The private part of the process was similar in these respects to the public part. The commission staff went through the motions of engagement with the intelligence community, but very much on the staff's terms and with little effect on the end result. When the staff provided a draft of its statement on intelligence to the community for prepublication review, the community offered some thirty pages of comments, with suggested corrections regarding the many errors and omissions in the draft. The staff ignored most of the comments. Of the few changes it made, most were workarounds designed not to correct the underlying error but instead to preserve the story line while preempting possible objections to it. Passages were reworded to avoid an explicitly false statement while continuing to convey the desired impression. The commission staff was using some of the drafting skills that would win it plaudits for its highly readable final report.

As the staff statements were converted into a draft of that report, the intelligence community had one more opportunity to comment on the section concerning its performance. It once again offered many comments, but most of them were again ignored. None of these exchanges were part of the public face of how the commission conducted its business. Had this been an unrestrained inquiry in which the prosecution case really were subject to questioning and examination—as in a real trial—then the intelligence community's comments would have been made part of a record for all to see. But they never were.

STRATEGIC SUCCESS

The spectator sport approach, in which the intelligence community's performance is critiqued with no attention to how a different performance might or would have affected U.S. policy and U.S. interests, was very much in evidence in the commission staff's work. For example, the commission's report includes as part of its appealing theme of "failure of imagination" a section that says that the intelligence community (and the CTC in particular) did not exercise its imagination enough about the tactic of using airplanes as cruise missiles.[26] In fact, the tactic had been not only imagined but actually considered by real terrorists. Algerian terrorists had planned to use this tactic in Paris in 1994 before French commandos retook the hijacked airplane during a refueling stop in Marseilles. And Ramzi Yousef, leader of the 1993 attack on the World Trade Center, had talked of crashing a plane into the CIA's headquarters. More important, this tactic was only one of dozens of comparably plausible, imaginable, and highly destructive terrorist tactics. The commission never addressed what good all this imagining—of one possibility or dozens of them—would do in helping policymakers or security managers make hard decisions about defensive measures and counterterrorist priorities. Moreover, the principal security measure against the cruise missile tactic—namely, keeping terrorists and their weapons off airplanes—is the same security measure needed against the old, familiar fly-me-to-Beirut variety of hijacking that was rampant in the 1970s and 1980s. That tactic not only was imagined but also became the basis for erecting a security system using X-ray machines and metal detectors at airports. The 9/11 terrorists defeated the system not because their tactic was not imagined, but instead because enforcement of the system had become lax.

The commission staff's portrayal of the intelligence community's performance was not only irrelevant in some respects but inaccurate in others. The errors occurred in topics as diverse as collection, planning, and budgets—hence the many pages of corrections provided in the community's response to the draft report. Consider strategic analysis of the jihadist terrorist threat represented by al-Qa'ida. One reason for selecting this topic in particular to discuss as a sample of errors is its importance as a standard of intelligence performance; although even the best intelligence service cannot be expected to uncover the details of every terrorist plot, a good service ought to be able to identify and describe the larger threat of which any one plot is a part. A second reason is that this topic concerns the part of pre-9/11 intelligence work with which I am most familiar and thus can write about most authoritatively. A third reason is that in presenting this topic the commission staff had to make the biggest adjustments from reality to support its preferred narrative. In other words, this topic is where the staff's account was most wrong and misleading.

The strategic intelligence on the terrorist threat that manifested itself in the 9/11 attacks was strong. The intelligence community identified and highlighted in the early 1990s the terrorist threat from the radical Sunni Islamist network as a growing phenomenon that was different in important respects from the state- and group-instigated terrorism of the 1970s and 1980s. Intelligence community analysts—in the CIA and other agencies—were writing about this network and more specifically the "Afghan Arabs" during this early part of the decade and by 1993 about the specific threat posed by Usama bin Ladin. The recognized significance of bin Ladin's role in the network was great enough to create in January 1996—despite this period being a nadir of funding for counterterrorism as for other aspects of national security—a first-of-a-kind center devoted solely to learning everything possible about bin Ladin, his activities, his associates, and his connections. The intelligence community's continued accumulation of knowledge about bin Ladin's organization, based in part on this center's work, was reflected in its swift determination of responsibility for the bombings of the U.S. embassies in Kenya and Tanzania in 1998.

Through much of the 1990s and into 2001, the community conveyed its analysis on bin Laden and al-Qa'ida in a wide range of written assessments, briefings for senior policymakers, and deliberations within the interagency Counterterrorism Security Group chaired by Clarke. What intelligence was saying in these classified fora was reflected in public statements as well. Tenet highlighted bin Ladin and al-Qa'ida as leading threats to U.S. security in each of his annual statements to Congress on worldwide threats from 1999 onward. In his statement in February 2001, he described the threat from terrorism as "real," "immediate," and "evolving." He said that bin Ladin and his network of associates were "the most immediate and serious threat" and were "capable of planning multiple attacks with little or no warning."[27] Throughout the subsequent summer, the CTC delivered repeated briefings and warnings about the imminent threat of an attack by bin Ladin, including a possible attack within the United States.

That policymakers absorbed the intelligence community's messages on the threat from bin Ladin and al-Qa'ida is confirmed by the policymakers' statements, including to the 9/11 Commission. Those policymakers include Clarke—who, given his position during this period, was the principal consumer of intelligence on terrorism—and his bosses, National Security Adviser Sandy Berger and President Bill Clinton.[28] The absorption of the message by these and other senior officials also is confirmed by the enormous time and attention they devoted over several years (a story told most fully in Steve Coll's Pulitzer Prize–winning book *Ghost Wars*) trying to do something about the threat in the face of innumerable diplomatic, logisti-cal, military, and other complications.[29] This effort included a sustained program of covert action against bin Ladin beginning in 1997 and a CIA plan—ready by early 1998—to capture him. The plan was not executed because the odds of success were simply not great enough—certainly not because there was any lack of appreciation among the policymakers about the importance of the target. I participated in some of the briefings on the plan for senior policymakers.

On the danger from terrorism and al-Qa'ida, unlike many other subjects addressed in this book, intelligence played a significant role in helping to guide policy. It did so because, unlike with the Iraq War, the policymakers of the day did not bring to the subject their own peculiar objectives and preconceptions. And it did so because, unlike with the Iranian revolution, policymakers were not crippled by competing values and reservations but instead were united by the simple objective of trying to curb terrorism and save lives.

Clinton made his own appreciation of the terrorist threat publicly clear during the latter half of his presidency. He stated in 1998 that the United States was in "a long, ongoing struggle between freedom and fanaticism, be-tween the rule of law and terrorism."[30] In the same year, he told the United Nations General Assembly that "terrorism is at the top of the American agenda—and should be at the top of the world agenda."[31] If the strength of Clinton's commitment does not come through in the 9/11 Commission's re-port, it is because Zelikow—over the objections of several other members of the staff—deleted references to such statements lest Bush look unfavorable by comparison.[32]

As Clinton's administration came to a close, his national security team's appreciation of the terrorist threat was reflected in the advice the team members gave to their successors. Berger told Condoleezza Rice, "You're going to spend more time during your four years on terrorism generally and al-Qa'ida specifically than [on] any other issue."[33] Berger's deputy, Lieuten-ant General Donald Kerrick, left a memo for the new NSC front office identifying al-Qa'ida as one of the "things you need to pay attention to." In his elaboration about al-Qa'ida, he said, "We are going to be struck again."[34] Clarke, who would become a frustrated holdover under Bush, repeatedly sounded the same themes during the first months of the new administra-tion.[35] Another holdover, Tenet, in a briefing to Bush, Cheney, and Rice a week before the inauguration, identified the "tremendous threat" from al-Qa'ida as one of the three biggest national security challenges facing the new administration.[36]

However much 9/11 was by definition a tactical intelligence failure, any suggestion that it represented a strategic failure is clearly nonsense. The intelligence community's work in identifying early a possible nascent threat, focusing collection efforts to learn as much as possible about that threat, using the collected information to form a fuller understanding of the threat, and successfully imparting to policymakers that understanding and an appreciation of the serious of the threat—all years before the 9/11 tragedy—was a model of how strategic warning ought to work.

But this picture did not fit into the preferred narrative of 9/11. It conflicted with the satisfying notions that 9/11 happened because government in general and intelligence in particular failed to understand a new and potent threat and that fixing faulty government agencies thus would prevent a recurrence. If the fact that the intelligence community and its policymaking customers actually did understand the threat were to become a message emanating from the inquiry, the catharsis would be less complete and satisfying, and the support for "reform" of intelligence would be weaker. And so the commission staff tried to paint a different picture: of an intelligence community that either did not understand the threat or understood it but failed to communicate that understanding to policymakers. (The staff sometimes seemed to be making the first of these accusations and sometimes the second, apparently untroubled by the contradiction between the two.)

The staff used a variety of techniques to paint this picture, the main one being simply to omit mention of much of the intelligence community's work on the subject, including some very important work. If the commission did not mention an action or a product, then as far as the public was concerned, the action never occurred, and the product never existed. A complementary technique was to identify and narrowly define certain things the intelligence community did *not* do and thereby—because all the comparable work the community *did* do was left unmentioned—to leave the impression that the community had done nothing at all.

The staff employed these techniques even with their own commissioners. MacEachin, about a year into the staff's work, used what he later admitted was "wise-ass" theater in a briefing of the commissioners. He made an elaborate presentation, complete with PowerPoint slides, of what he said was a comprehensive and previously unearthed intelligence report on al-Qa'ida.

After getting the commissioners suitably excited about this wonderful detail-filled, dot-connecting report, MacEachin revealed that he had made it up himself—dramatically making his point that it was something the CIA should have done but didn't.[37] The trick could have been used on almost any topic, no matter how sound and vigorous the actual intelligence work had been. It is always possible, even without the advantage of hindsight, to contrive an imaginary intelligence report not entirely like any real one, no matter how much the real reports had performed comparable functions and presented similar material packaged differently. The impact of the wise-ass theater depends on the audience being kept in the dark about the real reports.

One of the most relevant of the real reports was a comprehensive briefing on bin Ladin's organization that the CTC prepared and that Tenet presented to President Clinton immediately after the bombings of the embassies in Nairobi and Dar es Salaam in 1998. The briefing was very much like MacEachin's, including the use of PowerPoint slides, although without the added touches that could come only with six more years of hindsight. The briefing covered the nature, objectives, past actions, and current strength of bin Ladin's group. And it represented the best possible way for strategic analysis to have an impact on policymakers' thinking and actions. It was presented directly to the president and his senior advisers at the moment they were about to take decisions regarding the group about which they were being briefed. It would have been pointless for MacEachin to attempt his stunt if the commissioners had seen the briefing, but the staff concealed it.

GREEN AND BLUE COVERS

In its final report and other public presentations, the commission staff's principal technique in disparaging the intelligence community's strategic analysis was to equate it with only a single written intelligence art form and to brush aside or ignore all the other forms it took. The technique was equivalent to saying that Chopin was a deficient composer because he did not write a symphony—or, to make the analogy more exact, that he was deficient because he did not compose a symphony in a particular key at a particular point in his musical career. The art form the commission staff seized upon is the NIE. For the staff's purposes, the NIE had the advantage of being one of the very few intelligence formats that people outside government have heard of (largely because the name has been in use longer than any of the other formats' names). That advantage gave the staff an opening to suggest that any analysis that was not part of an NIE wasn't strategic, comprehensive, authoritative, or influential, and that because there was not an NIE specifically on al-Qa'ida during the period they were examining, strategic intelligence analysis on terrorism was thus deficient.[38]

The suggestion was wrong on all counts. Despite the familiarity of the term *national intelligence estimate*, and despite controversies surrounding portions of some NIEs that have been made public, the art form has consistently been one of the least influential intelligence products. As early as the 1950s, a survey of the use of those products showed that the main users of NIEs were junior staff members who found them to be handy sources of briefing material. A series of biennial reviews of intelligence performance during George W. Bush's administration showed the pattern had not changed. When senior policymakers were asked which intelligence products they found most useful, NIEs consistently ranked last or next to last.[39] The surveys reflected the fact that NIEs are not path-breaking or agenda-setting documents. Whatever they contain that is important enough to warrant policymakers' attention has almost always already been conveyed to them in other forms. As the NIE on Iraqi weapons vividly demonstrates, even when NIEs cover a topic that has top priority, few policymakers read them.

For senior policymakers, intelligence (including strategic analysis) is most effectively portrayed in oral briefings or simply in conversation at a conference table.[40] On terrorism and al-Qa'ida in the years prior to 9/11, Tenet and his deputy John McLaughlin performed this function at countless morning briefings and meetings of national security principals. (Tenet supplemented the briefings with a series of eight letters, beginning in December 1998, to the president and the rest of the national security community, emphasizing the danger of further attacks from bin Ladin.)[41] At the subcabinet level, the same function was performed primarily in the frequent meetings of Clarke's Counterterrorism Security Group. Whatever integration was going to be achieved—between intelligence and policy, between comprehensive views of al-Qa'ida and strategy on what to do about it—was being achieved in such meetings, not in an NIE or in any other single intelligence document. The Counterterrorism Security Group's deliberations were often operational and tactical, but also (as I know from sometimes having sat in the intelligence chair) genuinely strategic.

Even among analytical intelligence papers, NIEs are only one of many different forms that have come and gone through the years, no one of which has a monopoly on comprehensiveness or any other virtue. The choice of an art form is often arbitrary and has little to do with the paper's content. The two assessments I initiated on consequences of the Iraq War are examples. They were at least as NIE-like as the estimate on Iraqi weapons or any other NIE, but I decided instead to call them intelligence community assessments (ICAs). The procedures for producing and coordinating either an NIE or an ICA were identical except that the former required one last meeting of what was then called the National Foreign Intelligence Board to bless the final product. Board meetings rarely resulted in significant changes to a paper, but their scheduling was problematic. It was not unusual for an estimate to be delayed a couple of months because a meeting could not be scheduled or the agenda for the next meeting was full. So in the interest of getting the papers out the door as much in advance of the war as possible (and because of a concern in the back of my head that one more meeting would give board members a chance to get cold feet about releasing assessments so much at odds with the assumptions underlying policy), I made them ICAs. Even the Republicans on the Senate Intelligence Committee, who later strove to downplay the significance of these papers, did not try to make an issue of the art form. They accepted them as no less authoritative a statement of the intelligence community than NIEs. But by the 9/11 Commission staff's standards, anything not called an NIE would be dismissed as no more significant than narrow and tactical pieces of current intelligence.

Particular offices or agencies in the intelligence community own particular art form brands. For the past three decades the NIC has owned the NIE brand. Thus, the NIE format is not normally used on subjects that normally do not involve the NIC. This is true of several topics that have their own special centers or staffs. In the early 1990s, terrorism became one of those topics. With the CTC's having established its effectiveness over the previous few years, the function of coordinating and producing communitywide assessments was transferred from the NIC to the CTC for the same general reasons of integration and synergy that other counterterrorist work had been transferred to the center. A Community Counterterrorism Board was established within the center to perform this function. The head of the board (usually a senior officer from a non-CIA agency such as the NSA or the State Department) functioned just like a national intelligence officer, chairing an Interagency Intelligence Committee on Terrorism—which had been in existence since the 1980s—that met regularly, exchanged information and insights, and approved community-coordinated assessments on terrorism. Because the board and the CTC did not own the NIE brand, its products instead had different names, such as "community counterterrorism assessments." If one looked for strategic analysis on terrorism in the years prior to 9/11, an NIE was one of the least likely formats in which one would find it.

The commission staff knew all about these distinctions but did not explain to their readers what it meant regarding the format of analytical products on terrorism. To do so would have undercut the tactic of highlighting NIEs as the sine qua non of strategic analysis and the supposed gap in the intelligence community's work. An irony is that the earlier transfer of responsibility for strategic community-coordinated analysis on terrorism to the Community Counterterrorism Board was exactly the sort of change that, if proposed by someone on the outside, would be touted as reform. Like the commission's own proposals, it centered around the concept of integrating work on terrorism—the whole idea behind the NCTC. But the commission staff did not count the earlier change as reform, nor did they ever even mention it. In determining what counted as strategic analysis, the staff pretended that this previous act of integration had never occurred.

Besides being a game about the supposed difference between papers with green and blue covers (as NIEs have) and functionally equivalent papers with covers of another color, the staff's fixation on NIEs was a way of downplaying the undeniably huge amount of intelligence work, including strategic analytic work, that the community had done on al-Qa'ida and the larger jihadist terrorist threat in the years prior to 9/11. "Thousands" of reports were circulated, the staff acknowledged. These reports included "a number of very good analytical papers" on topics ranging from bin Ladin's "political philosophy," his "command of a global network," and al-Qa'ida's "operational style" to the "evolving goals of the international extremist movement." In addition, "hundreds" of articles had been produced for morning briefings for the most senior policymakers.[42] Being unable, not surprisingly, to find any significant missing insight in this corpus of work, the commission staff instead contended that arranging insights in a certain way was what mattered. The staff asserted that "there were no complete portraits of his [bin Ladin's] strategy or of the extent of his organization's involvement in past terrorist attacks."[43] The notion was that if just one more paper—one that stapled together the findings from the other thousands of papers into a single "complete" package—were produced and were given a green and blue cover, it somehow would have made a difference. In true spectator sport fashion, this notion paid no heed to policymakers' needs or to the likely impact on policy. It ignored one of the most time-tested principles of intelligence analysis, which is that shorter and more specific papers have a better chance of being read and heeded than longer, more "complete" ones. It also ignored the extent to which the Clinton administration policymakers already were heavily engaged with the problem. By their last couple of years in office, they were certainly well past the need for a textbook introduction to al-Qa'ida.

Regardless of whether "complete portraits" could have made a difference, the assertion that there were none was false. The aforementioned briefing for President Clinton was one. Another was an assessment on al-Qa'ida approved by the Interagency Intelligence Committee on Terrorism that CTC analysts produced in the same year. This was a product of the reformed process for producing community-coordinated analysis on terrorism, managed by the Community Counterterrorism Board, which the commission staff ignored.

Yet another complete portrait had been written earlier and could be found in the threat assessment sections of findings authorizing covert action against al-Qa'ida. A covert-action finding probably is the most definitive statement of perceptions that senior policymakers and intelligence officers hold in common. It starts with the president's or his senior advisers' identification of a security problem and instructions to the CIA to develop a program to deal with the problem. The CIA drafts a covert-action finding that includes a detailed description of the threat to be countered, the proposed program to counter it, and the risks and costs the program may entail. The draft finding is exhaustively reviewed within the CIA and—because every covert action is sensitive—by senior officials at the White House, NSC, and relevant departments. Drafts are frequently sent back and forth between the CIA and the policymakers. The president signs the final version before it is briefed to selected members of Congress.

One of the commission's staff statements (not the one on the intelligence community's performance) noted that President Clinton signed "successive authorizations" for offensive covert action against bin Ladin and that "policymakers devoted careful attention" to these documents.[44] Having acknowledged these covert-action efforts—the very existence of which testified to how seriously the Clinton administration regarded the threat from bin Ladin—it would have been easy to have declassified the least sensitive part of the findings, which were the sections describing the threat. If the commission had done so, it would have revealed a forcefully worded picture of bin Ladin's objectives, his record as a terrorist to date, al-Qa'ida's operational capabilities and reach, and the very serious threat the organization posed to U.S. national security. But this picture would have sharply contradicted the commission staff's assertions both about there being no "complete portraits" of al-Qa'ida and about policymakers not fully understanding the seriousness of the threat. So the commission never revealed these threat assessments, even though—unlike most NIEs—the president and his senior advisers actually read them.

A THREAT UNDERSTOOD

Although the NIE brand was not one usually employed for strategic analysis on terrorism in the decade prior to 9/11, the NIC, as the brand owner, could still suggest imprinting the brand on work done by other components. It did this in 1995 when it proposed to the CTC an NIE on a topic relating to international terrorism. The resulting estimate was titled *The Foreign Terrorist Threat in the United States*. The very selection of that subject highlighted the danger of attacks by foreign terrorists within the U.S. homeland. The paper integrated much analytic work by the FBI as well as by the CIA and other agencies. It identified the radical Islamist network that had formed during the jihad against the Soviets in Afghanistan and that continued to rely on training facilities in Afghanistan as the principal threat. It warned that the growth of the network was "enhancing the ability of Islamic extremists to operate in the United States." The estimate judged the most likely targets of attack to be "national symbols such as the White House and the Capitol and symbols of U.S. capitalism such as Wall Street." It also pointed to civil aviation as an especially vulnerable and attractive target.[45]

The agencies involved in producing this document followed up to try to convey its messages where they might do some good. We in the CTC had worked closely with the Federal Aviation Administration (FAA) to ensure that questions of aviation security of most concern to the FAA were fully addressed. The FAA subsequently organized a pair of briefings for senior members of the aviation industry, including representatives of airlines, airport authorities, the Air Transport Association, and the pilots' and flight attendants' unions. An FBI officer and I were the briefers. The FAA hoped the briefings would help in its difficult task of convincing the industry of the need for costly additional security measures against terrorism. I later joined John O'Neill of the FBI to brief jointly to senior officials in the Department of Transportation our judgments about the terrorist threat to other forms of transportation infrastructure within the United States.

These presentations were as relevant to the 9/11 Commission's inquiry as just about anything else the U.S. government had done in the years prior to the 2001 terrorist attack. But they also were jarringly inconsistent with the preferred story line according to which the CIA and FBI were not working together and neither one was voicing sufficient concern about the foreign terrorist threat to the U.S. homeland. So the commission staff never mentioned the briefings, adding them to the other relevant events that, as far as the American public knew, never occurred.

In its statement for the hearing that addressed the intelligence community's performance (and from which most of the press coverage on this subject emanated), the commission staff also did not mention any of the judgments from the 1995 estimate that I cited earlier. Nothing about Islamist extremists' growing ability to operate in the United States, the Afghan roots of the threat, the focus on aviation, or the likelihood of Washington and Wall Street landmarks as targets. (The staff eventually mentioned some of these topics in its final report.) Instead, the staff cited only a line that referred to the major portion of the threat then as being from loosely affiliated terrorists such as the ones who had accomplished the first attack on the World Trade Center in 1993.[46] The choice of this line as the lone citation was part of a larger effort by the commission staff to portray the intelligence community as being slow to recognize the emergence of one specific terrorist group, al-Qa'ida.

The staff never addressed what difference any of this 1995 document made or should have made to policy. This document was, after all, an NIE— the intelligence art form that, if the staff were to be believed, has influence like none other. If one asks what initiatives the U.S. government might have taken beginning in the mid-1990s in response to the threat the estimate described and that could have made a difference in preventing 9/11, two things come to mind. One is a major beefing up of aviation security—much like what was implemented after 9/11. The other is military intervention in Afghanistan—again, like what happened after 9/11 but moved up several years. Neither of these initiatives depended on conclusions about whether a later threat would come from a single named group such as al-Qa'ida or from other Islamists. In either case, Afghanistan was the base and aviation in the United States a likely target.

As with so many other topics in foreign and security policy, initiatives were left untaken not because intelligence agencies did not identify a problem or policymakers did not understand the problem, but instead because of other constraints on what policymakers could do. The resistance to enhanced aviation security measures, which the FAA had hoped our briefings might help to overcome, was strongly rooted, especially in the airlines' financial interests. The need for the additional measures was recognized in several government reports, in particular that of the Gore commission on aviation security in 1996. But each additional bit of screening of passengers and bags would cost money, either directly or indirectly because of its impact on schedules. The same was true of other security measures, such as hardened cockpit doors. The latter subject was under discussion, and the Israeli airline El Al had fortified its doors, but heavier doors meant more weight and more fuel costs, so U.S. airlines resisted that change, too. The industry lobbied hard on these questions. Journalists noted a spike in the industry's political donations to Democrats following release of the first draft of the Gore commission's report. A conclusion of one academic study of this issue is that the security shortcomings that 9/11 demonstrated can be seen as a "market failure brought on by deregulation" in which short-term earnings of the airlines were the decisive factor.[47]

As for intervening in Afghanistan, until a shock as momentous as 9/11 there simply was nothing close to the public and political support that would have been needed to send U.S. troops to that half-forgotten land half a globe away. The closest thing to a window of opportunity prior to 9/11 for launching such an expedition was the aftermath of the bombings of the embassies in Africa in 1998. But the impact of twelve Americans dying at an overseas installation paled in comparison with the impact of almost three thousand killed in a spectacular attack on the U.S. homeland. Even a politically strong president would have had difficulty mustering support for anything more than the cruise missile strikes two weeks later that constituted the U.S. military response to the 1998 incident. The fact that

President Clinton, mired in the Monica Lewinsky scandal, was politically weak at the time only compounded the difficulty.

It is easy to forget how much even the missile strikes, which seem like a pinprick now, generated skepticism. On the morning of the strikes, I had the task of going to the Capitol to brief the staffs of the House and Senate intelligence committees on the intelligence that underlay the targeting of the al-Qa'ida facilities that the missiles struck. The one member who also attended—a Republican senator—showed little interest in what I had to say about the nature of al-Qa'ida's presence in Afghanistan, the group's relationship with the Taliban, the training that took place in the camps that were hit, and the terrorist capabilities that were supported there. He wanted only to question the timing of the missile strikes and whether it had more to do with the White House's political requirement of detracting attention from Clinton's embarrassments than with the intelligence that suggested bin Ladin would be at one of the camps. This suggestion was what became known as the "wag the dog" scenario, after the title of a then-popular movie in which the White House concocts a foreign war to divert attention from a presidential sex scandal.

Clinton's political vulnerabilities may have been unique to him, but the other realities and complexities of policymaking on Afghanistan continued into the first eight months of the Bush administration. However valid are Richard Clarke's and others' criticisms that the new administration was slow to focus on counterterrorism, the slowness was not, as the 9/11 Commission would have it, due to any failure to "imagine" the seriousness of the terrorist threat emanating from Afghanistan.[48] If anything, the focus on bin Ladin and al-Qa'ida was too sharp in the sense that prior to 9/11 it would have required a broader rationale, based also on the Taliban's egregious human rights record and barbaric treatment of women, to have had even a hope of garnering support for a military operation more decisive than the missile strikes. The Bush administration decision makers were not insensitive to these other issues but calculated that tackling the Taliban problem with too long an agenda lessened the chance of making progress on the number one issue on the agenda, which was bin Ladin and al-Qa'ida.

The realities and complexities that faced the Clinton and Bush administrations included, as so many difficult foreign-policy problems do, several different interests and objectives that are important to the United States. Acting against the Taliban and their al-Qa'ida guests would necessarily have involved Pakistan and thus would have affected other major U.S.

concerns about Pakistan—including nuclear weapons, Kashmir, the Indo–Pakistani conflict, and issues of democracy and stability within Pakistan itself. Afghanistan's potential role as a conduit for Central Asian energy resources (and not letting Russia corner those resources) also figured into at least the Clinton administration's thinking.[49] Whatever political capital and diplomatic chits are expended on behalf of one objective are unavailable for other objectives. And short of a politically unsupportable full-scale intervention, the options for using military or covert resources for disposing of the problem of bin Ladin and al-Qa'ida continued to offer little hope of success.[50]

That the failure to dispose of that problem before 9/11 was not due to any failure to understand, appreciate, or "imagine" the threat it entailed is demonstrated by the continuation of many of the same obstacles *after* 9/11. Bin Ladin and his partner Ayman al-Zawahiri remain at large—not because the United States gives them insufficiently high priority as targets but instead because they utilize the same security savvy and local sympathies they always have utilized. Many of the same operational difficulties that led Clinton administration officials not to pull the trigger on the 1998 capture operation continue today. A planned secret military operation in 2005 to seize several senior al-Qa'ida members, including Zawahiri, was aborted when Secretary of Defense Rumsfeld decided that it put too many American lives at risk and could cause a rift with Pakistan.[51] And concerns about Pakistan's nuclear weapons continue to complicate U.S. policy regarding Taliban influence and activity in northwestern Pakistan.[52]

The only way in which the judgmental distinction that the 9/11 Commission staff tried to play up regarding the 1995 estimate—whether the threat was coming mainly from a single group led by bin Ladin or from a larger movement—could have misguided U.S. policy was if policymakers subsequently gave insufficient attention to this one man and his group. But they clearly didn't. The single most prominent strand in U.S. counterterrorist efforts through the late 1990s was bin Ladin and more specifically efforts to capture him. This had been true even before the embassy bombings in 1998; the focus on this one man and his group became even more extreme immediately after that attack. In my last year as deputy chief of the CTC (1998–1999), the center chief and I spent far more of our time on this one topic than anything else. That emphasis reflected similar priorities in Clarke's office and elsewhere in the counterterrorist community.

A GROUP HALTINGLY EVOLVES

The commission staff's theme of slowness in recognizing the development of al-Qa'ida was mistaken about both the recognition and the development. The staff asserted that "while we now know that al Qaeda was formed in 1988, at the end of the Soviet occupation of Afghanistan, the intelligence community did not describe this organization, at least in documents we have seen, until 1999."[53] As already noted, the latter half of this sentence was a falsehood that depended on arbitrarily focusing on documents with certain formats but ignoring others.

The first half of the sentence was deceptive. It left the impression that an anti-U.S. terrorist group had been in operation for a decade before anyone in the U.S. government paid attention to it. There was no such group. Although the commission is hardly the only one to refer to 1988 as a birth date for al-Qa'ida, the only thing "formed" back then was an agreement among bin Ladin and some other Arabs in Afghanistan not to dissolve their part of the support apparatus that had helped to sustain the insurgency against the Soviets. They wanted to do something else and not just to let their achievement fade into history. They were unsure what that something would be, but for the time being it was not a terrorist group, let alone an anti-U.S. one. Lawrence Wright, in his account of the rise of al-Qa'ida, *The Looming Tower* (another Pulitzer winner), says of that time, "It was still unclear what the organization would do or where it would go after the jihad. Perhaps Bin Laden himself didn't know."[54] Coll notes that as of late 1989 "Bin Laden was not yet much of an operator. He was still more comfortable talking on cushions, having himself filmed and photographed, providing interviews to the Arabic language press, and riding horses in the outback."[55] Bin Ladin later claimed, to appear consistent, that he had considered the United States his enemy all along, but his earlier words and actions belied that assertion. During the Afghan insurgency, he had gone out of his way to thank the Saudi royal family for bringing the Americans into the fight against the atheist Soviets.[56]

The uncertainty about what would be done with the old Afghan support structure continued over the next several years. Wright summarizes the situation as of 1995 this way: "Al-Qaeda so far had come to nothing. It was another of his [bin Ladin's] tantalizing enthusiasms that had no leadership and no clear direction."[57] Nothing in the 9/11 Commission's own narrative of al-Qa'ida's history, elsewhere in its report, contradicts this picture.[58] The 1995 estimate's judgments about the nature of the Islamist terrorist threat at that time were not just sound "based on what was then known," as the commission report patronizingly put it.[59] They constituted an accurate picture of the actual Islamist threat.

The focused and virulently anti-U.S. terrorist group that we came to know as al-Qa'ida emerged mostly in the latter half of the 1990s. It was a response to frustration among radical Islamists from failing to overthrow earlier in the decade the Arab governments that had been their principal enemy all along—especially the one in Egypt, the target of Zawahiri's Egyptian Islamic Jihad before he joined forces with bin Ladin. Bin Ladin's stroke of strategic genius was to redirect efforts away from those near enemies and aiming them instead against the United States, thereby gaining support as the supposed champion of the entire Muslim *umma* (community) against the alleged predations of the U.S.-led Judeo-Christian West.

This history has led those who have studied it closely to reject talk of a 1988 "formation" of al-Qa'ida. Fawaz Gerges, the American scholar who has described that history in most detail, writes: "In the first half of the 1990s there existed no centralized structure for transnational jihad, and Al Qaeda, as a formal organization, had not been activated yet. It would be misleading to talk about Al Qaeda as a formal organization before 1996; its official birthday is widely recognized as the 1998 announcement establishing the World Islamic Front."[60]

The wide recognition Gerges mentions refers to the writings of Arab scholars and commentators who also have been deeply immersed in the subject—some of them as participating political Islamists—and who routinely consider bin Ladin's declaration in February 1998 (of what is sometimes rendered in English as the International Islamic Front to Combat Jews and Crusaders) as marking the birth of al-Qa'ida.[61]

Scholars and analysts still debate exactly how the formative years of al-Qa'ida should be characterized and to what extent its actions in the late 1990s had precursors in the early 1990s. But the 9/11 Commission's suggestion of a terrorist group fully hatching in the late 1980s is way off the mark. An accurate rendering of the development of al-Qa'ida reveals that the intelligence community's tracking of that development and of the events and circumstances underlying it kept pace remarkably well given the inherent obstacles to tracking any secret organization. What the commission staff portrayed as being behind the curve was, like the judgments of the

1995 NIE, actually ahead of it. When the CTC established at the beginning of 1996 its special unit to learn everything it could about bin Ladin, it gave the unit the cable abbreviation TFL for "Terrorist Financial Links" because bin Ladin at that time was still essentially a financier, albeit one with bigger but still mostly unrealized ideas. There were other things going on earlier in the 1990s in the world of Islamist terrorism that posed a threat to U.S. interests—as the 1993 attack on the World Trade Center demonstrated—but they were not the work of al-Qa'ida.

Even if one were to focus solely on 9/11, the story of the Islamist terrorist threat was not just a story of al-Qa'ida. Khalid Sheikh Mohammed (or KSM, as he became known in the counterterrorist community) was the mastermind who conceived and organized the attack and was therefore at least as much responsible for it as bin Ladin. KSM, an uncle and associate of Ramzi Yousef, was a major target of U.S. counterterrorist operations through the 1990s. But he did not join bin Ladin's group until late 1998 or early 1999.[62]

In its retrospective effort to find any delay between the availability of source material and appearance of that material in intelligence analysis, the commission staff zeroed in on a very narrow slice of time: basically a few months beginning in 1997. The staff did not address whether whatever delay it found was unreasonable or out of the ordinary in painting a picture of something like a nascent terrorist group. More important, the staff never addressed what difference any of this made to policy or to the possibility of preventing 9/11. The unstated and unsupportable assumption involved whether a judgment or piece of analysis offered in, say, 1997 rather than 1998 would have made the difference in heading off a terrorist attack in 2001.

The commission staff was not finished treating papers with green and blue covers as the only intelligence analysis that mattered. The NIC occasionally issues short updates on estimates and other assessments it has issued. In 1997, it engaged the CTC to produce such an update to the 1995 NIE. The update revalidated the estimate's warnings about Islamist terrorism inside the United States and incorporated additional insights gained over the intervening two years. The commission staff's statement about intelligence performance asserted, however, that this update "failed to reflect" new information about al-Qa'ida and its efforts to mount attacks against the United States.[63] That assertion was false. The update referred explicitly to bin Ladin's discussion of plans to attack inside the United States and assessed—in the key judgments in the front of the paper—that heightened threats and surveillance by bin Laden's organization overseas might be the prelude to attacks inside the United States. In the later full commission report, the staff finally acknowledged what the update had said about the threat from bin Ladin's organization, but it counted the sentences referring to bin Ladin, pronounced them to be too few, and noted that recent raw intelligence had not been included in the paper.[64] The staff did not explain that this brief paper was a presentation of judgments, not raw reporting, and that like the NIE it was updating (and like most other NIEs) it was a distillation of a much larger amount of analytic work that was presented in fuller form in other products.

MISLEADING TACTICS

The commission staff employed other techniques to mislead. One was to use language strongly suggesting a preferred but false conclusion while stopping short of stating a falsehood directly. For example, the staff referred to information that bin Ladin's organization "quite possibly" was involved in the bombing of the U.S. military training mission in Riyadh in 1995 and that analysts had not "worked through answers to questions about links between bin Ladin and his associates" with regard to the bombing of the World Trade Center in 1993 and the plot to blow up airliners over the Pacific in 1994.[65] Given the staff's other assertions about the intelligence community's allegedly not catching on to the existence and nature of al-Qa'ida, the very strong implication for any reader who did not know better was—although the staff was careful not to say this explicitly—that bin Ladin's group was responsible for those attacks. It was not, based on everything known both then and now.

Other techniques were versions of wordplay. One concerned the name "al-Qa'ida," which was not in widespread use by either the terrorists or counterterrorist specialists or anyone else until very late in the period in question. Even bin Ladin's fatwas (ostensibly religious decrees) and "declarations of war" in the late 1990s did not use the term. So the commission staff would not consider a paper to have addressed al-Qa'ida if the paper did not use that name, even if the group that eventually would be known by that name was clearly the subject. Even such terminology as "bin Ladin's organization" or "bin Ladin and his associates" did not seem to make a paper count.

A related type of wordplay concerned references to bin Ladin as a "financier." That label frequently was applied to bin Laden through much of the 1990s because it was his financial role that had first made him visible and because without a widely recognized group name the usual way of identifying terrorist leaders (such as "Sendero Luminoso leader Abimael Guzman") was not suitable. This default label gave the commission staff the opportunity to say in its draft of Statement Number 11, on intelligence performance, that "as late as 1997, the CTC characterized Usama Bin Ladin as a financier of terrorism, rather than the head of a terrorist organization," with a footnote reference to the 1997 update to the earlier NIE.[66] It did not seem to matter that many of the products that used the "financier" label (including that same NIE update) also spoke in the same breath about bin Ladin's involvement in the planning of terrorist operations. Nor did it matter that another part of the commission staff (evidently not on message) wrote in a different statement that "by early 1997" the bin Ladin unit in CTC "knew that Bin Ladin was not just a financier but an organizer of terrorist activity."[67] In its review of the draft, the intelligence community helpfully pointed out the contradiction. The authors of Statement 11 responded by deleting the last eight words of their original sentence, leaving a statement that was narrowly correct regarding use of the label but that strongly—and falsely—implied that the intelligence community regarded bin Laden as *only* a financier.[68]

Another technique was to play a version of "gotcha." The commission staff plucked words or phrases from something an official had said in a staff interview or in writing and portrayed them as expressing a view that, based on everything else the same official had said and done, he clearly did not hold. The staff used this technique in depicting comments Deputy DCI John McLaughlin had made in his staff interview as expressing disdain for "comprehensive estimates." In fact, he had no such attitude, as anyone who had observed his earlier work as the official responsible for estimates in the NIC could attest. McLaughlin's point to the staff was instead that although such estimates have their role, they are only one of many possible vehicles—and often not the most effective vehicle—for the intelligence community to convey its strategic analysis to policymakers. As with most of the other corrections the intelligence community offered to the draft, the commission staff ignored this correction and retained the error in the published version of its statement.[69]

In its final report, the commission finally accurately attributed to McLaughlin one of the truths that he had communicated to the staff: that "the cumulative output of the Counterterrorist Center 'dramatically eclipsed' any analysis that could have appeared in a fresh National Intelligence Estimate."[70] But the commission staff evidently still was determined somehow to associate the deputy DCI with their story line about allegedly inadequate attention to strategic analysis because they irrelevantly added in the same sentence that he "conceded that most of the work of the Center's 30- to 40-person analytic group dealt with collection issues." One can only guess what kind of comment the staff misrepresented as such a "concession." But the point was totally wrong: the analytic group comprised those center analysts who did *not* deal primarily with collection issues but instead produced finished intelligence, including strategic assessments. Other analysts, assigned to operational branches, worked on collection. Anyone who had received even a cursory briefing about the CTC would know that.

Scratching Hard to Make the Case

The issue on which the commission staff had to scour hardest to find material and to apply the most creativity in depicting that material as supporting the prosecution case was the question of whether U.S. officials had sufficiently appreciated the seriousness of the threat that would be manifested by 9/11. The question was central to the case; many other issues, such as the adequacy of strategic intelligence analysis, were ultimately subsidiary to it. If there were any one thought that the American public most expected to hear from the commission and that the public could most easily understand when they heard it, that thought was, as the commission put it in its final report, that "the threat had not yet become compelling" to U.S. officials.[71] The staff contended that senior officials were bedeviled by "uncertainty" about how dangerous al-Qa'ida was and by a pre-9/11 "conventional wisdom" that underestimated the threat.[72] Despite the overwhelming evidence—including the presidential statements, the thousands of intelligence products, the hair-on-fire warnings from White House counterterrorist chiefs and intelligence directors, the risky capture plans and other covert-action efforts—that officials did indeed find the threat compelling, the commission staff searched and scratched to find something, however insignificant, to try to make a case in the other direction.

The staff found three things. One was a newspaper article from 1999 in which, as one discovers upon retrieving the article, the only uncertainty expressed is that of the journalist and not of U.S. officials, who are in fact cited as portraying bin Ladin as "the world's most dangerous terrorist."[73] (The journalist who wrote the article, Tim Weiner, later wrote a best-selling and unflattering book about the CIA. Not surprisingly, he made no mention in the book of his own cameo role in casting doubt on the official conclusion about the danger from bin Ladin.)[74]

The second item was a comment (another gotcha quotation from a staff interview) attributed to a deputy to Richard Clarke that the threat was seen as one that could cause "hundreds of casualties, not thousands." In its final report, the commission staff replaced the gotcha quote with a reference to a memo Clarke wrote to Rice that referred to the possibility of "hundreds" of dead. "He did not write 'thousands,'" the staff pointedly observed[75]—but there was no indication Clarke was positing any kind of limit to possible death and destruction from terrorist attacks in the United States. In fact, there were ample indications that Clarke, his superiors, and his subordinates saw themselves as striving to avert disasters of unbounded proportions. These and other officials working on counterterrorism did not devise strategies based on any such numerical line drawing, and they realized that precise death tolls would be a function of the terrorists' operational techniques and luck rather than of their declared and demonstrated intention to inflict maximum pain on the United States. The 1995 NIE assessed that the bombing of the World Trade Center in 1993—in which Yousef and his fellow bombers' objective was to topple the twin towers and to kill not just thousands but tens or even hundreds of thousands—probably had crossed a threshold for large-scale attacks in the United States.[76] (Yousef told interrogators he thought his operation would cause about 250,000 deaths.)[77] The Bremer Commission made essentially the same point in the opening pages of the report it published in 2000.[78]

The third item the staff used was a single word in something I had written. It was in a book, published in the spring of 2001, that primarily was a treatise on counterterrorism but also addressed the changing shape of the international terrorist threat. My book described bin Ladin's rise to an unprecedented position of prominence in the global jihadist movement, the reasons for that rise, and the growth of his influence over not only his own al-Qa'ida group, but also the wider movement. To depict this phenomenon, I coined the imagery of concentric circles, with bin Ladin and al-Qa'ida at the center and other parts of the movement occupying the larger circles.[79] Others who have written about international terrorism in the post-9/11 years have used the same imagery.[80] My 2001 book also discussed the increased role of religiously motivated and especially Islamist terrorism, the associated shift in terrorist objectives toward inflicting maximum pain and destruction rather than using terrorism in a more measured way for bargaining purposes, the related increase in the lethality of international terrorism, the increased role of the United States as the prime terrorist target, and the increased global reach of transnational terrorist groups such as al-Qa'ida. I assessed that the greater geographic reach and emphasis on inflicting maximum pain on Americans as well as a growing realization among terrorists that attacks within the United States were feasible was probably heightening the danger of foreign terrorist attacks against the U.S. homeland.[81] The September 11 attacks, which took place a few months after the book's publication, confirmed much of what was in the book and were consistent with virtually all of it. For a second edition published two years later, I left the original text unchanged, writing an additional introduction only to comment on counterterrorist measures taken since 9/11.

One of the judgments in the book that 9/11 confirmed concerned terrorist tactics and specifically whether terrorists would use chemical, biological, radiological, or nuclear (CBRN) tactics or non-CBRN tactics. I addressed this topic because there had arisen in the late 1990s such a strong and narrow focus on CBRN terrorism that, although certainly an important and valid concern, it threatened to suck the oxygen from the discussion of many other important counterterrorist issues. In this surge of interest in CBRN tactics, the term *catastrophic terrorism* (or sometimes *grand* or *super terrorism*) came to be used as a synonym for high-casualty CBRN attacks. This terminology was unfortunate because it led to a tendency to equate CBRN tactics with high casualties and to disregard the possibility that non-CBRN methods might have catastrophic results. I argued that CBRN terrorism was probably a growing threat but that this particular set of tactics was not to be equated with high casualties and that one of the reasons terrorists might forgo the attractions of CBRN methods is that they were quite capable of inflicting mass casualties through other methods.[82] That is why I kept the term *catastrophic* in quotation marks and eschewed the usual term *weapons of mass destruction* in favor of the less familiar but more precise *chemical, biological, radiological, or nuclear*.

An example of the commentary to which I was reacting was the article in 1998 in which Zelikow and his colleagues offered their proposal for a new terrorism intelligence center. The article was titled "Catastrophic Terrorism," and the authors explained in their opening pages what they meant by that term. The danger was that "terrorists may gain access to weapons of mass destruction, including nuclear devices, germ dispensers, poison gas weapons, and even computer viruses." All their hypothetical examples concerned such unconventional weapons. Whatever else the authors wish they had been thinking or would like to think now that they had been thinking then, their message was clear: being catastrophic was a matter of using unconventional weapons, specifically CBRN or cyberweapons. This was the threat they thought needed more attention. They reassured us that the United States already "takes conventional terrorism seriously, as demonstrated by the response to the attacks on its embassies in Kenya and Tanzania" that al-Qa'ida had just executed. The possibility that weapons as conventional as knives and tactics as conventional as hijacking might be used to cause catastrophic consequences was completely out of their picture.[83] That Zelikow and his coauthors had been wrong in equating highly destructive terrorism with a certain set of tactics was a further incentive—in addition to the intelligence community's having been right on the same issue—for the commission staff to obfuscate the distinction between choice of tactics and seriousness of the threat.

The term *catastrophic* invited such obfuscation: Despite the prior general usage that equated it with unconventional weapons, couldn't everyone now agree that 9/11 was a "catastrophic" event? So the staff, in its draft statement on the intelligence community's performance, said that "the head of analysis at the CTC until 1999"—meaning me, although I had moved up to become deputy chief of CTC in 1997—"regarded the Bin Ladin danger as still in the realm of past experience, discounting the alarms about a catastrophic threat."[84] This rendering was quite the opposite of what I had actually said and written about bin Ladin. The staff gave no hint that the use of the term *catastrophic* that it had seized upon referred specifically to CBRN tactics.

This twisting of specific terms became one more item in the catalog of errors that the intelligence community mentioned in its comments on the draft. The commission staff's response was to expand its earlier sentence so that in the published version of its statement I was described as "discounting the alarms about a catastrophic threat as relating only to the danger of chemical, biological, or nuclear attack which he downplayed, referring in 2001—before 9/11—to 'overheated rhetoric' on the subject."[85] The "as relating only" was one of the staff's more fiendish bits of syntax, with its false implication that I had questioned the likelihood of any sort of high-casualty attacks on the United States. I was instead criticizing the commentary that had equated highly destructive terrorism with the use of unconventional weapons only; a principal point of my criticism—which was specifically and explicitly about the narrow fascination with CBRN methods—was that these two things should *not* be equated.

The phrase "overheated rhetoric" was in the introductory chapter of my book, where I identified the gap in the literature on terrorism I intended to fill and appealed for more analysis and not just more emotion in discussing counterterrorism. The relevant paragraph noted that although "there are real dangers in CBRN terrorism and important issues to consider in any effort to defend against it," the intense preoccupation with this one contingency had "left a host of other important issues starved for attention by comparison." These issues included questions related not just to conventional terrorism, but also to "the effectiveness, cost, and consequences of measures taken (or that could be taken) to reduce all forms of terrorism, conventional and unconventional." I commented that "overheated rhetoric that has spun out ever more frightening and unusual ways" in which terrorists might use CBRN methods to kill people was no more helpful in formulating sound counterterrorist policy than dwelling on "nuclear winter" had been in developing sound policies on strategic arms.[86] None of these comments of mine had anything to do with the topic on which the commission staff had tried to stitch together an argument: how U.S. officialdom gauged the threat from terrorism and specifically from bin Ladin and al-Qa'ida.

In the commission's final report, the staff gave up on the phrases "in the past" and "overheated rhetoric" but did not give up its attempt to suggest that I had somehow pooh-poohed the possibility of high-casualty attacks from al-Qa'ida. The staff scoured for another sentence from my book to quote and used one—still from the section about CBRN tactics—that warned against redefining counterterrorism as solely a task of dealing with "catastrophic," "grand," or "super" terrorism.[87] My reference clearly was to CBRN methods; the sentences immediately before and after explicitly said CBRN. The preceding paragraph stated that CBRN terrorism was a legitimate cause for concern, a way in which terrorists might inflict major costs, and a risk that probably had risen in recent years, but that most actual CBRN attacks were likely to cause few rather than many casualties (as would prove to be true of the other terrorist attack in the United States in late 2001: the mailing of anthrax-contaminated letters, which killed five). Because the single quoted sentence did not happen to use the term *CBRN*, however, the staff's evident hope was that the reader would interpret it as blindness to the possibility of something like 9/11. This extended, tenacious effort by the commission staff to attribute views to an official who never held them was all just a play on two different usages of the word *catastrophic*.

This bit of wordplay was especially brazen in several respects. Anyone who bothered to look up the work the commission was referencing would quickly see that it did not say what the staff was suggesting it said. The reviewer of my book for the *New York Times*, writing shortly after 9/11 and referring to the same passages from which the commission staff extracted words, observed that the author was "prophetic in his insistence that we still have more to fear from conventional methods of terror like hijackings than from exotic forms like biological and chemical strikes."[88]

The judgment that the staff misrepresented, about the relative dangers of CBRN and non-CBRN methods, was one on which not just my book but also the intelligence community was correct: 9/11 had nothing to do with CBRN tactics. The attack was the most dramatic possible demonstration of how it was a mistake to redefine counterterrorism solely in CBRN terms. The 1995 estimate and other intelligence assessments through the late 1990s were right in assessing that although the chance of chemical or biological attacks was rising, foreign terrorists attacking in the United States were more likely to use conventional methods that could be, in the words of the NIE, "extremely destructive."[89]

This judgment was important because, if heeded, it could have done some good in setting priorities and guiding counterterrorist efforts (unlike what the commission had to say about "imagining" terrorist tactics). The fascination with CBRN scenarios skewed counterterrorist budgets at the local as well as national level in favor of programs (such as specialized equipment for first responders) that would be useless in anything other than a CBRN scenario. Resources and attention therefore were taken from other efforts that could have helped to counter all forms of terrorism, including what materialized on 9/11.[90] The widespread tendency (as illustrated by the article by Zelikow and his colleagues) to equate very high casualties from a terrorist attack with the use of unconventional weapons also contributed to the surprise and shock from an attack that achieved such casualties without the use of such weapons. Martha Crenshaw, the doyenne of American terrorism studies, has noted this mistaken equation: "A misdiagnosis of what the 'new' actually entails could lead to mistakes as grave as those attributed to lack of recognition. For example, the assumption that the sort of catastrophic terrorism that many defined as 'new' would necessarily involve the use of weapons of mass destruction turned out to be mistaken. The expectation was one factor in making surprise possible."[91] The 9/11 Commission said nothing about any of this.

The risible material that the commission staff offered as support for its contention about the threat not being seen as "compelling" was evidently the result of an effort to fill in a blank in Zelikow's preinquiry outline. There was to be a section in the report about how U.S. officials supposedly did not appreciate the seriousness of the threat, so the staff had to scrounge for material to fill in the section, no matter how much the record pointed overwhelmingly in the other direction. This explanation is certainly much more plausible than that the scrounged material was the basis for reaching the conclusion.

Sustaining the Mythology

In sum, the 9/11 Commission's report and other output constituted a badly flawed and highly inaccurate account of the U.S. intelligence community's work on international terrorism prior to 9/11. It was especially wrong regarding the question of strategic understanding of the threat. On this subject, the commission staff promoted three specific myths. One was that the intelligence community had long failed to discern the emergence of a menacing terrorist group called "al-Qa'ida." A second was that the community did not adequately convey its understanding of the group to policymakers. The third was that intelligence officers and policymakers alike did not understand that they were facing a serious threat. These myths fit comfortably into the existing American mythology of intelligence. None of them was true.

One confirmation that 9/11 was not the strategic intelligence failure that the commission staff endeavored so assiduously to portray it as comes from statements by Clinton administration policymakers. If the episode were such a failure, the policymakers would have every reason, in the interest of protecting their own records and reputations, to say so (much as the Bush administration shoveled as much blame for the Iraq War as it could onto the intelligence community for errors in evaluating Iraqi weapons programs). But they did not say so because they knew it would not be true and because saying so would be inconsistent with pointing out their own understanding of the threat and their major efforts to counter it.[92]

Another confirmation is that despite the commission's expensive inquiry over more than a year, the staff did not come up with a single intelligence judgment about al-Qa'ida or the broader terrorist threat that was incorrect or a single strategic insight about those topics that was missing. This lack of error makes the intelligence community's assessment of this subject different from its assessment of many other topics, including ones discussed in this book, where such errors or omissions by the community are readily apparent in retrospect: the work on Iraqi unconventional weapons, of course, as well as analysis on the Soviet Union in the 1980s, Iran before the revolution, and others. The editors of a volume dedicated to improving intelligence analysis lament in referring to the 9/11 Commission's output, "Sadly, professionals learn little from this well-written report." They point out that sound bites such as "lacked imagination" and "failed to connect the dots" are useless to intelligence officers seeking ways to improve intelligence analysis in the future.[93] The only lesson intelligence analysts can take away from the commission's report about what to do differently concerns ass covering—steps they might take not to perform the intelligence mission and to help guide policy but instead to make the community look good in retrospective inquiries or at least to impede the efforts of those determined to make it look bad. Such steps might include producing papers in certain formats that are unlikely to affect the making and execution of policy but that help to create a more impregnable paper trail. Ass covering is not a commendable use of intelligence resources.

Yet another indication that there was not a strategic failure is the tawdriness of the methods that the commission staff used to try to create the impression that there was. The staff members obviously were talented people who, given credible material, could construct a cogent argument. If there were a straightforward and honest story to tell of strategic failure, then the staff would presumably have told it in a straightforward and honest way. Perhaps the staff calculated—correctly, as it turned out—that if they constructed a story differently, they would not be called on it. But why even take the chance?

As indicated by the examples I have given, the commission staff constructed its portrait of this part of the intelligence community's performance by means of highly selective use of material, partial truths, irrelevant references, plays on words, quotations out of context, suggestive language that leads the reader to false inferences, and tenacious adherence to a story line even when its errors were pointed out. The biggest irony of the staff's account is that it purportedly was an evaluation of analysis. If an independent inquiry were to uncover that the intelligence community had used the same techniques, the community's analysis would be denounced, roundly and rightly, as shoddy. But the 9/11 Commission received a pass.

POLITICIZATION AGAIN

Zelikow had an opportunity to respond to much of what I have described in this chapter about how the commission addressed the issue of strategic analysis on terrorism. Four years ago the editor of a specialized journal on intelligence invited me to submit an article; I wrote about the commission's handling of this issue. My article cited many of the examples of wordplay, quotations out of context, highly selective use of material, and other tactics the commission staff had used to present an inaccurate picture of this part of the intelligence community's pre-9/11 work.[94] When the article was brought to Zelikow's attention, the former staff director wrote a long defense that was notable for what it did not say.[95] He ignored almost all of this record of misrepresentation, continuing the strategy evident in the commission's products of simply not mentioning anything that did not fit the preferred narrative. On the only items that Zelikow did mention, he ignored the details and essentially said, "We looked at this stuff—trust us." Most of Zelikow's missive, besides rebutting some subsidiary points in my article, was about how there was no "evidence" for my characterization of the misrepresentations as intentional. He did not define what would qualify as "evidence" beyond the record of the commission's own work. More explicit indications of intent—such as Zelikow's preinquiry, table-slapping declaration of a "massive" intelligence failure and the need for a director of national intelligence—had not yet been reported when I wrote the article.

I did not have space in the article to ruminate about intentions, but there are indeed other possible explanations beyond deliberate misrepresentation for the shape the commission's output took. Those explanations include the following: the staff allowed itself to be swept up in a popular mood; it lacked expertise about international terrorism; it was simply sloppy; or it had a mindset about there being only one possible way the intelligence community can perform its mission. The last explanation may have been a factor in how Douglas MacEachin addressed the community's output and in particular the role of NIEs. MacEachin had been responsible for CIA analysis on the Soviet Union in the 1980s. Working on the 9/11 Commission staff was an opportunity for him to be on the throwing rather than the receiving end of brickbats against the intelligence community and to show that he was not just a reflexive defender of the community's work but instead could be a tough prosecutor of it. Soviet strategic military forces during the Cold War was one of the few topics on which analytic work centered on NIEs; a series of annual estimates of the Soviet force took this form. So it was natural for MacEachin to think of this form even when addressing a subject on which strategic analysis instead took other forms. To borrow a slogan, the commission staff was stuck in a Cold War way of looking at the intelligence community's production even though the counterterrorist portion of the community had moved beyond that way years earlier.

Put most succinctly, the 9/11 Commission's work was highly politicized. I am using the term *politicization* as I have used it throughout this book. It is not limited to partisanship. Politicization includes shaping of analysis either to stay in the good graces of customers who want to hear certain messages or to help win support for certain favored policies. Two major influences politicized the commission's work. One was the very strong desire of the commission's customer, the public (represented most passionately by but not limited to the victims' families), to hear a message that 9/11 was preventable, that it occurred because government institutions and especially intelligence were to blame, and that "reform" of those institutions would preclude a recurrence.

The second major influence was the commission's own passionate advocacy of a particular public policy: its reorganization scheme. Any time the advocate for a proposal assembles the evidentiary picture relevant to that proposal, that picture is likely to be biased. The principle applies to commissions selling policy just as much as it applies to presidential administrations selling policy (although most commissions do not become fervent advocates of a particular proposal, as the 9/11 Commission did). In this case, the prosecution team functioned also as the jury that rendered the verdict and as the judge who devised the sentence. Almost no one has pointed out the conflict among these roles.[96]

Either of these two influences would have been sufficient to politicize the commission's output. Two other supplementary influences pushed in the same direction. One was the commission's fragile bipartisanship, which to be preserved required blame to be directed less at policymakers and more at the bureaucracy. The other was the commission staff's careerism and competing egos, which added to the incentive to sate the public hunger for certain kinds of findings.

As with any other instance of politicization, the politicizers' true beliefs may be uncertain. It is difficult to explain much of what I have described in this chapter as anything other than willful misrepresentation. But just because something is inaccurate does not necessarily mean members of the commission staff did not believe it, just as some proponents of the Iraq War probably believed that Saddam Hussein and al-Qa'ida were allies. And regardless of the original reason an inaccurate or misleading line of argument makes its way into a case, sheer hard work on the case (most members of the commission staff worked very hard in a high-pressure environment) is enough to inculcate a genuine belief, given the personal commitment that goes along with all the hard work.

What can be said with greater certainty is that staff members of blue-ribbon commissions find it just as hard as intelligence officers to admit that their own work has been politicized. They probably find it even harder because, unlike the intelligence officers and anyone else in a permanent bureaucracy, they cannot even claim that command influence was the reason.

The politics and public mood at the time the 9/11 Commission worked would have limited the choices of even a different staff and a different group of commissioners. But choices were available, including on how to handle something as sensitive as relations with the victims' families. During the Iranian hostage crisis of 1979–1981, National Security adviser Zbigniew Brzezinski intentionally avoided meetings with the hostages' families "in order not to be swayed by emotions."[97] The 9/11 Commission followed the opposite approach in giving victims' families not only reserved seats as a cheering (and booing) section at public hearings, but also seats at the witness table as a way of capitalizing on the emotion. The more swaying that occurred, the better.

The near-contemporaneous Silberman–Robb Commission demonstrated how ad hoc inquiries can make choices that are markedly different from how the 9/11 Commission decided to operate. No one can accuse the Silberman–Robb panel of pulling punches in its critique of the intelligence community's work: in the opening page of its report, it labeled the judgments about Iraqi WMD "one of the most damaging intelligence failures in recent American history."[98] But it produced a much more accurate and less politicized report than the 9/11 Commission because it behaved differently from the 9/11 Commission in several respects, one of which I already mentioned: it listened to intelligence officers and tried to learn from what they had to say. Another difference was not to make its proceedings a television show or to make its main objective the manipulation of public opinion. It went about its business quietly and seriously behind closed doors, issuing just enough in the way of interim statements to reassure the public that it was at work. Yet another difference is that it did not make itself an advocate by committing itself to any one proposal and defining it as the apotheosis of reform. It instead offered fresh observations and suggestions on many different matters, the great majority of which the Bush administration wound up accepting but with considerable latitude in implementation.

CONSEQUENCES

An obvious consequence of the 9/11 Commission's work is that history has been corrupted. The commission's product represents a missed opportunity in that its inquiry almost certainly will be the only occasion for a generously staffed and funded examination, with full access to classified materials, of the full story of the 9/11 attack and activities related to it. By shaping part of that story not as dispassionate history but as part of its campaign to build public support for its reorganization proposal, the commission deprived the public and scholars of what would have been an invaluable record that can be used confidently for years to come as the standard reference for everything having to do with 9/11. Some portions of the commission's report—especially those concerning the 9/11 plot itself—can still be so used (I have done so myself), but other portions, especially relating to what the intelligence community did, cannot.

The corruption of history extended not only to the politicized nature of the commission's own account, but also to the larger record it left—or didn't leave—for future historians. The deficiencies include the major omissions concerning the intelligence community's work and even the characterization of what officials said in staff interviews. The records of those interviews were not transcripts but rather notes the commission staff wrote. When intelligence officers later were given access to the notes on their own interviews (not to correct the notes—only to review them for declassification), some discovered, to their chagrin but not their surprise, that the notes were not accurate reflections of the interviews. Leading questions, for example, were omitted. If the staff had asked "Can this be considered a failure of imagination?" and the reply was "Well, I suppose so," the notes would record the entire exchange as "Interviewee said this was a failure of imagination." The prosecution team thus functioned not only as judge and jury, but also as court reporter.

Besides doing a disservice to history, the commission also left misimpressions about the nature and shape of international terrorism. By falsely implying that such operations as Yousef's bombing of the World Trade Center in 1993 were the work of bin Ladin's group, the commission contributed to the misperception (which the American public—given its tendency to think of its enemies as known, named individuals or organizations—is only too prone to hold) that the radical Sunni Islamist terrorist threat is to be equated only with that one group. That was not the case during the early 1990s; it was not the case even during al-Qa'ida's period of maximum strength several years later; and it certainly is not the case now: the radical Sunni Islamist movement is at least as decentralized (and as large) as ever.[99]

A more serious consequence of the commission's flawed portrayal is that it promotes the idea that the 9/11 attack occurred because of a problem that is in the power of Americans to fix and that once this problem is fixed, there will be no comparable disaster. The American public is predisposed to hold this belief also because of its historically based optimism about the country's ability to overcome any natural or manmade obstacle and to solve any problem if enough resources and smarts are applied to it. Here the 9/11 commission missed another opportunity—to educate the public that counterterrorism is not nearly that simple. The commission did not explicitly say it was that simple, but by centering its efforts on its reorganization proposal, bending its account to make intelligence look broken, and then lobbying for the proposal as if it were critical to counterterrorist success, that was one of its principal messages.

Other postattack inquiries have conveyed a more realistic message about the limits of counterterrorist intelligence. For example, the accountability review board chaired by retired Admiral William Crowe that examined the bombings of the U.S. embassies in Kenya and Tanzania in 1998 used part of its report to lecture security managers on the hazards of relying heavily on tactical warning.[100] The 9/11 Commission skipped that sort of lesson and kept the American public in its comfort zone by catering to its yearning for a fix to a fixable problem. The commission did not confront the public with an uncomfortable truth: that the 9/11 disaster occurred despite strong strategic warning, including warnings from the intelligence community, about the underlying threat and despite an appreciation within both intelligence and policymaking circles of the nature and seriousness of that threat. That truth was especially uncomfortable because it implicitly was in part a criticism of the public itself for not paying sufficient attention to—and not sufficiently supporting measures to counter—a threat that its government did understand. Making that unpopular point would have required some courage and would have made the commission itself less popular. Popularity won out over accuracy.

More specifically, by portraying reorganization of the intelligence community as *the* key to counterterrorist success, the commission fostered the illusion that the reorganization made Americans safer. It thereby made Americans that much less inclined to understand that even after such a reorganization the terrorist threat would remain undiminished. This illusion also made it more difficult to focus Americans' attention on other measures that stand a better chance of actually making them safer.

The 9/11 Commission addressed many other subjects, but none with the emphasis of the reorganization scheme, and there were glaring omissions of topics too politically hot to handle. The Iraq War was one of those topics; the commission report says almost nothing about it. Iraq has had major implications for international terrorism and specifically the terrorist threat to the United States, no matter what position one takes on the war. That would be so if everything the Bush administration had said about supposed ties between Saddam Hussein's regime and Islamist terrorists were true. And it would be so if—as is much more likely and as the intelligence community has subsequently assessed—the war has given a significant boost to Islamist terrorism.[101] But the commission's report leaves the impression that none of this matters as much as rearranging boxes on the intelligence community's organization chart. The report also gives almost no attention to that other perennial political third rail—one that has significant implications for international terrorism—the Arab–Israeli conflict.

Considering all these consequences, the 9/11 Commission represents one of the biggest disparities between the public esteem a body has enjoyed and the value it has added to public understanding and public policy. That's too bad because portions of the commission's output represent very good work by very capable people. And the commission's report really is a good read.

CHAPTER TEN

RESPONSES TO CATHARSIS

The response to the 9/11 Commission's work was almost total, immediate, unquestioned acceptance—even adulation. The same appetite for catharsis and thirst for accountability that had given rise to the commission in the first place were also major reasons for the automatic, unthinking response to its product. The political milieu was another, with Kean's strategy of tempting the parties to outbid each other in the midst of a presidential election campaign working flawlessly. The Democratic candidate, John Kerry, after barely enough time to turn the cover of the commission's report, called for all its recommendations to be adopted. His Republican opponent, President Bush, had to follow suit. The image the commission had created of a thorough, bipartisan study caused its report to be viewed not as the political document that it was, but instead as a careful and objective study. The 117 pages of footnotes in eye-straining small type encouraged the impression that the study was exhaustive and well grounded, more than it encouraged any cross-checking of the commission's material (most of which remained inaccessible to the public). The writing style of the commission's report, which was nominated for a National Book Award, impressed readers as being uncharacteristically lucid for an official report. Style helped to preempt any questions about substance, and it was forgotten that much—probably most—of the world's most beautifully written literature is fiction.

Richard Posner, the polymath from Chicago whose day job is as a judge on the U.S. Court of Appeals for the Seventh Circuit, is almost the only person to have subjected the 9/11 Commission's work and methods to careful scrutiny. Posner summarizes the reception of the report and the reasons for that reception this way:

> The commission's bipartisan composition, its unanimity, its sentimental alliance with (or perhaps one should say exploitation of) the families of the victims of the 9/11 attacks, the rhetorical adroitness and sheer heft of the report, journalists' aversion to complex and abstract issues of public policy (mirroring and reinforcing the ignorance and indifference of the public at large), the curious lack of interest in the subject by media-adept public intellectuals, the natural reticence of intelligence officers, the unpopularity of the intelligence agencies (which makes them natural scapegoats and is one of the factors contributing to the shaky morale of intelligence officers), a sense on the part of a number of members of Congress of both parties that the President had actually done little to strengthen the intelligence system in the wake of 9/11, the timing of the release of the commission's report in the midst of the Presidential election campaign, and its ensuing endorsement by both Presidential candidates, combined to paralyze most public and private criticism and confer holy-writ status on the report, including its recommendations.[1]

The writer John Updike made the holy-writ status more explicit when, a few months after the report's release, he referred in the New Yorker to the King James Bible as "our language's lone masterpiece produced by committee, at least until this year's 9/11 Commission Report."[2] The exalted status of the commission and its report has continued to this day. The report has become a common reference point, repeatedly cited as if there can be no source closer to the original truth about terrorism, about 9/11, and about everything else on which the report comments, including intelligence.

The near-universal acceptance of what the commission said about intelligence involves another irony. A common line of criticism of the intelligence community's work is that it reflects mindsets that are closed to different possibilities and perspectives. There is no clearer example of a broadly shared mindset than the unthinking, uncritical acceptance of the 9/11 Commission's message.

The Press Fails

Unquestioning acceptance of the commission's output represented a failure of the press. As in the run-up to the Iraq War, the press got swept up in a broad consensus, except in this case the consensus was even more broadly shared. There also was no immediate policy outcome as obvious as a war of choice riding on public perceptions of the issues at hand. It would have been hard for a journalist to find a hook on which to hang an inquiry into the commission's misrepresentations without sounding like an apologist for the intelligence community.

What little press coverage did attempt to look past the commission's outward conclusions and at its inner workings focused mostly on partisan politics and whether something worked for or against a particular administration. Zelikow's conflict of interest got some press attention; it would have been hard to avoid the subject. He was a collaborator (and coauthor of a book) with Condoleezza Rice, Bush's national security adviser at the time of 9/11. Seven months after release of·the 9/11 Commission's report, Rice, as secretary of state, appointed Zelikow to a senior position at the State Department. Even the commission's general counsel believed that because of the conflict of interest Zelikow never should have been hired as staff director.[3] The zero-sum nature of some of the issues that arose in the investigation, particularly relating to what the intelligence community had told the Bush administration, meant that massaging the story to make the Bush administration look better also meant making the intelligence community look worse.

One such issue that did eventually come to light was literally a he said/ she said dispute. A book that Bob Woodward published in 2006 revealed a meeting in July 2001—not mentioned in the 9/11 Commission's report—at which George Tenet warned Rice of an imminent threat of attack from al-Qa'ida.[4] Rice's public reaction to Woodward's account was that Tenet had presented nothing new, if in fact they ever had such a meeting. The reaction from members of the 9/11 Commission was their usual one whenever any revelation pertinent to their investigation has belatedly surfaced— indignation that they hadn't been told about it.[5] A day later, after records were checked, the story was: oops, Tenet had in fact told commission personnel about the meeting, in an interview in which Zelikow was one of the interviewers. Other records confirmed not only that Tenet had briefed Rice, but also that Rice evidently found the briefing significant enough to ask Tenet to give it as well to the secretary of defense and attorney general.[6]

Zelikow's looking out for the Bush administration's backside is a major theme of Philip Shenon's book *The Commission: The Uncensored History of the 9/11 Investigation*, which describes other instances in which this bias meant diminishing the significance of the intelligence community's work. Shenon tells of how the commission's staff director attempted (against the objections of one of the Democratic commissioners) to portray an item in the President's Daily Brief in August 2001 that warned of a current and serious threat from al-Qa'ida the way Rice was attempting to portray it: as mostly just "historical."[7] But neither Shenon nor any other journalist has asked, in light of these few instances that have come to light because a commissioner balked or because Bob Woodward happened to write about it, how much more the commission staff massaged its message in similar ways. And if this sort of political manipulation of findings—belying the idea that the commission's inquiry was an objective fact-finding exercise—was going on, how much more manipulation was occurring for reasons other than just protecting the Bush administration? How much was the portrayal of the intelligence community's performance manipulated in the interest of satisfying the popular desire for catharsis and for fixes to supposedly fixable problems? Based on the sample regarding strategic analysis (admittedly not an altogether representative sample), the answer to those last two questions is: a great deal. But the fourth estate never explored this subject.

When a partisan ox gets gored, the ox fights back, and the press does take notice. One instance of such a fight occurred two years after publication of the commission's report, when ABC television aired a "dramatization" of events leading up to 9/11 titled *The Path to 9/11*. The docudrama put fictional words in the mouths of real officials such as Madeleine Albright, Sandy Berger, Richard Clarke, and John O'Neill and did so in a way that, Democrats believed, portrayed the Clinton administration unfavorably and unfairly. The Democrats cried foul, and the issue got editorial attention.[8] Although Kean and Hamilton had until then functioned as Siamese twins, in this instance Hamilton broke with his partner and criticized

ABC's production.⁹ Kean, who was the miniseries' "coexecutive producer," of course defended it. His involvement was consistent with ABC's declaration that the program was based on "a variety of sources including the Sept. 11 commission report and other published materials and personal interviews."¹⁰

One lesson from the episode is that it often takes powerful political interests, offended by being misrepresented, to bring misrepresentation to light and to get media attention. Prominent Democratic political figures constitute such an interest; the intelligence community does not. A second lesson, which Kean's unapologetic involvement in ABC's fictionalized production underscores, is how much the work of the 9/11 Commission in itself constituted a docudrama. That work included the commission's televised hearings as well as its final report, with its smoothly flowing prose and novelistic chapter titles such as "We Have Some Planes" and "The System Was Blinking Red." The commission did not have to concoct dialogue as the television scriptwriters did, but it achieved similar purposes through its selective and creative depiction of material. The commission made its impact in an American culture in which the lines between fiction and nonfiction have become increasingly blurred. The contributions to that culture range from souped-up "biographies"¹¹ to Oliver Stone movies to docudramas. Much of the American public's impression of their leaders and their institutions has depended more on the dramatic and literary quality of the works of art (whether ostensibly fiction or nonfiction) that have depicted them than on any careful attention to facts and analysis.

There will be no mea culpas from the press for its failure to probe the 9/11 Commission's findings—unlike the confessions, which flowed after the Iraq War went sour, about failure to probe more deeply into the Bush administration's case for the war. Nothing coming out of the 9/11 Commission's work has anything like the immediate costs and anguish of that war that would be needed to stimulate such confessions. Public misunderstandings about intelligence do have serious costs, but they extend farther into the future and are harder to identify in specific and concrete terms.

Much of what the press could have probed in the commission's product but didn't had parallels with the Bush administration's pro-war case. For example, the innuendoes about al-Qa'ida's supposed responsibility for terrorist attacks earlier in the 1990s were remarkably similar to the hints in the pro-war campaign about connections between al-Qa'ida and the Iraqi regime. The commission staff's highly selective use of material also resembled the cherry-picking that characterized the Bush administration's sales pitch on the war.

The press would have faced the obstacle of not having direct access to most of the material the commission staff had and from which it made its selections. But the aggressive investigative reporting that caught fire once the Iraq War went bad shows what inspired and inventive journalists can do. Moreover, much of the commission's output easily could have been questioned and checked without gaining access to controlled material. For example, the press could have looked more closely into the commission's central contention that U.S. officials simply did not appreciate the seriousness of the terrorist threat. The material that the commission staff adduced, even if it said what the staff suggested it said, was conspicuously thin in contrast to everything else that officials were doing to counter the threat. And a quick check of the staff's unclassified source material would have shown that this material did not even say what the staff suggested. Instead, it showed that the intelligence community was right, while others outside government were wrong; that bin Ladin posed a very serious threat and that the intelligence community also was right, while again others were wrong; and that highly destructive terrorism in the United States was probably not going to use what were commonly called WMD. If this part of the prosecution case had received any scrutiny at all, it would have been laughed out of court. But like most other parts of the case, it received none.

ECHOES

The 9/11 Commission's enormous influence has been reflected in countless replays of its themes and citations of its conclusions. The power of suggestion that the commission staff skillfully employed is reflected in how much its story has been embellished and the errors in it compounded with each retelling. Suggestions have been turned into firm conclusions, and innuendo turned into fact. The process started with the 9/11 commissioners. Commissioner Tim Roemer, for example, took the staff's bait about use of the "financier" label when he falsely charged that the intelligence community "thought bin Ladin was a financier of terrorism *rather than* one of the heads of terrorism."[12] Heavy and unthinking reliance on the commission's report has repeatedly compounded errors in a similar fashion in media commentary, academic writing, and general discourse. For example, the commission staff's references to an absence of "complete, authoritative" portraits of bin Ladin's strategy or role in past attacks—which refer only to the art form it selected to prioritize, the NIE—have led even scholars who claim to have studied this subject to slide into the quite false statement that *no* intelligence assessments addressed these topics.[13] The commission's story is damage to public understanding that keeps on inflicting harm.

COPYCAT INQUIRY

The commission's heavy influence also has shaped other official inquiries—most notably a congressionally requested report by the CIA inspector general on individual responsibility related to 9/11. The inspector general's office was in an uncomfortable position as it performed this task. It faced all the same accountability-seeking, finger-pointing public pressures that the 9/11 Commission had faced. In addition, it felt the pressure of the commission's report, with its emphasis on faults in intelligence. Given the wide, unquestioned acceptance of the commission's findings, for the inspector general to issue a report that appeared to differ even slightly with the commission would inevitably subject him to charges of being soft on his own agency and of covering up misdeeds of fellow intelligence officers.

The inspector general's office faced an additional complication. In August 2001, only one month before the 9/11 attacks, it had completed an inspection report about the CIA's work on counterterrorism, part of its regular cycle of comprehensive evaluations of offices and functions within the agency. The report was very favorable. Its principal conclusion was: "The DCI Counterterrorist Center is a well-managed component that successfully carries out the Agency's responsibilities to collect and analyze intelligence on international terrorism and to undermine the capabilities of terrorist groups." The report commented positively on the CTC's integrative, communitywide functions. It said, "CTC fulfills interagency responsibility for the DCI by coordinating national intelligence, providing warning and promoting effective use of Intelligence Community resources on terrorism issues." The report drew special attention to how "relationships with the FBI have been vastly improved" and how "CTC's relationship with NSA has improved dramatically since the last inspection." The report had no changes to suggest in either operations or analysis. Its sole recommendation concerned a minor administrative matter.[14] The report was drastically at odds with the picture the 9/11 Commission would purvey, especially considering that a very large proportion of the counterterrorist work that the inspector general had inspected was focused on Islamist terrorism and especially on bin Ladin and al-Qa'ida.

The inspector general faced an unpleasant choice. His office could respond to the congressional request by producing its new report in an honest and straightforward way, consistent with its previous findings (and there is no reason to suppose that its August 2001 report, prepared free of any post-9/11 emotions and recriminations, was anything other than honest and straightforward). If it did, the office would be publicly pilloried for being so out of step with the story line that the 9/11 Commission propounded and that the nation had unquestioningly accepted. Or the inspector general's office could get in step with that story line and produce a report that reflected the commission's report, even though that would be diametrically opposed to its own recent findings. The resulting contradiction in the inspector general's own work could lead to charges either that in its earlier inspection it had incompetently overlooked grossly poor performance, or—the valid explanation—that in its new report it was bending to the political wind and to popular appetites, as conveyed by the 9/11 Commission.

The inspector general chose the latter course, anticipating (correctly) that few people would focus on or even be aware of his office's earlier report. Although the inspector general's office routinely refers in its inspection reports to any earlier reports it had produced on the same subject, this time it did not mention that it had so recently examined the agency's work on terrorism. When a declassified version of the second report's executive summary was released in 2007,[15] the only public indication that the first report existed came in a statement issued by George Tenet, then in retirement. Ever since Tenet had been quoted as saying "slam dunk," he had trouble getting people to pay attention to anything else he said, no matter how informative his other statements may have been. The press coverage and statements by members of Congress about release of the second document all referred to "the" inspector general's report, as if it were the only one on the subject. Readers of the released summary did not seem to realize that what they were reading is one of the starkest 180-degree reversals in the history of inspectors general.[16]

The inspector general's office unashamedly did an about-face, with no explanation, on matters it had addressed in its first report. What it previously described as up, it now portrayed as down; what had been white was now black; what had been good was now bad. For example, the new report reversed the office's assessment of a decision by senior CIA management to devote a portion of counterterrorist funds not to the CTC but instead (still earmarking the money for counterterrorism) to other elements of the Directorate of Operations to develop additional human sources—a recognition that developing more such sources was one of the biggest counterterrorist needs. The first report mentioned this allocation approvingly as one of the ways the agency was making effective use of added counterterrorist funding in the late 1990s; the second report mentioned this same allocation as an instance of "not effectively managing" counterterrorist funds. On relations between the CIA and NSA, there was likewise no mention in the second report of how, in the words of the first report, the relationship had "improved dramatically"; instead, the second report mentioned only "persistent strain," differences that "remained unresolved," and the "negative impact" this strain had on performance of the mission. And so on. On some topics, such as strategic analysis, the inspector general's second report simply aped themes from the 9/11 Commission.

The second report used any matter on which CIA officials had exercised management discretion as a point of criticism, but with no credible explanation of why the course officials chose was worse than the alternatives. The most extreme example of this approach concerned the CTC's special focus on Khalid Sheikh Mohammed as a target to be captured and brought to justice. The report suggested that because KSM was followed primarily by a unit whose mission was to effect such a capture, analysts were not fitting him adequately into a larger picture of al-Qa'ida. It is worth reflecting for a moment on what the inspector general's office was saying: that it was *bad* for intelligence officers to have handled KSM as a case of special importance, with the intention of putting the eventual mastermind of 9/11 out of business, rather than treating him as just one more object of analysis. Of course, if the CTC had decided not to handle KSM that way, the second report almost certainly would have found fault with that decision instead.[17]

The effect such fault-finding mischief can have on broader public perceptions is illustrated by a reference to this same subject in *The Economist* after the summary of the second report was released in 2007. The magazine stated that the report had "revealed" that a supposed failure of units within the CIA to work together had allowed KSM "to slip through the net."[18] *The Economist*'s readers could be forgiven for assuming this assertion meant that CIA officers had simply not paid sufficient attention to this terrorist.

Readers would be astonished to learn that, quite the opposite, the sole basis for the allegation that KSM had "slipped through the net" was that the agency had considered him so important that it devoted special efforts to catching him. Such absurdities are made possible when inquiries such as those of the 9/11 Commission and the CIA inspector general are determined to find fault and press the limits of their creativity in doing so. They also are made possible when members of the press do not stop to consider whether what they are reporting even begins to make sense.

The writers of the second inspector general report did not carry the burden of making the final determination of the fates of the CIA officers involved. The writers could preserve their own public standing by conforming to the popular story line as propounded by the 9/11 Commission and then buck the issue to the agency's director. The director at the time, Porter Goss, had every personal and political reason to go with the flow as well and to let heads roll where they may. The events in question had not happened on his watch, and he had been appointed director in part to tighten up what allegedly had become an undisciplined ship amid the acrimony over the Bush administration's selling of the Iraq War. Only one thing inclined him in the other direction: the patently contrived nature of the report. So Goss did the only fair and honorable thing, which was to keep the report classified and to disapprove its recommendation to convene an accountability board to mete out discipline.

Goss's successor, Michael Hayden, had similar incentives to go along with the report's recommendation; the events also had not happened on his watch at the CIA, and he was receiving other pressures from Congress relating to his previous directorship of the NSA. But he reaffirmed Goss's decision for the same reason Goss had made it. When Hayden eventually was forced, under heavy congressional pressure, to release a redacted version of the report's summary, he said to CIA employees that "there are very different perspectives on this report," adding that "our colleagues referred to in the document, and others who have read it, took strong exception to its focus, methodology, and conclusions."[19] This was about as close as the head of any department or agency ever comes to renouncing publicly the work of his own inspector general. The second report was one of the factors that convinced Hayden it was necessary to inspect the inspectors, which he did by directing his senior counselor to look into how the inspector general's office conducted its business. As he surely must have anticipated, this directive subjected him to even more criticism from members of Congress, who accused him of trying to intimidate a watchdog.[20]

Much of the commentary, investigations, finger pointing, and blame mongering directed primarily at the intelligence community would have occurred even if the 9/11 Commission had never existed or if different people had performed its work. These responses were rooted in long-standing American habits of dealing with setbacks and tragedy. But the commission and how it decided to use the enormous attention it enjoyed certainly influenced greatly the shape and direction of all the other reactions to 9/11. When the summary of the second inspector general report was released, Philip Zelikow praised it and observed that it was consistent with the 9/11 Commission's findings.[21]

ACCOUNTABILITY

The commission-driven response to 9/11 has solidified and extended the American mythology of intelligence. The September 11 attack has joined the Iraq War as the second great example in the recent bastion of common wisdom about intelligence failure. The common wisdom persists despite the most direct evidence refuting it. The single most authoritative piece of evidence comes from the intelligence community's annual statement to Congress on worldwide threats to U.S. interests—the intelligence product that, given its comprehensiveness and regularity, would most deserve to be called a "national intelligence estimate" if that name had not already been applied to an older ad hoc art form. In particular, that evidence comes from the 2001 edition of this statement—the most recent one before 9/11 and before President Bush decided to launch the Iraq War—which described (as had the previous couple of editions) terrorism by al-Qa'ida as the number one threat to U.S. national security and which did not even mention Iraqi nuclear weapons as a possibility or make any mention of stockpiles of Iraqi unconventional weapons. Purveyors of the common wisdom according to which the intelligence community did not convey the seriousness of the terrorist threat but did misguide the Bush administration into a war do not seem to have noticed.

A final thought about the 9/11 episode concerns a concept that became much in vogue in discussion of it: accountability—or, rather, a lack of it.

Commissions enjoy the extra status that comes from being in effect a temporary fourth branch of government, but they bear none of the accountability that most of the permanent government does. The 9/11 Commission staff wrote about the performance of the intelligence community knowing the commission would not be held accountable, at least anytime soon, for the accuracy of its story or the integrity of its methods. With almost no scrutiny of the commission's own work, full accounting of its performance will come only in the future, when it becomes an object of history and not a writer (or rewriter) of it. Future historical judgments, rendered after more Americans fall victim to international terrorism, will need to consider how the 9/11 Commission will share responsibility for those tragedies because it fostered public misunderstanding of what underlay 9/11 and pushed for changes that, as I describe in the next chapter, made U.S. counterterrorism no better and may only have made it worse.

CHAPTER ELEVEN

THE ILLUSION OF REFORM

The reorganization plan that the 9/11 Commission made the centerpiece of its work and that Congress enacted after hasty consideration and in slightly modified form in December 2004 was a response to the national yearning for catharsis, not a response to any careful analysis of what actually had happened before 9/11. There is no reason to suppose that what is cathartic is also effective in other respects. The 9/11 Commission's plan exemplifies this principle.

The commission never explained how, even if its politicized report were taken at face value, most of the shortcomings in the intelligence community's performance would have been avoided or mitigated if its plan had been in effect. Even specific and unmistakable errors by intelligence officers, such as much-noted tardiness in placing two of the 9/11 hijackers on a watch list, were not a problem of organization charts or interagency communication. The necessary procedures were all in place, even if in this specific instance officials faced with a flood of reporting were not as prompt as they should have been in using those procedures. The commission's prosecution case against the intelligence community was not logically connected to its proposal, but instead impressionistically and emotionally connected to it by fostering public support for intelligence "reform." Because reorganization is a visible and thus favorite Washington way of reforming, and because in this instance some reorganization ideas already were on the shelf, reorganization it was destined to be.

Richard Posner's trenchant critique of the 9/11 Commission's work focuses on the reorganization plan and the thinking that should have gone into it but did not. One can do no better in understanding the plan than to read Posner's analysis of it.[1] I do not duplicate that analysis here but instead highlight the principal characteristics of the plan and add some observations based on personal experience. Posner notes that many of the serious flaws in the scheme can be traced to the commission's failure to avail itself of relevant sources of insight, including organization theory, the history of reorganization of government agencies, and foreign experiences in organizing intelligence services.[2]

A study of the foreign experiences alone would suggest that the commission's scheme was largely change for the sake of change. An Israeli commission that studied failures prior to Egypt's surprise military attack on Yom Kippur in 1973, for example, concluded that Israeli intelligence was too centralized and that a more pluralistic intelligence system would be better at preventing such surprises—the opposite of the 9/11 Commission's conclusion.[3] Whatever the current system is, the imperative is to make it different, to respond to the urge to "do something" in response to defeat or tragedy. Clichés tripping over each other demonstrate the illogic in much of this view. A House intelligence subcommittee report in 2006 that criticized the intelligence community for a "lack of urgency" in addressing its failures said that the analytical portion of that community was still "subject to groupthink."[4] If groupthink were applicable to that community, no one explained how centralizing the community *more* would ameliorate the problem rather than make it worse.

The 9/11 Commission's closed, noninquisitive manner of operating meant a failure to examine changes taking place in the absence of reorganization. This failure was yet another contrast with how the Silberman–Robb Commission conducted its business. One of the suggestions I made to the latter commission was to look (as that commission in fact did) at the changes the intelligence community already had implemented on its own as a result of lessons learned from failures on Iraqi unconventional weapons. The most important of those changes was to require senior intelligence officials to certify explicitly the reliability of source material that their agencies had collected and to do so as part of the final review of any community-coordinated assessment that used the material. In one of the last such assessments I managed before retiring, some reporting was deleted as a direct result of this requirement. If the revised procedure had been in effect in 2002, the spurious reports from the infamous informant Curveball almost certainly would have been screened out. The change was a major improvement, and it had nothing to do with any reorganization. The 9/11 Commission's relative lack of interest in improvements the intelligence community was making on its own was probably less a simple absence of curiosity than part of a pattern of wanting to hear only certain things. The more that experience showed improvement can occur without reorganization, the weaker would be the case for reorganization.

A New Layer of Bureaucracy

As intelligence officers come to work each day, they do not, as their first order of business, study the organization chart on their cubicle walls to determine how they will do their jobs. Instead, they perform their assigned missions using whatever contacts and resources are available to them, whether inside or outside their own component or agency. This certainly has been true of intelligence officers dealing with terrorism. Officers working on the subject in the CIA, NSA, FBI, State Department, and elsewhere exchange as many phone calls and emails with each other as with members of their own agencies and departments. They also share the same fundamental mission, which, simply put, is to reduce terrorism and to save lives. One of the elements of unreality in most discussions of intelligence organization—and in the adoption by the 9/11 Commission and Congress of the old proposal to create a DNI—is that the discussions are largely divorced from the real workaday world of intelligence officers. Those officers know they have important jobs to perform, and they get on with their jobs. The lines on the upper parts of the organization chart hardly matter for the great majority of things they need to do.

To the extent that the head of the entire intelligence community does matter, there already was such a position before December 2004: that of DCI. The position was associated with leadership of the CIA because, as the word *central* implies, the CIA was the only intelligence organization not part of some other government department. Many of the other organizations in the intelligence community exist because they function as the intelligence staff for an individual department such as State, Defense, Treasury, or Energy—a function the heads of departments undoubtedly would insist they retain no matter how ruthless a reorganization the rest of the intelligence community might undergo. If the head of the community needed more clout, the obvious response would have been to grant more authority to the DCI. But that would have looked too much like a reward to the CIA to be a politically attractive measure after 9/11.

The DNI as established by the reorganization legislation has little more power than the DCI had. The second DNI, Mike McConnell, openly complained about having insufficient authority.[5] Limiting the DNI's control over such things as transfers of personnel was the main respect in which Congress put its stamp on the 9/11 Commission's proposal after only a cursory review of the plan. The result is a job whose responsibilities and expectations exceed its authorities. Robert Gates was smart—from the standpoint of preserving his own reputation—to turn down the opportunity to become the first DNI. Those who, unlike Gates, nevertheless have been willing to take the job deserve the nation's gratitude for doing so.

The odd and undefined nature of the DNI's position is underscored by one of the frequent arguments heard in favor of it: that the DCI's job had to be split up because leading both the CIA and the intelligence community was too big a job for one person to handle. The DCI, like any other senior leader in either government or the private sector, did not personally do everything, though; he delegated. To help run the CIA, he had an executive director of the agency as well as a deputy DCI who focused much of his time on agency business. A second deputy DCI was concerned solely with communitywide business, assisted by an intelligence community staff. If such delegation does not negate the "too big" argument, then what does it imply about the DNI? If he really is in charge of the whole intelligence community, then his job is every bit as big as the DCI's was. If he is not fully in charge of it, then what did the reorganization accomplish?

The specific task that consumed as much of the DCI's time and attention as any other was to serve as the president's principal intelligence adviser, which in recent years has carried with it direct involvement in the president's morning intelligence briefing. When the DCI's job was divided, that function went to the DNI. As long as the DNI performs that job, he or she will never be able to devote anything close to full time attention to leadership and management of the community.

Creation of the DNI did not consolidate the intelligence community and bring different agencies in it together. Instead, it created yet another agency, called the Office of the Director of National Intelligence (ODNI), to sit precariously on top of the other agencies in the community. This outcome was predictable from previous ostensibly centralizing reorganizations. Robert McNamara's creation of the Defense Intelligence Agency in 1961 did not achieve the hoped-for consolidation of military intelligence but instead created one more organization to coexist as a first among equals in the continuing intelligence activities of the individual military services. Moreover, it is understandable and reasonable for a senior leader burdened with broad responsibilities to want sufficient staff to assist him in discharging those responsibilities. That outcome, too, can be seen in how the military operates. Creation of any new military command has always entailed creation of a full staff to go with it.

The 9/11 Commission and Congress devoted remarkably little attention to these issues and thus to what the ODNI would inevitably look like. I felt one effect of this inattention during my last three months of government service, which also was the first three months of the new agency after it went into operation under the first DNI, John Negroponte, and his principal deputy, Michael Hayden. One of the tasks they assumed was participation in senior interagency policy meetings. Preparation for the meetings requires a significant amount of staff work, including researching the issues to be discussed, communicating with the NSC and contacting other departments to identify departmental positions, writing briefing books, and briefing the principals. When the DCI and his principal deputy attended the policy meetings, they relied on CIA offices to do most of this work. The DNI and his deputy could not do likewise without appearing to be an appendage of this one agency. They turned to the only substantive staff they had—the NIC, the small office whose mission is to manage interagency assessments. I was the member of the council responsible for the Near East and South Asia, so about half the policy meetings fell in my area. Preparation for the meetings overwhelmed everything else my staff and I had to do. So for those three months (and beyond), work on interagency assessments in my area of responsibility—including NIEs, the art form the 9/11 Commission had touted as supposedly being especially important—ground almost to a halt. Later adjustments in staffing would enable the NIC to cope with the problem, but this specific outcome exemplified the lack of thought that went into the reorganization scheme.

The rapid growth of the ODNI into a full agency has incurred criticism, including from members of the 9/11 Commission, who claim they had in mind something leaner and meaner.[6] This commentary is misplaced for the reasons just given. The criticism also illustrates how intelligence "reform" and the arguments that support it can become self-sustaining and self-reinforcing. Critics castigate the growth of the ODNI as an example of the intelligence community's stodgy, ponderous, overbureaucratized habits that have made reform necessary, but without realizing or acknowledging that it was a commission's attempt at "reform" that caused the problem in the first place.

Another example of this self-reinforcing cycle concerns exactly which of the functions and authorities of the now-divided DCI job were to devolve to the DNI and which would stay with the director of the CIA. Those functions and authorities had accumulated over several decades of legislation and executive orders. The hastily prepared reorganization legislation did not come close to detailing which authorities went where. Government lawyers have been negotiating over this division ever since. Added to the uncertainty over division of functions has been the ODNI's natural tendency to make full use of the one solid line of control on the new organization chart that extends downward from the DNI to a previously existing agency: the one to the CIA. The lines to the intelligence community components that continue to reside inside other departments are only dotted. This line of control has resulted in such bureaucratically ineffective and friction-inducing steps as the ODNI's booting CIA representatives off interagency committees in which the CIA had played a part for years and still had a major interest so that the ODNI could claim the seat.

One area of friction that has gotten public notice concerns whether overseas intelligence representatives should be representing the CIA or the DNI.[7] This argument and similar tussles generated by the uncertainties of the reorganization of 2004 have come across as more of the kind of petty squabbling among turf-conscious intelligence bureaucrats that proponents of reform like to point to as the main reason the intelligence community needs to be overhauled.[8] The proponents of reform do not mention, however, that the tussles result directly from the 9/11 Commission's "reform."

Whatever members of the commission and the Congress may have hoped for in the way of greater communitywide work habits, their reorganization has done little to promote that goal. The redrawing of lines on the organization chart has done little to enhance what the military calls a "purple-suit mentality"—thinking of joint missions ahead of individual service responsibilities. One of my last initiatives before retiring from the NIC was to recruit an experienced officer from one of the intelligence agencies to fill a new position to help discharge the suddenly suffocating responsibility of preparing the DNI and his principal deputy for policy meetings. The officer was well qualified for the task and eager to do it. I told his home agency that this job was an important one in which although the officer would be a deputy to me, he would in effect be working much of the time directly for the DNI and deputy DNI. The home agency balked at the reassignment, and a deputy agency director said in essence that his agency's needs came before the DNI's. I had to enlist the DNI's chief of staff to do additional lobbying and to appeal the decision to the agency's director before I could get the assignment approved.

There has long been much purple-suit thinking in the intelligence community—especially regarding counterterrorism—but most of it has nothing to do with reorganization. Informal lines of communication and cooperation and the attitudes and work habits of officers and their managers are ultimately much more important than lines on an organization chart. Agencies in the intelligence community have taken many steps through the years, such as cross assignments of personnel, that have encouraged communitywide perspectives without reorganizing anything. The CIA, for example, made what is known informally as an "out of body experience"— an assignment outside the agency—a requirement for promotion to its senior intelligence service.

The establishment of the ODNI, besides being an old idea that could be dusted off to help satisfy the urge to "do something" following 9/11, also represents a swing of a rhetorical pendulum between sharing information across agencies and safeguarding it. The next espionage case that is serious enough to become a scandal and in which the spy is found to have exploited access to multiple databases will see the replacement of commentary about the need to share information more widely across the government with recriminations over how one disloyal person could have been allowed such access. The pendulum already began to swing back in 2010 in response to the release of hundreds of thousands of classified U.S. government documents by the organization WikiLeaks. The chairwoman of the Senate Select Committee on Intelligence, Diane Feinstein (D–Calif.) acknowledged that "part of the problem" leading to the huge leaks was the broad distribution of information that had been promoted heavily in the wake of 9/11.[9]

A CENTER OF CONFUSION

It is very difficult to identify any advantage offered by the other major feature of the 9/11 Commission's reorganization scheme—creation of the NCTC—that had not already been offered by the one reorganization of counterterrorist intelligence that made a major difference: the establishment of the CTC nearly a quarter-century ago. The CTC incorporated all the advantages of synergy and cross-fertilization that come from integrating into a single component counterterrorist functions ranging from disruption of terrorist cells to strategic analysis of worldwide threats. The integration was not just multifunctional but multiagency. The participating agencies included not only those in the intelligence community, but also others involved in counterterrorism. The most important relationship was with the FBI, whose role in the integration included the assignment of a senior special agent as a deputy chief of the CTC as well as the assignment of numerous other FBI personnel at various levels. Customs, immigration, the Secret Service, and several other nonintelligence organizations with responsibilities related to counterterrorism also participated.

The CTC demonstrated how a function such as counterterrorism can evolve and improve without redrawing any lines on an organization chart. The relationship between the CIA and the FBI is the best specific example of this conclusion. I saw that relationship change, during the six years I worked on counterterrorism, from distrust sometimes bordering on disdain to an extensive collaboration with deep mutual understanding of each service's mission and challenges and, most important, mutual respect. This collaboration was the "vastly improved" relationship to which the first CIA inspector general's report—the one not shaped by hindsight and by the 9/11 Commission's version of events—referred.

In contrast, the creation of the NCTC has generated confusion, despite the efforts of the talented people who work there. The confusion begins with the odd combination of intelligence analysis and policy planning that the center embodies, along with its related double reporting chain to higher authority. The unusual structure reflects the hard bargaining between the 9/11 Commission's staff director, who was determined to create such a center, and the commission's vice chairman, who sensed the downsides of the proposal but reluctantly agreed to it after imposing additional conditions that complicated the organization chart even further. Just as the nation should be grateful to those who have agreed to serve as DNI, it also should be grateful to anyone who becomes chief of the NCTC with its binary responsibilities and two different bosses.

Even greater confusion concerns where NCTC's responsibilities begin and those of continuing counterterrorist components, especially the CTC, end—especially with regard to analysis. I have asked officers in each of these centers how the responsibility for that function is divided, and the most frequent response has been a shrug of shoulders. The commission might have anticipated the problem if it had paid more attention to how the NCTC's precursor, the Terrorist Threat Integration Center, had already created similar confusion. Some understandings appear to have been reached over time, and the shoulder shrugs have become slightly less marked. To the extent that officers in each center have managed to draw some lane lines and to clarify some of their responsibilities, it has been in spite of, not because of, the organizational hand they were dealt.

The NCTC embodies one of the major disconnects between the 9/11 Commission's narrative and its supposed remedy. The narrative had much to say about information getting stuck in stovepipes and not flowing as smoothly and quickly as it might have across agency lines. And yet the commission's plan created one more stovepipe—NCTC is in effect yet another agency in the intelligence community—and one additional set of bureaucratic lines across which information must flow. It is unsurprising that improvement in the intragovernmental flow of terrorism-related information is not readily apparent now and continues to be a focus of criticism in outside studies.[10]

No doubt some information is flowing quite nicely among officers from the FBI, CIA, and other agencies who are sitting around the same tables at the NCTC. But flow of information is one of the many subjects in intelligence and in counterterrorism that present trade-offs. What might assist the flow between agencies may impede it within agencies—and the latter, as the 9/11 narrative itself suggests, can be just as important as the former. By separating bureaucratically and physically the counterterrorist analysts in the NCTC from analysts in agencies such as the CIA who do not have "counterterrorism" as part of their titles but are doing related work, the reorganization lessened the prospects of identifying emerging terrorist threats early.

An episode from 1995 illustrates this point: the Japanese cult Aum Shinrikyo's attack on the Tokyo subway system with sarin gas. At the time of the attack, the group was not on the screens of the U.S. counterterrorist community. That fact represents a strategic intelligence failure—quite the opposite of the attention the intelligence community already was giving, even at that early date, to bin Ladin. As chief of the analytic group in the CTC at the time, I bear at least as much responsibility for that failure as anyone. The failure did not receive attention because it did not involve the deaths of Americans or a large number of deaths of anyone else. But it might have. Aum Shinrikyo's bizarre ideology envisioned an Armageddon between Japan and the United States, which the group thought it might have to stimulate. If the Japanese police had not begun disrupting Aum's activities (the proximate stimulus for the attack on the subway), there is no telling how much lethal anti-U.S. mayhem the group might have caused.

The failure was in part a matter of resources; our coverage of East Asian terrorist groups at the time was embarrassingly meager. The year 1995 was a nadir of funding for counterterrorism,[11] and the CTC's gearing up of its concentrated effort against bin Ladin was stretching resources available for coverage of other targets even more thinly. But another lesson of the episode is the importance of communication between counterterrorist officers and analysts covering topics that may involve precursors to terrorism. (The main impact of the Tokyo incident on most nongovernmental American thinking about terrorism was unfortunately instead to amplify the fascination with chemical, biological, and other unconventional weapons.) Aum Shinrikyo was well known to anyone following Japanese political and social phenomena but was not being looked at from a counterterrorist perspective. The reorganization that created the NCTC has increased, not decreased, the chance of this kind of failure in the future.

SELF-DELUSION

Skilled, dedicated officials at the NCTC, ODNI, and other components affected by the creation of these offices are making the structure that the 9/11 Commission and Congress imposed work despite the significant faults of that structure. They are making it work precisely because they are skilled and dedicated and because they are adaptable, the more experienced of them having lived and worked through previous reorganizations. That something can be made to work is not the same as saying it ever should have been imposed in the first place or that it constitutes an improvement over what came previously. On balance, the reorganization of 2004 is probably more damaging than helpful. This is especially true when the disruption that imposes major costs in any reorganization, this one certainly included, is taken into account. It is all the more true when the confusion—about roles, powers, and responsibilities—that continues to this day is also taken into account. A question the 9/11 Commission staff rhetorically posed— "Who is in charge of intelligence?"—is, as far as counterterrorism is concerned, harder to answer now than when there was a DCI.[12]

Enactment of the 9/11 Commission's reorganization plan was an exercise in national self-delusion. Americans, eager to do something visible after 9/11 and yearning for a fix that they would like to believe would prevent a recurrence of the tragedy, bought the commission's sales pitch that rearranging boxes on the intelligence community's organization chart would make them safer. It has not made Americans safer. It may have made them less safe—if not because of the flaws in the reorganization itself, then because of the huge diversion of attention it represents away from things that really will affect the likelihood that Americans will fall victim to terrorism in the future.

Failure Redux

The failure of the commission's reorganization scheme to improve counterterrorism was highlighted by the next terrorist incident salient enough to cause uproar in Washington: a near-miss in December 2009 in which a Nigerian terrorist unsuccessfully attempted to detonate an explosive aboard a Northwest Airlines flight from Amsterdam to Detroit. The incident touched off recriminations that replayed the ones heard after 9/11, with the same familiar themes about strands of information not being put together and dots not being connected. Only this time the cast of bureaucratic characters was different, with the 9/11 Commission's creations, the DNI and especially the NCTC, being prime targets of the recriminations.[13]

Those who had been involved in the commission did not acknowledge what the incident underscored: that the scheme adopted five years earlier that was supposed to fix problems underlying such failures clearly did not do so. The former commission chairman, Thomas Kean, instead indulged in the hindsight that as usual dominated the recriminations. A visit by the Nigerian's father to the U.S. embassy in Abuja "should have been enough to set off all kinds of alarms," said Kean,[14] as if a father's request for help in locating a wayward son, with mention of some radical comments but no mention of involvement in terrorism, ought to have caused this tip to send the Nigerian terrorist's name zooming to the top of the list of half a million names that the NCTC maintains. Kean's main theme after the incident was that "despite the best efforts of the 9/11 commission and other intelligence reformers," churlish or incompetent bureaucrats were keeping the machinery from working right. "Turf battles persist among intelligence agencies," he said,[15] without identifying any way in which a battle over turf figured into the latest incident and without noting that the principal turf battles in recent years resulted directly from the commission's "reform."

A few who reflected on the incident involving the flight to Detroit began to ask the unavoidable question of whether that much-ballyhooed "reform" really was an improvement after all. Fewer still—and no one in a position of authority—voiced the main lesson: that maybe, just maybe, at least some such incidents reflect the inherent challenges of the business and the normal and for all practical purposes unavoidable shortcomings exhibited by even extensively reformed bureaucracies and by even skillful and diligent officers who work within those bureaucracies.

It would be political poison for any politician or senior government official to utter that lesson. It is politically imperative to express indignation at anything less than perfection in counterterrorism. It is all the more imperative when one's opponents are poised to pounce on anything that might be construed as acquiescence in failure. Republicans vigorously exploited the Detroit incident to portray the Obama administration as weak on security in general and on terrorism in particular.[16] President Obama consequently had to express his own indignation at the performance of intelligence and security agencies.[17] Most of the measures the president announced as supposedly corrective steps were, by their very nature, further evidence of how uncorrectable is the fundamental challenge of identifying terrorist needles amid what is not just a haystack, but instead a stack of other, nonterrorist needles. The steps he mentioned included vague exhortations—such as that the DNI should "take further steps to enhance the rigor and raise the standard of trade craft of intelligence analysis"—that reflected the difficulty of coming up with anything new and different.[18]

The most useful step the president announced was to have the NSC staff lead a review of the criteria for placing names on watch lists. Much of the hindsight-filled hand wringing after the December 2009 incident had to do with why the would-be bomber was on the NCTC's long list but not added to much shorter lists of people to be given special scrutiny before be-ing allowed to fly or barred from airplanes altogether. The criteria to apply to such listing constitute a policy decision. They are not for intelligence and security agencies alone to decide. The criteria represent a national decision about how much security to buy at the price of decreased privacy or increased inconvenience to the traveling public. The decision changes with the national mood, which in turn changes according to how much time has transpired since the most recent terrorist incident. In the couple of years prior to the 2009 incident, there were complaints that too many, not too few, people were being placed on the restrictive lists.

EPISODIC RESPONSES

The 9/11 Commission's reorganization plan and the largely unthinking adoption of it were an unusually intense and politicized chapter in the un-ending story of intelligence "reform." In other respects, however, the chap-ter was typical of the rest of the story. One of those respects is the tendency to equate change with reform. Another is that the post-9/11 response drew from a single event implications that were far broader than that one event and led to changes that have even broader effects. Such "reform" is driven not by the seriousness of problems ostensibly being corrected but instead from the public anguish over the latest incident to give rise to demands for reform. Loss of human life is one of the main things that produces such anguish.

This pattern is hardly unique to intelligence. It also applies, for exam-ple, to NASA's space program. Recrimination and demands for reform followed the losses of the space shuttles *Challenger* and *Columbia* mainly because people died. The inquiries into these accidents received much at-tention, with indelible images such as the one of physicist Richard Feyn-man, a board of inquiry member, using his glass of ice water to demonstrate how cold temperatures could cause failure of the O-rings that doomed *Challenger*. Contrast the response to the *Challenger* accident with the after-math of the accident (involving explosion of an oxygen tank) that imper-iled the moon mission *Apollo 13* in 1970. The engineering errors that caused that accident were no less serious than the ones underlying the space shuttle incidents, but the Apollo astronauts survived, in part because of luck; if the same accident had occurred later in the mission, after jettisoning the lunar module that could serve as a lifeboat, the astronauts probably would have perished. There was a fact-finding inquiry after that accident, of course, but it did not receive nearly as much attention as the ones convened after the space shuttle incidents. There were no images of Nobel laureates dipping pieces of rubber into water glasses. A popular movie about *Apollo 13* highlighted the astronauts' fortitude and the ground-based engineers' ingenuity; it ended triumphantly with the safe return of the crew to Earth, not with any postincident investigation.

Intelligence agencies, at least as much as the space program, make mistakes every week. The mistakes range from the trivial to the major. Many can be attributed to nothing more than human fallibility; others might point to a correctable institutional weakness. Most cause no harm; others have negative consequences. Only some of the latter become apparent even to the agency's senior management, and only a tiny fraction of those ever become public knowledge. Which fraction becomes public is a function of luck, circumstance, and the nature of the subject matter. There is little correlation between the intrinsic seriousness of mistakes and the seriousness of their consequences, and almost no correlation between the seriousness of errors and the likelihood of their becoming publicly known intelligence failures. There also is almost no correlation between public knowledge and the degree to which mistakes are due to institutional flaws that some reform can ameliorate. Not only are publicly known intelligence failures highly unrepresentative of an intelligence service's entire body of work, but they also are unrepresentative of what the intelligence service is doing wrong.

Episodic "reform" in response to what become salient, publicly known failures (or what are perceived as failures) is thus likely to be misplaced. This is so also because of the inherent trade-offs: the conflicts between different objectives and different criteria of good performance. (The issue of interagency versus intra-agency communication is just one example.) Even the best-intentioned and most carefully designed fix to one problem is apt to exacerbate some other problem, which might actually be more serious and more likely to lead to ill consequences in the future even though it has not yet become associated with any publicly known failure. Or the "fix" might create a new problem altogether.[19]

Dealing prudently with the trade-offs inevitably involves compromises among competing objectives. The most workable and least damaging compromises usually evolve gradually, with slow tinkering that can be adjusted as experience shows what works and what doesn't as well as what unforeseen side effects are appearing. There is no reason to believe that a fully hatched plan imposed from outside would represent an improvement. There is much more reason to expect that such a plan, not tested against experience, would give rise to unforeseen problems.

Model and Reality

The periodic crisis- or tragedy-inspired bursts of public demand for fixing intelligence are only part of the intelligence-reform story. There also is the more constant, year-in and year-out drone of commentary on the subject that, for the reasons discussed in an earlier chapter, continues without end. The commentary has a depressing sameness. Its oft-repeated themes constitute what one might call—with apologies to particle physicists—the standard model of intelligence reform. It goes something like the following:

> The intelligence community should be aggressive in hiring people with the backgrounds and skills required to understand foreign countries. It needs more language ability. It needs to develop deeper knowledge of foreign cultures. It has to be more creative in techniques for collecting intelligence, such as making greater use of people outside embassies. Analysts need to be rigorously trained in sophisticated analytic techniques. They need to be taught to overcome their mindsets and biases. They need to develop deep expertise in their subjects. Barriers between agencies must be broken down, and information must flow freely. Innovative methods much be used for exploiting different sources of data. Advanced information technology must be fully exploited. Alternative analysis should be fostered. Differing analytic perspectives should be fostered and not suppressed. Outstanding performance should be rewarded, and mediocre performance penalized.

Add a few bits of verbiage about how the intelligence community needs to be less risk averse, bureaucratic inertia must be overcome, groupthink must be avoided, new threats must be focused on, and the community must get beyond a Cold War way of doing business, and you have the CliffsNotes version of the most of what is said or written in the United States about intelligence reform.

The standard model contains legitimate and important objectives. U.S. intelligence can and should be improved, and there are many fronts—including ones reflected in the standard model—where improvement can occur. But most who invoke the model show little practical sense of how the intelligence community actually operates and what this implies regarding how the model can be applied. The pro-reform commentary specifically has three major gaps.

One gap is a lack of awareness (and lack of acknowledgment) of what the intelligence community already is trying or has tried. The community has been working on every topic in the standard model, in most cases for a long time. If the commentary is intended as preaching to the community, then it is preaching to the choir. On helping analysts to overcome mindsets and biases, for example, Richard Betts observes (writing in 2007), "The intelligence community in the past few years has undertaken a breathtaking array of training programs, conferences, and experiments aimed at making analysts confront unconscious biases and unscientific habits of mind."[20] The only modification to make to this observation is that the community has been doing this sort of thing much longer than just the past few years.

Statements by the intelligence community's own leaders add to the misperception that the community has only recently focused on many aspects of the standard model. Each leader has an interest in touting his own "reform" efforts, and the public and Congress expect him to talk in such terms anyway. In an article in 2007 titled "Overhauling Intelligence," then-DNI Mike McConnell, for example, made all the requisite comments about how intelligence needs to be changed in the post–Cold War era and about efforts to hire a more diverse workforce, to share information better, to promote advanced analytic techniques, and the like.[21] Such comments help to create the impression that these efforts are related to the reorganization of 2004, but almost all of them go back much earlier. McConnell's successor, Dennis Blair, in an article published one week before the attempted bombing of the Northwest airliner, also struck all the expected themes about how the reorganization of 2004 had made a difference in the "massive" job of "reinventing our intelligence structure."[22]

A second major gap in the commentary is lack of attention to why, given that these efforts have been in train for so long, more has not been accomplished. Inherent limitations and drawbacks do not get addressed. An example is the enhancement of foreign-language ability, which U.S. intelligence agencies have been emphasizing for decades through incentive pay, facilitation of language training, and focused recruitment of employees already having fluency. Twenty or fifty years from now, language ability will still be a major theme, both of the agencies' efforts and of commentary about intelligence reform. There never will seem to be enough of it. Issues of job satisfaction and alternative opportunities complicate recruitment and retention. Very few intelligence jobs (such as case officers recruiting human sources) make regular use of a foreign language as part of a challenging professional function. Most of the intelligence community's use of foreign-language ability is for uninspiring tasks such as translation of transcripts.

Another example is the use of nonofficial cover by intelligence officers operating overseas. Expanding that use is another common theme in the commentary, and it also has been another focus of decades-long effort by the intelligence agencies. Overlooked in the commentary is the much greater cost and difficulty of convincingly living an unofficial cover story. Also overlooked is that such cover does not buy any more access than the official variety to the targets that matter most—such as terrorist groups, whose members usually trust only those who can be vouched for by family members or by friends whose relationships date back to childhood.

A third gap in discussion of the standard model is a lack of appreciation of how much any model, however earnestly one tries to apply it, inevitably differs from reality. In any organization, real pressures and fears can screw up management's best-laid plans and negate the most careful recruitment and training of employees. And in intelligence, as in many other businesses, the high-pressure situations are most likely to be seen, at least in retrospect, as the moments of truth. Think of preparation of the estimate on Iraqi unconventional weapons, when all the training and doctrine about analytic methods to which the officers involved had been thoroughly exposed mattered less than the politics, policy preferences, and urgency of that particular moment.

In some lines of work, the organization can prepare its people for that kind of moment. A well-trained infantry squad not only has received classroom instruction in patrol formations and has sharpened marksmanship on the firing range but also has had realistic field exercises in which it practices reacting to the smoke, noise, confusion, and stress of battle. The squad's well-practiced reaction becomes instinct more than intellect. The members of the squad reflexively drop into firing positions from which they can immediately engage the enemy and cover other members. Repeated drills on the practice field accomplish the same purpose in sports such as football. The payoff comes as players react instinctively and effectively when the practiced situation arises in a game, with opposing players about to crash into them and no time to think about what to do.

Intelligence doesn't work that way. For intelligence officers to rely on reflex or instinct when under pressure (such as when policymakers are about to crash into them) is likely to yield worse rather than better results. Intelligence officers need to continue to use their intellect. Consistent use of the techniques they learned in the training courses—about overcoming biases, using alternative analyses, and all the rest—is about intellect, not instinct. Even the most thorough application of the standard model will not prepare intelligence officers for their moments of truth.

The standard model points to worthwhile principles for operating a sound intelligence service, but the repeated invocation of the model is ultimately an unhelpful diversion. By pretending that the principles are different from what the intelligence community has long been endeavoring to do, and by overlooking inherent limitations to applying the principles, unending reference to the model merely perpetuates the myth of a reformist nirvana that someday can end intelligence failures.

CHAPTER TWELVE

REAL REFORM

Two sets of possible measures, hitherto virtually ignored, would be much better able to improve the guiding images of American foreign and security policy than the prevailing misguided "reform" of intelligence. One would focus on the most serious correctable impediment to sound work by the intelligence community. The other would focus on sources of images that have far more effect on policy than does anything the intelligence community produces.

Countering Politicization

We saw earlier that politicization was a major part of the story of intelligence and the Iraq War, a significant factor in other issues such as the Vietnam War and Soviet military forces, and an influence on work ranging from missiles in Cuba to prospects for the shah of Iran. But the latest round of recrimination over intelligence failure barely addressed politicization and resisted even acknowledging its existence. The reorganization of 2004 did nothing to ameliorate the problem; the DNI is in the same position relative to politics and the policymakers as the DCI was. This outcome is especially unfortunate because politicization is one malady about which reform—and more specifically that favorite variety of reform, reorganization—could make a difference. Who reports to whom and to whom people owe their jobs matter.

Making the intelligence community less vulnerable to politicization would yield two general benefits. In a direct way, it would help to safeguard the integrity of the community's own work. In an indirect way, it would make it at least marginally more difficult for policymakers to politicize intelligence-based cases for their policies.

As with alcoholism and other afflictions, the first step in correcting the problem is to acknowledge it exists. The United States has not taken that first step—not in any official statements or findings. Acknowledgment not only would be a prerequisite to concrete corrective steps, but would itself be at least modestly corrective. Official acknowledgment would help to discourage those who in the future might attempt to politicize and to encourage those who would need to resist politicization.

As difficult as acknowledgment is (for politicizers as well as for alcoholics), the next steps in trying to reduce politicization get even more difficult. They run up against more of the trade-offs that abound in the intelligence business, in which correcting one problem often means exacerbating a different problem. The principal trade-off involved is one that intelligence officers have debated among themselves for decades: whether to maintain distance from the policymaker in the interest of preserving policy-neutral integrity or to get close to the policymaker in the interest of making intelligence more relevant.[1] Although the U.S. intelligence community in its earliest days hewed more to the "keeping one's distance" school of thought, the greater emphasis for most of its subsequent history has been on cultivating close relations with policymakers in the hope of buying relevance.[2] George Tenet embodied this outlook as DCI and saw schmoozing with his senior policymaking customers as essential to doing his job well.[3] The bitter experience over the Iraq War has rekindled but not settled the closeness versus distance debate among intelligence cognoscenti. Some contributors to that debate, in particular ones approaching the subject from the policymaking side, warn against overreacting to the Iraq experience by insulating intelligence officers from policy.[4]

Tenet's finger-burning experience with the selling of the Iraq War led him to depict a different sort of trade-off in this rather inconclusive advice to his successors: "I advise future directors of the Agency to be wary of the pitfalls when engaging with policy makers on intelligence related to their policies. On the one hand, if you keep hands off, chances are the intelligence may be misused. On the other, if you engage, you run the risk of seeming to support policy even when you strive for neutrality."[5]

Tenet and the intelligence community—as well as the nation—got the worst of both sides of this trade-off. He engaged, and the community did indeed seem to be supporting a particular policy. But the Bush administration policymakers misused intelligence in their selling of the war, anyway, nearly as much as they would have if Tenet had not engaged them at all. Moreover, closeness to policymakers bought the intelligence community no influence over policy on the war. And beyond this problem is the issue of how much the intelligence community's work actually was politicized, not just how much it seemed to be. The Iraq War experience alone is reason enough for a serious national examination of politicization and of reform that might reduce it, but such an examination has yet to take place.

A debate on this question that includes more than just intelligence cognoscenti would be useful. *Debate* is the proper term because the discussion would have to address contradictory conceptions of the intelligence community's role and mission. The issue is highlighted by Henry Kissinger's reaction to the community's assessment of Iran's nuclear program in 2007. The release of unclassified judgments from this assessment, which referred to a prior cessation of nuclear weapons design work, was widely perceived as having the political effect of taking off the table, at least for a time, the option of a military strike against the Iranian program.[6] Kissinger commented, "I am extremely concerned about the tendency of the intelligence community to turn itself into a kind of check on, instead of a part of, the executive branch."[7] Such concern is reasonable, and Kissinger is not the only one to have expressed it.[8] The view is consistent with the "close is better than distant" school of intelligence–policy relations. But being a check on the executive is exactly what many expected, at least retrospectively, from the intelligence community regarding the Bush administration's selling of the Iraq War. Many Americans did not expect better from the Bush administration but believed the intelligence community had fallen down on the job in allowing the administration to sell the country a bill of goods about Iraq. Intelligence officers are thus entitled to ask, "What do you want us to do, America—to check or not to check?" The intelligence community cannot answer this question on its own, and it should not try to do so.

The absence of a consensus answer to this question and the related "close versus distant" question argues for keeping an open mind, pending the kind of national debate I am suggesting. Until such a debate occurs— and don't hold your breath waiting for one—the trend toward cozying up to the policymaker should be reversed, and U.S. intelligence should be given an institutional status that makes it more of an assuredly independent, unpoliticized voice.

Institutionalizing Independence

Even if we accept the objective of greater independence for U.S. intelligence, there is no school solution for achieving it. We need to avoid the mistake of the 9/11 Commission in promoting one formula as the sine qua non of reform. Insights can be gained from studying other parts of government. Experiences from some of them can be applied in part. I have suggested as a model the Federal Reserve, a quasi-autonomous body within the executive branch.[9]

I hasten to acknowledge the uncertainties and downsides of any such suggestion. If analysts are moved to a more autonomous part of the government to help insulate them from policy influence, then do operational components (such as the CIA's National Clandestine Service) come with them? Not including them might undo much of the beneficial enhancement of communication between analysts and operators that the intelligence community has achieved over the past quarter-century. If the operators move, then how might this move affect their essential cooperation with other parts of the executive branch, such as the military? Such questions are not a reason to give up trying to correct the problem of politicization; they are reasons to be careful in devising solutions. The partially autonomous Fed (which, by the way, is a consumer of some of the intelligence community's products) can still work closely with other parts of the executive branch such as the Department of the Treasury, as it did during the financial crisis beginning in 2008.[10] Making the intelligence community more autonomous and less vulnerable to politicization than it is now would not preclude similar operational collaboration between it and other parts of the executive branch.

Two features of the Fed would be especially worth applying in modified form to the intelligence community. One would be to give the head of the community a long, fixed term. Another would be to create a collective body, somewhat akin to the Federal Reserve Board of Governors, which would have the last substantive say on any of the community's output or any part of it the board deemed sufficiently important to weigh in on. Unlike the current National Intelligence Board, which consists of component heads subject to the same pressures as anyone else embedded in the bureaucracy, the new board would be structured to emphasize its independence. Its members would be appointed according to explicitly nonpolitical criteria to fixed (probably nonrenewable) terms, subject to Senate confirmation, and with probably not all nominations in the hands of the president. The members would be beholden to no one, with their only reference point the broader national interest.

I am not recommending another reorganization of the intelligence community any time soon. The costs of disruption inherent to such reorganizations are substantial, as the costs of the most recent reorganization demonstrate. But the ever-spinning wheel of intelligence failure and demands for reform will continue to turn. After the next failure prominent enough to stimulate a new round of such demands, the problems with the previous "reform" can be addressed. The problem of politicization can also be addressed on this occasion.

CONGRESS AND THE PUBLIC AS CUSTOMERS

Another deterrent to the politicization of intelligence is for the intelligence community to feel responsible not only to the chief executive, but also to a coequal branch of government. The role of Congress therefore is critical—as a consumer of intelligence, not only as an overseer of it. My conversations with members of both houses of Congress indicate that members underestimate the potential for expanding that role. They do not appreciate how seriously the intelligence community takes what few requests for assessments they do receive from Congress. They overestimate the extent to which a more active congressional role would be negated by automatic intelligence community deference to the White House—a defeatist attitude regarding politicization. I have encouraged members to make more substantive requests of the intelligence community. This means, for both the majority and the minority, making such requests early and often—not waiting, as in the case of Iraqi unconventional weapons, until the executive's policy is firmly set and a vote is about to be taken to confirm it.

One of the items in Robert McNamara's catalog of mistakes leading to the Vietnam War was that "we failed to draw Congress and the American people into a full and frank discussion and debate of the pros and cons of a large-scale U.S. military involvement in Southeast Asia before we initiated the action."[11] The same failure has occurred in other instances, most conspicuously with the Iraq War. To avoid such failure and for Congress to play effectively its role as discussant and debater, it also needs to play more actively the role of full-fledged consumer of intelligence. Diluting the executive's political influence on the intelligence community would be a further important benefit of Congress's doing so.

The partisanship and inattention that have impeded the performance of so many of Congress's other functions will, of course, continue to impede this function as well. That is why another idea involving Congress is worth considering: creation of a congressional intelligence office—a permanent, nonpartisan watchdog modeled after the Government Accountability Office and the Congressional Budget Office. It would not replace the normal oversight functions of the intelligence committees but instead would be the principal locale in the legislative branch of scrutiny and vigilance regarding the substantive use and misuse of intelligence, including politicization. A couple of years ago I was pleasantly surprised to discover that a congressional staffer had independently come up with the same idea for such an office and had even written a first draft of legislation to create it. I commended the proposal to his boss, a member who was well positioned to work on the issue, but I detected little interest.

Beyond Congress is the public that it represents. The role of the public as a consumer of intelligence (or, more precisely, of unclassified intelligence-based judgments) needs to be readdressed. This topic is unpleasant for most intelligence officers, who, because of experiences such as the brouhaha over the Iranian nuclear issue, have come to see unclassified releases of their products as more of a headache than they are worth. They have legitimate concerns, especially over analysts' becoming reticent if they fear their work will become fodder for partisan debate.[12] The problems, however, stem in large part from the infrequency and irregularity of releases of the intelligence community's work beyond a few periodic products such as the annual statement on worldwide threats. It is hard not to release something without the release's being seen as the pursuit of someone's policy agenda. More comprehensive—regular and expected—sharing of judgments with the public would tend to reduce this problem. The public's right to know is one important reason for more generously sharing the intelligence community's judgments. More informed public participation in debate over important issues—part of the shortfall that McNamara noted about the Vietnam War—is another. Yet another reason, most pertinent to our current subject, is that such sharing would help to counter politicization by diversifying the intelligence community's customer base and getting away from the sense that intelligence is owned by whoever happens to occupy the White House.

REDUCING COGNITIVE IMPAIRMENT

So much for reforming intelligence. We need to remember that intelligence by itself is ultimately unimportant; accurate images and well-guided policies based on those images are important. What reforms might increase the accuracy of the images that really matter—the ones that actually guide or misguide U.S. foreign and security policy?

To the extent those images are rooted in American history and culture, as to a large extent they are, they are resistant to change. They do evolve, however, as the nation adds to its experiences. The aversion to foreign wars that became known as the Vietnam syndrome, besides being a change in national strategy, also represented a correction of some of the mistaken images that underlay the U.S. intervention in Vietnam, including images of the structure of worldwide communism, the receptivity of non-Western people to Western values, and foreign responses to the application of U.S. military force. The passage of time, victory in the Cold War, and arrival of the unipolar moment reversed some of this evolution, particularly regarding the perceived applicability of democratic principles and efficacy of military force. The Iraq War and possibly the war in Afghanistan may reverse it again.[13]

Although these sorts of changes show that even perceptions rooted in national culture are not immutable, they hardly constitute a reassuring corrective to mistaken and influential images. The correction may occur only after a costly tragedy such as the wars in Vietnam and Iraq. Moreover, the correction—in Americans' characteristically discontinuous, episodic way of reacting to their forays into the outside world—may be an overcorrection. Mistaken images may be replaced by new ones that are mistaken in a different way. Ronald Reagan and many other American conservatives thought the Vietnam syndrome was one such overcorrection.[14]

There is no feasible reform, no national counseling session, that would enable Americans to become collectively and quickly aware of the blinders they wear as a result of their shared national experience. The blinders generally slip off only with the passage of even more time, after the experiences that shaped them are well in the past. Americans can now understand that the Spanish–American War, the most recent major offensive war that the United States launched prior to the Iraq War, was fought less because of an explosion on the battleship *Maine* (which, if it occurred today, would of course immediately be assailed as an "intelligence failure") than because of jingoistic politics and the application of ideas about Manifest Destiny to expansion abroad. A century from now the Iraq War will be explained in history books less in terms of aluminum tubes and phantom biological weapons labs than in terms of larger forces and moods in American politics, including the ascendancy of neoconservatism and flawed beliefs about the efficacy of military power during the unipolar moment and about foreign populations' receptivity to democratic ideals and practices.

Adoption of the antipoliticization suggestions I made earlier, in particular those involving Congress and the public, would help somewhat by providing a counterpoint to many mistaken images stemming either from popular moods or from policymakers' salesmanship, but it would have little or no direct effect on mistaken images in the heads of the policymakers themselves. The great majority of the examples adduced in the classic work on cognitive errors in foreign policy, Robert Jervis's *Perception and Misperception in International Politics*, concern policymakers rather than intelligence services.[15] Jervis, one of the most distinguished American political scientists, also has contributed valuable work on intelligence, including how and why it can go wrong.[16] But it is significant that the thinking that provides the substance of his seminal book is far more that of policymakers than of intelligence officers.

A leading diplomatic historian (who would later serve in the ODNI), Richard Immerman, concludes that regardless of any benefit from reform of the intelligence community,

> the effect on policy is likely to be slight so long as the makers of that policy remain cognitively impaired and politically possessed. Our colleagues in political science have spent careers diagnosing these pathologies and prescribing antidotes. One must wonder, nevertheless, whether the same attributes that enable someone to achieve the presidency of

the United States, or a position almost as high up the political food chain, militate against his or her receptiveness to information and advice that is discordant with his or her existing beliefs, images, and even values. Electoral success normally requires holding strong beliefs or convincing the electorate that beliefs held are strong—and sound. How likely is it, one must therefore ask, for those who are politically successful to learn from intelligence once in office that these beliefs are unfounded?[17]

It is hard to disagree with this depressingly pessimistic observation, with regard to both the described affliction and the poor prospects for curing it. The making of many of the major foreign-policy decisions described in this book has been in large part a story of policymakers' being cognitively impaired and politically possessed. The story contains numerous examples that can serve as "how not to do it" case studies in those courses the intelligence community conducts for its analysts on correct methods for assessing overseas situations. The rigor the courses impart—about making assumptions explicit, critically examining the evidence on which judgments are based, using alternative analysis, counteracting one's own perceptual biases, and utilizing other aspects of good methodological discipline—has been conspicuously absent from the making of some of the most momentous decisions in U.S. foreign policy. Policymakers instead have constructed their most important policy-guiding images through unquestioned, gut-based intuition or casual use of analogies or personal experience. When policies have been successful, it has usually been because the intuition happened to be correct, as with Reagan's perception of the Soviet Union, rather than because the procedure was sound.

The nonprocess through which the Bush administration decided to go to war in Iraq is the extreme case of lack of rigor. Consider how one of the chief promoters of the war, Paul Wolfowitz, arrived at his governing images—especially in light of the 9/11 Commission's theme of "failure of imagination." Two months before the invasion, Wolfowitz—in dismissing General Eric Shinseki's estimate that several hundred thousand troops would be required for the job—said it was "hard to imagine" that providing stability in Iraq would require more troops than needed to topple Saddam.[18] When asked after the invasion began how Iraqis would receive U.S. troops, Wolfowitz said, "I imagine they will be welcomed."[19] In justifying the war decision amid an emerging insurgency in the summer of 2003, he said it had been "difficult to imagine" before the war that such fighting would continue after Saddam was overthrown.[20] When asked the following year, as the violence and casualties mounted, whether a different course could be set in Iraq, Wolfowitz replied, "I can imagine a different approach, but I can't imagine it working."[21] Such views clearly represent one of the costliest failures of imagination from which the United States has suffered in recent times. But the failure was not insufficient use of imagination; it was too much use of it. It was needless reliance on imagination when there were more firmly based sources of insight available, both inside and outside the government. Imagination was substituting for rigor and disciplined inquiry.

The launching of the Iraq War was not just a case of one official's imagination running wild, though. Despite how much the 9/11 Commission's theme of "failure of imagination" appealed to the American public's imagination, more use of imagination is not a cure for cognitive impairment. In fact, it can make that impairment worse. Research on political judgment demonstrates that although exercises using imagined scenarios may help in contingency planning, they do not improve forecasting.[22]

Policymakers might learn a great deal from the courses the intelligence analysts take. Experience shows that policymakers have the greatest need for such instruction, and it is among policymakers that the methodological insights the courses teach would have the greatest benefit in improving the accuracy of images that guide policy. If Americans were serious about making U.S. foreign policy better guided, they would make policymakers take the courses or equivalent ones designed especially for them.

This suggestion may sound far-fetched, but why should it be? A training blitz the CIA's analytical directorate conducted in the 1990s was administered to everyone in the directorate, regardless of grade or experience. Office directors and the agency deputy director who headed the entire directorate took the same course as the most junior analysts. If the agency's seniors can make time for such training, why can't their counterparts in policy agencies? Professional education in the military services extends into the general officer ranks. Freshman members of Congress receive a weeklong course that covers such topics as decorum, pay and benefits, and relations with the media.[23] Isn't how to make sound and well-informed decisions about national policy—including how to form accurate images as the basis for foreign policy—at least as important for incoming legislators to know as any of those other topics?

From a realistic perspective, policymakers in neither the executive nor the legislative branch are going to take courses to reduce their cognitive impairment. They would consider themselves too senior, too important, too intellectually experienced, and too busy to subject themselves to such instruction. And even if they did, the limitations on transferring insights from the classroom to real-world decision making would be at least as great for them as for intelligence analysts. Amid multiple tasks, tight deadlines, and political pressures, the textbooks tend to be forgotten, and reliance is placed on intuition and preexisting worldviews.

STRUCTURE AND PROCESS

With little hope for reducing individual policymakers' cognitive impairment, perhaps structural solutions might help to counteract the effects of that impairment. In contrast to the enormous attention given to the structure of the intelligence community, far less attention has been given to the policymaking machinery whose images have had much greater effect on foreign-policy decisions. That machinery's generation of images of overseas situations is inseparable from other aspects of the policymaking process, including the identification of national interests and objectives at stake and the selection of strategies to pursue those objectives. Rigorous procedures that are more likely to select good strategies also are more likely to develop accurate images.

Good and bad examples of procedures for making U.S. foreign policy are easy to find. The NSC ExComm of the Cuban Missile Crisis, despite its shortcomings, still ranks as one of the best examples. But President Kennedy quickly disbanded it after the crisis, and nothing comparable continued during the rest of his administration. Perhaps the best structural innovation of a more permanent type was the NSC Planning Board that President Eisenhower created. Staffed by senior planners from all the relevant departments, the board was charged with debating the costs and benefits of alternative foreign-policy strategies.[24] The board's approach reflected the superlative organizational and planning skills Eisenhower had displayed during his military career.[25] (The Kennedy administration discontinued the board, hoping to make the NSC more flexible.)

Two key features distinguish a policymaking process that maximizes the chance that the guiding images will be accurate and that inaccurate images will be weeded out. One is thoroughness: comprehensive consideration given to all underlying assumptions and relevant evidence and to all the costs and benefits of all the available alternatives. The other is competitiveness: the assurance that no single image, no matter how influential the person who holds it, will go unchallenged.[26]

Whether policymaking displays these attributes depends on the person at the top. If the president wants a procedure that makes it more likely policy will rest on accurate images of the world abroad, he or she can establish it. That is a big "if." No one has ever been elected president of the United States on a platform of improving the foreign-policy decision-making process. And even if the chief executive accepts in principle the need for a rigorous process, in practice he or she will tend to fall back on the beliefs and instincts that got him or her to the top in the first place. Below the top, a similar retreat from rigor occurs. Each new administration comes into office by erecting a seemingly detailed and well-defined apparatus for making national security policy; the apparatus and the procedures associated with it become less important over time than personalities and informal patterns of power.

In a democracy, the ultimate sanction to misguided policies is to cashier the policymakers. That is an unreliable and ineffective way, however, of dealing with the problem of inaccurate images flowing from inadequate policy processes. The electorate that would do the cashiering may share the mistaken images, as they have with regard to many issues in the past. Turning leaders out of office also is an extremely blunt instrument—too late to avoid rather than respond to disasters, useless against second-term presidents, and insensitive to the good that an incumbent is doing along with the bad.

The poor prospect for substantially improving the foreign-policy-relevant images inside American policymakers' heads is a reason to favor a model of intelligence–policy relations that would enable the intelligence community, when necessary, to function as a check on the executive and not just a partner of it.

The Political Layer

A related, distinctly American reason why certain images drive foreign policy and other ones do not concerns the staffing of the executive branch of the U.S. government. The United States, unlike other industrialized democracies, has a huge number of political appointees. The typical structure of government departments in other democracies includes a small political stratum consisting only of a minister and a few junior ministers and personal assistants atop a career bureaucracy that extends all the way up to someone with a title such as permanent undersecretary. In contrast, the number of political appointees in the United States, which has been growing more rapidly than the government as a whole, was more than three thousand by the end of George W. Bush's presidency.

A large layer of people that has a big role in shaping policy thus belongs to neither the ministerial level of elected politicians nor the professional bureaucracy. Those with the most influence on policy are in-and-outers, who separate their stints in government with time at law firms, think tanks, corporations, or academia. Those selected for policy positions are picked in part because of prior connections with those making the selections and in part because they have made names for themselves in a policy-prescriptive sense. So they come into their jobs with an agenda, tinged with partisanship. They measure success not in terms of managing a component of the government well, but instead in terms of policy accomplishments consistent with that agenda. This system accentuates the tendency for objectives to shape beliefs rather than vice versa.

The existence of this large layer of appointees means that the topmost decision makers are getting most of their facts and analysis not from disinterested people who are trying to paint an unbiased picture of situations overseas. They are instead getting it from people with policy agendas, often strong agendas. The agendas may be similar to those of the top decision makers, although not always. In any event, images of what is going on overseas get presented by or filtered through advocates of particular policies.

The stratum of in-and-outers constitutes a huge blurring of the distinction between politics and policy, on one hand, and dispassionate interpretation of overseas reality, on the other. The blurring reached a grotesque extreme in the unit in the Pentagon that labored to find links between Iraq and al-Qa'ida and then presented its case to senior policymakers as if it were an alternative intelligence analysis. Even in less extreme forms, the in-and-outers both personify and exacerbate the tendency for policy objectives to shape factual and analytical perceptions rather than the other way around. Because of the enormous number of political appointees, whose positions extend far and deep throughout the bureaucracy, they also personify a partial politicization of the bureaucracy itself.

The system leads to unavoidable tension between the in-and-outers and the professional bureaucrats.[27] The two groups compete not only for the ears of senior policymakers but sometimes for the same jobs. The bureaucrats may resent the political appointees as having been parachuted in above them, lament the politicization of the bureaucracy they represent, and distrust the slanted, policy-inspired way in which they handle information. The political appointees detect these negative vibrations, which intensifies whatever disdain the appointees already had for the bureaucrats and any suspicion they already had toward anyone not seen to be a true believer in the policy. The suspicions and ill will further impair the flow of ideas and insights and restrict the range of image-shaping information that policymakers accept or to which they are exposed.

Neither the bureaucrats nor the appointees can claim intrinsically superior brainpower or wisdom. In one important respect, however, the latter are more susceptible than the former to the sort of oversimplified, faulty images that often have underlain misguided policies. Isaiah Berlin described in his classic essay *The Hedgehog and the Fox* the two types of thinking involved. His inspiration was a line from the ancient Greek poet Archilochus: "The fox knows many things, but the hedgehog knows one big thing."[28] The foxes among human thinkers accept the inevitable contradictions and ambiguities of life and search for greater understanding unrestrained by commitment to any single theme or tradition of inquiry. Hedgehogs, in contrast, seek understanding by fitting diverse phenomena into a grand explanatory idea—the "one big thing." Hedgehogs are more inclined than foxes toward action and sometimes are exasperated by the foxes' seemingly unending investigation of complexity.

Berlin had past philosophers, not U.S. government officials, in mind when he explored this distinction, but the distinction corresponds to predominant habits of thinking among bureaucrats on one hand and political appointees on the other. This divide is largely a matter of self-selection of different careers by different types of people and partly a matter of reinforcing culture once they are in those careers. Intelligence analysts are prototypical foxes; they are in their element when examining ill-fitting pieces to whatever puzzle they are working on and searching for more clues to solving it, especially if unburdened by the need to come to closure soon and to make clear decisions. In-and-outers are more likely to be hedgehogs; they came to their jobs committed to whatever big concepts are associated with the parties and ideologies with which they identify. To push through policy initiatives during their short time in office, they need simplifying, image-shaping grand ideas that keep them from getting waylaid by uncertainties, complexities, and doubts.

Extensive research by psychologist Philip Tetlock on what causes some experts to be better than others in forecasting events (especially political events) has yielded mostly null results. Almost the only distinction Tetlock found useful in separating good forecasters from poor ones is the distinction between foxes and hedgehogs. "If we want realistic odds on what will happen next, coupled with a willingness to admit mistakes," Tetlock says, we are better off turning to people who think like foxes. In contrast, he found that "hedgehogs have repeatedly emerged as the higher-risk candidates for becoming 'prisoners of their preconceptions.'"[29]

Mistaken estimates and forecasts thus have misguided U.S. foreign policy in part because hedgehogs have been in positions from which they can inject their images into the policymaking process more readily than foxes can inject theirs. The top decision makers have varied in their thought patterns, but they probably have included many hedgehogs.[30] The faith-based, mission-driven, detail-discarding George W. Bush surely ranked very high on the hedgehog scale.

Regardless of any one president's pattern of thinking, all presidents welcome the sort of assurance and confidence in their advisers that hedgehogs are more likely than foxes to provide. Harry Truman, tired of hearing "on one hand, on the other hand" analysis from his economic advisers, famously wished for a one-armed economist. The yearning to simplify, to push aside doubts, and to overlook complications stems in part from the top decision maker's need for reassurance that he is doing the right thing. It also stems from the need to gather broader backing for policy, a process in which doubts and complications are unhelpful. The mustering of support for American foreign policy has chronically involved the overselling both of threats and of proposed remedies to meet the threats.[31] The hedgehoglike interpretation of events overseas in terms of grand ideas and "big things" can furnish confidence and support, but often at the price of inaccuracy.

Slash the Political Layer

Despite the ample grounds for pessimism about improving the images that most guide and misguide American foreign policy, there is one reform—in addition to the counterpoliticization measures described earlier—that would help significantly. It is a step I have no realistic expectation of seeing anytime soon, but others have also suggested it,[32] and it seems not quite as quixotic as trying to enroll senior policymakers in courses in analytic methods: curtail greatly the number of political appointees in the executive branch of the U.S. government.

This reform would undo the damaging effects of the bloated and ever-increasing political stratum. It would facilitate the flowing of insights and information to top policymakers without being filtered through appointees with their own policy agendas. It would sharpen the distinction between policy advocacy and policy-neutral analysis. It would increase the visibility and availability of judgments by foxes, who are more likely to discern the complexities of overseas situations than are the hedgehogs who dominate policymaking environments. It would, in short, be a step toward more accuracy and objectivity in the formation of images that guide policy.

The reform, by clarifying the distinction between politicians and bureaucrats, between the temporary and the permanent parts of government, would increase trust and cooperation between the two. They would not be competing with each other. The bureaucrats would know that the most senior of their number have direct access to cabinet-level policymakers and are not cut off by a filtering layer of appointees. Bureaucrats would know they can provide candid insights to the policymakers without having their loyalty questioned because in a system with such well-defined roles that is part of what bureaucrats are supposed to do. They would also know that for the system to work and for them to retain their access, they must be scrupulously apolitical and ready and willing to execute the policies of whoever is in power. The policymakers would know the bureaucrats know that, and they would thus not have reason to feel threatened or suspicious. The more trusting relationship would improve the flow of information and thereby enhance the accuracy of policy-relevant images as well as the smooth operation of government generally.

As with any other reform, though, one has to look for trade-offs and downsides in this reform. One argument sometimes made in favor of a large appointed stratum is that it injects fresh perspectives into government with the advent of each new administration. True, but fresh perspectives can be had through a variety of means without appointing people who hold those perspectives. Government departments obtain such perspectives all the time through consultancies and other arrangements. And there is a big difference between an outside perspective's being obtained as an input to an impartial process of forming images and a particular perspective's becoming the image that will guide policy, which is more often the case with the current system of a large appointed layer. Moreover, most of the perspectives that come with appointees are not very fresh. There is much intellectual inbreeding in the think tanks and related circles from which most of the appointees come.[33]

A more mundane reason for having so many appointed jobs is that many of them are rewards for having advised or assisted in political campaigns. It is also the main reason why the reform I have suggested has meager chances of being adopted; no candidate wants to be the only candidate to tell his advisers and supporters that they can stop thumbing through the *Plum Book* because their efforts are not going to entitle them to any of the jobs listed. Of course, if the supporters of *all* campaigns knew that, American democracy would be no less strong and fair than it is now.

Another rationale for the huge appointed stratum is that letting the president seed his people all through the executive branch helps to ensure that his preferences will be honored and his policies executed. But that rationale assumes away the whole concept of a loyal and apolitical civil service, part of whose defining mission is to do exactly that. To assume it away and to push the political layer ever farther down into the bureaucracy merely generates the sort of distrust that makes the assumption self-fulfilling.

Rather than assuring that policy will conform to what the American people thought they were getting when electing a president, the bloated layer of appointees tends to have the opposite effect because the appointees have their own policy agendas, those agendas are not all the same, and the process that determines who gets appointed and who does not is haphazard. The process is a game of personal connections, getting in early with the right candidate during the primary season, and luck. Who wins and who loses in this game go a long way toward shaping policy.

The Iraq War provides an outstanding example. One of the few perceptive observations about the war that Richard Perle, one of its strongest supporters, has made is that the war would not have happened if enough other supporters had not succeeded in getting appointments. "Let's put it this way," said Perle. "If Bush had staffed his administration with a group of people selected by Brent Scowcroft and Jim Baker, which might well have happened, then it could have been different, because they would not have carried into it the ideas that the people who wound up in important positions brought to it. The ideas are only important as they reside in the minds of people who were involved directly in the decision process."[34] Columnist Tom Friedman made a similar point when, sitting in Washington shortly after the war began, he said, "I could give you the names of 25 people (all of whom are at this moment within a five-block radius of this office) who, if you had exiled them to a desert island a year and a half ago, the Iraq war would not have happened."[35]

Who could have predicted that the biggest difference the outcome of the 2000 presidential election would make for U.S. foreign policy would be an offensive war in Iraq? I certainly didn't. Few would have predicted it even if they had been able to anticipate the other major event that made it politically possible: the 9/11 terrorist attack. The fact that the Bush administration was able, through its Herculean sales campaign and the manipulation of images that went with it, to persuade even many Democrats to go along with the war had nothing to do with fulfilling an electoral mandate.

Two other effects of greatly cutting back the layer of political appointees would be beneficial. One would be to increase competence and effectiveness in government. This aspect of the overall suggestion is not just related to the highly publicized instances of ineffectiveness, such as the federal response to Hurricane Katrina led by the much-maligned Michael Brown. And it goes beyond egregious cases where political loyalty has taken precedence over everything else—such as the staffing of the Coalition Provisional Authority in Iraq, in which an internship at the Heritage Foundation was considered a more important entry on a résumé than knowing anything about the Middle East.[36] One study of performance of federal programs, using an evaluation system administered by the Office of Management and Budget under the Bush administration, found that programs led by career bureaucrats significantly bested in performance those led by political appointees even though the appointees had more impressive individual credentials, including being better educated on average, than the career managers.[37] Another study found that federal agencies that were more successful at "strategic change" had smaller proportions of political appointees than agencies that were less successful.[38]

An issue of competence that is directly related to the formation of images of situations overseas concerns ambassadorial appointments. Over the past fifty years, approximately 30 percent of U.S. ambassadors have been noncareer appointees.[39] A few of them have brought genuine expertise and stature to their jobs, but most of these appointments have been rewards for contributions to political campaigns. Fifty-three of the 124 people George W. Bush appointed to foreign posts had raised at least $100,000 each for his campaigns.[40] The pattern of political patronage does not seem to have changed under President Obama; a majority (46 out of 82) of the ambassadors he appointed in his first nine months in office were not career foreign-service officers.[41] The damage from this practice is mitigated by the concentration of many of the political appointments in posts that have high comfort but relatively low importance, such as Luxembourg or the Bahamas, and by the ability of deputy chiefs of mission and other professional staff to do the work of an embassy even with an inert ambassador. Nonetheless, ambassadors gain some access that other embassy officers do not, and events can quickly turn seemingly unimportant posts into important ones. Observations and reporting from ambassadors provide important input to images that help to guide U.S. foreign policy, and the damage from using so many of these positions as political rewards is real.

Another beneficial effect of this reform would be to reduce the tremendous disruption to the functioning of government when much of the upper echelon of the executive branch is purged each time a new president is elected. Every presidential transition is followed by months of drift as many vacancies remain unfilled, often with the White House and Senate blaming each other for the delays.[42] The worldwide interests of the United States continue, but this aspect of the staffing of its government seems to assume that those interests—as well as the threats, opportunities, and relationships that go with them—start from scratch with each change of occupancy at the White House. This practice, too, has a direct deleterious effect on the accuracy of images that are input to foreign policy. Knowledge is lost, lessons learned by the old crew have to be relearned by the new one, and patterns that are discernible only with the passage of time go unnoticed.

MISDIRECTION

The reforms that have been promoted as a response to the problem of poorly guided American foreign and security policy have been as misdirected as the common diagnosis of the problem. The narrow focus toward reform—extremely narrow in the case of fixation on the intelligence community's organization chart—has missed most of the images that shape policy and most of the reasons those images are often flawed. Some of the roots of those flaws run so deep it would be difficult for any reform to cut them out. Other possible reforms would substantially improve the accuracy of the images, but the political will to enact them has been lacking. This lack of support and the misdirected nature of changes that do have political support constitute more grounds for pessimism about ever breaking the cycle of failure and recrimination over misguided foreign policy. Some of the "reform" already enacted fuels the cycle by perpetuating the misdirection and providing more material for future recrimination.

All of this constitutes one of the reasons U.S. foreign policy will never be made with the benefit of full and accurate images of the world with which it is supposed to deal. Policy itself must take account of that fact.

ADAPTING POLICY TO UNCERTAINTY

The makers of American foreign policy will never know much of what they would like to know or would be useful for them to know in dealing with the world abroad. Moreover, much of what they might think they know will be wrong. One reason for this harsh prognosis is the unlikelihood that the United States will adopt any of the few measures most likely to improve the accuracy of the images that guide its policy. The most fundamental reasons, though, are that foreign adversaries will withhold secrets that are impenetrable to even the most skilled efforts to obtain them and that much of what would be most useful to know involves the complex interplay of innumerable forces and factors, the outcome of which is unpredictable. A large amount of uncertainty is an inevitable, inescapable fact of life in the guiding and making of foreign and security policy.

Neither intelligence nor any other source of images can eliminate that uncertainty. Intelligence can, among its other functions, help to manage the uncertainty. It can define the scope of the uncertainty, specifying what is known and not known and what is likely to stay unknown. It can distinguish true uncertainty from simple ignorance by systematically assembling all available information. It can identify possible outcomes and perhaps give a sense of the relative likelihood of each one. It can identify variables that will increase or decrease the likelihood of each possibility. It can identify indicators that would show that particular possibilities are becoming more likely. And it can analyze the implications of each of the possibilities, including the implications for U.S. national interests.

Americans often expect more from intelligence than what I have described here. They expect intelligence not only to delimit and interpret uncertainty, but also to make specific judgments in the face of it. In principle, there is no reason not to continue to have these expectations. Intelligence officers represent a source of expertise, and tax dollars are paying for that expertise, so why shouldn't we try to get the most for our money by pressing them to make judgments no matter how great the uncertainty? That's fine as long as we fully realize what we are doing as we press. We are calling on the officers to give their best shots in answering a question even though some of those shots will miss. Sometimes they will be wrong. The more specific the sort of judgment we demand of them, the more likely their shots will miss. We need to remember these limitations and that what intelligence officers have to say about the scope of uncertainty and about other possibilities may be at least as important as whatever judgment we demand of them about the most likely possibility. If we cannot remember these things, it would be better not to press them for specific judgments at all.

Americans and the makers of their foreign policy not only need to discard the vain hope that uncertainty can be eliminated, whether through reforming intelligence or through the oversimplifying processes churning away in our own minds. Foreign policy needs to be constructed in full awareness and full acceptance of the uncertainty. The policy must adapt to the uncertainty. Policy needs to work well over a range of possible outcomes, not just to work well with whatever is judged to be the most likely outcome. A single judgment is insufficient to characterize whatever situation we confront, not only because the judgment may be wrong, but also because it may miss important variables. Even if we correctly judge that a river's average depth is four feet, it would be unwise to try to wade across it.[1]

CRAVING CERTAINTY

It is hard for Americans, at least as far as national policy is concerned, to accept this much uncertainty. The resistance begins with humans' tendency to overestimate their own ability to estimate. We think we face less uncertainty than we really do because we think we know more than we really do. Another universal tendency that psychologists have demonstrated in their laboratories is an emotional aversion to uncertainty. Not knowing whether something painful will occur upsets us more than knowing that the same painful something definitely will occur. In one experiment, subjects who knew that only some of the electric shocks they were about to receive would be intense sweated more heavily and had faster heartbeats than other subjects who would receive the same number of shocks and knew that all of them would be intense.[2]

People—perhaps intelligent, creatively thinking people in particular—search for order and comprehensive explanations rather than accept that they cannot know everything and that errors are inevitable. An experiment demonstrating this characteristic involved trying to predict on which side of a T-maze food would appear. The experiment pitted a single rat against a group of Yale undergraduates. The rat won. The food appeared 60 percent of the time on one side and 40 percent on the other, in what was otherwise a random sequence. The rat learned to go to the favored side every time and thus attained the maximum possible success rate of 60 percent. The human subjects tried to discern a nonrandom pattern, selecting each side of the maze some of the time and being successful only 52 percent of the time.[3]

Leo Tolstoy, the principal subject of Isaiah Berlin's essay about hedgehogs and foxes, exhibited the same yearning for certainty, order, and understanding. Tolstoy was acutely aware that, as Berlin puts it, "the areas of our knowledge are incredibly small compared to what is uncharted and (Tolstoy vehemently insists on this) unchartable." Tolstoy also believed, in what can begin to describe politicization, that "we know too few facts, and we select them at random and in accordance with our subjective inclinations." Tolstoy was a highly perceptive fox, and yet he wished to be a hedgehog, longing for some universal principle that would explain the highly varied human experience for which he had such a keen eye.[4]

The craving for certainty is even stronger with policymakers. They want to accomplish the policy agenda with which they came to office; they do not want to be diverted by the unexpected.[5] The wish becomes father to the belief. The same craving that leads policymakers to favor hedgehogs' simplifying images and explanations also leads them to believe that they live in a world certain enough for the images to be accurate and the explanations to be valid.

Elected policymakers' political needs push their wants and beliefs in this same direction. Acceptance of uncertainty implies acceptance of the principle that good decisions can lead to bad results. That is not how politics works. Voters have little patience for a leader who tries to explain that his policy was sound based on what was known at the time he made it, but that what was unknown did not happen to break in their favor. Not only does the electorate not accept the implications of uncertainty, but they do not want leaders who sound uncertain. Uncertainty is associated with weakness. Citizens want their leaders to describe with certainty and clarity what the country is facing and what needs to be done about it and to evince confidence that they will get the desired outcome.

Similar tendencies pervade pundits and scholars' armchair strategizing. The grand strategies they offer—at least the ones with a chance of gaining interest and support—boldly explain the challenges of the world in terms of clear and simple concepts characterizing a particular era. Especially since the end of the Cold War, the ranks of strategists have been filled with George Kennan wannabes hoping to offer the next great concept to catch on, even though Kennan himself never intended his own concept of containment to be applied as indiscriminately as it came to be applied.[6] What does not sell is an outlook that reminds us that "history is one damned thing after another" and that we need to stay alert and nimble enough to cope with the next thing that history throws at us.

Recognition and acceptance of uncertainty in foreign affairs need not be a matter of weakness, and it assuredly need not involve a lack of rigor. Beginning with an insight from an eighteenth-century English clergyman named Thomas Bayes, who devised a mathematical formula for using information to adjust estimates of probabilities, an entire subdiscipline has been constructed for rigorously making such estimates and making decisions in conditions of uncertainty.[7] And yet with foreign affairs, adjusting estimates and decisions in line with that discipline still tends to get associated with weakness, ignorance, and indecision. When the intelligence community, for example, uses new information to adjust its assessments, this procedure is less likely to be seen as good Bayesian analysis than as an admission of error and an inability to get a grip on the situation (as happened with reactions to successive intelligence estimates on Iran's nuclear program). Policymakers making similar adjustments receive a similar reaction. (Think of how Jimmy Carter was lambasted for publicly suggesting that the invasion of Afghanistan taught him something about the Soviet Union.)

These tendencies are especially apparent in the United States. Acceptance of uncertainty is the opposite of the sense of clear challenges, clear enemies, and clear victory that the world wars of the twentieth century and the Cold War did so much to foster among Americans. Adapting to uncertainty is the opposite of the sense of being in control—which America's history has imparted to its citizens more than the history of other nations, buffeted by the actions of others, has imparted to theirs. And of course, acknowledgment of uncertainty is the antithesis of the belief that a nation as successful as the United States ought to be able to figure out everything that is going on outside its borders. But it cannot. One more entry in Robert McNamara's litany of errors underlying the Vietnam War is worth noting: "We did not recognize that neither our people nor our leaders are omniscient."[8]

SUCCESSFUL ADAPTATION

Other American habits and experiences provide some offsetting basis for optimism about the prospects for coming to terms with uncertainty. Outside matters of public policy, Americans have shown a willingness and ability to deal with uncertainty and to do so carefully and strategically. A host of business and investment decisions demonstrate this ability. Some of those decisions are structured and researched so that the decision maker is facing a calculable risk—rather like legalized gambling, in which Americans bet some $600 billion each year, but with better odds for making a profit. Many other decisions involve true uncertainty, which is not calculable although subjective probabilities can be assigned to different possible outcomes. The uncertainties can be political as well as economic. A bevy of consulting firms offer political risk assessments to help clientele making overseas investment decisions to identify and manage uncertainties involving political events abroad.

Many products of the financial services industry, such as futures contracts, are tools for managing uncertainty. And of course all sorts of insurance policies are also tools for shedding risk. With each one of these tools, someone else is on the other end of the transaction, not shedding risk but taking it on—and taking it on with eyes wide open as part of a business or investment strategy that makes sense.

In short, there is plenty of experience in the private sector in which uncertainty is not bemoaned amid futile expectations that it somehow can be eliminated. Instead, strategies are designed around it. The strategy adapts to the uncertainty. With foreign policy, the response all too often unfortunately involves bemoaning and holding futile expectations.

Some American statesmen have been exceptions to this pattern, providing wholesome examples for others to follow. Two prime examples were secretaries of state near the end of the Cold War: George Shultz and James Baker. Shultz formed some specific ideas of his own about Soviet conduct and the future of the Soviet Union, but his main advice to President Reagan was not to let any one image of Soviet behavior or the USSR's destiny shape U.S. policy. The policy, he believed, had to protect U.S. interests no matter which image turned out to be correct. He wrote in a memo to Reagan in 1983: "While the Soviet response to a successful demonstration of our resolve is not entirely predictable, I believe that the Soviet leadership might conclude that it had no alternative but to come to terms with us. In that event, opportunities for a lasting and significant improvement in U.S.–Soviet relations would be better than they have been for decades. If the Soviets remained intransigent, we would have nevertheless taken the essential steps needed to ensure our security."[9]

Shultz maintained this posture in the late 1980s, even as speculation accelerated about what was going on inside the Soviet Union under Gorbachev. "Fascinating" though it was to indulge in that speculation, said Shultz, U.S. policy should not be based on it. "Our knowledge was thin," he observed later. "We could be wrong."[10]

When Baker's policy-planning staff presented him in 1989 with alternative scenarios for the Soviet Union's future, as he later wrote, "The wide range of potential scenarios made it clear that we needed a strategy that could manage the growing uncertainties regarding the Soviet future."[11] Baker's policy, under President George H. W. Bush, of "locking in" a changed relationship with Gorbachev was based on his recognition that no one could predict the Soviet leader's future. It made sense to reach agreements that would advance U.S. interests regardless of whether Gorbachev stayed or was ousted and regardless of whether perestroika was a fundamental shift in direction for the USSR or merely an attempt by Soviet leaders to gain breathing space. The uncertainties included not only whether Gorbachev would stay or go, but also whether any successor would be comparably willing to make concessions. So Baker executed the policy to gain as many of those concessions as possible "without frivolously irritating," as he put it, potential successors to Gorbachev, such as Boris Yeltsin.[12]

The policy was an excellent example of effective adaptation to uncertainty. It distinguished clearly between what could be known and what could not as well as between what the United States could count on and what it could not. It was designed to maximize U.S. gains and to minimize U.S. losses regardless of which of several possible futures unfolded. The policy did not rest on the accuracy of any one image of the USSR, and the policymakers did not dwell on whether any one group of analysts covering the USSR was getting it right or getting it wrong.

U.S. foreign policy needs to emulate Shultz and Baker's outlook and to be more consistently sensitive to uncertainty than it has been in the past. An uncertainty-sensitive foreign policy, by its very nature, is not reducible to the kind of simplifying concepts that all those would-be Kennans have offered. Such a policy is not itself a strategy, but rather more an open frame of mind and a way of approaching the construction of policy on any of the innumerable and diverse problems that policymakers are forced to address. Although not easily definable, an uncertainty-sensitive foreign policy would reflect, among other things, the observations and advice I give in the upcoming sections.

Expect Tactical Surprise

We should not be surprised to be surprised—and I refer here to tactical surprise, which is harder to reduce, let alone eliminate, than strategic surprise, chiefly because it involves unobservable and perhaps unattainable things such as an adversary's secret plans. Enemy attacks of various sorts constitute the most consequential form of tactical surprise, but such surprises may originate with something else, such as a natural disaster. Things go bump in the night, no matter how much we try to lower the chance of this happening.

Prudent policy would reflect thinking about threats and trends that might generate tactical surprise, about how to mitigate damage to U.S. interests if such surprise occurs (or how to exploit opportunities because some surprises are good), and how to do so without unacceptable negative consequences for other U.S. interests. This does not mean aimless imagining of the many ways in which others might do us harm. It means focusing on practical steps that can be taken to maximize gains or to minimize losses if the unexpected should occur.

An uncertainty-sensitive policy would not have concentrated the Pacific fleet at Pearl Harbor in December 1941—not because the tactical details of a Japanese attack should have been predictable, but instead because such details usually are *not* predictable. A Japanese military attack of some sort was a significant possibility. Having the fleet that would be needed to conduct a war against Japan at any one place, be it Pearl Harbor or anywhere else, reflected insufficient recognition of the potential for tactical surprise.

Similar issues might be raised about some deployments of U.S. military forces today. What about the twenty-eight thousand U.S. troops in South Korea? Kim Jong Il's North Korea is a bundle of possible bad surprises waiting to happen. Might some of those surprises, possibly involving nuclear weapons, have Pearl Harbor–scale consequences for U.S. personnel on the peninsula?

One of the biggest issues relevant to tactical surprise is terrorism. The United States needs to discard the unattainable hope of obtaining enough tactical information to eliminate the surprise that any terrorist attack entails. The problem of overreliance on tactical warning, about which the Crowe panel investigating the bombings of the U.S. embassies in Kenya and Tanzania warned a decade ago, persists. We should heed the panel's observation that unwarranted reliance on tactical warning has distracted the United States from other steps that have a better chance of reducing the likelihood of and damage from terrorist attacks.

An uncertainty-sensitive counterterrorist policy would have undertaken prior to 9/11 most of the security measures that were taken afterward; there certainly was a sufficient strategic threat to warrant doing so. Such a policy would not have adopted stoplight charts or similar ways of expressing levels of threat, not only because citizens have been confused about how to respond but also because such measures perpetuate the notion that counterterrorism can and should be ramped up or ramped down according to the threat information du jour. Most counterterrorist measures need to be sustained indefinitely because the threat is indefinite. A counterterrorist policy built operationally and rhetorically on the realization that there will be more tactical surprises has the further benefit of reducing the psychological impact on the citizenry when an attack does occur.

Friends Might Change

An uncertainty-sensitive foreign policy involves taking to heart Lord Palmerston's dictum about nations having no permanent friends, only permanent interests. The possibility of major and perhaps sudden change among friends and allies is one of the contingencies for which it is important to prepare, even if judged unlikely in any one case. Revolutionary overthrow of a regime is one type of change. Its inherent unpredictability argues against strategic or economic policies that depend heavily on a continued alliance with the existing regime. The uncertainty also argues against cozy relationships that should a regime be deposed would magnify problems the United States would have with its successor. The required outlook is one that never would have led the United States to become irretrievably dependent on the shah of Iran in the 1970s.

U.S. relations with current regimes in some other Middle Eastern countries raise similar issues. The oil-lubricated partnership with Saudi Arabia is one key relationship. It would be a mistake to undermine King Abdullah, who is one of the best things going both for the relationship and for the Saudis' long-term interests. But the fragility of this politically medieval, family-owned state requires thinking about the unthinkable and about how the United States might minimize the damage to its interests if the unthinkable were to occur. The United States already has done some prudent things, such as reducing its military dependence on the Saudis and their territory.

Egypt is another important case—a heavyweight in the Arab world, but with a muddling, increasingly authoritarian regime. A U.S. policy that fully recognizes the uncertainty of Egypt's future would use the $1.5 billion in U.S. military and economic aid to Egypt in ways that would make it more apparent that the United States was a friend to all Egyptians and not just to the regime. Such a policy also would not foreclose the possibility, should the current regime crumble, of good relations with its most credible successors, including the Muslim Brotherhood.

Unfavorable and even sudden change also can occur when a regime reevaluates its policies, not just when it is overthrown. Prudent U.S. policy would avoid placing much stock in any one image of a given regime's friendship both because the image might be wrong and because even if it were correct at one time, the underlying reality might change. An uncertainty-sensitive approach would not have shaped policy toward

Russia around looking into the Russian president's eyes and seeing his soul. It would not have been petulant about France and Germany's opposing the Iraq War because it seemed like a betrayal by friends, and it would not tend to bifurcate the world into friends and enemies in the first place. An uncertainty-sensitive approach would be braced for possible unfavorable changes of a more permanent sort among major powers. With regard to the Far East, for example, it would be prepared for policy changes by China comparable to the ones of the 1970s or even for Japan's retreat from friendship with the United States, which peaked under the Elvis-loving Junichiro Koizumi from 2001 to 2006.

ADVERSARIES MIGHT NOT BE SO ADVERSARIAL

Images of foes are even harder to get right than images of friends. Our image of an adversary might be wrong from the outset because there are fewer sources of information to exploit, less direct interaction from which to learn, more incentive on the other side to deceive, and more tendency on our side to stereotype. Even if the image was correct at one time, it may become incorrect because foes, like friends, can change. Some of the most important elements of the image of an adversary are inherently unknowable—and changeable—because they involve decisions the adversary has not yet taken.

Prudent U.S. policy would recognize that an adversary might move or evolve in any of several different directions and would be designed to maximize U.S. gains and minimize U.S. losses no matter what direction the adversary takes. Just as important, prudent policy would *allow* the adversary to move in more favorable directions. The policy would not be based on a single unfavorable image that becomes self-fulfilling because it effectively closes the adversary's other options. Sound, uncertainty-sensitive policy would not only reduce the risk of harm from unfavorable contingencies but also increase the chance of exploiting favorable ones and even of bagging some pleasant surprises. Adversaries should be approached in the spirit expressed by Nassim Nicholas Taleb, exponent of the concept of black swans, when he says, "There are so many things we can do if we focus on antiknowledge, or what we do not know. Among many other benefits, you can set yourself up to collect serendipitous Black Swans (of the positive kind) by maximizing your exposure to them."[13]

U.S. policy toward states (or other political entities) that Americans view as adversaries has unfortunately too often been based on a single, unfavorable image. This has been true of much U.S. policy in the Middle East, most conspicuously during the eight years of George W. Bush's administration. Adversaries have been assumed to be incorrigible and have been the object of policies that have left them little opportunity to be anything but incorrigible.

It has also been true of much American thinking about Iran, including on the preoccupying issue of Iran's nuclear program. Failure to appreciate that the most important Iranian decisions about that program have yet to be taken has led to failed policies such as a peremptory demand to cease all uranium enrichment and has prevented full exploration of formulas that might satisfy each side's requirements with neither side caving in. Sensitivity to uncertainty is needed even more with regard to Iran's internal politics. But here again much American discourse about Iran exhibits either-or, single-image thinking: either we accept the mullahs and hardliners as here to stay, or we trust in the ability of the Iranian opposition to overcome them. But no one can predict the future political evolution of Iran, and it would be foolish to base a policy on the assumption that we can. Moreover, the dichotomy is false. Foreign engagement with a government need not weaken internal opposition to it. Engagement can take forms that reduce the negative consequences of hostility between the United States and Iran without reducing the chances for favorable political evolution and even pleasant surprises inside Iran.

Most American attitudes toward Syria have been based on a similar negative image in which the regime is bent on supporting violence against Israel, maintaining an alliance with Hizballah in Lebanon, and condoning cross-border trouble making in Iraq. There are good reasons to believe that Damascus is not wedded to any of those things, that return of the Golan Heights is the preeminent objective of its foreign and security policy, and that everything else is instrumental to that end and is negotiable. But the policies of most of the past several years have given no opportunity to discover if these variables are true. Different policies, involving more active engagement with Damascus, would enable the United States to find out if they are true, while risking little or nothing even if they were not.

Policies toward the Palestinian Islamist political organization Hamas provide perhaps the clearest example of a self-fulfilling assumption of incorrigibility, although U.S. and Israeli policies toward the group are probably based less on any image than on a visceral dislike for dealing with a group that has used terrorist attacks to kill innocent Israelis. Whatever the mixture of emotion and calculation, U.S. support for Israeli efforts to undermine Hamas in every way possible—even after it won a fair election—only encourages the group not to abandon violent means for pursuing its objectives. The self-interest of Hamas leaders who want to exercise political power over Palestinians suggests considerable possibilities for the group to pursue that primary objective peacefully if it were allowed to do so, with a long-term truce, or *hudna*, with Israel leading to further favorable evolution of attitudes and political relationships. Again, sound policy would be based not on an assumption that this or any other single scenario necessarily would unfold, but instead on minimizing damage and maximizing favorable opportunities given that any of several possibilities might occur. For Hamas to hold or share power in a Palestinian state or quasi-state and to be recognized as doing so would pose no more danger (even to Israeli interests, let alone to U.S. ones) than it does now even if the image of incorrigibility turned out to be correct. And this posture toward Hamas would allow more favorable possibilities to unfold that prevailing policies have foreclosed altogether.

Don't Draw to an Inside Straight

Any move that depends on the cards falling just right—on an uncertainty being resolved a certain way—can be dangerous. This does not mean such moves never make sense. But a foreign-policy decision that advances the national interest only if a particular uncertain proposition about events beyond our borders turns out to be true is likely to be a bad bet, given how difficult it is to resolve many uncertainties relevant to foreign policy and given the many reasons the relevant images that policymakers hold may be wrong. Just how bad a bet depends, among other things, on the consequences if the cards don't happen to break right.

A clear example is preemptive war—what the Bush administration said it was waging in Iraq. (Or, more accurately, the administration's claim was instead that its invasion was a *preventive* war, the idea being that if the Iraqi regime were not deposed, it eventually would do something nasty and aggressive even if it were not on the verge of doing so.) *Preemptive* war, if it is to make sense at all, requires highly specific and timely information about the adversary's intentions and preparations. This requirement is usually beyond intelligence services' ability to fulfill. The requirements for preventive war are not as severely specific but usually involve decisions the adversary has not yet made and in that respect may be even harder to fulfill.

Cold War strategists agonized at length over these problems. In the context in which the United States and the USSR confronted each other with nuclear weapons, a preemptive strike in response to an accurate image that the adversary was about to strike might save the nation. But if the image were inaccurate, the result would be a nuclear war that no one wanted. In most contemporary situations of preemption or prevention, the negative consequences of an inaccurate image would not be that catastrophic. They can be major, however, as the Iraq War has demonstrated. As we saw in an earlier chapter, the actual motivations for the war had less to do with either preemption or prevention and more to do with a desire to remake the political order of the Middle East. But the hoped-for result of acting on that desire, too, rested on an assumption that key cards would break the right way—that a new political order in Iraq would smoothly fall into place and that this outcome would set off a democratic domino effect in the region.

Salvage Some Benefit Even When We're Wrong

Foreign policy should be formulated not just to realize our highest hopes or to assuage our worst fears if the variables of most interest to us turn out as we expect, but also to limit the damage and even to realize some gain if they turn out differently. The consequences that matter in foreign affairs are typically numerous and varied, which means that more sophisticated policies are needed than would apply to a simpler situation such as the experiment with the food in the T-maze. For the rat always to go where food was more likely was the best strategy because the rat was not going to starve to death (and neither would the students) when the food instead appeared at the other end of the maze. In foreign affairs, we need to consider not only what we think has a 60 (or even 80 or 90) percent chance of happening, but also the consequences of less likely but still possible alternatives. The answer lies not in the futile attempt to find predictable order in unpredictable events, but instead in finding ways to hedge bets and to get out of the binary tyranny of the T-maze altogether. Such ways usually can be found in the real world of foreign policy.

In the Middle Eastern examples cited earlier, prudent policies are ones that would leave the United States better off even if the dominant images that drive the policies turn out to be wrong and the maximum hopes for those policies go unrealized. Engagement with adversaries such as Iran or Syria, even if they prove to be intransigent and no major deals are struck, at least would provide more credible grounds for expecting international support in confronting the intransigence. Vigorous effort to secure an Israeli–Palestinian peace, even if it produces no breakthrough agreement, would beneficially change regional attitudes toward the United States and at least marginally increase willingness to cooperate with Washington. The opposite policies (no engagement, passivity about a peace settlement) offer no benefit and only missed opportunities if the images that guide them turn out to be wrong. Debates over policy should not just be—as they far too often are—arguments over whose image is correct, but rather explorations of what the balance of gains and losses for U.S. interests will be, given that anyone's image might be incorrect.

The benefit to be salvaged might be unrelated to the original problem we were trying to address. For example, a cogent reason for taking additional measures to safeguard the civilian population against biological terrorism is not that the threat of such terrorism is severe, but instead that even if such a threat never materialized, the measures would still be beneficial in protecting against natural or accidental outbreaks of disease.[14] The specific steps might include greater stockpiling of vaccines and other needed bolstering of the public-health system. The wisdom of such measures would not depend on the accuracy of any one image of terrorist threats.

Policymakers should, as James Baker did in contemplating the fragile USSR at the end of the 1980s, carefully distinguish the certain from the uncertain—what the United States can count on and what it cannot. They should pocket certain gains and discount (but not discard) uncertain hoped-for ones. Some options should be favored not because the gains they offer are more important than the gains that other options may offer, but instead because they are less uncertain. This outlook was unfortunately absent from most of the debate in 2006 and 2007 on what to do about the mess in Iraq before the Bush administration finally agreed with the Iraqi government in 2008 on a schedule for the withdrawal of U.S. troops. Sophisticated arguments were advanced about continuing missions for U.S. forces and what might befall Iraq if the troops were not there to perform the missions. The arguments were not necessarily invalid, but the scenarios they offered were highly uncertain. No one could confidently predict the future of Iraq, with or without U.S. troops. The opposing pro-withdrawal position, pejoratively labeled "cut and run," deserved more weight than it got because the direct benefit it offered of stanching the loss of American blood and treasure was more certain.

CONSIDER *ALL* THE UNCERTAINTIES

Being cognizant of the different ways the few variables of most interest to us might break is not enough. Most foreign-policy problems of any importance involve many uncertainties, not just a few. How each of the many variables breaks is important, individually and collectively, to the success or failure of policy. We do not have the luxury of focusing on only one uncertainty or a few of them and ignoring the rest.

Much of the thinking that has gone into policymaking, however, and certainly into the selling or rationalizing of policy has paid attention to only one or a few uncertainties rather than to all of them. A prime example is Dick Cheney's concept that even just a one percent chance that Saddam Hussein had WMD was sufficient reason to wage war to depose him. Although at first glance the former vice president's reference to a percentage seems to be an admirable acknowledgment of uncertainty—and even a heeding of my advice to pay attention to the consequences of less likely possibilities and not just the most likely one—many other uncertainties besides the one about unconventional weapons would determine the success or failure of the Iraq War and whether launching the war was wise or foolish. Those other uncertainties involved the costs of securing and reconstructing Iraq, the building of a new Iraqi political order, the impact of the war on political extremism and on attitudes toward the United States, and much else. The makers of the war either ignored those other uncertainties or wished them away with best-case assumptions.

Cheney's one percent idea was almost certainly not part of any rigorous calculation of risks but instead merely a rhetorical device for expressing and justifying his preference for the use of force to topple Saddam. But suppose for a moment that it were part of a careful calculation. Suppose also that unconventional weapons actually had been the main motive for launching the war. Even if one believed that a one percent chance of Saddam's having the feared weapons was reason enough to invade Iraq, what if the estimated probability of this outcome were only one-tenth of a percent? One-hundredth of a percent? At some level of probability, even the war makers' sunniest assumptions about the course of the war would presumably not have made the cost and bother of launching it seem worthwhile. The less sunny the assumptions, the higher the percentage below which the war would be unattractive. One implication is that decision makers deal with subjective probabilities, not just possibilities, all the time, even if not expressed in mathematical terms. Another implication is that careful and complete input to a decision would involve weighing all the risks implied by all of the relevant variables, not just one variable that happens to have caught our attention or to have become a focus of public discourse or fears. If such a careful and complete decision process had taken place prior to the Iraq War, the conclusion would have been that the war was a foolish gamble—worthwhile only if the United States were lucky enough to draw several of the right cards, not just one particular card.

A narrow focus on only one risk rather than on all the relevant risks has also characterized much discussion and debate about the Iranian nuclear program and specifically the possibility of using military force to retard it. The uncertainty that has gotten the most attention is the status of the program and the timetable for Iran to be able to make a nuclear weapon if it chooses to do so. Some attention (but not enough) has been given to the Iranian leadership's future decisions about building a weapon. How malleable and how well defined are Tehran's intentions, and what changes in Washington's policy toward Iran might lead Tehran to abandon a weapons program? Some attention (but not nearly enough) has been given to the impact an Iranian nuclear weapon would have on regional security. How exactly would possession of a nuclear weapon change Iran's behavior and affect U.S. interests? In particular, why would deterrence, which has kept nuclear peace with other adversaries, not work with Iran?

Many more uncertainties than those are relevant to any use of military force against the Iranian program. A host of questions, many of which have barely entered public discussion, would have to be addressed in any thorough consideration of whether the military option would make sense.[15] Given the likely hardening, concealment, and dispersal of Iran's nuclear facilities, what would be the physical impact of a military strike on the program? How much would Iran's nuclear efforts be set back, especially given that bombs are not very good at destroying knowledge and expertise? Would the Iranian response to this setback be appreciably different from that of

Iraq to Israel's bombing of its nuclear reactor in 1981, after which Iraq re-doubled its nuclear efforts while turning to different methods for producing fissile material? How would Tehran respond to an act of war? What terror-ism might it launch against the United States, using either its own agents or its ally Hizballah? How would it exploit U.S. vulnerabilities next door in Iraq, where it has barely begun to exploit the influence it has assiduously been cultivating? What other military action might it take, with the risk of a wider war in the Persian Gulf? How much would the direct assertion of U.S. hostility strengthen Iranian hardliners, whose policies are in part pre-mised on such hostility? How much would it add to all Iranians' list of his-torical grievances against the United States and adversely affect relations with future governments in Tehran? What would be the impact on the oil market (especially if the Iranian response were to lead to a wider conflict in the gulf), and what would be the subsequent consequences for the global economy? What would be the impact on other Middle Eastern states' will-ingness to cooperate with the United States? Would a military strike exac-erbate the damage the Iraq War dealt to the standing of the United States worldwide? My own contemplation of these questions leads me to the con-clusion that a military strike would be folly. But the pertinent point for our present purposes is that all these uncertainties are relevant to such an ac-tion and that the costs and risks entailed in all of them—not just in some of them—would need to be considered.

Paul Wolfowitz once said, "There is a constant bias toward inaction, because the risks are less obvious."[16] The war that he championed demon-strated otherwise. The scary possibilities if Saddam were allowed to remain in power were embedded into Americans' thinking about Iraq; it was the risks of the war to overthrow him that did not get sufficient attention. Wol-fowitz's statement is incorrect not just because the Bush administration's selling of the Iraq War made it wrong in that specific case, but also in a more general sense. It is the risks of action that tend to be less obvious be-cause the action itself changes the situation, and more variables and uncer-tainties come into play than we observe in contemplating the status quo.

Uncertainties need to be analyzed collectively, not just individually. The costs and risks they involve are at least additive and sometimes multi-plicative. Some possible problems exacerbate other problems, as was the case in Iraq. Insecurity within Iraq made economic reconstruction slower and more expensive and made political reconciliation more difficult. The political divisions and the frustrations related to a shattered economy in turn encouraged resort to violence and exacerbated the insecurity. All of the problems inside Iraq reduced the chance of a democratic domino effect by souring other Middle Easterners on the idea of political transformation. The psychological tendency to overestimate the cumulative probability of a series of events—in this case, the probability that all of the several uncertainties will break in our favor—must be overcome.[17] An initiative that might seem like a worthwhile bet when weighed against any one risk may be revealed to be a bad gamble when considered with all the risks together.

REMEMBER WHOSE INTERESTS ARE AT RISK

Behavioral economists would remind us that any discussion of good and bad gambles and of prudent and imprudent approaches to uncertainty must confront the fact that attitude toward risk is an individual preference. A bet that is unattractive to a risk-averse person may look fine to a risk-acceptant one. That distinction raises the question of how much risk policymakers, acting not as individuals but on behalf of a nation, *ought* to accept. In the private sector, especially in business and financial decisions, some of the biggest rewards go to those who assume the biggest risks. Should the United States do the same and reach for the brass ring?

The makers of U.S. foreign policy would be better advised to try to shun risk rather than to accept it. In general, they should favor courses of action that pose fewer uncertainties over those that pose many. One reason to do so is that the consequences of failure in U.S. foreign policy are potentially far greater than those of failure in the private sector. The biggest consequences of risky and unsuccessful decisions in the private sector, as illustrated in the financial crisis of 2008, have concerned companies deemed "too big to fail." The United States, by far the most important actor in international politics and security, is always too big to fail. If it gets into trouble, the impact is much greater than even the largest investment bank's or hedge fund's going bust.

Another reason to shun risk is that the makers of U.S. policy face incalculable uncertainties, not calculable risks. They always will have fewer bases for making intelligent decisions to accept risk than does the most risk-acceptant financial gunslinger on Wall Street. It is not just a matter of exposing the nation to the risk of failure, but instead of never fully knowing just what those risks are, or at least the magnitude of them. Moreover, given the tenuous equilibria that characterize so much of international politics and security, uncertainty-heavy actions are likely to encounter more bad surprises than pleasant ones.

A third reason concerns the proper role of government. The policy-makers in charge of the government at any one moment are stewards or custodians of interests much larger and more permanent than their own. As they make foreign and security policy, they are playing with other people's money as well as with other people's lives. Because, as with most government activities, there is an element of compulsion (paying taxes for foreign wars being a clear example), government should perform what is necessary rather than what stems from an expansive and voluntary assumption of risk. There is no sound philosophical or moral basis for the temporary stewards to impose their own propensity for risk on the rest of the nation. There is even less basis for them to lead the nation to take big risks on behalf of their own favored ideologies or experiments.

A useful comparison is with debates over privatizing Social Security. The choice is usually framed as between government controlling the money and keeping it in low-risk government securities or letting individuals control it and having the option to put it in riskier investments. What has not received any significant support is for the government to control the money *and* to put it in high-risk investments. The Iraq War, which was contrary to the advice I am offering here about avoiding policies that involve many uncertainties, was the foreign-policy equivalent of doing just that. It was a gamble akin to putting the Social Security trust fund into naked short sales, subprime mortgages, and out-of-the-money options on hog bellies. Even that does not fully capture the magnitude of the gamble, which entailed a multitude of incalculable uncertainties rather than a fixed number of quantifiable risks.

PUT A PRICE ON INFORMATION

A foreign policy that is fully sensitive to uncertainty would include an integrated, two-way view of intelligence and policy, eschewing the all-too-common spectator sport approach toward intelligence. Such a policy would acknowledge that we can know only some of the things it would be useful to know, that we can know only some of those things through intelligence, and that we are unlikely ever to know other things. It also would acknowledge that further efforts to collect information and to improve the detailed accuracy of our images are apt to have diminishing returns. Such a policy would kick the habit of responding to policy conundrums by automatically calling for intelligence to collect more and better information. The habit is long-standing. The report in 1971 of a review of intelligence led by James Schlesinger noted, "Seldom does anyone ask if a further reduction in uncertainty, however small, is worth the cost."[18]

An uncertainty-sensitive foreign policy would frequently ask that question. In answering it, policymakers should carefully consider exactly what use they would or would not make of additional information if they had it. They should do the kind of deliberation Dean Rusk did in deciding that more detailed information about the timing of China's first nuclear test would not have affected his actions anyway. Policymakers should be aware that further efforts to reduce uncertainty may include not only the monetary costs of intelligence or other information-gathering operations, but also other costs, such as possibly ruffling relations with another government. They should be aware that adaptation may in many instances be a better response to uncertainty than efforts—costly and possibly futile—to reduce it.

An integrated view of intelligence and policy includes acknowledgment of trade-offs between some actions intended to cope with a problem and the chance of collecting more information on the same problem. This old dilemma arose in classic form with major intelligence breakthroughs of the past. How could the Western allies in World War II exploit information from decoded German messages without tipping off the Germans that their codes had been broken?[19] It has arisen more recently in less classic and thus less acknowledged form, such as how a demarche to India about nuclear tests would tip off the Indians about U.S. ability to monitor preparations for future tests. It also has arisen when policy decisions have led to the expulsion of international arms inspectors from North Korea or Iraq and thus to loss of an important source of information on the programs they were inspecting.[20] In all such cases, recognizing the trade-off entails putting a price on additional information, with part of that price being the forgoing of what might otherwise be a useful policy action.

Expect Unknown Unknowns

Not only is the world that the makers of foreign policy have to face filled with uncertainties, but it is also uncertain which uncertainties the policymakers will have to face. They not only should not expect to know the answers to many important questions but should also not expect to know all of the questions that will turn out to be important. U.S. presidents cannot set all of their own foreign-policy agenda. They generally set less and less of it the farther they get into their presidencies as new problems or new twists on old problems demand responses and overshadow whatever ambitions the presidents brought with them into office.

This meta-uncertainty stems in part from all the unpredictable things going bump in the night, some subset of which will, for equally unpredictable reasons, turn out to be important and demand responses. It also stems from changes in the international system, which might be somewhat more predictable because they involve larger trends and forces rather than troublesome aberrations. The forecasting of such changes is something of a discipline and a business. My former organization, the NIC, has offered its own series of futuristic reports, each looking out about fifteen years.[21] The NIC appropriately describes its efforts as less a prediction than a discussion of trends and variables. But even that modest variety of forecasting confronts the fact that not only do the challenges the world throws at policymakers change, but the reasons for the change—or even the *types* of reasons for the change—themselves change. Think back half a century and ask what the most important changes in the global system over the twenty years before that were. One might respond: the advent of nuclear weapons, the onset of the Cold War, and the erection of international organizations to make the post–World War II order more orderly than what came before. Ask the same question today about the most recent twenty years and the character of the answer would be quite different: maybe something about economic interdependence and security concerns regarding nonstate actors such as terrorist groups. Look out another half-century or perhaps even just a decade or two into the future, and the answer is apt to have yet a different flavor.

Uncertainties swirling around uncertainties do not, by their very nature, lead to clear and specific policy advice. But they do suggest two more general admonitions. One is to avoid trying to tailor processes and institutions around finding the answers to certain questions, however important those questions may seem. The questions are apt to be eclipsed, sooner than we think, by other questions that we cannot now anticipate. It would be a mistake, for example, to focus counterterrorist efforts exclusively on the groups and ideologies of most concern to us at the moment because doing so would come at the expense of compromising our ability to detect future terrorist threats from other directions.

The other admonition is that the United States needs to maintain reserves—of resources, of international goodwill, and of its policymakers' time and attention—to deal with unforeseeable issues and problems. This means not letting the part of the national agenda that policymakers control get too crowded so there is room for the addition of items not under their control. It means avoiding initiatives that might become all consuming, as the wars in Vietnam and Iraq did in expending vast amounts of human, monetary, and political capital. It means consciously conserving economic and military capabilities for rainy days. In brief, it means not trying to press the envelope of what even a superpower can accomplish.

GRAND STRATEGY REVISITED

Although the advice in this chapter does not constitute a grand strategy, it suggests some criteria for assessing strategies that have been adopted or proposed.[22] We should be wary of any strategy that has high requirements for information and whose success depends on the accuracy of particular images. This wariness is most clearly applicable to any strategy that emphasizes preemptive or preventive war. It also applies to some other elements of U.S. strategy that were most apparent in but not unique to the George W. Bush administration's mixture of assertive nationalism and neoconservatism. We should be wary of extensive reliance on military force generally—among other reasons because successful use of it often imposes informational requirements we are unlikely to be able to meet and because the commitments involved tend to consume much of our reserves of attention and resources needed to meet other, unforeseeable challenges. We should be skeptical of strategies that assume that any one way the world works is likely to endure and that something like the unipolar moment will be more than just a moment. We should be similarly skeptical of any strategy that sorts other regimes into unchanging categories of friends and foes.

In general, we should be circumspect about assertive strategies that seek to impose U.S. will or expand U.S. presence, upsetting whatever patterns have evolved from the undirected vicissitudes of world politics. This advice means calling into question much of the direction of U.S. strategies over the past several decades, which one student of grand strategy has lumped together under the label "extraregional hegemony."[23] The advice means favoring the cautious and agnostic over the bold and confident, given that there is very little in the world about which we can justifiably be very confident.

The perspective in this chapter also calls for circumspection about the whole idea of grand strategy or at least about how much any such strategy should guide U.S. foreign policy. Policy should not be entirely reactive. As Yogi Berra reminded us, if you don't know where you're going, you might end up someplace else. But simple, overarching principles, although intrinsic to any grand strategy, are antithetical to much of what I have said here about unavoidable uncertainty. Guidance that claims to be generally applicable is likely to be misguidance in some specific cases, some of which—and we cannot know in advance which ones—turn out to be important. To a large extent, policymakers would do well to expect that to a large degree history really is one damned thing after another.

The simplifying, overriding, doctrinally enshrined tenets of a grand strategy have another unfortunate effect: once enshrined, they discourage debate, dissent, and healthy skepticism. They become unquestioned and often unstated assumptions. They generate images that, although possibly inaccurate, are taken for granted. And they encourage politicization, in which contrary information is either ignored or shaped to conform to the strategy.[24]

THE CHOICE

The United States can do much to improve the images that guide its foreign policy and to minimize the damage to its policy from images that are inaccurate or missing. Americans, or at least their elected representatives, might begin by understanding whence come the images that most influence policy—not from some part of the government bureaucracy, but instead from their leaders' innards, from the workings of their political system, and from their own culture and historical experiences. They might acknowledge that politicization exists and use that acknowledgment as the first step in trying to reduce it. They might implement the recommendations in the previous chapter on behalf of that objective and to bring more accurate images before senior policymakers. They might accept that they will never know many things important to foreign policy and follow the advice in the current chapter to advance U.S. interests despite that uncertainty.

Or, in contrast, Americans might continue to treat these topics as they have treated them for decades. Doing so would mean little or no acknowledgment of the sources of images, the biases, the politicization, or the limits of knowledge. It would mean continuing to support policies that outstrip those limits. It would mean that failed policies and inaccurate images would continue to be blamed on "intelligence failure," leading to still more iterations in the endless cycle of recrimination and demands for "reform." And it would mean American foreign policy would be no better guided than previously.

The second scenario is unfortunately much more likely than the first. It has prevailed for too long and reflects attitudes that are too deeply rooted to warrant optimism about the prospects for change. The most recent iterations of the cycle have shown the attitudes to be as firmly entrenched as ever. The response to 9/11 demonstrated that Americans would rather be reassured than be right. They also would rather not mar the national self-image of an America capable of doing whatever it puts its mind to, including figuring out what is going on outside its borders. Harry Howe Ransom, in the final sentence of a book on intelligence he wrote more than fifty years ago, appealed for "humility required in the face of all that American government leaders need to know but which even the best of intelligence services today cannot tell them."[25] Given that this lesson in humility has not been learned in the past half century, it is unlikely to be learned anytime soon.

If there is a basis for offsetting optimism, it lies with the hope that Americans can dig more deeply into another part of their political tradition and culture—the part that values openness and the free exchange of ideas and that holds that open competition of differing views is the best way to expose error. Americans still cannot eliminate uncertainty and know the unknowable, but a fuller application of this part of their tradition to foreign policy would at least make it less likely for misconceptions to prevail. It also would reduce political elites' ability to use their powers of persuasion to impose their own version of events.

Inscribed in a wall by the entrance to the CIA headquarters building is a biblical verse: "And ye shall know the truth, and the truth shall make you free" (John 8:32). Some have questioned the applicability of this quotation to intelligence on grounds that intelligence is not to be equated with truth. Of course it should not be. But the quotation can be interpreted as containing some concepts closely related to ideas in this book. One is that, knowable or not, there is such a thing as the truth. I mean an objective truth, not someone's created reality and not something growing out of particular preferences or policies. Another concept is the link with freedom. In this case, the concept of truth might refer to the importance of an accurate understanding of the outside world for protecting the national security of the United States and with it American values, including freedom. This idea is probably what whoever selected the inscription had in mind. It also can refer to freedom that inheres more directly in knowing the truth—the freedom of not having to subscribe to someone else's version of reality. And then there is the future tense: we "shall" know the truth. We may not have attained truth, and on many matters we may never attain it, but it is worthwhile to strive for it and to come as close to it as we can.

1. Introduction

1. Walter Russell Mead, *Special Providence: American Foreign Policy and How It Changed the World* (New York: Routledge, 2002), 8.

2. Joseph Frankel, *The Making of Foreign Policy: An Analysis of Decision Making* (London: Oxford University Press, 1963), 105.

3. Alexis de Tocqueville, *Democracy in America*, trans. Henry Reeve, 2 vols. (New York: Schoken, 1961), 2:37–39.

4. Stephen Peter Rosen, *War and Human Nature* (Princeton, N.J.: Princeton University Press, 2005), 57–58.

5. Robert Jervis, *Why Intelligence Fails: Lessons from the Iranian Revolution and the Iraq War* (Ithaca, N.Y.: Cornell University Press, 2010), 170.

6. For an overview, see John G. Benjafield, *Cognition* (Englewood Cliffs, N.J.: Prentice Hall, 1992), chap. 2.

7. Doris Kearns, *Lyndon Johnson and the American Dream* (New York: Harper and Row, 1976), 258.

8. For further discussion of this element of the mythology, see Paul R. Pillar, "Great Expectations: Intelligence as Savior," *Harvard International Review* 27, no. 4 (Winter 2006): 16–21.

9. George Tenet, *At the Center of the Storm: My Years at the CIA* (New York: HarperCollins, 2007), 45.
10. Quoted in "Soldier for Sailor," *Time*, August 28, 1950, 14.
11. Mead, *Special Providence*, 61.

2. Weapons of Mass Destruction and the Iraq War

1. Quoted in Ron Suskind, *The One Percent Doctrine: Deep Inside America's Pursuit of Its Enemies Since 9/11* (New York: Simon and Schuster, 2006), 225.
2. Quoted in Nicholas Lemann, "Remember the Alamo: How George W. Bush Reinvented Himself," *New Yorker* (October 18, 2004), 157.
3. Bob Drogin, *Curveball: Spies, Lies, and the Con Man Who Caused a War* (New York: Random House, 2007).
4. Lewis D. Solomon, *Paul D. Wolfowitz: Visionary Intellectual, Policymaker, and Strategist* (Westport, Conn.: Praeger Security International, 2007), 67.
5. Zalmay M. Khalilzad and Paul Wolfowitz, "Overthrow Him," *Weekly Standard*, December 1, 1997.
6. The text of this letter is available at http://www.newamericancentury.org/iraqclintonletter.htm.
7. The text of this letter is available at http://www.iraqwatch.org/perspectives/rumsfeld-openletter.htm.
8. Robert Kagan, "On Iraq, Short Memories," *Washington Post*, November 20, 2005.
9. Statement of Principles, Project for the New American Century, available at http://www.newamericancentury.org/statementofprinciples.htm.
10. President George W. Bush, speech to the American Enterprise Institute, February 26, 2003, available at http://georgewbush-whitehouse.archives.gov/news/releases/2003/02/20030226-11.html.
11. George W. Bush, Inaugural Address, January 20, 2005, available at http://georgewbush-whitehouse.archives.gov/news/releases/2005/01/20050120-1.html.
12. Quoted in Bob Woodward, *Plan of Attack* (New York: Simon and Schuster, 2004), 412.
13. Joshua Muravchik, "Can the Neocons Get Their Groove Back?" *Washington Post*, November 19, 2006.
14. Charles Krauthammer, "The Unipolar Moment," *Foreign Affairs* 70, no. 1 (1990–1991), 33.

15. George Packer, *The Assassins' Gate: America in Iraq* (New York: Farrar, Straus and Giroux, 2005), 36.

16. Ivo H. Daalder and James M. Lindsay, *America Unbound: The Bush Revolution in Foreign Policy* (Washington, D.C.: Brookings Institution Press, 2003), 15.

17. Michael R. Gordon and Bernard E. Trainor, *Cobra II: The Inside Story of the Invasion and Occupation of Iraq* (New York: Pantheon, 2006), 64.

18. Paul R. Pillar, "Intelligence, Policy, and the War in Iraq," *Foreign Affairs* 85, no. 2 (March–April 2006), 16.

19. The responses to the work on this subject by John J. Mearsheimer and Stephen M. Walt, presented most fully in their book *The Israel Lobby and U.S. Foreign Policy* (New York: Farrar, Straus and Giroux, 2007), included reckless charges of anti-Semitism. An example of such a response is Eliot A. Cohen, "Yes, It's Anti-Semitic," *Washington Post*, April 5, 2006.

20. An objective and complete assessment of Israeli interests with the benefit of hindsight might alternatively lead to the conclusion that on balance the war has hurt those interests by boosting international terrorism and extremism in the Middle East, increasing Iranian influence, and weakening and distracting the strongly pro-Israel administration of George W. Bush. See some of the Israeli second thoughts cited in Michael Abramowitz, "Bush's Legacy on Israel Debated on Eve of Visit," *Washington Post*, May 13, 2008. But pro-Israeli champions of the war were not voicing these considerations before the invasion.

21. Douglas J. Feith, "Withdrawal Process, Not Peace Process," *Middle East Quarterly* 3 (March 1996), 20.

22. Study Group on a New Israeli Strategy Toward 2000, *A Clean Break: A New Strategy for Securing the Realm* (Jerusalem: Institute for Advanced Political and Strategic Studies, 1996), available at http://www.iasps.org/strat1.htm.

23. Douglas J. Feith, "A Strategy for Israel," *Commentary* 104, no. 3 (September 1997): 21–29.

24. David Wurmser, *Tyranny's Ally: America's Failure to Defeat Saddam Hussein* (Washington, D.C.: AEI Press, 1999), 81, 91–92, 95–99, 106, 137.

25. Packer, *The Assassins' Gate*, 30–31.

26. Quoted in Jeffrey Goldberg, "A Little Learning: What Douglas Feith Knew, and When He Knew It," *New Yorker* (May 9, 2005), 38–39.

27. Thomas E. Ricks, *Fiasco: The American Military Adventure in Iraq* (New York: Penguin Press, 2006), 16.

28. Solomon, *Paul D. Wolfowitz*, 10.

29. Janine Zacharia, "All the President's Middle East Men," *Jerusalem Post*, January 19, 2001.

30. Bret Stephens, "Man of the Year," *Jerusalem Post*, Rosh Hashana 2003, available at http://info.jpost.com/C003/Supplements/MOTY/art.01.html.

31. Mearsheimer and Walt, *The Israel Lobby and U.S. Foreign Policy*, 243.

32. David D. Kirkpatrick, "For Evangelicals, Supporting Israel Is 'God's Foreign Policy,'" *New York Times*, November 14, 2006.

33. Ron Suskind, *The Price of Loyalty: George W. Bush, the White House, and the Education of Paul O'Neill* (New York: Simon and Schuster, 2004), 70–75.

34. Ibid., 85–86.

35. Quoted in Packer, *The Assassins' Gate*, 40.

36. Suskind, *The Price of Loyalty*, 184.

37. Woodward, *Plan of Attack*, 26; Michael Isikoff and David Corn, *Hubris: The Inside Story of Spin, Scandal, and the Selling of the Iraq War* (New York: Crown, 2006), 80; and Suskind, *The Price of Loyalty*, 187–88.

38. Quoted in Gordon and Trainor, *Cobra II*, 15.

39. The text of the letter is available at http://www.newamericancentury.org/Bushletter.htm.

40. Bob Woodward, *State of Denial* (New York: Simon and Schuster, 2006), 83–85.

41. Quoted in Richard A. Clarke, *Against All Enemies: Inside America's War on Terror* (New York: Free Press, 2004), 32.

42. Woodward, *Plan of Attack*, 1–3.

43. Ibid., 53–65.

44. President George W. Bush, State of the Union Address, January 29, 2002, available at http://georgewbush-whitehouse.archives.gov/news/releases/2002/01/20020129-11.html.

45. Woodward, *Plan of Attack*, 87. Bush later wrote that even after the addition of the references to Iran and North Korea, he still intended the "axis" to refer to a link between WMD and terrorism. See George W. Bush, *Decision Points* (New York: Crown, 2010), 233.

46. Quoted in Richard N. Haass, *War of Necessity, War of Choice: A Memoir of Two Iraq Wars* (New York: Simon and Schuster, 2009), 5.

47. The text of the Downing Street memo is available at http://www.timeson line.co.uk/tol/news/uk/article387374.ece.

48. For example, President Bush's comments at a press conference in Berlin on May 23 are available at http://archives.cnn.com/2002/US/05/23/gen.war

.on.terror/, and his remarks at a cabinet meeting on July 31 are reported by
Woodward in *Plan of Attack*, 137.

49. Deputy Secretary of Defense Paul Wolfowitz, interview, *Vanity Fair* (May
    2003), transcript available at http://www.defenselink.mil/transcripts/transcript
    .aspx?transcriptid=2594.

50. Quoted in Isikoff and Corn, *Hubris*, 412.

51. Woodward, *Plan of Attack*, 12.

52. DCI George J. Tenet, statement, U.S. Senate, *Worldwide Threat 2001: Na-
    tional Security in a Changing World, Hearings Before the Select Committee on
    Intelligence*, 107th Cong., 1st sess., February 7, 2001, available at https://
    www.cia.gov/news-information/speeches-testimony/2001/UNCLAS-
    WWT_02072001.html.

53. Based on observations by Secretary of the Treasury Paul O'Neill. Suskind,
    Price of Loyalty, 160–61.

54. Secretary of State Colin Powell, statement, U.S. Senate, *Foreign Operations,
    Export Financing, and Related Programs Appropriations for Fiscal Year 2002,
    Hearing Before the Subcommittee on Foreign Operations, Appropriations Com-
    mittee*, 107th Cong., 1st sess., May 15, 2001, available at http://frwebgate.ac
    cess.gpo.gov/cgi-bin/getdoc.cgi?dbname=2002_sapp_for_1&docid=f:70754
    .pdf.

55. Woodward, *Plan of Attack*, 247–50. Woodward confirms in *State of Denial*
    that the "slam dunk" conversation was about the public marketing of the
    war (303).

56. George Tenet, *At the Center of the Storm: My Years at the CIA* (New York:
    HarperCollins, 2007), 473–74.

57. Ibid., 449–50; Woodward, *State of Denial*, 97; Suskind, *The One Percent Doc-
    trine*, 177; and Eric Lichtblau, "2002 Memo Doubted Uranium Sale Claim,"
    New York Times, January 18, 2006. On the repeated White House efforts to
    use the report despite repeated warnings not to, see also Isikoff and Corn,
    Hubris, 86, 100, 144, 299. On previous CIA testimony to Congress, see Bar-
    ton Gellman and Dafna Linzer, "A 'Concerted Effort' to Discredit Bush
    Critic," *Washington Post*, April 9, 2006.

58. Suskind, *The One Percent Doctrine*, 246–47.

59. President George W. Bush, State of the Union Address, January 28, 2003,
    available at http://georgewbush-whitehouse.archives.gov/news/releases/
    2003/01/20030128-19.html.

60. Walter Pincus, "Records Could Shed Light on Iraq Group," *Washington Post*,
    June 9, 2008.

61. Quoted in Elisabeth Bumiller, "Bush Aides Set Strategy to Sell Policy on Iraq," *New York Times*, September 7, 2002.

62. Woodward, *Plan of Attack*, 163; Vice President Dick Cheney, address to the VFW convention, Nashville, August 26, 2002, available at http://georgewbush-whitehouse.archives.gov/news/releases/2002/08/20020826.html. Scowcroft expressed his opposition in an op ed, "Don't Attack Saddam," *Wall Street Journal*, August 15, 2002, available at http://www.wagingpeace.org/articles/2002/08/15_scowcroft_dont-attack.htm.

63. Bob Graham, "What I Knew Before the Invasion," *Washington Post*, November 20, 2005.

64. A White House spokesman acknowledged this at a background briefing for reporters on July 18, 2003; a transcript of this briefing is available at http://www.fas.org/irp/news/2003/07/wh071803.html.

65. Bush, *Decision Points*, 52n. Rove says Bush read ninety-four books. Karl Rove, remarks at Duke University, December 3, 2007, cited at http://projects.newsobserver.com/under_the_dome/rove_beats_bush_in_book_race.

66. Woodward, *Plan of Attack*, 174.

67. Cheney, address to the VFW convention, August 26, 2002.

68. Bush used the mushroom cloud imagery in an address in Cincinnati on October 7, 2002; text available at http://georgewbush-whitehouse.archives.gov/news/releases/2002/10/20021007–8.html. Rice used the same imagery in an interview on CNN's *Late Edition*, September 8, 2002; transcript available at http://transcripts.cnn.com/TRANSCRIPTS/0209/08/le.00.html.

69. Cheney, address to VFW convention, August 26, 2002.

70. Ibid., emphasis added.

71. Ibid.

72. Secretary of Defense Donald Rumsfeld, statement, U.S. Senate, *Department of Defense Appropriations for Fiscal Year 2003, Hearing Before the Subcommittee on Defense, Appropriations Committee*, 107th Cong., 2d sess., May 21, 2002, emphasis added, available at http://frwebgate.access.gpo.gov/cgi-bin/getdoc.cgi?dbname=2003_sapp_def_1&docid=f:78465.wais.

73. DCI George Tenet, letter to Senate Intelligence Committee chairman, *New York Times*, October 9, 2002.

74. President George W. Bush, address in Cincinnati, October 7, 2002, available at http://georgewbush-whitehouse.archives.gov/news/releases/2002/10/20021007–8.html.

75. Woodward, *Plan of Attack*, 176.

76. Quoted in Gordon and Trainor, *Cobra II*, 72.

77. UNMOVIC executive chairman, statement to the United Nations Security Council, February 14, 2003, available at http://www.un.org/Depts/unmovic/new/pages/security_council_briefings.asp#6; IAEA director general, statement to the United Nations Security Council, February 14, 2003, available at http://www.iaea.org/NewsCenter/Statements/2003/ebsp2003n005.shtml.

78. UNMOVIC executive chairman, statement to the United Nations Security Council, March 7, 2003, available at http://www.un.org/Depts/unmovic/new/pages/security_council_briefings.asp#7; IAEA director general, statement to the United Nations Security Council, March 7, 2003, available at http://www.iaea.org/NewsCenter/Statements/2003/ebsp2003n006.shtml.

79. Deputy DCI John McLaughlin, remarks at Texas A&M University, cited in Jeffrey T. Richelson, *Spying on the Bomb: American Nuclear Intelligence from Nazi Germany to Iran and North Korea* (New York: Norton, 2007), 529.

80. Richelson, *Spying on the Bomb*, 509.

81. See, for example, the interview of President Bush on NBC's *Meet the Press*, February 8, 2004; transcript available at http://www.msnbc.msn.com/id/4179618/.

82. Glenn Frankel, "From Memos, Insights Into Ally's Doubts on Iraq War," *Washington Post*, June 28, 2005.

83. For additional analysis supporting this point, see Michael C. Desch, "America's Liberal Illiberalism: The Ideological Origins of Overreaction in U.S. Foreign Policy," *International Security* 32, no. 3 (Winter 2007–2008), 38.

84. Quoted in Suskind, *The One Percent Doctrine*, 62.

85. See my colloquy with Marvin Kalb at a public forum in 2006, recounted in Isikoff and Corn, *Hubris*, 412.

86. Johndroe quoted in Scott Shane and Mark Mazzetti, "Ex-C.I.A. Chief, in Book, Assails Cheney on Iraq," *New York Times*, April 27, 2007.

3. Alternative Visions of the Iraq War

1. President Bush used this term in, for example, his speech on the aircraft carrier *Abraham Lincoln* on May 1, 2003, when he declared the end of major combat operations in Iraq; text available at http://georgewbush-whitehouse.archives.gov/news/releases/2003/05/20030501-15.html.

2. "Overview of State Sponsored Terrorism," in U.S. Department of State, *Patterns of Global Terrorism 2000* (Washington, D.C.: U.S. Department of State, April 30, 2001), available at http://www.state.gov/s/ct/rls/crt/2000/2441.htm.

3. U.S. Department of State, *Patterns of Global Terrorism 2001* (Washington, D.C.: U.S. Department of State, May 2002), 65–67.

4. The polling data are cited in Paul R. Pillar, *Terrorism and U.S. Foreign Policy*, paperback ed. (Washington, D.C.: Brookings Institution Press, 2003), xviii.

5. Eric Schmitt and Thom Shanker, "Pentagon Sets Up Intelligence Unit," *New York Times*, October 24, 2002.

6. George Packer, *The Assassins' Gate: America in Iraq* (New York: Farrar, Straus and Giroux, 2005), 106.

7. Quoted in Inspector General, U.S. Department of Defense, *Review of the Pre–Iraqi War Activities of the Office of the Under Secretary of Defense for Policy*, report no. 07-INTEL-04 (Washington, D.C.: U.S. Department of Defense, February 9, 2007), appendix E. A redacted version of the report is available at http://levin.senate.gov/newsroom/supporting/2007/SASC.DODIGFeith report.040507.pdf.

8. Quoted in ibid., 11.

9. Douglas Feith, letter to Senator John Warner and Representative Jane Harmon, June 21, 2003, quoted in ibid., 2.

10. Douglas J. Feith, "Tough Questions We Were Right to Ask," *Washington Post*, February 14, 2007.

11. Inspector General, *Review of the Pre–Iraqi War Activities*, iii, 3, 7–8.

12. A redacted version of the briefing slides is available at http://levin.senate .gov/newsroom/supporting/2007/SASC.Feithslides.040507.pdf.

13. Quoted in Inspector General, *Review of the Pre–Iraqi War Activities*, 36.

14. For a concise review of the evidence, see Peter Bergen, "Enemy of Our Enemy," *New York Times*, March 28, 2006.

15. Ron Suskind, *The One Percent Doctrine: Deep Inside America's Pursuit of Its Enemies Since 9/11* (New York: Simon and Schuster, 2006), 196–97; and George Tenet, *At the Center of the Storm: My Years at the CIA* (New York: HarperCollins, 2007), 372.

16. Quoted in Bruce B. Auster, Mark Mazzetti, and Edward T. Pound, "Truth and Consequences," *U.S. News & World Report*, June 9, 2003, 14.

17. President George W. Bush, address to the Saban Forum, Washington, D.C., December 5, 2008, available at http://georgewbush-whitehouse.archives.gov/ news/releases/2008/12/20081205-8.html.

18. Quoted in Caroline Wyatt, "Bush and Putin: Best of Friends," BBC, June 16, 2001, available at http://news.bbc.co.uk/2/hi/europe/1392791.stm.

19. Quoted in Michael Abramowitz, "Bush's Gut Feeling on Maliki Is Positive," *Washington Post*, June 18, 2006.

20. Quoted in Suskind, *The One Percent Doctrine*, 2.

21. Bush, in his memoir, quotes Cheney as saying in one of their weekly lunches, "Are you going to take care of this guy [Saddam Hussein] or not?" Bush says that Condoleezza Rice gave her opinion to him in private and that she was a strong supporter of inspections, but that she "reluctantly concluded that the only way to enforce the UN resolution would be to use the military option." George W. Bush, *Decision Points* (New York: Crown, 2010), 251.

22. Bob Woodward, *State of Denial* (New York: Simon and Schuster, 2006), 90.

23. Quoted in Bob Woodward, *Plan of Attack* (New York: Simon and Schuster, 2004), 251–52.

24. Quoted in Eric Schmitt, "Pentagon Contradicts General on Iraq Occupation Force's Size," *New York Times*, February 28, 2003.

25. Quoted in ibid.

26. Quoted in Packer, *The Assassins' Gate*, 117.

27. Woodward, *Plan of Attack*, 149–52.

28. Quoted in ibid., 271.

29. Ibid., 283–84.

30. Michael C. Desch, "Bush and the Generals," *Foreign Affairs* 86, no. 3 (May–June 2007): 97–108.

31. Packer, *The Assassins' Gate*, 111–12.

32. Alan Wolfe, "Academia (Kind of) Goes to War: Chomsky and His Children," *World Affairs* (Winter 2008), available at http://www.worldaffairsjournal.org/articles/2008-Winter/full-academia-war.html.

33. For an apt summary of the administration's decision-making method on Iraq, see James Dobbins, "Who Lost Iraq? Lessons from the Debacle," *Foreign Affairs* 86, no. 5 (September–October 2007), 64.

34. Michael J. Mazarr, "The Long Road to Pyongyang: A Case Study in Policymaking Without Direction," *Foreign Affairs* 86, no. 5 (September–October 2007), 78.

35. Thomas E. Ricks, *Fiasco: The American Military Adventure in Iraq* (New York: Penguin, 2006), 99.

36. Quoted in Michael Isikoff and David Corn, *Hubris: The Inside Story of Spin, Scandal, and the Selling of the Iraq War* (New York: Crown, 2006), 198.

37. Quoted in Jeffrey Goldberg, "A Little Learning: What Douglas Feith Knew, and When He Knew It," *New Yorker* (May 9, 2005), 41.

38. Dobbins, "Who Lost Iraq?" 65.

39. Lawrence Wilkerson, interview, *NewsHour*, PBS, November 4, 2005, available at http://www.pbs.org/newshour/bb/white_house/july-dec05/wilk_11-4.html.

40. National Intelligence Council, *Principal Challenges in Post-Saddam Iraq* (Washington, D.C.: National Intelligence Council, 2003); and National Intelligence Council, *Regional Consequences of Regime Change in Iraq* (Washington, D.C.: National Intelligence Council, 2003). Redacted versions of these assessments are available at http://intelligence.senate.gov/11076.pdf.

41. National Intelligence Council, *Principal Challenges in Post-Saddam Iraq*, 5.

42. Quoted in Dale Van Natta Jr., "Bush Was Set on Path to War, Memo by British Adviser Says," *New York Times*, March 27, 2006.

43. Alex Roberto Hybel and Justin Matthew Kaufman, *The Bush Administrations and Saddam Hussein: Deciding on Conflict* (New York: Palgrave Macmillan, 2006), 101–4.

44. National Intelligence Council, *Principal Challenges in Post-Saddam Iraq*, 17.

45. National Security Council, *National Security Strategy* (Washington, D.C.: National Security Council, September 17, 2002), available at http://georgewbush-whitehouse.archives.gov/nsc/nss/2002.

46. President George W. Bush, address to the National Endowment for Democracy, Washington, D.C., October 6, 2005, transcript available at http://georgewbush-whitehouse.archives.gov/news/releases/2005/10/20051006-3.html.

47. Assistant Secretary of Defense Paul Wolfowitz, statement, U.S. House of Representatives, *Department of Defense Budget Priorities for Fiscal Year 2004, Hearing of the House Committee on the Budget*, 108th Cong., 1st sess., February 27, 2003, available at http://frwebgate.access.gpo.gov/cgi-bin/getdoc.cgi?dbname=108_house_hearings&docid=f:85421.wais.

48. Secretary of Defense Donald Rumsfeld, interview, *NewsHour*, PBS, February 20, 2003, available at http://www.pbs.org/newshour/bb/middle_east/jan-june03/rumsfeld_2-20.html.

49. Vice President Dick Cheney, interview, *Meet the Press*, NBC, March 16, 2003, transcript available at http://www.mtholyoke.edu/acad/intrel/bush/cheneymeetthepress.htm.

50. Quoted in Eric Rosenberg, "Rumsfeld Retreats, Disclaims Earlier Rhetoric," *Ocala Star Banner*, November 9, 2003, reproduced at http://www.truth-out.org/article/rumsfelds-wmd-denials-prove-false.

51. Vice President Dick Cheney, interview, *Meet the Press*, NBC, September 14, 2003, available at http://www.msnbc.msn.com/id/3080244/default.html.

52. Goldberg, "A Little Learning," 40.

53. For example, see Paul Wolfowitz's speech to the VFW, March 11, 2003, text available at http://www.defense.gov/speeches/speech.aspx?speechid=359.

54. Ricks, *Fiasco*, 97.

55. Bob Davis, "Bush Economic Aide Says Cost of Iraq War May Top $100 Billion," *Wall Street Journal*, September 16, 2002.

56. Elisabeth Bumiller, "Threats and Responses: The Cost; White House Cuts Estimate of Cost of War with Iraq," *New York Times*, December 31, 2002.

57. Paul Krugman, "Secretary, Protect Yourself," *New York Times*, June 2, 2006.

58. Estimate based on data in Amy Belasco, *The Cost of Iraq, Afghanistan, and Other Global War on Terror Operations Since 9/11*, report no. RL33110 (Washington, D.C.: Congressional Research Service, September 28, 2009), available at http://www.fas.org/sgp/crs/natsec/RL33110.pdf. On the likely total direct and indirect costs, see Joseph E. Stiglitz and Linda J. Bilmes, *The Three Trillion Dollar War: The True Cost of the Iraq Conflict* (New York: Norton, 2008).

59. Wolfowitz, statement, U.S. House of Representatives, *Department of Defense Budget Priorities for Fiscal Year 2004*.

60. Quoted in Woodward, *State of Denial*, 145.

61. Douglas J. Feith, *War and Decision: Inside the Pentagon at the Dawn of the War on Terrorism* (New York: Harper, 2008), 332–35.

62. Quoted in Woodward, *Plan of Attack*, 206.

63. H. R. McMaster, *Dereliction of Duty: Lyndon Johnson, Robert McNamara, the Joint Chiefs of Staff, and the Lies That Led to Vietnam* (New York: HarperCollins, 1997), 315.

64. Quoted in Woodward, *State of Denial*, 99.

65. Quoted in Packer, *The Assassins' Gate*, 117.

66. Robert Jervis, "The Remaking of a Unipolar World," *Washington Quarterly* 29, no. 3 (Summer 2006), 15.

67. *ABC News/Washington Post* poll, available at http://www.washingtonpost.com/wp-dyn/content/custom/2006/02/02/CU2006020201345.html.

68. President George W. Bush, remarks at religious broadcasters' convention, Nashville, February 10, 2003, available at http://georgewbush-whitehouse.archives.gov/news/releases/2003/02/20030210-5.html.

69. Presidential debate, Tempe, Arizona, October 13, 2004, transcript available at http://www.debates.org/index.php?page=october-13-2004-debate-transcript.

70. Ivo H. Daalder and James M. Lindsay, *America Unbound: The Bush Revolution in Foreign Policy* (Washington, D.C.: Brookings Institution Press, 2003), 88.

71. President George W. Bush, remarks at John Cornyn for Senate reception, Houston, September 26, 2002, available at http://georgewbush-whitehouse.archives.gov/news/releases/2002/09/20020926-17.html.

72. Woodward, *State of Denial*, xii–xiii, 21–22.
73. An example of the genre, as it has been applied to several former presidents, is Alexander L. George and Juliette L. George, *Woodrow Wilson and Colonel House: A Personality Study* (New York: Dover, 1964).

4. CONGRESS AND THE POLITICS OF THE IRAQ WAR

1. Quoted in Michael Isikoff and David Corn, *Hubris: The Inside Story of Spin, Scandal, and the Selling of the Iraq War* (New York: Crown, 2006), 124–25.
2. Thomas E. Ricks notes this pattern in *Fiasco: The American Military Adventure in Iraq* (New York: Penguin, 2006), 62.
3. Kenneth M. Pollack, *The Threatening Storm: The Case for Invading Iraq* (New York: Random House, 2002), chap. 8.
4. Isikoff and Corn, *Hubris*, 126.
5. Lincoln D. Chafee, "The Senate's Forgotten Iraq Choice," *New York Times*, March 1, 2007.
6. Ricks, *Fiasco*, 61–63.
7. Byrd made this statement on February 12, 2003, *Congressional Record* 149 (2003), S2268.
8. Dana Priest, "Congressional Oversight of Intelligence Criticized," *Washington Post*, April 27, 2004.
9. Quoted in Isikoff and Corn, *Hubris*, 133–34.
10. Bob Graham, "What I Knew Before the Invasion," *Washington Post*, November 20, 2005.
11. Ricks, *Fiasco*, 85.
12. Senator Bill Nelson, comments, U.S. Senate, *Current and Future Worldwide Threats to the National Security of the United States, Hearing Before the Committee on Armed Services*, 108th Cong., 2d sess., March 9, 2004, p. 74.
13. U.S. Senate, Select Committee on Intelligence, *U.S. Intelligence Community's Prewar Intelligence Assessments on Iraq*, S. Report 108-301 (Washington, D.C.: U.S. Government Printing Office, July 9, 2004), available at http://intelligence.senate.gov/108301.pdf.
14. U.S. Senate, Select Committee on Intelligence, *Prewar Intelligence Assessments About Postwar Iraq*, S. Report 110-76 (Washington, D.C.: U.S. Government Printing Office, May 25, 2007), available at http://intelligence.senate.gov/11076.pdf.

15. Quoted in David Rose, "Neo Culpa," *Vanity Fair* online, November 5, 2006, available at http://www.vanityfair.com/politics/features/2006/12/neocons 200612.

16. U.S. Senate, Select Committee on Intelligence, *Whether Public Statements Regarding Iraq by U.S. Government Officials Were Substantiated by Intelligence Information*, S. Report 110-345 (Washington, D.C.: U.S. Government Printing Office, June 5, 2008), available at http://intelligence.senate.gov/pdfs/110345.pdf.

17. U.S. Senate, *U.S. Intelligence Community's Prewar Intelligence Assessments on Iraq*, S. Report 108-301, 286.

18. Ibid., 288.

19. Ibid., 286.

20. Ibid., 293.

21. White House, *A Decade of Deception and Defiance* (Washington, D.C.: U.S. Government Printing Office, September 12, 2002), available at http:// georgewbush-whitehouse.archives.gov/news/releases/2002/09/iraqdecade. pdf.

22. Ricks, *Fiasco*, 89.

23. "From the Editors: The *Times* and Iraq," *New York Times*, May 26, 2004.

24. Michael Getler, "A Parting Thought on Iraq, Again," *Washington Post*, October 9, 2005.

25. "Buying the War," *Bill Moyers Journal*, April 25, 2007; transcript available at http://www.pbs.org/moyers/journal/btw/transcript1.html.

26. For example, see Warren P. Strobel, Jonathan S. Landay, and John Walcott, "Some in Bush Administration Have Misgivings About Iraq Policy," published in several Knight-Ridder newspapers on October 8, 2002.

27. John Mueller, *Overblown: How Politicians and the Terrorism Industry Inflate National Security Threats, and Why We Believe Them* (New York: Free Press, 2006), 80.

28. David Halberstam, *The Best and the Brightest* (New York: Random House, 1969).

29. David Halberstam, *The Making of a Quagmire* (New York: Random House, 1965), 315, 319.

30. Neil Sheehan, *A Bright Shining Lie: John Paul Vann and America in Vietnam* (New York: Random House, 1988).

31. Neil Sheehan, "Much Is at Stake in Southeast Asian Struggle," *New York Times*, August 16, 1964.

32. Michael R. Gordon and Judith Miller, "U.S. Says Hussein Intensifies Quest for A-Bomb Parts," *New York Times*, September 8, 2002.

33. Tim Weiner, "U.S. Long View on Iraq: Patience in Containing the Ever-Deadlier Hussein," *New York Times*, January 3, 1999.

34. *Comprehensive Report of the Special Advisor to the DCI on Iraq's WMD*, vol. 1: *Key Findings* (Washington, D.C.: U.S. CIA, September 30, 2004), available at https://www.cia.gov/library/reports/general-reports-1/iraq_wmd_2004/chap1.html#sect1.

35. Vice President Dick Cheney, interview, *Meet the Press*, NBC, September 10, 2006, transcript available at http://www.msnbc.msn.com/id/14720480/page/2/. Douglas Feith makes the same argument in his book *War and Decision: Inside the Pentagon at the Dawn of the War on Terrorism* (New York: Harper, 2008), 225–27.

36. Richard K. Betts, *Enemies of Intelligence: Knowledge and Power in American National Security* (New York: Columbia University Press, 2007), 115–16.

37. Ibid., 122.

38. Vice President Dick Cheney, address to the VFW convention, Nashville, August 26, 2002, available at http://georgewbush-whitehouse.archives.gov/news/releases/2002/08/20020826.html; President George Bush, speech, Cincinnati, October 7, 2002, available at http://georgewbush-whitehouse.archives.gov/news/releases/2002/10/20021007-8.html.

39. Richard Cohen, "When Peace Is No Better Than War," *Washington Post*, March 11, 2003.

40. Richard Cohen, "Why We Need Leakers," *Washington Post*, February 21, 2006.

41. Paul R. Pillar, *Terrorism and U.S. Foreign Policy*, paperback ed. (Washington, D.C.: Brookings Institution Press, 2003), xvii.

42. President George W. Bush and Prime Minister Ayad Allawi, press conference, September 21, 2004, transcript available at http://georgewbush-whitehouse.archives.gov/news/releases/2004/09/20040921-9.html.

43. On this topic, see Paul R. Pillar, "Great Expectations: Intelligence as Savior," *Harvard International Review* 27, no. 4 (Winter 2006): 16–21.

5. GREAT DECISIONS AND THE IRRELEVANCE OF INTELLIGENCE

1. Glenn D. Paige, *The Korean Decision* (New York: Free Press, 1968), 124; and Ernest R. May, *"Lessons" of the Past: The Use and Misuse of History in American Foreign Policy* (New York: Oxford University Press, 1973), 70.

2. Harry S. Truman, *Memoirs*, vol. 2: *Years of Trial and Hope* (Garden City, N.Y.: Doubleday, 1956), 334.

3. Dean Acheson, *Present at the Creation: My Years in the State Department* (New York: Norton, 1969), 405.

4. Dean G. Acheson, "Crisis in Asia—An Examination of U.S. Policy," *Department of State Bulletin* 22, no. 551 (January 23, 1950), 116.

5. Truman, *Years of Trial and Hope*, 337.

6. Ibid., 337, 339–40.

7. Harry S. Truman, *Memoirs*, vol. 1: *Year of Decisions* (Garden City, N.Y.: Doubleday, 1955), 119–21.

8. Truman, *Years of Trial and Hope*, 332–33.

9. May, *"Lessons" of the Past*, 81, 84–85.

10. Truman, *Years of Trial and Hope*, 339–40.

11. See the chart in Paige, *The Korean Decision*, 291.

12. The use of historical analogy in the crisis is discussed in Richard E. Neustadt and Ernest R. May, *Thinking in Time: The Uses of History for Decision-Makers* (New York: Free Press, 1986), 5–6.

13. Barbara Tuchman, *The Guns of August* (New York: Macmillan, 1962). The influence of Tuchman's book on the president is mentioned in Robert F. Kennedy, *Thirteen Days: A Memoir of the Cuban Missile Crisis* (New York: Norton, 1971), 40, 105.

14. Graham T. Allison, *Essence of Decision: Explaining the Cuban Missile Crisis* (Boston: Little, Brown, 1971).

15. Ibid., 204.

16. Ibid., 50–52, 194–95.

17. Michael Dobbs, "Cool Crisis Management? It's a Myth. Ask JFK." *Washington Post*, June 22, 2008.

18. This idea inspired the title of a three-decades-old but still incisive study of how such a process can nonetheless yield such a tragic outcome: Leslie H. Gelb and Richard K. Betts, *The Irony of Vietnam: The System Worked* (Washington, D.C.: Brookings Institution Press, 1979). Gelb directed the official classified study that became known as the *Pentagon Papers*.

19. *The Pentagon Papers*, Senator Gravel ed., 4 vols. (Boston: Beacon Press, 1971), 1:266–67.

20. Ibid., 1:243, 267.

21. "Transcript of President Eisenhower's Press Conference, with Comment on Indo-China," *New York Times*, April 8, 1954.

22. President John F. Kennedy, interview, *Huntley–Brinkley Report*, NBC, September 9, 1963.

23. Lyndon Baines Johnson, *The Vantage Point: Perspectives of the Presidency 1963–1969* (New York: Holt, Rinehart, and Winston, 1971), 120, 136.

24. *Pentagon Papers*, 2:107.

25. Ibid., 3:178–79.

26. Harold P. Ford, *CIA and the Vietnam Policymakers: Three Episodes 1962–1968* (Washington, D.C.: CIA History Staff, 1998), 56.

27. See, for example, a report in November 1964 by Assistant Secretary of State William Bundy and Assistant Secretary of Defense John McNaughton in the *Pentagon Papers*, 3:657, and a memorandum by McNaughton in March 1965, quoted in H. R. McMaster, *Dereliction of Duty: Lyndon Johnson, Robert McNamara, the Joint Chiefs of Staff, and the Lies That Led to Vietnam* (New York: HarperCollins, 1997), 236–37.

28. Johnson, *The Vantage Point*, 151–52.

29. Daryl G. Press, *Calculating Credibility: How Leaders Assess Military Threats* (Ithaca, N.Y.: Cornell University Press, 2005).

30. *Pentagon Papers*, 3:293.

31. Ibid., 3:294.

32. Ibid., 3:399.

33. Bruce Palmer Jr., "U.S. Intelligence and Vietnam," *Studies in Intelligence* 28 (1984), 34–35.

34. *Pentagon Papers*, 3:169.

35. Ibid., 3:295.

36. Robert S. McNamara, *In Retrospect: The Tragedy and Lessons of Vietnam* (New York: Times Books, 1995), 162.

37. See the estimates by the army chief of staff General Harold K. Johnson and the Marine Corps commandant General Wallace Greene, cited in McNamara, *In Retrospect*, 176–77; the estimates are also given in McMaster, *Dereliction of Duty*, 304.

38. Johnson, *The Vantage Point*, 64.

39. McNamara, *In Retrospect*, 154–55.

40. On all these dimensions of Johnson's approach to the war, see especially Doris Kearns, *Lyndon Johnson and the American Dream* (New York: Harper and Row, 1976).

41. Henry F. Graff, *The Tuesday Cabinet: Deliberation and Decision on Peace and War Under Lyndon B. Johnson* (Englewood Cliffs, N.J.: Prentice-Hall, 1970).

42. Irving Janis, *Groupthink: Psychological Studies of Policy Decisions and Fiascoes*, 2d rev. ed. (Boston: Houghton Mifflin, 1983), 101; Graff, *The Tuesday Cabinet*, 6, 178; and Robert L. Gallucci, *Neither Peace nor Honor: The Politics of American Military Policy in Viet-Nam* (Baltimore: Johns Hopkins University Press, 1975), 133.

43. McNamara, *In Retrospect*, 39.

44. *Pentagon Papers*, 3:314.

45. Henry Kissinger, *White House Years* (Boston: Little, Brown, 1979), 54.

46. Deborah Welch Larson, "Learning in U.S.–Soviet Relations: The Nixon–Kissinger Structure of Peace," in George W. Breslauer and Philip E. Tetlock, eds., *Learning in U.S. and Soviet Foreign Policy* (Boulder, Colo.: Westview Press, 1991), 351, 358.

47. Quoted in Kissinger, *White House Years*, 11.

48. Thomas Powers, *The Man Who Kept the Secrets: Richard Helms and the CIA* (New York: Alfred A. Knopf, 1979), 230.

49. Ibid., 231–32; and Kissinger, *White House Years*, 36.

50. Kissinger, *White House Years*, 163–64.

51. Ibid., 805–6.

52. Ibid., 189–90.

53. James Mann, *About Face: A History of America's Curious Relationship with China, from Nixon to Clinton* (New York: Knopf, 1999), 24; and Robert S. Ross, *Negotiating Cooperation: The United States and China, 1969–1989* (Stanford, Calif.: Stanford University Press, 1995), 33.

54. One leaf that Kissinger admits missing was an invitation from Mao to Edgar Snow, an American journalist with longstanding contacts among the Chinese leadership, to be on the reviewing stand for China's national-day parade in October 1970. See Ross, *Negotiating Cooperation*, 28; Kissinger, *White House Years*, 698–99; and Raymond Garthoff, *Détente and Confrontation: American–Soviet Relations from Nixon to Reagan*, rev. ed. (Washington, D.C.: Brookings Institution Press, 1994) 254–55.

55. Mann, *About Face*, 30.

56. Text in ibid., 13–14.

57. Kissinger, *White House Years*, 913.

58. Richard M. Nixon, *RN: The Memoirs of Richard Nixon* (New York: Grosset and Dunlap, 1978), 530.

59. On the relationship with Gandhi, see Kissinger, *White House Years*, 848.

60. Ibid., 867.

61. Powers, *The Man Who Kept the Secrets*, 236.

62. Nixon, *RN*, 527–28.

63. Christopher Van Hollen, "The Tilt Policy Revisited: Nixon–Kissinger Geopolitics and South Asia," *Asian Survey* 20, no. 4 (April 1980), 350–52.

64. Ibid., 359–60; and Garthoff, *Détente and Confrontation*, 320–21.

65. Cyrus Vance, *Hard Choices: Critical Years in America's Foreign Policy* (New York: Simon and Schuster, 2004), 388.

66. Zbigniew Brzezinski, *Power and Principle: Memoirs of the National Security Adviser 1977–1981* (New York: Farrar Straus Giroux, 1983), 430.

67. President Jimmy Carter, interview by Frank Reynolds, ABC News, December 31, 1979.

68. Brzezinski, *Power and Principle*, 3, 147–48, 346, 426–27.

69. Ibid., 429; see also George Urban, "A Long Conversation with Dr. Zbigniew Brzezinski: The Perils of Foreign Policy," *Encounter* 56, no. 5 (May 1981), 21.

70. President Jimmy Carter, State of the Union Address, January 23, 1980, text available at http://www.jimmycarterlibrary.org/documents/speeches/su80jec.phtml.

71. Such a case is made in Ralph K. White, *Fearful Warriors: A Psychological Profile of U.S.–Soviet Relations* (New York: Free Press, 1984).

72. Brzezinski, *Power and Principle*, 64.

73. Anthony Lewis, "Reagan on War and Peace," *New York Times*, October 20, 1980.

74. Ronald Reagan, *An American Life* (New York: Simon and Schuster, 1990), 267.

75. Ibid., 297, 552, 594, 637.

76. George P. Shultz, *Turmoil and Triumph: My Years as Secretary of State* (New York: Scribner, 1993), 1133.

77. See Weinberger's testimony on this subject in U.S. Senate, *Department of Defense Authorization for Appropriations for Fiscal Year 1982, Hearings Before the Committee on Armed Services*, 97th Cong., 1st sess., March 4, 1981, 545.

78. Reagan, *An American Life*, 550.

79. Shultz, *Turmoil and Triumph*, 507.

80. Ibid., 490, 691.

81. Ibid., 864.

82. Robert M. Gates, *From the Shadows: The Ultimate Insider's Story of Five Presidents and How They Won the Cold War* (New York: Simon and Schuster, 1996), 340, 344, 377, 565.

83. Richard J. Kerr, "The Track Record: CIA Analysis from 1950 to 2000," in James B. Bruce and Roger Z. George, eds., *Analyzing Intelligence: Origins,*

Obstacles, and Innovations (Washington, D.C.: Georgetown University Press, 2008), 41.

84. Gates, *From the Shadows*, 197.

85. James A. Baker III, *The Politics of Diplomacy: Revolution, War, and Peace, 1989–1992* (New York: Putnam, 1995), 69. For the distribution of views within the administration, see also Gates, *From the Shadows*, 473–75.

86. Baker, *The Politics of Diplomacy*, 475.

87. Gates, *From the Shadows*, 529.

88. Ibid., 471.

89. Quoted in David Arbel and Ran Edelist, *Western Intelligence and the Collapse of the Soviet Union* (London: Frank Cass, 2003), 255–56.

90. Richard H. Immerman, a leading diplomatic historian who later would work in the intelligence community, reaches the same conclusion in "Intelligence and Strategy: Historicizing Psychology, Policy, and Politics," *Diplomatic History* 32, no. 1 (January 2008), 7.

6. POLITICIZATION

1. Roger Hilsman, *To Move a Nation: The Politics of Foreign Policy in the Administration of John F. Kennedy* (Garden City, N.Y.: Doubleday, 1967), 172–73.

2. Graham T. Allison, *Essence of Decision: Explaining the Cuban Missile Crisis* (Boston: Little, Brown, 1971), 189–91.

3. George W. Allen, *None so Blind: A Personal Account of the Intelligence Failure in Vietnam* (Chicago: Ivan R. Dee, 2001), 142–43.

4. The incident is described in Allen's book *None so Blind*, 142.

5. Harold P. Ford, *CIA and the Vietnam Policymakers: Three Episodes 1962–1968* (Washington, D.C.: CIA History Staff, 1998), 12–17.

6. Ibid., 18.

7. Edited transcript in Michael R. Beschloss, *Taking Charge: The Johnson White House Tapes, 1963–1964* (New York: Simon and Schuster, 1997), 495.

8. Ibid., 500.

9. Edwin E. Moise, *Tonkin Gulf and the Escalation of the Vietnam War* (Chapel Hill: University of North Carolina Press, 1996).

10. Quoted in ibid., 143.

11. Quoted in ibid., 144.

12. Patrick McGarvey, *CIA: The Myth and the Madness* (New York: Saturday Review Press, 1972), 17.

13. Robert J. Hanyok, "Skunks, Bogies, Silent Hounds, and the Flying Fish: The Gulf of Tonkin Mystery, 2–4 August 1964," *Cryptologic Quarterly* 19, no. 4 and 20, no. 1 (Winter 2000–Spring 2001): 1–55; the study is available in declassified form at http://www.nsa.gov/public_info/_files/gulf_of_tonkin/articles/rel1_skunks_bogies.pdf.

14. Hanyok, "Skunks, Bogies, Silent Hounds, and the Flying Fish," 38, 49.

15. Ibid., 38.

16. Allen, *None so Blind*, 144–45, 243.

17. Ibid., 247–49, 254.

18. Quoted in ibid., 251.

19. Bruce Palmer Jr., "U.S. Intelligence and Vietnam," *Studies in Intelligence* 28 (1984), 50–51.

20. Allen, *None so Blind*, 252; and Sam Adams, *War of Numbers: An Intelligence Memoir* (South Royalton, Vt.: Steerforth Press, 1994), 123, 127.

21. Quoted in Adams, *War of Numbers*, 124.

22. Allen, *None so Blind*, 252.

23. Quoted in Adams, *War of Numbers*, 169.

24. Quoted in Robert L. Gallucci, *Neither Peace nor Honor: The Politics of American Military Policy in Viet-Nam* (Baltimore: Johns Hopkins University Press, 1975), 61.

25. Based on Allen's account in *None so Blind*, 236–37. See also Ford, *CIA and the Vietnam Policymakers*, 111.

26. Gallucci, *Neither Peace nor Honor*, 71.

27. Allen, *None so Blind*, 235.

28. A detailed account of Kissinger's handling of the SLBM issue is in Raymond L. Garthoff, *Détente and Confrontation: American–Soviet Relations from Nixon to Reagan*, rev. ed. (Washington, D.C.: Brookings Institution, 1994), 183–87.

29. Cf. John Prados, *The Soviet Estimate: U.S. Intelligence Analysis and Soviet Strategic Forces* (Princeton, N.J.: Princeton University Press, 1986), 250–51, 294–95.

30. Anne Hessing Cahn, "Team B: The Trillion Dollar Experiment," *Bulletin of the Atomic Scientists* 49, no. 3 (April 1993), 24–25.

31. Richard K. Betts, *Enemies of Intelligence: Knowledge and Power in American National Security* (New York: Columbia University Press, 2007), 88; and Cahn, "Team B," 26–27.

32. Prados, *The Soviet Estimate*, 252–53.

33. Pavel Podvig, "The Window of Vulnerability That Wasn't: Soviet Military Buildup in the 1970s—a Research Note," *International Security* 33, no. 1 (Summer 2008), 125–30.

34. *Intelligence Forecasts of Soviet Intercontinental Attack Forces: An Evaluation of the Record*, in Gerald K. Haines and Robert E. Leggett, *CIA's Analysis of the Soviet Union, 1947–1991* (Washington, D.C.: Center for the Study of Intelligence, CIA, 2001), 291.

35. Podvig, "The Window of Vulnerability That Wasn't," 137–38.

36. Robert M. Gates, *From the Shadows: The Ultimate Insider's Story of Five Presidents and How They Won the Cold War* (New York: Simon and Schuster, 1996), 199, 286, 332.

37. This description of the preparation of the estimate is based on my own observations while I was working at the time in the NIC as well as on published accounts in Bob Woodward, *Veil: The Secret Wars of the CIA 1981–1987* (New York: Simon and Schuster, 1987), 124–29; Raymond Garthoff, *The Great Transition: American–Soviet Relations and the End of the Cold War* (Washington, D.C.: Brookings Institution, 1994), 24–26; and Gates, *From the Shadows*, 203–6.

38. "Excerpts from Haig's Remarks at First News Conference as Secretary of State," *New York Times*, January 29, 1981.

39. Claire Sterling, *The Terror Network: The Secret War of International Terrorism* (New York: Holt, Rinehart, and Winston, 1981); the accusations regarding the Soviets and Western intelligence services are in chapter 16.

40. Ibid., 287, 291.

41. Claire Sterling, *The Time of the Assassins* (New York: Holt, Rinehart and Winston, 1984).

42. Gates, *From the Shadows*, 355.

43. Quoted in Joseph E. Persico, *Casey: From the OSS to the CIA* (New York: Viking, 1990), 286–88.

44. Woodward, *Veil*, 129.

45. David Johnston: "The Gates Hearings: Documents Show C.I.A. Feud on Papal Shooting," *New York Times*, October 2, 1991.

46. Quoted in Garthoff, *The Great Transition*, 308.

47. See especially the database of false statements compiled by the Center for Public Integrity at http://www.publicintegrity.org/WarCard. See also U.S. House of Representatives, Government Reform Committee, *Iraq on the Record: The Bush Administration's Public Statements on Iraq*, March 16, 2004, prepared by the committee's minority staff, available at http://permanent.access.gpo.gov/lps60698/pdf_admin_iraq_on_the_record_rep.pdf. Another useful review of discrepancies between public statements about Iraqi weapons and actual evidence is Joseph Cirincione, Jessica Mathews, and George

Perkovich, *WMD in Iraq: Evidence and Implications* (Washington, D.C.: Carnegie Endowment, January 2004), available at http://www.carnegie endowment.org/files/Iraq3FullText.pdf. Many of the deceptions in the Bush administration's pro-war campaign are described in Frank Rich, *The Greatest Story Ever Sold: The Decline and Fall of Truth from 9/11 to Katrina* (New York: Penguin, 2006).

48. Powell's observation is in Bob Woodward, *Plan of Attack* (New York: Simon and Schuster, 2004), 292.

49. Vice President Dick Cheney, interview, *Meet the Press*, NBC, September 8, 2002, transcript available at http://www.mtholyoke.edu/acad/intrel/bush/meet.htm.

50. See James Risen, "Prague Discounts an Iraqi Meeting," *New York Times*, October 21, 2002.

51. Vice President Dick Cheney, interview, *Meet the Press*, NBC, September 14, 2003, transcript available at http://www.msnbc.msn.com/id/3080244/.

52. National Security Adviser Condoleezza Rice, interview, *NewsHour*, PBS, September 25, 2002, transcript available at http://www.pbs.org/newshour/bb/international/july-dec02/rice_9-25.html.

53. Walter Pincus, "Newly Released Data Undercut Prewar Claims," *Washington Post*, November 6, 2005.

54. See, for example, President Bush's statement at a news conference on April 13, 2004, containing the incomplete description of violence in Iraq; transcript available at http://www.nytimes.com/2004/04/14/politics/14BTEX.html?ex=1397361600&en=08ad8f3a11fe7650&ei=5007&partner=USERLAND.

55. White House, *A Decade of Deception and Defiance* (Washington, D.C.: U.S. Government Printing Office, September 12, 2002), available at http://georgewbush-whitehouse.archives.gov/news/releases/2002/09/iraqdecade.pdf.

56. Stephen F. Hayes, "Case Closed," *Weekly Standard*, November 24, 2003.

57. Vice President Dick Cheney, interview by M. E. Sprengelmeyer, *Rocky Mountain News*, January 9, 2004.

58. Jeffrey Travers and Stanley Milgram, "An Experimental Study of the Small World Problem," *Sociometry* 32, no. 4 (December 1969): 425–43.

59. Military intelligence official quoted in Thomas E. Ricks, *Fiasco: The American Military Adventure in Iraq* (New York: Penguin, 2006), 51.

60. Secretary of Defense Donald H. Rumsfeld, statement to the U.S. Senate, Armed Services Committee, 107th Cong., 2d sess., September 19, 2002.

61. Quoted in Ron Suskind, *The One Percent Doctrine: Deep Inside America's Pursuit of Its Enemies Since 9/11* (New York: Simon and Schuster, 2006), 124.

62. Additional views from Vice Chairman John D. Rockefeller IV, Senator Carl Levin, and Senator Richard Durbin, appended to U.S. Senate, *Report of the Select Committee on Intelligence on the U.S. Intelligence Community's Prewar Assessments on Iraq*, S. Report 108-301 (Washington, D.C.: U.S. Government Printing Office, July 9, 2004), 456.

63. For a general discussion, see David Dadge, *The War in Iraq and Why the Media Failed Us* (Westport, Conn.: Praeger, 2006).

64. Michael Getler, "A Parting Thought on Iraq, Again," *Washington Post*, October 9, 2005.

65. Howard Kurtz, "The *Post* on WMDs: An Inside Story," *Washington Post*, August 12, 2004.

66. Brian Stelter, "Was Press a War 'Enabler'? 2 Offer a Nod from Inside," *New York Times*, May 30, 2008.

67. Ibid.

68. Tom Shales, "A Media Role in Selling the War? No Question," *Washington Post*, April 25, 2007.

69. See Rockefeller, Levin, and Durbin views appended to U.S. Senate, *Report of the Select Committee on Intelligence on the U.S. Intelligence Community's Prewar Assessments on Iraq*.

70. U.S. Senate, *Report of the Select Committee on Intelligence on the U.S. Intelligence Community's Prewar Assessments on Iraq*, 357–63.

71. Commission on the Intelligence Capabilities of the United States Regarding Weapons of Mass Destruction, *Report to the President of the United States* (Washington, D.C.: Commission on the Intelligence Capabilities of the United States, March 31, 2005) (hereafter *WMD Commission Report*), 188.

72. Ibid., 189.

73. Steven R. Weisman, "Ex-Official Says Nominee Bullied Analyst on Arms," *New York Times*, April 13, 2005.

74. Additional press reports of Bolton's behavior as revealed in his ambassadorial confirmation hearings include Douglas Jehl, "Bolton's Nomination Is Questioned by Another Powell Aide," *New York Times*, April 30, 2005; and David Ignatius, "Bolton's Biggest Problem," *Washington Post*, April 22, 2005.

75. George Tenet, *At the Center of the Storm: My Years at the CIA* (New York: HarperCollins, 2007), 349.

76. Shane Harris, "National Intelligence Memo Details Transition Efforts," *National Journal*, November 6, 2008, available at http://lostintransition .nationaljournal.com/2008/11/letter-national-intelligence-s.php.

77. Jack Davis, "Why Bad Things Happen to Good Analysts," in Roger Z. George and James B. Bruce, eds., *Intelligence Analysis: Origins, Obstacles, and Innovations* (Washington, D.C.: Georgetown University Press, 2008), 167.

78. Gregory F. Treverton, "Intelligence Analysis: Between 'Politicization' and Irrelevance," in George and Bruce, eds., *Intelligence Analysis*, 95.

79. Quoted in Michael Isikoff and David Corn, *Hubris: The Inside Story of Spin, Scandal, and the Selling of the Iraq War* (New York: Crown, 2006), 135–36.

80. *WMD Commission Report*, 190.

81. Many of these indications are reviewed in Jacob Weisberg, "No Politics, Please—We're Spies," *Slate*, April 5, 2005, available at http://www.slate.com/ id/2116260/.

82. *WMD Commission Report*, 107.

83. Ibid., 75.

84. "State/INR Alternative View of Iraq's Nuclear Program," available at http:// www.dni.gov/nic/special_keyjudgements.html.

85. Tenet, *At the Center of the Storm*, 336.

86. Quoted in Bob Woodward, *State of Denial* (New York: Simon and Schuster, 2006), 287.

87. Joseph C. Wilson IV, "What I Didn't Find in Africa," *New York Times*, July 6, 2003.

88. David Ignatius, "A Failed Cover-up," *Washington Post*, February 2, 2007.

89. Quoted in Isikoff and Corn, *Hubris*, 300.

90. Paul R. Pillar, *Terrorism and U.S. Foreign Policy* (Washington, D.C.: Brookings Institution Press, 2001), especially chap. 6.

91. "Senior Intelligence Officer Blasts President's Speech," *Insight*, February 22, 2002.

92. "'Stupid' Intelligence," *Wall Street Journal*, October 3, 2003. For another *Journal* editorial on the same theme, see also "Iraq and al Qaeda," September 22, 2003.

93. John Diamond, "Reports Warned of Violent Postwar Iraq, Official Says," *USA Today*, September 28, 2004.

94. Douglas Jehl, "U.S. Intelligence Shows Pessimism on Iraq's Future," *New York Times*, September 16, 2004.

95. President George W. Bush and Prime Minister Ayad Allawi, press conference, September 21, 2004, transcript available at http://georgewbush-white house.archives.gov/news/releases/2004/09/20040923-8.html.

96. Robert D. Novak, "CIA vs. Bush," September 27, 2004, available at http://townhall.com/columnists/RobertDNovak/2004/09/27/cia_vs_bush.

97. "The CIA's Insurgency," *Wall Street Journal*, September 29, 2004.

98. See, for example, the editorial "Finessing Terrorism," *Washington Times*, October 1, 2004.

7. Scapegoats and Spectator Sport

1. Ken Adelman, "Cakewalk in Iraq," *Washington Post*, February 13, 2002.

2. Ken Adelman, "'Cakewalk' Revisited," *Washington Post*, April 10, 2003.

3. Quoted in David Rose, "Neo Culpa," *Vanity Fair*, November 3, 2006, available at http://www.vanityfair.com/politics/features/2006/12/neocons200612.

4. Quoted in ibid.

5. Glenn D. Paige, *The Korean Decision* (New York: Free Press, 1968), 146–47.

6. Henry L. Stimson and McGeorge Bundy, *On Active Service in Peace and War* (New York: Harper and Brothers, 1948), 188.

7. Mark M. Lowenthal, *Intelligence: From Secrets to Policy*, 2d ed. (Washington, D.C.: Congressional Quarterly Press, 2003), 11.

8. Gallup poll, July 10–11, 2001, available at http://www.gallup.com/poll/4696/Americans-Still-Moderately-Favorable-Opinion-FBI.aspx.

9. Gallup Governance Survey, September 8–10, 2003, available at http://www.gallup.com/poll/9367/Federal-Scorecard-Americans-Rate-US-Agencies.aspx.

10. Commission on Organization of the Executive Branch of the Government, *Intelligence Activities: A Report to the Congress* (Washington, D.C.: U.S. Government Printing Office, June 1955), 15, 63.

11. Quoted in Harry Howe Ransom, *Central Intelligence and National Security* (Cambridge, Mass.: Harvard University Press, 1958), 182–83.

12. David S. Robarge, *Richard Helms: The Intelligence Professional Personified* (Washington, D.C.: Center for the Study of Intelligence, CIA, 2007), available at https://www.cia.gov/library/center-for-the-study-of-intelligence/csi-publications/csi-studies/studies/vol46no4/article06.html.

13. Richard A. Posner, *Countering Terrorism: Blurred Focus, Halting Steps* (Lanham, Md.: Rowman and Littlefield, 2007), 71–72.

14. For a more general comment on how marketplaces of ideas can fail in similar ways, see Philip E. Tetlock, *Expert Political Judgment: How Good Is It? How Can We Know?* (Princeton, N.J.: Princeton University Press, 2005), 231–32.

15. Quoted in David Arbel and Ran Edelist, *Western Intelligence and the Collapse of the Soviet Union* (London: Frank Cass, 2003), 256.

16. Charles Babington, "Some GOP Legislators Hit Jarring Notes in Addressing Katrina," *Washington Post*, September 10, 2005.

17. Lyndon Baines Johnson, *The Vantage Point: Perspectives of the Presidency 1963–1969* (New York: Holt, Rinehart, and Winston, 1971), 294.

18. Raymond L. Garthoff, *Détente and Confrontation: American–Soviet Relations from Nixon to Reagan*, rev. ed. (Washington, D.C.: Brookings Institution Press, 1994), 406–10.

19. Richard M. Nixon, *RN: The Memoirs of Richard Nixon* (New York: Grosset and Dunlap, 1978), 920.

20. Ibid., 941.

21. Robert F. Kennedy, *Thirteen Days: A Memoir of the Cuban Missile Crisis* (New York: Norton, 1971), 7.

22. Zbigniew Brzezinski, *Power and Principle: Memoirs of the National Security Adviser 1977–1981* (New York: Farrar Straus Giroux, 1983), 430.

23. James A. Baker III, *The Politics of Diplomacy: Revolution, War, and Peace, 1989–1992* (New York: Putnam, 1995), 273.

24. Quoted in CNN, "India's Nuclear Tests: U.S. Intelligence 'Failure' Seen," May 13, 1998, available at http://www.cnn.com/WORLD/asiapcf/9805/13/india.cia.update/.

25. Speculation and unsubstantiated reporting about a flash off southern Africa that was detected by a U.S. surveillance satellite in 1979 have included the possibility that it was an Israeli nuclear test. The nature and origin of what the satellite detected are still unresolved. For a discussion, see Jeffrey T. Richelson, *Spying on the Bomb: American Nuclear Intelligence from Nazi Germany to Iran and North Korea* (New York: Norton, 2007), chap. 7.

26. Richard J. Kerr, "The Track Record: CIA Analysis from 1950 to 2000," in James B. Bruce and Roger Z. George, eds., *Getting It Right: Expanding the Frontiers of Intelligence Analysis* (Washington, D.C.: Georgetown University Press, 2008), 46.

27. For example, see the statements of BJP president Lal Krishna Advani reported in "Hindu Nationalist Wants India to Go Nuclear," *Agence France Presse*, December 11, 1997.

28. Miriam Jordan, "Indian Opposition Party Would Assert Nuclear Capability If It Gains Power," *Wall Street Journal*, April 2, 1996.

29. Richelson, *Spying on the Bomb*, 163.

30. Emily Wax and Rama Lakshmi, "Dissent Threatens U.S.–India Nuclear Cooperation Deal," *Washington Post*, August 26, 2007.

31. Quoted in Rama Lakshmi, "A Secondary Role for U.S. in India's Nuclear Future," *Washington Post*, September 2, 2008.

32. Quoted in Richelson, *Spying on the Bomb*, 446.

33. George Tenet, *At the Center of the Storm: My Years at the CIA* (New York: HarperCollins, 2007), 44–45.

34. Leonard A. Kusnitz, *Public Opinion and Foreign Policy: America's China Policy, 1949–1979* (Westport, Conn.: Greenwood Press, 1984), 110.

35. Michael R. Gordon and David S. Cloud, "U.S. Knew of China's Missile Test, but Kept Silent," *New York Times*, April 23, 2007.

36. North American Air Defense Command data cited by T. S. Kelso at http://celestrak.com/events/asat.asp.

37. National Aeronautics and Space Administration, "Chinese Anti-Satellite Test Creates Most Severe Orbital Debris Cloud in History," *Orbital Debris Quarterly News* 11, no. 2 (April 2007), 2–3, available at http://orbitaldebris.jsc.nasa.gov/newsletter/pdfs/ODQNv11i2.pdf.

38. Gordon and Cloud, "U.S. Knew of China's Missile Test."

39. On the strength of Chinese motivation, see Ashley Tellis, *Punching the U.S. Military's "Soft Ribs": The Chinese Antisatellite Weapon Test in Strategic Perspective*, Policy Brief no. 51 (Washington, D.C.: Carnegie Endowment for International Peace, June 2007).

40. See, for example, Brzezinski, *Power and Principle*, 394, 396; and Cyrus Vance, *Hard Choices: Critical Years in America's Foreign Policy* (New York: Simon and Schuster, 1983), 325–26.

41. Gary Sick, *All Fall Down: America's Tragic Encounter with Iran* (New York: Random House, 1985), 21.

42. Jimmy Carter, *Keeping Faith: Memoirs of a President* (New York: Bantam, 1983), 440.

43. Sick, *All Fall Down*, 21.

44. Ibid., 40–41.

45. Ibid., 41.

46. Vance, *Hard Choices*, 325, 329.

47. Brzezinski, *Power and Principle*, 358, 396.

48. Sick, *All Fall Down*, 60.

49. Brzezinski, *Power and Principle*, 354.

50. Ibid., 355.

51. Vance, *Hard Choices*, 331.

52. Brzezinski, *Power and Principle*, 397.

53. Carter, *Keeping Faith*, 449.

54. Ibid., 443–44, 446. For Sullivan's version of his relationship with the White House, see William H. Sullivan, *Mission to Iran* (New York: Norton, 1981), especially 194.

55. Vance, *Hard Choices*, 328.

56. See Gary Sick's conclusion that even with "perfect understanding" of the situation in Iran, it is quite possible that U.S. policy decisions "would have been much the same, with the same results" (*All Fall Down*, 168).

57. Alexander L. George, *On Foreign Policy: Unfinished Business* (Boulder, Colo.: Paradigm, 2006), 106.

58. Harold P. Ford, *CIA and the Vietnam Policymakers: Three Episodes 1962–1968* (Washington, D.C.: CIA History Staff, 1998), 121–23; Johnson, *The Vantage Point*, 381–82; George W. Allen, *None So Blind: A Personal Account of the Intelligence Failure in Vietnam* (Chicago: Ivan R. Dee, 2001), 257; and Don Oberdorfer, *Tet!* (Garden City, N.Y.: Doubleday, 1971), 19–20.

59. Oberdorfer, *Tet!* 120.

8. The Never-Ending Issue

1. Richard A. Best Jr., *Proposals for Intelligence Reorganization, 1949–2004* (Washington, D.C.: Congressional Research Service, updated September 24, 2004), available at http://www.fas.org/irp/crs/RL32500.pdf; and Michael Warner and J. Kenneth McDonald, *US Intelligence Community Reform Studies Since 1947* (Washington, D.C.: Center for the Study of Intelligence, April 2005).

2. Richard K. Betts, *Enemies of Intelligence: Knowledge and Power in American National Security* (New York: Columbia University Press, 2007), 143.

3. James B. Bruce and Roger Z. George, "Conclusions: The Age of Analysis," in Roger Z. George and James B. Bruce, eds., *Analyzing Intelligence: Origins, Obstacles, and Innovations* (Washington, D.C.: Georgetown University Press, 2008), 295.

4. Dan Eggen and Walter Pincus, "Spy Chief Gets More Authority Over FBI," *Washington Post*, June 30, 2005.

5. John Solomon, "FBI Reorganizes Effort to Uncover Terror Groups' Global Ties," *Washington Post*, September 26, 2007.

6. All quotes from "Former CIA Chief Blasts Intelligence Reform Plan," CNN, August 24, 2004, available at http://www.cnn.com/2004/ALLPOLITICS/08/23/intel.reform.reax/index.html.

7. Paul Burka, "Agent of Change," *Texas Monthly* (November 2006), 154.

8. "President Bush Nominates Dr. Robert M. Gates to Be Secretary of Defense," November 8, 2006, available at http://georgewbush-whitehouse.archives.gov/news/releases/2006/11/20061108-4.html.

9. A good example of this outlook is Amy B. Zegart, *Spying Blind: The CIA, the FBI, and the Origins of 9/11* (Princeton, N.J.: Princeton University Press, 2007).

10. Jessica T. Mathews, "Power Shift," *Foreign Affairs* 76, no. 1 (January–February 1997): 50–66.

11. Paul R. Pillar, "Adapting Intelligence to Changing Issues," in Loch Johnson, ed., *Handbook of Intelligence Studies* (London: Routledge, 2007), 148–62.

12. On these themes, see Richard E. Neustadt and Ernest R. May, *Thinking in Time: The Uses of History for Decision-Makers* (New York: Free Press, 1986), 257–58.

13. John Mueller, *Overblown: How Politicians and the Terrorism Industry Inflate National Security Threats, and Why We Believe Them* (New York: Free Press, 2006).

14. Martha Crenshaw, "'New' vs. 'Old' Terrorism: A Critical Appraisal," in Rik Coolsaet, ed., *Jihadi Terrorism and the Radicalisation Challenge in Europe* (Aldershot, U.K.: Ashgate, 2008), 24.

15. Francis J. Gavin, "Same As It Ever Was: Nuclear Alarmism, Proliferation, and the Cold War," *International Security* 34, no. 3 (Winter 2009–2010), 21–23.

16. Philip Jenkins, *Images of Terror: What We Can and Can't Know About Terrorism* (New York: Aldine de Gruyter, 2003), chap. 3.

17. Crenshaw, "'New' vs. 'Old' Terrorism," 35.

18. Townsend Hoopes, *The Limits of Intervention* (New York: David McKay, 1969), 9–13.

19. Graham Allison and Peter Szanton, *Remaking Foreign Policy: The Organizational Connection* (New York: Basic Books, 1976), x and chap. 3.

20. Bruce D. Berkowitz and Allan E. Goodman, *Strategic Intelligence for American National Security* (Princeton, N.J.: Princeton University Press, 1989), 14–17.

21. See, for example, Zegart, *Spying Blind*, 69–89, in which a review of intelligence adaptations in counterterrorism starts in 1991 and thus conveniently omits the establishment of the CTC.

22. Quoted in David Arbel and Ran Edelist, *Western Intelligence and the Collapse of the Soviet Union* (London: Frank Cass, 2003), 157.

23. Joseph E. Persico, *Casey: From the OSS to the CIA* (New York: Viking, 1990), 284.

24. Berkowitz and Goodman noted these challenges two decades ago in *Strategic Intelligence for American National Security*, 157–61.

25. Chris Edwards, "Federal Pay: Myth and Realities," *Washington Post*, August 13, 2006.

26. Excluding postseason play and all-star games.

27. Constance Hays, *The Real Thing: Truth and Power at the Coca-Cola Company* (New York: Random House, 2004), 125; and Mark Pendergrast, *For God, Country, and Coca-Cola* (New York: Basic Books, 1994), 362–64.

28. Kenneth N. Gilpin, "Coke Trims Pay Package of Chairman," *New York Times*, March 10, 1993.

29. Erin Scottberg, "NASA Says Shuttle Risk Overstated, Yet Some Risk Unavoidable," *Popular Mechanics* online news, June 30, 2006, available at http://www.popularmechanics.com/blogs/science_news/3259521.html.

30. Daniel Byman, *The Five Front War: The Better Way to Fight Global Jihad* (Hoboken, N.J.: Wiley, 2008), 98.

31. The latter point refers to the "signal-to-noise" problem. The best-known treatment of it with respect to a particular intelligence failure is Roberta Wohlstetter, *Pearl Harbor: Warning and Decision* (Stanford, Calif.: Stanford University Press, 1962), esp. 386–95.

32. Edward N. Lorenz, "Deterministic Nonperiodic Flow," *Journal of the Atmospheric Sciences* 20, no. 2 (March 1963), 141.

33. Robert Sobel, *For Want of a Nail: If Burgoyne Had Won at Saratoga* (New York: Macmillan, 1973).

34. Alexander Woodcock and Monte Davis's *Catastrophe Theory* (New York: E. P. Dutton, 1978) offers a nontechnical introduction to this subject.

35. Stephen Jay Gould, *Dinosaur in a Haystack: Reflections in Natural History* (New York: Harmony Books, 1995), esp. chaps. 10 and 11.

36. Nassim Nicholas Taleb, *The Black Swan: The Impact of the Highly Improbable* (New York: Random House, 2007), xx.

37. David S. Fogelsang, *America's Secret War Against Bolshevism* (Chapel Hill: University of North Carolina Press, 1995), 144, 229.

38. Larry J. Bockman, *The Spirit of Moncada: Fidel Castro's Rise to Power, 1953–1959*, (Quantico, Va.: United States Marine Corps Command and Staff

College, April 1, 1984), available at http://www.globalsecurity.org/military/library/report/1984/BLJ.htm.

39. Daniel L. Byman and Kenneth M. Pollack, "Let Us Now Praise Great Men: Bringing the Statesman Back In," *International Security* 25, no. 4 (Spring 2001): 107–46.

40. Michael C. Thomsett, *The German Opposition to Hitler: The Resistance, the Underground, and Assassination Plots* (Jefferson, N.C.: McFarland, 2007), 212–36; and Denis Rigden, *Kill the Fuhrer: Section X and Operation Foxley* (Gloucestershire, U.K.: Sutton, 1999), 1–10, 166–70.

41. Mackinlay Kantor, *If the South Had Won the Civil War* (New York: Forge Books, 2001).

42. Neustadt and May, *Thinking in Time*, 259–61.

43. Stephen Peter Rosen, *War and Human Nature* (Princeton, N.J.: Princeton University Press, 2005), 182.

44. Philip E. Tetlock, *Expert Political Judgment: How Good Is It? How Can We Know?* (Princeton, N.J.: Princeton University Press, 2005), chap. 2.

45. Robert Jervis, *Perception and Misperception in International Politics* (Princeton, N.J.: Princeton University Press, 1976), 54–57.

46. Betts, *Enemies of Intelligence*, 51, 125.

47. Ibid., 68.

48. See the comments of an Israeli intelligence officer in Michael J. Totten, "On the Record with IDF Intelligence," March 7, 2007, available at http://www.michaeltotten.com/archives/001399.html.

49. Jennifer E. Sims, "Understanding Friends and Enemies: The Context for American Intelligence Reform," in Jennifer E. Sims and Burton Gerber, eds., *Transforming U.S. Intelligence* (Washington, D.C.: Georgetown University Press, 2005), 15.

50. On projection, see Jan Grant and Jim Crawley, *Transference and Projection: Mirrors to the Self* (Buckingham, U.K.: Open University Press, 2002), 18–23.

9. CATHARSIS AND 9/11

1. U.S. House of Representatives and U.S. Senate, *Counterterrorism Efforts and the Events Surrounding the Terrorist Attacks of September 11, 2001, Joint Hearing of the House and Senate Select Intelligence Committees*, 107th Cong., 2d sess., October 8, 2002.

2. Thomas H. Kean and Lee H. Hamilton, *Without Precedent: The Inside Story of the 9/11 Commission* (New York: Alfred A. Knopf, 2006), 26.

3. Ibid., 15.

4. Ibid., 289ff.

5. Ibid., 18–19, 26–27, 45, 49, 128, 158.

6. Ibid., 145.

7. Representative Thomas Kean, testimony before the U.S. House of Representatives International Relations Committee, 108th Cong., 2d sess., August 24, 2004.

8. Kean and Hamilton, *Without Precedent*, 300.

9. See the 9/11 Public Discourse Project at http://www.9-11pdp.org/about/index.htm.

10. Kean and Hamilton, *Without Precedent*, 134–35.

11. Philip Shenon, *The Commission: The Uncensored History of the 9/11 Investigation* (New York: Twelve, 2008), 172.

12. Kean and Hamilton, *Without Precedent*, 190.

13. Quoted in Shenon, *The Commission*, 78.

14. Ibid., 155.

15. Ibid., 388–89. Ernest May from Harvard, whom Zelikow had enticed to assist in writing the report, was also involved in preparing the outline.

16. Ashton Carter, John Deutch, and Philip Zelikow, "Catastrophic Terrorism: Tackling the New Danger," *Foreign Affairs* 77, no. 6 (November–December 1998), 84.

17. Shenon, *The Commission*, 69–70, 83–85, 90, 131.

18. Kean and Hamilton, *Without Precedent*, 286–87.

19. A list of the hearings and witnesses is in appendix C of the commission's report: National Commission on Terrorist Attacks Upon the United States, *The 9/11 Commission Report* (New York: Norton, 2004).

20. Shenon appears to favor this explanation for why Zelikow called Mylroie as a witness, as did some members of the commission staff. See Shenon, *The Commission*, 128, 134, 321–23, 380.

21. Peter Bergen, "Armchair Provocateur," *Washington Monthly* (December 2003), 28.

22. Shenon, *The Commission*, 256–61.

23. Kean and Hamilton, *Without Precedent*, 133.

24. Ibid., 154.

25. Ibid., 272.

26. National Commission on Terrorist Attacks, *9/11 Commission Report*, 344–348.

27. DCI George J. Tenet, statement, U.S. Senate, *Worldwide Threat 2001: National Security in a Changing World, Hearings Before the Select Committee on Intelligence*, 107th Cong., 1st sess., February 7, 2001, available at https://www .cia.gov/news-information/speeches-testimony/2001/UNCLAS WWT_02072001.html.

28. See National Commission on Terrorist Attacks, *Eighth Public Hearing*, March 23–24, 2004, available at http://govinfo.library.unt.edu/911/hearings/ hearing8.htm.

29. Steve Coll, *Ghost Wars: The Secret History of the CIA, Afghanistan, and Bin Laden, from the Soviet Invasion to September 10, 2001* (New York: Penguin, 2004).

30. President Bill Clinton, Address to the Nation, August 20, 1998, available at http://www.state.gov/www/regions/africa/strike_clinton980820a.html.

31. President Bill Clinton, remarks to the Fifty-third United Nations General Assembly, September 21, 1998, available at http://daccess-dds-ny.un.org/ doc/UNDOC/GEN/N98/858/28/PDF/N9885828.pdf?OpenElement.

32. Shenon, *The Commission*, 397.

33. Quoted in Barton Gellman, "A Strategy's Curious Evolution," *Washington Post*, January 20, 2002.

34. Quoted in Daniel Benjamin and Steven Simon, *The Age of Sacred Terror* (New York: Random House, 2002), 336.

35. Clarke's own account is in Richard A. Clarke, *Against All Enemies: Inside America's War on Terror* (New York: Free Press, 2004).

36. Bob Woodward, *Bush at War* (New York: Simon and Shuster, 2002), 34. The other two challenges Tenet identified were the rise of China and the proliferation of WMD.

37. Shenon, *The Commission*, 312–13.

38. See especially pages 341–43 of National Commission on Terrorist Attacks, *9/11 Commission Report*.

39. Mark M. Lowenthal, "He Blames the Israel Lobby. But the Job Wasn't Worth It," *Washington Post*, March 15, 2009.

40. Richard K. Betts, *Enemies of Intelligence: Knowledge and Power in American National Security* (New York: Columbia University Press, 2007), 68.

41. George Tenet, *At the Center of the Storm: My Years at the CIA* (New York: HarperCollins, 2007), 122–23.

42. National Commission on Terrorist Attacks Upon the United States, *The Performance of the Intelligence Community*, Staff Statement no. 11 (Washington, D.C.: National Commission on Terrorist Attacks Upon the United States, final version released April 13, 2004), available at http://www.9-11commission.gov/staff_statements/staff_statement_11.pdf; and National Commission on Terrorist Attacks, *9/11 Commission Report*, 342.

43. National Commission on Terrorist Attacks, *9/11 Commission Report*, 342.

44. National Commission on Terrorist Attacks Upon the United States, *Intelligence Policy*, Staff Statement no. 7 (Washington, D.C.: National Commission on Terrorist Attacks Upon the United States, 2004), 4, available at http://www.9-11commission.gov/staff_statements/staff_statement_7.pdf.

45. This NIE is discussed and quoted in Paul R. Pillar, "A Scapegoat Is Not a Solution," *New York Times*, June 4, 2004.

46. National Commission on Terrorist Attacks, *The Performance of the Intelligence Community*, 4.

47. Max H. Bazerman and Michael D. Watkins, *Predictable Surprises: The Disasters You Should Have Seen Coming, and How to Prevent Them* (Boston: Harvard Business School Press, 2004), 37. The other observations in this paragraph about industry resistance are from chapter 2 of this book. Appendix A lists a series of pre-9/11 reports by the General Accounting Office on the need for enhanced aviation-security measures.

48. For this perspective from the 9/11 Commission, see Ernest R. May and Philip D. Zelikow, "Sins of Commission? Falkenrath and His Critics," *International Security* 29 (Spring 2005), 208–9.

49. Coll, *Ghost Wars*, 305, 463.

50. Ibid., 499–500.

51. Mark Mazzetti, "U.S. Aborted Raid on Qaeda Chiefs in Pakistan in '05," *New York Times*, July 8, 2007.

52. Thom Shanker and David E. Sanger, "Pakistan Is Rapidly Adding Nuclear Arms, U.S. Says," *New York Times*, May 17, 2009.

53. National Commission on Terrorist Attacks, *9/11 Commission Report*, 341.

54. Lawrence Wright, *The Looming Tower: Al-Qaeda and the Road to 9/11* (New York: Alfred A. Knopf, 2007), 133.

55. Coll, *Ghost Wars*, 204.

56. Wright, *The Looming Tower*, 151–52.

57. Ibid., 199.

58. National Commission on Terrorist Attacks, *9/11 Commission Report*, 55–70.

59. Ibid., 341.

60. Fawaz A. Gerges, *The Far Enemy: Why Jihad Went Global* (Cambridge, U.K.: Cambridge University Press, 2005), 55.

61. See a compendium of such scholars' comments by Khalil Al-Anani, an Egyptian political analyst most recently at the Brookings Institution, at http://islamists2day-e.blogspot.com/2007/11/jihad-revisions-is-it-too-late.html. See also Nathan Field, "The Al-Qaida We Don't Know: The Limits of the Counterterrorism Approach," *World Politics Review*, October 26, 2008, available at http://www.worldpoliticsreview.com/article.aspx?id=2820.

62. National Commission on Terrorist Attacks, *9/11 Commission Report*, 149–50.

63. National Commission on Terrorist Attacks, *The Performance of the Intelligence Community*, 4.

64. National Commission on Terrorist Attacks, *9/11 Commission Report*, 341–42.

65. National Commission on Terrorist Attacks, *The Performance of the Intelligence Community*, 4.

66. Draft of National Commission on Terrorist Attacks, *The Performance of the Intelligence Community*, April 5, 2004, 3–4.

67. National Commission on Terrorist Attacks, *Intelligence Policy*, 4.

68. National Commission on Terrorist Attacks, *The Performance of the Intelligence Community*, 3–4.

69. Ibid., 5.

70. National Commission on Terrorist Attacks, *9/11 Commission Report*, 342.

71. Ibid., 343.

72. National Commission on Terrorist Attacks, *The Performance of the Intelligence Community*, 5.

73. Tim Weiner, "U.S. Hard Put to Find Proof Bin Laden Directed Attacks," *New York Times*, April 13, 1999.

74. Tim Weiner, *Legacy of Ashes: The History of the CIA* (New York: Doubleday, 2007).

75. National Commission on Terrorist Attacks, *9/11 Commission Report*, 343–44.

76. Pillar, "A Scapegoat Is Not a Solution."

77. Coll, *Ghost Wars*, 273.

78. National Commission on Terrorism, *Countering the Changing Threat of International Terrorism* (Washington, D.C.: National Commission on Terrorism, 2000), 2.

79. Paul R. Pillar, *Terrorism and U.S. Foreign Policy* (Washington, D.C.: Brookings Institution Press, 2001), 52–55.

80. For example, Richard A. Clarke, "A War of Ideas," *Washington Post Book World*, November 21, 2004.

81. Pillar, *Terrorism and U.S. Foreign Policy*, 20–21, 45–48, 57–69, 130–32.

82. Ibid., 22.

83. Carter, Deutch, and Zelikow, "Catastrophic Terrorism," 80–82.

84. Draft of National Commission on Terrorist Attacks, *The Performance of the Intelligence Community*, April 5, 2004, 5.

85. National Commission on Terrorist Attacks, *The Performance of the Intelligence Community*, 5.

86. Pillar, *Terrorism and U.S. Foreign Policy*, 5.

87. National Commission on Terrorist Attacks, *9/11 Commission Report*, 343.

88. Robert D. Kaplan, "The Faceless Enemy," *New York Times Book Review*, October 14, 2001.

89. Pillar, "A Scapegoat Is Not a Solution."

90. Despite the non-CBRN nature of 9/11, this misdirection of resources and attention is still a problem. See Daniel Byman, *The Five Front War: The Better Way to Fight Global Jihad* (Hoboken, N.J.: Wiley, 2008), 154.

91. Martha Crenshaw, "'New' vs. 'Old' Terrorism: A Critical Appraisal," in Rik Coolsaet, ed., *Jihadi Terrorism and the Radicalisation Challenge in Europe* (Aldershot, U.K.: Ashgate, 2008), 36.

92. See Clarke's comments about CIA warnings to the White House in Richard A. Clarke, "The Trauma of 9/11 Is No Excuse," *Washington Post*, May 31, 2009.

93. James B. Bruce and Roger Z. George, "Intelligence Analysis: The Emergence of a Discipline," in Roger Z. George and James B. Bruce, eds., *Analyzing Intelligence: Origins, Obstacles, and Innovations* (Washington, D.C.: Georgetown University Press, 2008), 4.

94. Paul R. Pillar, "Good Literature and Bad History: The 9/11 Commission's Tale of Strategic Intelligence," *Intelligence and National Security* 21, no. 6 (December 2006): 1022–44.

95. This defense is part of a correspondence with Shenon that Zelikow made public; the letter can be found at http://www.fas.org/irp/news/2008/02/zelikow.pdf.

96. A rare exception is Richard A. Posner, *Preventing Surprise Attacks: Intelligence Reform in the Wake of 9/11* (Lanham, Md.: Rowman and Littlefield, 2005), 6.

97. Zbigniew Brzezinski, *Power and Principle: Memoirs of the National Security Adviser 1977–1981* (New York: Farrar, Straus and Giroux, 1983), 481.

98. Commission on the Intelligence Capabilities of the United States Regarding Weapons of Mass Destruction, *Report to the President of the United States* (Washington, D.C.: U.S. Government Printing Office, March 31, 2005), 3.

99. Paul R. Pillar, "The Diffusion of Terrorism," *Mediterranean Quarterly* 21, no. 1 (Winter 2010): 1–14.

100. Letter of transmittal to the secretary of state, January 8, 1999, accompanying *Report of the Accountability Review Boards on the Bombings of the US Embassies in Nairobi, Kenya, and Dar es Salaam, Tanzania on August 7, 1998*, available at http://www.state.gov/www/regions/africa/board_letter.html.

101. Declassified key judgments of *National Intelligence Estimate, Trends in Global Terrorism: Implications for the United States* (April 2006), available at http://www.dni.gov/press_releases/Declassified_NIE_Key_Judgments.pdf.

10. Responses to Catharsis

1. Richard A. Posner, *Preventing Surprise Attacks: Intelligence Reform in the Wake of 9/11* (Lanham, Md.: Rowman and Littlefield, 2005), 56–57.

2. John Updike, "The Great I Am," *New Yorker* (November 1, 2004), 100.

3. Philip Shenon, *The Commission: The Uncensored History of the 9/11 Investigation* (New York: Twelve, 2008), 170.

4. Bob Woodward, *State of Denial* (New York: Simon and Shuster, 2006), 49–52.

5. Philip Shenon, "Sept. 11 Panel Wasn't Told of Meeting, Members Say," *New York Times*, October 2, 2006.

6. Dan Eggen and Robin Wright, "Tenet Recalled Warning Rice," *Washington Post*, October 3, 2006; and Philip Shenon and Mark Mazzetti, "Records Confirm C.I.A. Chief Warned Rice on Al Qaeda," *New York Times*, October 3, 2006.

7. Shenon, *The Commission*, 374–79.

8. "The Fictional Path to 9/11," *New York Times*, September 12, 2006.

9. Howard Kurtz, "Clinton Administration Officials Assail ABC's 'The Path to 9/11,'" *Washington Post*, September 7, 2006; and Dana Milbank, "With 9/11 Film, Kean Finds Tough Critic in Hamilton," *Washington Post*, September 12, 2006.

10. Quoted in Shaun Waterman, "ABC Airs Edited Docu-drama," UPI, September 11, 2006.

11. Perhaps the most glaring example of such a biography is Edmund Morris, *Dutch: A Memoir of Ronald Reagan* (New York: Random House, 1999).

12. Representative Tim Roemer, interview, CNN, August 10, 2004, emphasis added, available at http://transcripts.cnn.com/transcripts/0408/10/lol.03.html.

13. See, for example, Amy B. Zegart, "How Intelligent Is Intelligence Reform?" *International Security* 30, no. 4 (Spring 2006), 207.

14. Quotations from the inspector general office's report are in an unclassified and unpublished statement that George Tenet released on August 21, 2007, available at http://www.nytimes.com/2007/08/21/washington/21cnd-tenet.html.

15. The declassified version of this summary is at https://www.cia.gov/library/reports/Executive%20Summary_OIG%20Report.pdf.

16. A rare exception is an article by a former government attorney who had worked at different times for the congressional joint inquiry and for the CIA: Catherine Lotrionte, "The Fault, Dear Brutus, Is Not in Individuals, but in Our System: CIA's Inspector General Seeks to Find Individuals Accountable for 9/11 and Misses an Opportunity for Effective Intelligence Reform," *SAIS Review* 28, no. 1 (Winter–Spring 2008): 109–37.

17. Ibid., 116–17.

18. "The World This Week," *The Economist*, August 25, 2007, 8.

19. CIA Director's Statement on the Release of the 9/11 Inspector General Report Executive Summary, August 21, 2007, available at http://www.fas.org/irp/news/2007/08/cia082107.html.

20. Scott Shane and Mark Mazzetti, "Lawmakers Raise Concerns Over Call for Investigation of C.I.A. Watchdog's Work," *New York Times*, October 13, 2007; and Walter Pincus, "Lawmakers Criticize CIA Director's Review Order," *Washington Post*, October 13, 2007.

21. Mark Mazzetti, "C.I.A. Lays Out Errors It Made Before Sept. 11," *New York Times*, August 22, 2007.

11. The Illusion of Reform

1. See especially Richard A. Posner, *Preventing Surprise Attacks: Intelligence Reform in the Wake of 9/11* (Lanham, Md.: Rowman and Littlefield, 2005); and Richard A. Posner, *Uncertain Shield: The U.S. Intelligence System in the Throes of Reform* (Lanham, Md.: Rowman and Littlefield, 2006), chap. 3.

2. Posner, *Preventing Surprise Attacks*, 10.

3. Ibid., 84–85.

4. Quoted in Mark Mazzetti, "Report Faults Speed of Intelligence Overhaul," *New York Times*, July 28, 2006.

5. "Director Wants More Authority in Intelligence," *New York Times*, April 5, 2007.

6. Scott Shane, "In New Job, Spymaster Draws Bipartisan Criticism," *New York Times*, April 20, 2006; and John Lehman, "We're Not Winning This War," *Washington Post*, August 31, 2006.

7. Pamela Hess, "CIA, Intel Director Locked in Spy Turf Battle," Associated Press, May 27, 2009; and David Ignatius, "Duel of the Spy Chiefs," *Washington Post*, June 11, 2009.

8. Mark Mazzetti, "Five Years After Overhaul, U.S. Spy Chiefs Still Fight Over Turf," *New York Times*, June 9, 2009.

9. Quoted in Shaun Waterman, "'Obstructionists' Hinder WikiLeaks Probe," *Washington Times*, December 2, 2010, available at http://www.washington times.com/news/2010/dec/2/obstructionists-hinder-wikileaks-probe/ ?page=1.

10. Karen DeYoung, "GAO Faults Agencies' Sharing of Terror Data," *Washington Post*, April 19, 2006; and Eric Schmitt and Thom Shanker, "Hurdles Stymie Counterterrorism Center," *New York Times*, February 23, 2010.

11. Steve Coll, *Ghost Wars: The Secret History of the CIA, Afghanistan, and Bin Laden from the Soviet Invasion to September 10, 2001* (New York: Penguin Press, 2004), 253, 317.

12. The question comes from National Commission on Terrorist Attacks Upon the United States, *The Performance of the Intelligence Community*, Staff Statement no. 11 (Washington, D.C.: National Commission on Terrorist Attacks Upon the United States, final version released April 13, 2004), available at http://www.9-11commission.gov/staff_statements/staff_statement_11.pdf, 12. A good journalistic review of some of the confusion is in Karen DeYoung, "A Fight Against Terrorism—and Disorganization," *Washington Post*, August 9, 2006.

13. The conclusions of the principal congressional inquiry into the 2009 incident are in U.S. Senate, Select Committee on Intelligence, *Unclassified Executive Summary of the Committee Report on the Attempted Terrorist Attack on Northwest Airlines Flight 253* (Washington, D.C.: U.S. Government Printing Office, May 18, 2010), available at http://intelligence.senate.gov/100518/1225report .pdf.

14. Scott Shane, "9/11 Shadow Is Cast Again," *New York Times*, December 30, 2009.

15. Thomas H. Kean and John Farmer Jr., "How 12/25 Was Like 9/11," *New York Times*, January 6, 2010.

16. Philip Rucker, "Republicans See Political Opportunity," *Washington Post*, December 30, 2009.

17. "Remarks by the President on Strengthening Intelligence and Aviation Security," January 7, 2010, available at http://www.whitehouse.gov/the-press-office/remarks-president-strengthening-intelligence-and-aviation-security.

18. *Presidential Memorandum Regarding 12/25/2009 Attempted Terrorist Attack* (January 7, 2010), available at http://www.whitehouse.gov/the-press-office/presidential-memorandum-regarding-12252009-attempted-terrorist-attack.

19. See Richard K. Betts, *Enemies of Intelligence: Knowledge and Power in American National Security* (New York: Columbia University Press, 2007), 18.

20. Ibid., 134.

21. Mike McConnell, "Overhauling Intelligence," *Foreign Affairs* 86, no. 4 (July–August 2007): 49–58.

22. Dennis C. Blair, "Strengthening Our Front Line of Defense," *Washington Post*, December 18, 2009.

12. REAL REFORM

1. Mark M. Lowenthal, *Intelligence: From Secrets to Policy*, 2d ed. (Washington, D.C.: Congressional Quarterly Press, 2003), 14.

2. Richard K. Betts, *Enemies of Intelligence: Knowledge and Power in American National Security* (New York: Columbia University Press, 2007), 76–77.

3. Bob Woodward, *Plan of Attack* (New York: Simon and Schuster, 2004), 67–68.

4. See, for example, James B. Steinberg, "The Policymaker's Perspective: Transparency and Partnership," in Roger Z. George and James B. Bruce, eds., *Analyzing Intelligence: Origins, Obstacles, and Innovations* (Washington, D.C.: Georgetown University Press, 2008), 87; and James Dobbins, "Who Lost Iraq? Lessons from the Debacle," *Foreign Affairs* 86, no. 5 (September–October 2007), 68.

5. George Tenet, *At the Center of the Storm: My Years at the CIA* (New York: HarperCollins, 2007), 363.

6. The unclassified version is *Iran: Nuclear Intentions and Capabilities* (November 2007), available at http://www.dni.gov/press_releases/20071203_release.pdf.

7. Henry A. Kissinger, "Misreading the Iran Report," *Washington Post*, December 13, 2007.

8. In "Who Lost Iraq?" Dobbins makes essentially the same point.

9. Paul R. Pillar, "Intelligence, Policy, and the War in Iraq," *Foreign Affairs* 85, no. 2 (March–April 2006), 27.

10. Indeed, some have criticized the Federal Reserve's leadership (in particular former chairman Alan Greenspan) for not being as independent of the administration of the day as it ought to be. See, for example, Paul Krugman, "Sad Alan's Lament," *New York Times*, September 17, 2007.

11. Robert S. McNamara, *In Retrospect: The Tragedy and Lessons of Vietnam* (New York: Times Books, 1995), 322.

12. Mark M. Lowenthal, "Intelligence in Transition: Analysis After September 11 and Iraq," in George and Bruce, eds., *Analyzing Intelligence*, 236.

13. John Mueller, "The Iraq Syndrome," *Foreign Affairs* 84, no. 6 (November–December 2005): 44–54.

14. See Reagan's speech to the VFW convention, August 18, 1980, Chicago, available at http://www.reagan.utexas.edu/archives/reference/8.18.80.html.

15. Robert Jervis, *Perception and Misperception in International Politics* (Princeton, N.J.: Princeton University Press, 1976).

16. Most recently in Robert Jervis, *Why Intelligence Fails: Lessons from the Iranian Revolution and the Iraq War* (Ithaca, N.Y.: Cornell University Press, 2010).

17. Richard H. Immerman, "Intelligence and Strategy: Historicizing Psychology, Policy, and Politics," *Diplomatic History* 32, no. 1 (January 2008), 23.

18. Testimony, U.S. House of Representatives, *Department of Defense Budget Priorities for Fiscal Year 2004, Hearings Before the House Committee on the Budget*, 108th Cong., 1st sess., February 27, 2003, available at http://frwebgate.access.gpo.gov/cgi-bin/getdoc.cgi?dbname=108_house_hearings&docid=f:85421.wais.

19. U.S. Department of Defense, news briefing, M2 PressWire, April 3, 2003.

20. Quoted in Matt Kelley, "U.S. Shows Photos of Saddam's Dead Sons," Associated Press, July 24, 2003.

21. Quoted in Mark Bowden, "Wolfowitz: The Exit Interviews," *The Atlantic* (July–August 2005), available at http://www.theatlantic.com/magazine/archive/2005/07/wolfowitz-the-exit-interviews/4078/.

22. Philip E. Tetlock, *Expert Political Judgment: How Good Is It? How Can We Know?* (Princeton, N.J.: Princeton University Press, 2005), chap. 7.

23. Lyndsey Layton, "The Grand Tour of Their New House," *Washington Post*, November 14, 2006.

24. Aaron L. Friedberg, "The Long Haul: Fighting and Funding America's Next Wars," *Foreign Affairs* 86, no. 4 (July–August 2007), 146.

25. Another great military planner, George C. Marshall, also displayed the approach that makes for more accurate images and more successful foreign

policy. See the favorable reference to Marshall in Richard E. Neustadt and Ernest R. May, *Thinking in Time: The Uses of History for Decision-Makers* (New York: Free Press, 1986), 252–53.

26. On the importance of competitive views' making their way to the president in the Cuban Missile Crisis, see Robert F. Kennedy, *Thirteen Days: A Memoir of the Cuban Missile Crisis* (New York: Norton, 1971), 94. A more recent perspective on the value of building competition into the policymaking process is given in David Brooks, "Building a Team of Rivals," *New York Times*, November 23, 2006.

27. This problem is not new. See, for example, Graham Allison and Peter Szanton, *Remaking Foreign Policy: The Organizational Connection* (New York: Basic Books, 1976), 89–90.

28. Isaiah Berlin, *The Hedgehog and the Fox* (New York: Mentor Books, 1957), 7.

29. Tetlock, *Expert Political Judgment*, 2, 75–81, 163.

30. Ibid., 143.

31. Theodore J. Lowi, *The End of Liberalism: Ideology, Policy, and the Crisis of Public Authority* (New York: Norton, 1969), 170–86.

32. For example, see Paul C. Light, *The Decline of the Federal Service and How to Reverse It* (Cambridge, Mass.: Harvard University Press, 2008), 225; and Dobbins, "Who Lost Iraq?" 67.

33. Alan Wolfe, "Academia (Kind of) Goes to War: Chomsky and His Children," *World Affairs* (Winter 2008), available at http://www.worldaffairsjournal.org/articles/2008-Winter/full-academia-war.html.

34. Quoted in George Packer, *The Assassins' Gate: America in Iraq* (New York: Farrar, Straus and Giroux, 2005), 41.

35. Quoted in Ari Shavit, "White Man's Burden," *Haaretz*, April 6, 2003.

36. Rajiv Chandrasekaran, "Ties to GOP Trumped Know-How Among Staff Sent to Rebuild Iraq," *Washington Post*, September 17, 2006.

37. David F. Lewis, "Testing Pendleton's Premise: Do Political Appointees Make Worse Bureaucrats?" *Journal of Politics* 69, no. 4 (November 2007): 1073–88.

38. Booz Allen Hamilton, *What It Takes to Change Government* (MacLean, Va.: Booz Allen Hamilton, Spring 2009).

39. Data from the American Foreign Service Association, available at http://www.afsa.org/ambassadorsgraph2.cfm.

40. Jonathan Salant and Julianna Goldman, "Obama Offers Prime Posts to Top Campaign Contributors," *Bloomberg News*, May 29, 2009.

41. Albert R. Hunt, "Some Holdouts to Obama's Vow to Change," *Bloomberg News*, October 25, 2009.

42. For commentary on the most recent round of this drift, see Paul C. Light, "Nominate and Wait," *New York Times*, March 24, 2009; and David S. Broder, "Running on Empty," *Washington Post*, March 5, 2009.

13. ADAPTING POLICY TO UNCERTAINTY

1. The river-crossing analogy is in Nassim Nicholas Taleb, *The Black Swan: The Impact of the Highly Improbable* (New York: Random House, 2007), 161.
2. Daniel Gilbert, "What You Don't Know Makes You Nervous," *New York Times*, May 21, 2009.
3. Philip E. Tetlock, *Expert Political Judgment: How Good Is It? How Can We Know?* (Princeton, N.J.: Princeton University Press, 2005), 40.
4. Isaiah Berlin, *The Hedgehog and the Fox* (New York: Mentor Books, 1957), 11, 43, 58.
5. James B. Steinberg, "The Policymaker's Perspective: Transparency and Partnership," in Roger Z. George and James B. Bruce, eds., *Analyzing Intelligence: Origins, Obstacles, and Innovations* (Washington, D.C.: Georgetown University Press, 2008), 83.
6. Derek Chollet and James Goldgeier, "Kennan Had a Vision: Things Aren't So Clear Now," *Washington Post*, July 13, 2008.
7. A standard treatment of decision-making theory is given in Howard Raiffa, *Decision Analysis: Introductory Lectures on Choices Under Uncertainty* (Reading, Mass.: Addison-Wesley, 1968).
8. Robert McNamara, *In Retrospect: The Tragedy and Lessons of Vietnam* (New York: Times Books, 1995), 323.
9. George P. Shultz, *Turmoil and Triumph: My Years as Secretary of State* (New York: Scribner, 1993), 266.
10. Ibid., 1003.
11. James A. Baker III, *The Politics of Diplomacy: Revolution, War, and Peace, 1989–1992* (New York: Putnam, 1995), 143.
12. Ibid.
13. Taleb, *The Black Swan*, xxi.
14. Gregory Koblentz, "Pathogens as Weapons: The International Security Implications of Biological Warfare," *International Security* 28, no. 3 (Winter 2003–2004), 121.
15. Paul R. Pillar, "What to Ask Before the Next War," *Washington Post*, February 4, 2007.

16. Quoted in Lewis D. Solomon, *Paul D. Wolfowitz: Visionary Intellectual, Policymaker, and Strategist* (Westport, Conn.: Praeger Security International, 2007), 6.

17. On how this tendency encourages a belief in domino theories, see Jack Snyder, *Myths of Empire: Domestic Politics and International Ambition* (Ithaca, N.Y.: Cornell University Press, 1991), 29–30.

18. *A Review of the Intelligence Community* (March 10, 1971), 11, redacted version available at http://www.gwu.edu/~nsarchiv/NSAEBB/NSAEBB144/document%204.pdf.

19. F. W. Winterbotham, *The Ultra Secret* (New York: Harper and Row, 1974).

20. Richard K. Betts, *Enemies of Intelligence: Knowledge and Power in American National Security* (New York: Columbia University Press, 2007), 16.

21. The most recent installment is National Intelligence Council, *Global Trends 2025: A Transformed World* (Washington, D.C.: National Intelligence Council, November 2008), available at http://www.dni.gov/nic/PDF_2025/2025_Global_Trends_Final_Report.pdf.

22. For a brief summary of some leading-candidate grand strategies for the United States, see Daniel W. Drezner, "The Grandest Strategy of Them All," *Washington Post*, December 17, 2006.

23. Christopher Layne, *The Peace of Illusions: American Grand Strategy from 1940 to the Present* (Ithaca, N.Y.: Cornell University Press, 2006), 3.

24. Leslie H. Gelb and Richard K. Betts draw a similar lesson from the Vietnam War in *The Irony of Vietnam: The System Worked* (Washington, D.C.: Brookings Institution Press, 1979), 362–67.

25. Harry Howe Ransom, *Central Intelligence and National Security* (Cambridge, Mass.: Harvard University Press, 1958), 216.